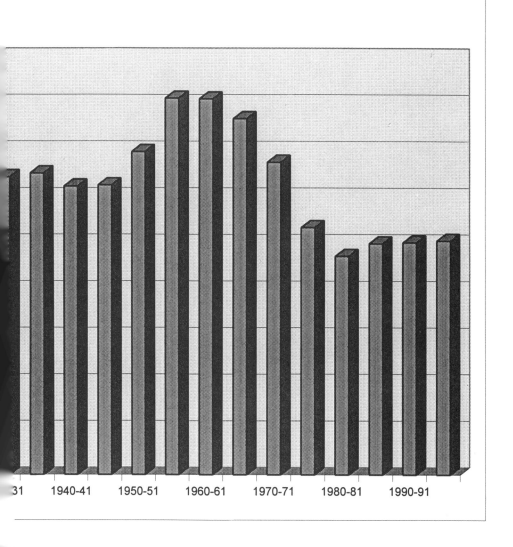

31   1940-41   1950-51   1960-61   1970-71   1980-81   1990-91

ity School District 1890 - 1995

CULTURE CLASH
AND ACCOMMODATION

CULTURE CLASH AND ACCOMMODATION

PUBLIC SCHOOLING IN
SALT LAKE CITY, 1890–1994

Frederick S. Buchanan

*Smith Research Associates
in association with Signature Books
San Francisco / Salt Lake City*

To the thousands of teachers
who made Salt Lake City public schools possible
and to the numerous newspaper reporters
who made much of this history possible.

Library of Congress Cataloging-in-Publication Data
Buchanan, Frederick Stewart
Culture clash and accommodation: public schooling in
Salt Lake City, 1890-1994 / Frederick S. Buchanan
p. cm.
Includes index.
ISBN 1-56085-082-5 (cloth)
1. Public schools—Utah—Salt Lake City—History.
2. School superintendents—Utah—Salt Lake City—History.
I. Title.
LA375.S2B83 1996
371'.01'09792258—dc20   95-40863
CIP

CONTENTS

PREFACE

This history was written as part of the public celebration of the 1990 centennial of the establishment of the public school system in Salt Lake City. It was not meant to be an exhaustive treatment of all aspects of public school development in the Salt Lake School District. My intent was to write a history which would communicate some understanding of how the schools came into being, the important changes that occurred and the issues and problems which were faced during the first century.

My decision to focus on the superintendents of the schools from 1890 to 1990, was dictated in part by the availability of primary documents and by the fact that newspaper accounts tended to stress the issues surrounding the board and the superintendents, rather than the work of teachers in the day-to-day activities of classrooms. It is regrettable that very few accounts of teachers' work in classrooms have been recorded or are readily available for use by historians. Even the reminiscences of students who attended the schools during century one would add unique insights not recorded elsewhere. I made a number of attempts to uncover such accounts through radio and newspaper appeals without success. If alternative sources were available, the history of the schools as told from the perspective of classroom teachers and students would be a quite different history from one based on the records of the board and the superintendents. Perhaps some future historian will find what is written here a stimulus to writing a history of Salt Lake City's public schools focusing on the teachers, the principals, the curriculum or the students.

One might also look at the schools through the lenses of race, ethnicity, gender or social class and present an account of how these issues shaped the schools of Salt Lake. While I have touched on these issues, a major thread of this history has been the way in which the schools became the battleground for the historic culture clash between Mormons and non-Mormons during the past century. During much of that time, the political struggle over who should control the schools had a decidedly Mormon/gentile orientation. For many years the elections to the board of education were clearly Mormon versus non-Mormon. Only in the last thirty years has this been muted and less acerbic than it was in, say, the years from 1898 to 1915.

There are still, however, tensions in the public schools between Mormons and those of other religions and beliefs. Frequently this occurs on a personal level as when non-Mormon students feel excluded by virtue of their being a minority. Some non-Mormon parents view the Salt Lake public schools as Mormon "parochial" schools because of their perceived reflection of Mormon values and hesitate to have their children attend them. From time to time the issue of teaching Utah history (with its obvious Mormon themes) raises hackles on both sides of the "objectivity" issue. More significant, from a school policy perspective at least, is the long-standing practice of public school choirs (consisting of Mormons and non-Mormons) singing in Latter-day Saint worship services. In such circumstances, the religious minority may feel pressured to participate, even though such participation may be "voluntary." While these tensions are not dealt with directly in this history, perhaps this centennial account of public schooling in Salt Lake City will provide some historical perspective for students of such contemporary issues. Given the nature of our society, the tensions between majorities and minorities will continue for many years as will the need to resolve them creatively and amicably.

In addition to the religious/cultural dimension which pervaded much of what happened in the public schools of Salt Lake, I believe this study is unique as an account of the growth and development of public schools in a medium-sized western city, as distinguished from the histories of urban education which are based on the development of public schools in the east or mid-west. Even though national programs initiated in the east had an influence on the west, this study suggests that there was always a considerable molding of these reforms or movements to meet the needs of the western educational landscape—of which "Mormon Country" is a part.

The principal sources used in writing this history have been annual school reports, minutes of board meetings and newspaper accounts of school related activities. However, time and time again I found board minutes deficient whenever tensions rose in the community over Mormon/gentile conflicts. Hours of serious and sometimes acrimonious debate would be summed up with a terse and bland "A discussion followed." The work of intrepid investigative newspaper reporters helped fill in the lacuna caused by the board's unwillingness to "go public" with controversy. I have also attempted to compensate for too much reliance on official records by using oral histories. These interviews with the last four superintendents and with a few teachers and students were an invaluable source of insights. The willingness of two of the late D. H. Christensen's children—Dean K. Christensen and Kathleen Christensen Hall—to share their father's professional and personal papers enriched my understanding of the role of the superintendent in the Salt Lake City school district.

I also benefited from three master's theses done many years ago on aspects of the district's history and gratefully acknowledge the work of Karl E. Lingwall, Catherine J. Rogers, George B. Robinson for their contribution to my understanding of events in the 1890s, 1920s, and 1930s, respectively. Five graduate students, Allan Payne, Dale Rees, Jack Monnett, Dee Darling, and Brian Hardy contributed to my understanding of the Mormon response to public schooling through their Ph.D. dissertations. A recent Ph.D. dissertation by Patricia McLeese was of immense value in interpreting the issues of school governance in Salt Lake City during the 1970s and 1980s.

I appreciate the efforts of a number of my graduate classes in the history of education for assistance in finding relevant materials in the Salt Lake City newspapers. The newspaper references they identified frequently gave me a jump start on a variety of topics and issues.

It should be added that the task of writing this history would have been greatly facilitated had the scrapbooks of newspaper articles dealing with the school district from around 1925 to the 1970s been preserved. Unfortunately, someone, in a fit of presentism and disregard for historical record keeping, disposed of these bound volumes sometime in the mid-1970s and only a few survived. Unless otherwise indicated, source materials (or copies thereof) may be found in the Frederick S. Buchanan Papers, Special Collections, Marriott Library, University of Utah. Minutes of the Board of Education are on microfilm at the district office in Salt Lake City.

A word about Mormon terminology: the Church of Jesus Christ of Latter-day Saints is referred to in this history as the "Mormon church," the "LDS church," or simply "the church." It is presided over by a president and two counselors known collectively as "The First Presidency." Next in authority is the Quorum of the Twelve Apostles. The church is divided up geographically into wards (equivalent to a parish), presided over by a bishop and two counselors. A group of wards makes up a stake (roughly equivalent to a diocese), presided over by a stake president and two counselors. The term "ward" is also used to refer to civic precincts in Salt Lake City, but these are not the same entities as the ecclesiastical wards. Finally, the term "gentile" was commonly used in Utah in the nineteenth and early twentieth centuries to refer to people who were not members of the LDS church.

I am indebted to many people for their help in making this history possible. John and Sylvia Bennion first broached the idea as part of the centennial celebration and have been supportive of my efforts throughout. The Board of Education has been generous in providing financial support which, when combined with resources from the Graduate School of Education and the Department of Educational Studies, allowed me to have two free quarters to pursue my research. The Board also helped underwrite some of the costs of publication. The University of Utah Research Committee provided me with funds which enabled me to hire Dianna Campanella as a research assistant. Her painstaking combing of newspapers, obituaries and the Masonic membership lists were invaluable. Gregory Thompson, Assistant Director for Special Collections at the University of Utah's Marriott Library, generously arranged for the transcription of the oral history interviews which I conducted in the course of my research. Jan Keller and Juanita Barclay Wainwright of the superintendent's office helped locate numerous hard to find records. Sue Southam and Hilary Bertagnole, English teachers par excellence at Highland High School, gave me the benefit of their skill and perspectives in reading some of the chapters. Zane G. Alder, Professor Emeritus of English at Brigham Young University, and William Mulder, Professor Emeritus of English at the University of Utah, provided me with helpful critiques of early chapters of the book. The reference librarians at the University of Utah and at the LDS Historical Department in Salt Lake City were always gracious and helpful in tracking down obscure citations and references. As always, my wife Rama and our five sons were supportive of my research and writing.

I am very grateful for the support and encouragement of my department chair, Ralph E. Reynolds and for the advice and practical assistance of Ann S. Curtis, one of the departmental secretaries. On numerous occasions she kept me from being lost in the electronic labyrinth of word processing and frequently responded to the content of what I was writing. One could not wish for a better support staff than exists in the Department of Educational Studies. They have my sincere thanks for their skill and patience. I deeply appreciate the sensitive collegial spirit of Robert V. Bullough, Jr., and his consistent encouragement of the project. I am also indebted to Harvey Kantor for his expert critiques of a number of chapters. His insightful commentary helped me focus my research and gave the book some of its dominant themes.

Ultimately, of course, I am responsible for the interpretation placed on the records I have used in writing this history. What is presented is a reflection of some of my own personal interests and biases as an educator and as an historian. I have written it in the hope that it may promote reflection on the part of those who read it: reflection about the complex social institution—public schools—which we take so much for granted in our present era; reflection about the promises which schools have often made which are never (or only partially) realized; reflection about the need for continual examination of our schools in terms of what we do expect from them and what we should reasonably expect from them. Lastly, I hope that this account will stimulate reflection on the demands and challenges confronting those who shaped and guided the Salt Lake City schools through their first century.

The time spent on researching and writing this book is my professional contribution as an historian of education to the history of my adopted city and state. It is also an expression of this Scottish emigrant's gratitude for the many undreamed of opportunities which have come my way through my involvement in American education as a student, teacher, and professor.

1

"MORMON COUNTRY" SCHOOLS

THE CULTURAL CONTEXT OF UTAH'S SCHOOLS

When the Salt Lake District produced its golden jubilee history in 1940, not a word (except the term "Ward Schools") referred to the fact that these schools prior to 1890 were vital components of Mormon culture. Indeed, a person unfamiliar with the larger context of the schools would not know that the Mormon church, its members and leaders, played a dominant role in the development of these schools. Even references to the early years, when Mormons were the only Europeans in Utah, keep from mentioning the notorious "M" word. Nor, on the other hand, would a newcomer reading such an account realize the early role played by Protestant mission schools. And there is no hint that behind the facade of unity and progress were numerous confrontations between Mormons and those of other faiths (the vaguely defined "non-Mormons" or "gentiles")—contestants perceiving elections to the board of education as struggles to determine whether the "insiders" or "outsiders" should control school policies in Utah's capital city.[1]

A balanced history of schooling in Salt Lake City—or in Utah in general—cannot ignore ways in which Mormonism's interactions with other groups influenced Utah's educational institutions. From Salt Lake's initial settlement in 1847 to the establishment of the first public schools in 1890 to the present, the history of education in the city was molded first by the dominant presence of the Church of Jesus Christ of Latter-day Saints and second, by the resistance from those of other persuasions, secular or religious, who tenaciously opposed Mormon dominance in the affairs of the city's public schools.

Prior to the passage of Utah's 1890 free public school law, Salt Lake City had 21 school districts, each coterminous with the city's 21 Mormon wards (or parishes) and each with its own elected three-person school board. While a few teachers and trustees were "gentiles," the vast majority were Mormons, and the schools were in effect quasi-public Mormon district schools, controlled by local ecclesiastical wards, supported by local taxes and tuition fees, and catering mainly to the city's Mormon majority.

In 1890 this changed when the city became one consolidated school district with some 21 ungraded schools (designated even by the non-Mormon board as First Ward School through Twenty-First Ward School) and the Salt Lake High

---

1. *Fifty Years of Public Education* (Salt Lake City, Board of Education, 1940). This volume was actually the *Fiftieth Annual Report, School Year 1939-1940*.

School, all controlled by an elected board made up of two trustees from each of the city's six municipal wards and supported by territorial appropriations and local taxes. Within a few years school names were changed to represent American political and literary heroes such as Lincoln, Jefferson, Sumner, Whittier, and Bryant, symbolizing an effort to make them mainline, secular institutions. Even if Mormons had objected to renaming the schools, there would have been little they could have done about it: the first city-wide school board election in July 1890 gave the city a predominately gentile board consisting of seven non-Mormons and three Mormons.[2]

While the elections of the 1890s included debates on efficiency, the best heating and toilet facilities, financial accountability, and free text books, the overriding issue in all eight campaigns for board seats can be reduced to one statement made in the aftermath of the first election: "Our people must control their own schools," a statement meaning something quite different to each of the opposing groups.

THE REDEMPTIVE COMMUNITY AT RISK

While Mormons feared that gentile-controlled schools would not confirm their children's faith, gentiles feared that Mormon-controlled schools would become proselyting agencies of the dominant religion. At the more crucial level of cultural continuity, the Mormons feared that secular public schools would discretely separate the secular from the sacral, something the Mormons' integrated community resisted. For them, as for the Mennonites and the Amish, the close-knit Mormon community was a "redemptive community" within which the faithful would not only find peace for their souls, but food for their stomachs. Naturally, schools for the Mormons would be expected to reinforce rather than challenge this way of life.

The fear that the community would be disrupted is at the root of the Mormon resistance to schools that would *not* reflect their community values of, for example, egalitarian cooperation, even if these were weakening as the nineteenth century drew to a close. Underlying this is a tenet from Joseph Smith's revelations which sets out the close correlation in nineteenth-century Mormonism between spiritual and material spheres: "if ye are not equal in earthly things ye cannot be equal in obtaining heavenly things" (Doctrine & Covenants 78:6). Earthy and heavenly things were all one for early Mormons, as their sixth president, Joseph F. Smith, succinctly expressed for a non-Mormon publication, *Out West*, in 1905: "It has always been a cardinal teaching with the Latter-day Saints that a religion which has not the power to save people temporally and make them prosperous and happy here, cannot be depended upon to save them spiri-

---

2. Sources for the election campaigns for the Salt Lake Board of Education are the city's major newspapers—the Mormon *Deseret News*, and the *Salt Lake Tribune*, which generally supported the non-Mormons in school and other social issues. The coverage for board elections appeared in July issues of the papers for 1890 and thereafter in November and December issues.

tually, to exalt them in the life to come."[3] When this notion is extrapolated to the political realm, it is easy to understand why the Mormons resisted gentile efforts to clearly distinguish between the two. Only a few documented instances can be found in which the Mormons used the Bible and other Mormon sacred texts in the ward schools. Nevertheless, the fact that the schools met in the LDS meeting-house and almost all teachers and students were Mormon made even the supposedly secular district schools a reflection of the Mormon community and its values. In such circumstances, the hidden curriculum of the Latter-day Saints was pervasive. As far as non-Mormons were concerned it was also probably intrusive. Prior to 1890 prayers were part of the school routine, and gentiles were convinced that Mormonism "by the devices of its schools aims to educate only to that extent as to produce faithful contributions to the one institution." Which was, of course, the traditional aim of many religious schools.[4]

A concrete example of the public schools acting as extensions of the Mormon community is the 1889 book, *The School and Primary Songster*, designed for use in *both* the public schools and in the "Primary," the weekday religious education program organized for LDS children. The book contains secular songs, as well as LDS hymns. The gentile objection to Mormon dominance can perhaps be understood when one realizes that one such hymn said: "Hail to the brightness of Zion's glad morning, Joy to the lands that in darkness have lain, Hush'd be the accents of sorrow and mourning, Zion in triumph begins her glad reign." The overt purpose of the *Songster* was to teach music; its covert purpose was to reinforce Mormon ideology, with "Zion" really a code word for the Mormon church. Given the role schools from Horace Mann's time have played in displacing the local community's value system, it is not surprising that Mormons resisted the gentile desire to tear asunder what they thought should stay together. And just as stoutly did the gentiles resist the Mormon insistence on having the school reflect Mormon values. As Carmon Hardy has observed, "Next to polygamy, Mormon attitudes toward education were probably cited . . . more often than anything else as evidence of Mormonism's alien and backward condition."[5]

The election of trustees to the Salt Lake City Board of Education in the 1890s vividly illustrates the opposition between Mormons and gentiles. It also shows that these conflicts were not simply local, precinct-level fights, but indicators of radically different value systems. One set derived from a sacral orientation rooted in the American Puritan heritage and the other from a secular orientation that downplayed religious values in the affairs of the modern state. Ralph Waldo Emerson, after visiting Utah and Brigham Young in 1871 opined that Mormon-

3. Joseph F. Smith (1905), cited in Leonard J. Arrington and Davis Bitton, *The Mormon Experience* (New York: Alfred E. Knopf, 1979), 262.

4. C. Brian Hardy, "Education and Mormon Enculturation: The Ogden Public Schools, 1849-1896," Ph.D. diss., University of Utah, 1995, 53-54, 182; *Salt Lake Tribune,* 7 May 1881, citing an article in the *Washington Republican.*

5. Evan Stephens, *The School and Primary Songster* (Salt Lake City: Coalter & Snelgrove, 1889), 103-104. Carmon B. Hardy, "The Schoolboy God: A Mormon-American Model," *Journal of Religious History* 9 (Dec. 1976): 179.

ism "was the after-clap of Puritanism."[6] Perhaps, but it was no minor distant rumbling in the Western skies. As a self-proclaimed "city on a hill" it attracted more than its share of secular lightning, both within Utah and nationally.

Similar tensions between public schools and religious communities can be seen in the cases of Roman Catholics in New York, the Old Order Amish in Ohio, and the Russian Mennonites in Minnesota. But the Utah case was exacerbated by high-profile Mormon proselyting, the Mormon hold on civic government in Utah, and large-scale emigration from Northern Europe and the British Isles as part of the LDS doctrine of "the gathering." Unlike other groups, the Mormons were not content to draw boundaries around "Mormon Country" and await the second coming; they intended to expand Zion's boundaries to encompass the whole earth, and schooling would play a role in this hegemonic enterprise. Mormons, in shaping public schools to their own ends, were protecting a cooperative community at odds with individualized industrial America.

WHAT ARE SCHOOLS FOR?

Those who opposed Mormonism in the nineteenth century denigrated the Mormons as ignorant, credulous, and naive. Some claimed they owed their success to a policy of intellectual bondage. In the words of one disaffected Mormon of 1874: "The rule is [among the Mormons]: them that is Ignorent keep them Ignorent Or they will cause trouble."[7] Such an interpretation, popular as it was, ignores the fact that Mormons *did* establish and support a system of quasi-public schools from the late 1840s to the 1880s. In common with most nineteenth-century Americans, Mormons favored schooling in general; the problem arose, in Utah and elsewhere, in determining what purposes schools should serve, what should be taught beyond the rudiments, who should go to school, how the system should be supported financially, and the extent to which religious influences should permeate the actions of those who managed the schools and those who taught the community's children.[8] In a society still unsure of the route it should follow, attempts to answer these questions often stirred acrimonious debates—as they still do—over competing notions of the school as change agent and the schools as preserver of the status quo. The central issue in such disputes, historically and currently, is whether tax-supported, public schools should promote values contrary to those of large segments of the population. Before the common school became a widely accepted and highly centralized public institution, diverse communities in the early nineteenth-century United States had created a

---

6. Cited in William Mulder and A. Russell Mortensen, eds., *Among the Mormons: Historical Accounts by Contemporary Observers* (New York: Alfred A. Knopf, 1969), 382-4.

7. John MacNeil to Ann MacNeil and Elizabeth Thompson, 11 Feb. 1874, in Frederick S. Buchanan, ed., *A Good Time Coming: Mormon Letters to Scotland* (Salt Lake City: University of Utah Press, 1988), 177.

8. For an extended discussion of Mormon attitudes toward public schools in Utah, see my article "Education Among the Mormons: Brigham Young and the Schools of Utah," *History of Education Quarterly* 22 (Winter 1982): 435-459; also Charles S. Peterson, "The Limits of Learning in Pioneer Utah," *Journal of Mormon History* 10 (1983): 65-78.

potpourri of quasi-public schools supported by a combination of local taxes, charitable societies, religious groups, and local boosters. These locally controlled schools reflected the needs of individual communities. Many, in fact, resisted the tendency of the new Massachusetts style common schools to accommodate the larger state community. Even with their localist perspective, some early institutions were very good; but whether adequate or inadequate, they reflected a popular notion that schools should mirror their societal roots.[9]

What non-Mormons perceived as a Mormon conspiracy against public schooling can be viewed as an extension of this earlier American impulse to establish schools that served constrictive religious, economic, and community needs. Michael Katz's use of the term "democratic localism" in describing the locally controlled school systems that dotted the landscape in the first half of the nineteenth century, can also be applied to the schools that emerged in Utah under the auspices of Mormon culture between 1847 and the 1880s.[10] This type of locally controlled school was in direct contrast to the system urged on America by Horace Mann and other educational leaders, which tended to be liberal, secular and more expansive in its notion of community.

In retrospect, the much criticized Mormon-established schools, operating from the 1840s to the 1880s, represent a culture lag similar to that experienced in other areas of the United States before the secular, tax-supported, compulsory Common Schools became the norm. In nineteenth-century Utah, the Mormons, although enjoying a significant degree of local control in their semi-theocratic society, nevertheless perceived themselves as being treated as second class citizens by the dominant secular society centered in the East.

SCHOOLS OF THE KINGDOM

Mormon opposition to free public schools can be summed up in Brigham Young's own words: "Would I encourage free schools by taxation? NO! That is not in keeping with the nature of our work."[11] The perception of the school's role in Mormon society reflects the Mormons' notion that they were a chosen people whose religious obligation was to establish on earth a religious commonwealth known to them as the "Kingdom of God." This "kingdom" would eventually take the place of "man-made" governments and prepare the way for the imminent second coming of Christ. The drive to establish earlier "redemptive communities" in Kirtland, Ohio, and in Independence, Missouri, in the 1830s and in Nauvoo, Illinois, in the early 1840s precipitated conflict between Mormons and their neighbors in these areas. Mormon community building (which included schools)

---

9. For an overview of the quasi-public schools in the United States prior to the establishment of public common schools, see Carl F. Kaestle, *Pillars of the Republic: Common Schools and American Society, 1780-1860* (New York: Hill & Wang, 1983), 13-61.

10. Michael B. Katz, *Class, Bureaucracy, and School: The Illusion of Educational Change in America* (New York: Praeger, 1975), 15-22.

11. *Journal of Discourses*, 26 vols. (Liverpool: F. D. & S. W. Richards, 1854-86; Reprint, 1967), 18:357.

led ultimately to an "extermination order" issued against them in Missouri in 1838 and in their expulsion from Illinois in 1846. The church's dominant role in the political, economic, and social aspects of the communities they controlled was strenuously objected to by those who did not accept the Mormon claim that they were building the Kingdom of God.

In the American West, under Brigham Young's vigorous leadership, the Mormons took advantage of the sparsely populated, wide-open spaces, establishing hundreds of communities ranging from San Bernardino in southern California to Franklin in southern Idaho. Like early Puritans, Mormons made few distinctions between church and state. Given the dominance of Mormons in the area, no one seemed to challenge the practice or the assumptions on which they were based. Faithful Mormons saw no conflict in having the president of their church, Brigham Young, serve also as the civil governor of the territory, or the president of the Quorum of Twelve Apostles, John Taylor, serve as the superintendent of common schools.

Although Protestant critics in the 1870s and 1880s made much of the intermingling of public and private domains in Utah, objecting to schools that reflected Mormon values, throughout America Protestants supported public schools in large measure because they sustained a generic Protestant ideology. Public schools in nineteenth-century America were by no means neutral with respect to religious preference, although it was usually interpreted by Protestants as "non-denominational Christianity." The dichotomy between public and private ideology in the common schools was not as clear cut as their boosters claimed.[12]

Utah's unique settlement by one cohesive religious community tended to create in critics a demand for a greater separation between the things of God and the things of Caesar. However, for Mormons to back away from what they considered to be divine mandate would have been tantamount to denying their belief that they had been chosen to fulfill the divine will in establishing the Kingdom of God. Consequently, much of Utah's history in the late nineteenth century reflects the conflict between these competing conceptions of the role of private versus public religious values, most evident as the Mormons sought, without initial success, the status of statehood.

Given their commitment to a revelation-led community, it is no wonder that the Mormons perceived their children's schools as necessary aspects of kingdom building. Schools were, as already noted, needed to reinforce beliefs and practices. In the 1880s, as schools gradually evolved toward the free school model, they could not *formally* inculcate the tenets of the Mormon religion. At the same time, neither could they (in Mormon thought) threaten the community's values or undermine faith in its leaders. Following Brigham Young, Mormon leaders in

---

12. Kaestle, *Pillars of the Republic*, 74-79; Michael B. Katz, *Reconstructing American Education* (Cambridge: Harvard University Press, 1987), 132-35. For an account of one Protestant group's attempt to combat Mormon controlled schools in Utah, see Dee R. Darling, "Culture in Conflict: Congregationalism, Mormonism, and Schools in Utah, 1880-1893," Ph.D. Diss., University of Utah, 1991.

the late 1880s took the position that compulsory schools maintained by public taxes would eventually become "Godless" institutions. As such they would reflect the values of a federal government that had waged a relentless crusade for over a decade to destroy Mormon economic, political, and social hegemony in Utah. The struggle saw six rejected attempts for statehood before it was finally achieved in 1896.[13]

The federal crusade against Mormon "plural marriage," consensus politics, and cooperative economics, convinced the Mormon leadership that dominant, direct influence over the public schools of Utah had ended. In April 1886 the First Presidency of the church declared it essential for Mormons to "keep their children away from the influence of the sophisms of infidelity and the vagaries of the sects" by "establish[ing] schools taught by those of our faith, where being free from the trammels of State aid, they can unhesitatingly teach the doctrines of true religion combined with the various branches of general education."[14] That same month, George Q. Cannon, First Counselor in the First Presidency, criticized the Mormon-controlled territorial legislature for imposing a tax on the people for the support of public schools. "Latter-day Saints through their own unwise legislation," Cannon said, had created a situation in which schools, supported by taxes levied on Mormons, were teaching everything but religion: "Thus it is that all our schools are secularized, and the Bible, the Book of Mormon and all our Church books are rigidly excluded from our schools. No teacher is permitted to inculcate any religious doctrine, and no one is required to teach even morality, lest in doing so would trench on the domain of religion."[15]

As a direct consequence of the leadership's disapproval of public secondary schools, a private Mormon secondary school system emerged during the late 1880s. However, no Mormon elementary school system developed parallel to the free public schools, perhaps because of the church's economic difficulties or because local elementary schools were less threatening than the more sophisticated secondary schools. Perhaps most Mormon parents simply did not want, or could not afford, to set up a costly parallel private school system, although some did try.

"A SCHOOL INDEPENDENT OF THE DISTRICT SYSTEM"

One such attempt at providing a parallel system was made in 1884 when the Mormon Eighteenth Ward decided to construct a new school building adjacent to its chapel. The impetus for this project came from the bishop of the ward, Orson F. Whitney, who believed the ward should have a "school independent of the District System, where the children might be taught the principles of truth and

---

13. An insightful analysis of the struggle between Mormons and non-Mormons in Utah during the latter half of the nineteenth century is Edward Leo Lyman, *Political Deliverance: The Mormon Quest for Statehood* (Urbana: University of Illinois Press, 1986).

14. Epistle of 6 April 1886, cited in James R. Clark, "Church and State Relations in Education in Utah," Ed.D. diss., Utah State University, 1958, 246.

15. [George Q. Cannon], "Topics of the Times," *Juvenile Instructor* 21 (Apr. 1886): 134.

virtue while they are young."[16] At another meeting Whitney emphasized to parents that a "fear of God should be instilled into the minds of children as the very basis of education." While the new school would promote the development of physical, musical, and intellectual faculties, Whitney left no doubt that the "most important of all is the spiritual."[17]

However, even before the Eighteenth Ward Seminary in Salt Lake City opened, doubts arose as to whether the school could be locally supported. After almost four years of construction, the ward asked church president Wilford Woodruff to allow a tenth of the tithing collected in the ward to help support the school. The request was rejected, as the church could not allow other wards similar leeway. This reluctance is understandable; given the Church's extreme financial difficulties, general church support of academies was minimal.[18]

Eventually the Eighteenth Ward raised $6,083.84 to help pay building debts, and by the end of August 1889, some $11,239 had been paid. However, every year revealed a thousand-dollar deficit due to operating expenses. Notwithstanding such financial strictures, the first class began in September 1889— one year before all the other ward/district schools in the city would automatically become public schools. Though the patrons who supported the "Latter-day Saints' Seminary of the Eighteenth Ward" were drawn from wards other than the Eighteenth, the vast majority of the students registered in its first year of operation were residents of the Eighteenth Ward—twenty-five students were even turned away because of lack of room. Students from outside the Eighteenth Ward were required to pay higher tuition fees: for example, Preparatory students from the ward were assessed $1.75 per term; those from outside the ward, $3.00 per term. With the exception of one or two non-Mormons, almost all the 211 pupils were LDS, ranging in age from six to twenty: sixty of whom were Preparatory students; eighty-four, Intermediate, and sixty-seven, Primary. The rolls listed children of a number of LDS general authorities (including the daughters of Apostle Heber J. Grant) and children with prominent Mormon family names such as Kimball, Romney, Reynolds, Toronto, Pyper, and Clawson. Notes in the student register record that some students dropped out because they were not doing adequate work—Howard Snelgrove withdrew because he came in "last in theological exercises" to which was added a clear cut reason for his failure: "refused to take." In the second year, entries indicate that some children were withdrawing to attend public schools in the city, and by the beginning of the third year (1892-93) requests for volunteers to make good on their pledges to meet the deficit were being made in the ward. At the end of the third year it was apparent that meeting the deficit was becoming a perennial difficulty. At this time

---

16. Eighteenth Ward Board, Minutes, 16 Mar. 1884. Microfilm copy of original minutes in Historical Department of the Church of Jesus Christ of Latter-day Saints, Salt Lake City, Utah. Hereafter cited as LDS Historical Department.

17. Eighteenth Ward Board, Minutes, 11 May 1884.

18. For a detailed account of the emergence of the LDS academies, see John D. Monnett, Jr., "The Mormon Church and its Private School System in Utah: The Emergence of the Academies, 1880-1892," Ph.D. diss., University of Utah, 1984.

an editorial appeared in the Mormon publication the *Juvenile Instructor* which actually sealed the fate of this parochial school in one of Salt Lake City's most prestigious and wealthiest Mormon wards.[19]

The straight-forward editorial, probably written by George Q. Cannon, cautioned the Saints against establishing ward seminaries. An astute businessman, Cannon was well aware that good intentions could not make up for depleted resources. Recognizing the need for schools in which children would not be led astray, many Mormons had concluded that the church should establish schools for all Latter-day Saint children. Desirable as this might be, financial circumstances would not permit it. Nor, given the need to be perceived as less exclusive, was it politically astute for Mormons to be seen as withdrawing from the public schools, which would leave them open to the common charge that the Church was opposed to education.

The *coup de gras* to ward-sponsored seminaries came when Cannon stated that although the church would help maintain academies for older students, because "Latter-day Saints paid their taxes the same as other citizens" they should also use the public elementary schools. Members simply could not afford to pay taxes *and* school fees. Apparently referring to difficulties in the Eighteenth Ward, Cannon noted that some Salt Lake City schools were "admirably conducted," and that Mormons could now "avail themselves of the district schools and thus be relieved from the necessity of paying tuition fees." After-school religion classes and Sunday Schools could mitigate against the children's religious instruction being neglected. Of course, if some wards were able and willing to pay taxes *and* school fees they were entitled to do so, but most Latter-day Saint children would have to attend public school.[20]

After reading the editorial, the Eighteenth Ward leadership requested a meeting with the First Presidency to ask if it applied to their seminary. The "Brethren" reiterated the position carefully outlined in the Cannon editorial: that if any ward wanted to support such schools it was "all well and good," but no support from the Church would be forthcoming. The ward leaders reported to the membership that the First Presidency "could see no reason why we should not take advantage of the free schools which had been established." With a deficit of some $443 before the school even began in September 1893, it was moved, seconded, and carried that, in view of financial distress, "we do not endeavor to conduct the School during the coming year." On 19 February 1894 the Mormon school on the Avenues was disbanded.

This effort on the part of a group of Latter-day Saints to establish their own school was made in response to many statements by Mormon leaders which seemed to encourage such schools. But it was the exception rather than the rule

---

19. Eighteenth Ward Board, Minutes, 10 Sept. 1888; 22 Dec. 1888; 6 May, 6 June 1889; 18 May 1891; 2 Sept. 1892; 4 Aug. 1893; also, "Latter-day Saints' Seminary," *Deseret Evening News*, 29 Aug. 1889. Details about the students attending the Eighteenth Ward Seminary can be found in the "Eighteenth Ward Seminary Student Register," microfilm copy of original, LDS Historical Department. I am indebted to Gordon Irving of the LDS Historical Department for bringing this material to my attention.

20. [George Q. Cannon], "Topics of the Times," *Juvenile Instructor* 28 (15 June 1893): 392-94.

in Utah in the late 1880s. As Monnett points out in his study of the rise of the Mormon academies, in spite of a stereotypical expectation to the contrary, Mormons have not always been willing or perhaps economically able to give over their decision-making prerogatives to the "Brethren"; a majority of Mormon parents simply did *not* respond to continual entreaties to support the academy movement. Nor did the Eighteenth Ward experiment serve as a prototype for other ward elementary schools. Even the centerpiece of the Mormon educational system—the Brigham Young Academy—had difficulty rousing enthusiastic support: "prominent and influential men in Provo . . . whispered in the ears of students not to listen to the 'old Dutchman' [Karl Maeser, founder and President of Brigham Young Academy]" and "to make matters still worse [those same] influential men in the community not only had no confidence in the stability of the new venture, but openly opposed it by using their influence against it."[21] The "prominent and influential" people in Provo of the 1890s were certainly committed members of the LDS church; it was not simply the laity in rural areas who resisted the Brethren's advice regarding the expansion of "higher education."

THE CAMEL'S NOSE IN ZION'S TENT

Nineteenth-century Mormon leaders and members did not so much oppose the idea of public schools or the acquisition of new knowledge as they did the *different* moral, social, and religious values which might be communicated through the schools. Of course, those convinced that the "different" value orientation of the Mormon people was in fact an irrational (as distinguished from a non-rational) perspective on life concluded that these values could only be sustained by ignorance and credulity. However, the existence of a relatively urbane and educated group among the faithful Mormons of Utah in the nineteenth century indicates that not all Mormons can be stereotyped as ignoramuses.[22] Nonetheless, given the "spiritual" emphasis present in conversion, it is understandable why some would oppose, or at least be loath to embrace, a secular system of instruction which *excluded* the teaching of particular spiritual experiences. Along with other conservative religious groups, some Mormons thought too much focus on "book learning" was impractical and might undermine faith. In addition to fears that orthodox religion might be undermined by secular schools, leaders such as Brigham Young and George Q. Cannon had reservations about tax money being used to support public schools, which went contrary to their ideological assumption that individual families, not the public treasury, should be the basis for funding schools. During an 1890 meeting on the issue of free schools

---

21. Reinhard Maeser, as cited in Monnett, "The Mormon Church and Its Private School System in Utah," 180.

22. See, for example, Dr. John A. Widtsoe's response to the charge that Utah's Mormon-oriented schools were of inferior quality. He cited his own record at Harvard, "of which I am not ashamed," as evidence that the church schools of the 1880s did a credible job of preparing him and others for rigorous university work. His "list of similar cases would fill several columns of your paper," he claimed. See "Widtsoe Upholds Standards Maintained by Utah Schools," *Salt Lake Tribune*, 26 Nov. 1921.

between Mormon legislators and church "authorities" in Salt Lake City, it was recalled that "Brigham Young always opposed free schools because he feared [they] would pauperize the people and make them feel that the state owed them an education."[23] This, of course, was a fairly common position expressed when the public school movement was being established in the East and Midwest in the 1840s and certainly not unique to the Mormons in Utah. In many rural areas in the nation, and in Utah, there was considerable resistance to common public schools, which were not viewed as necessary to an agrarian society. Similarly, there was an almost universal revulsion to government control of children and the "awful monster"—taxation.[24]

Another factor creating a lag in Utah's development of public schools was the failure of the federal government to contribute financially to territorial schools. The original Organic Act of 1850, which created the territory of Utah, stipulated that two sections of land in each township should be reserved for schools. However, this promise was never fulfilled. For political and other ideological reasons, federal authorities opposed granting these lands for school use during the 1870s and 1880s and ignored frequent appeals for the release of this "federal aid" to Utah schools.[25] From the remarks of Robert L. Campbell, Utah territorial superintendent of schools between 1862 and 1874, it appears that some territories *did* have their lands released to them prior to statehood. Unfortunately, opposition in the administrative and legislative branches of the federal government prevented Utah from getting school funds until statehood was granted in 1896. Consequently, some Mormons interpreted the refusal as a deliberately punitive act, part of the colonial mentality that pervaded much of the federal system of administering the western territories. Until 1869 Congress refused to establish a land office which would make Mormon land claims legitimate, and even then they only did so when a large gentile population demanded it. The lack of an official government survey also hindered the process of granting land to the territorial government and subsequently to the district schools.[26]

The coming of the railroad in 1869 and the discovery of silver in 1873 attracted large numbers of non-Mormons to the territory. By 1880 some twenty percent of the population was listed in the census as being non-Mormon. As early as 1874 one quarter of Salt Lake City's population was non-Mormon, claiming a greater say in the city's affairs by virtue of the fact that their property taxes

---

23. Abraham H. Cannon, Journal, 15 Jan. 1890, photocopy of original in possession of H. Stanley Cannon, Salt Lake City.

24. The popular notion that all Americans were enthusiastic about having tax-supported public schools is challenged by Wayne E. Fuller in his *The Old Country School* (Chicago: University of Chicago Press, 1982), 38-41.

25. Laverne C. Bane, "The Development of Education in Utah (1870 to 1896)," Ed.D. diss., Stanford University, 1940, 48-49.

26. John C. Moffitt, comp., "Reports of the Superintendents of Public Schools, 1861-1895." Typescript volume in Brigham Young University Library and copy in Special Collections, University of Utah, 6, 22. See also Calvin S. Smith, "Public School Land Policies of the State of Utah," Ph.D. diss., University of Chicago, 1978, 1-41; Dean L. May, *Utah: A People's History* (Salt Lake City: University of Utah Press, 1987), 116.

and licenses for businesses provided almost half of the city's budget of $110,000.[27] Although non-Mormons were not able to achieve a majority in any of the city and school board elections until the 1890s, cultural pluralism became more of a reality in Salt Lake City in the 1880s and gentile citizens began to make their opinions and values known.

The twenty-one district schools which had attempted to serve the needs of the predominantly Mormon Salt Lake City community were viewed by non-Mormons as inadequate partly because they were staffed almost entirely by Mormon teachers. Quite apart from the fact that some Mormon teachers were competent, their allegiance to the Latter-day Saint faith was enough to disqualify them in the eyes of non-Mormon citizens. And just as clearly and with as much logic, in 1867 Brigham Young expressed his feelings about the tendency of some Mormon bishops to ignore Mormon teachers in favor of outsiders. They were unwilling, he claimed, to pay a local Mormon "possessing the best talent we have among us . . . [b]ut bring a poor, miserable, rotten-hearted, cursed gentile, and they will lick the dust off his shoes to have him keep school, when he does not know half as much as the Elders in Israel know." At the same conference Young referred to these imported teachers as "miserable little, smooth-faced, beardless, good-for-nothing Gentiles."[28] James Clark succinctly sums up the reasons for Brigham Young's strong denunciation of some bishops for allowing the "camel's nose" in the form of gentile teachers into the Mormon tent. Given the Mormon claims to being the chosen people, "one can readily understand the concern of Brigham Young as Mormon control of the education of its children began to slip through their fingers. To the Mormons more than the three R's was at stake. President Young felt that the eternal salvation of the children sent to school under such 'Gentile' teachers was at stake."[29] Interestingly enough, the first non-Mormon day school, St. Mark's Day School, was established in Salt Lake City by the Episcopal Church only two months after these denunciations. As Episcopalians, Presbyterians, Congregationalists and other Protestants established private schools as a countervailing balance to the Mormon controlled district schools, their explicit purpose was to wean the Mormon children away from their parents by "Christianizing" them. There can be little doubt that such explicit aims were perceived as a threat to the Mormon community and its values.

THE TEACHER CORPS IN SALT LAKE CITY

Although the University of Deseret's original charter made that institution a "Parent School" for the preparation of teachers, lack of resources led to the dissolution of the fledgling university (and its potential as a teacher preparation program) only a year after its founding in 1850. Over the next twenty to thirty years Utah's "schools drifted to a low ebb because of an insufficient number of quali-

---

27. Thomas G. Alexander and James B. Allen, *Mormons and Gentiles: A History of Salt Lake City* (Boulder, CO: Pruett, 1984), 92-93.
28. *Journal of Discourses* 11:353, 12:406-407.
29. Clark, "Church and State," 194.

fied people who could provide learning experiences of a high quality."[30]

In spite of much contemporary rhetoric to the contrary, Utah was not widely recognized as a center of academic or scholarly activity during the nineteenth century. Nor was there a general interest in promoting high quality teacher education. Schools and their teachers reflect in large measure the societies which produce them—and teacher preparation was neglected in Utah as elsewhere because of lack of interest, lack of money, or lack of will. As Utah historian Charles Peterson expressed it, "[t]here was a dearth of qualified teachers in the early Utah years; and many who were educated either could not afford to teach or were diverted from it by pioneering, concern with salvation, or the conviction that the great teachers, after all, were life's experiences and the Holy Ghost."[31] Although meant as a humorous jest, the comment of R. W. Ashton reflects what was a common perception of teacher preparation in Utah in much of the nineteenth century: "The principal qualifications of a teacher in those days were well-developed biceps, long finger nails, square-toed shoes and the ability to hold a spelling book right side up." [32]

Through the 1860s, a major theme of the Territorial Superintendent of Common Schools, Robert L. Campbell, was that the "greatest lack . . . is that of qualified teachers." Partly as a result of Campbell's efforts, within a few years of the re-establishment of the University of Deseret in 1870, provision was made for the organization of a Normal School designed to prepare teachers for the territory's school districts. In typical fashion, however, rhetoric exceeded reality and the Normal School was given no financial aid. Campbell and his successor, Dr. Obadiah Riggs, made repeated requests for support, but not until 1876 was there an appropriation of five thousand dollars given to the university for the preparation of teachers. This aid was given on condition that forty potential teachers annually would be instructed free of charge in the normal department of the university. Students assisted in this way were required to teach one year in the district schools for each year of free tuition received.[33]

In 1880 the law was changed so that any student graduating from the normal division of the University of Deseret would be entitled to teach in any district school, provided that the county board of examination was able to "attest to the moral character" of the graduate, but graduation from a normal program was not at this time a requirement for teaching. There were apparently too many teachers needed and too few candidates to make such certification mandatory. Most teachers were certified to teach on the basis of successfully completing an examination set by the county board of examinations regardless of what their formal schooling had been. Indeed, not until 1910 were elementary teachers re-

---

30. John C. Moffitt, *The History of Public Education in Utah* (n.p., 1946), 280.

31. Charles S. Peterson, "A New Community: Mormon Teachers and the Separation of Church and State in Utah's Territorial Schools," *Utah Historical Quarterly* 48 (Summer 1980): 295.

32. "Surprise and Banquet," *Deseret News* 11 Sept. 1891. This comment was made at a dinner honoring William M. Stewart, the outgoing superintendent of Salt Lake County Schools.

33. Moffitt, *History*, 280-86.

quired to have four years of high-school work.[34]

In the absence of organized programs in teacher education it was left to the initiative of teachers themselves to help prepare the current and future cadre of teachers. As early as the 1873 Robert L. Campbell was advocating that teachers should be involved in what came to be known as "in service training," as a means of improving their skills as teachers. At the initial meeting of the Teacher's Association in Salt Lake City in 1870, the President of the University of Deseret, John R. Park, commented that the forming of the association was a "happy blending of theory and practice" which would "give teaching a tone and respectability which it so justly deserves." The minutes of the new association went on to say that the group "[s]ustained the idea of Dr. Park that school teachers should be professionals" and "[s]poke disparagingly of the present rather inconsistent manner of teaching our common schools." Eleanor J. Pratt noted that it was "great toil and displeasure" to instruct children" in the old manner of mixed graded schools" and urged the adoption of better gradation of pupils in the schools. In words that are repeated in the regular cycle of school reform rhetoric, it was also recommended that more progressive approaches to the teaching of spelling be adopted other than "the too common method of arbitrary memorizing." There was also the perennial urging that the Deseret Alphabet (Brigham Young's attempt to reform English "orthography") should be adopted in the schools. However, it was also noted that including the Deseret Alphabet as part of the curriculum had an adverse affect on student spelling. At the November meeting in 1871 Mary E. Cook read an address of the Superintendent of Public Schools in St. Louis, Missouri, William T. Harris, "on the bearing of the political state of society of the present day upon education." At the other end of the theory-practice spectrum, at the next meeting Miss Cook read materials and led a discussion on "tardiness and cleanliness."[35]

Eventually these meetings evolved into Teacher's Institutes where teachers could receive instructions from veterans such as Karl Maeser, John R. Park, Warren and Wilson Dusenbury and Mary and Ida Cook. Such meetings were usually well attended and provided an "interchange of ideas" which helped promote a sense of solidarity among teachers and helped stimulate the emergence of teaching as "a distinct and well-defined profession." As might be expected, the expenses incurred by these institutes were borne by the teachers. In 1886 Parley L. Williams, the federally appointed territorial Commissioner of Schools, campaigned vigorously for public financial assistance for these professional development institutes. Some support was given in 1890 and for a number of years attendance was even made mandatory, but by 1916 the institutes gave way to college attendance and participation in a standardized teacher education program.[36]

34. Ibid., 309.
35. Minutes of meeting of the Salt Lake Teacher's Association held in "Council House" Salt Lake City, 18 Oct. 1870; 22, 29 Nov. 1871, Utah State Archives, Salt Lake City.
36. Moffitt, "Reports," 259; Moffitt, History, 293-97.

Such a standardized program was in place at the University of Deseret by 1890. The program for prospective teachers at the University's Normal Department was "designed for those intending to become teachers in our district schools." The brochure noted that anyone having the care of children could find "this course of study and discipline a profitable one," including parents. In addition to the required courses in pedagogy (the science of education, history of education, principles of master teachers, school management), mathematics, geography and history, science, English, vocal music and drawing were taught "with special reference to the work of the teacher."[37]

The ultimate power to grant teaching certificates was lodged securely in the county educational offices during the 70s and 80s (and after 1890 in the city boards of education), but with the coming of statehood in 1896, the trend towards standardization continued and the program for the preparation of teachers at what was now the University of Utah became more centralized. All graduates from the normal course received a five-year teaching certificate and if they received an academic degree they were entitled to teach in the elementary and high schools of the state. Given the university's location in Salt Lake City there was a considerable degree of cooperation between it and the Salt Lake City Schools in the preparation of teachers.[38]

During the long period in which an institution for teacher preparation emerged there were individual teachers who were well-trained among the Mormons; one thinks of John R. Park, teacher par excellence in Draper, the Dusenbury brothers in Utah County and the Cook sisters in Salt Lake, who had received their education in the East and had settled among the Mormons as teachers before joining the Mormon Church.[39] Most professional educators seem to have brought their expertise with them and it was not until the late nineteenth century that locally trained teachers from the University of Utah and Brigham Young Academy began to meet the needs of the burgeoning public school movement. With the establishment of free public schools the need for more and better teachers increased rapidly. When Salt Lake City's schools opened in the fall of 1890 a major problem was simply finding competent teachers; previously the community had called upon whomever was willing to bear the burden of educating future generations.

At the beginning of the nineteenth century most classroom teachers in the United States were men, but by mid-century a majority were women. In 1870 some 60 percent were women, increasing to 70 percent by 1900, peaking with 86 percent around 1920 and dipping to 66 percent in 1978.[40] The following

37. *Annual of the University of Deseret 1890-91* (1890), 26-29.
38. Moffitt, *History*, 287, 289.
39. For sketches of Park and the Dusenburys, see Peterson, "A New Community," 308-9, 299-300; Jill Mulvay, "The Two Miss Cooks: Pioneer Professionals for Utah Schools," *Utah Historical Quarterly* 43 (1975): 396-409.
40. David B. Tyack and M. Stroher, "Jobs and Gender," in *Educational Policy and Management: Sex Differentials*, Patricia Schmuck et al., eds. (New York: Academic Press, 1981), 133.

chart shows the proportion of males to females teaching in the Salt Lake Valley during the years prior to the adoption of the free public school system.[41]

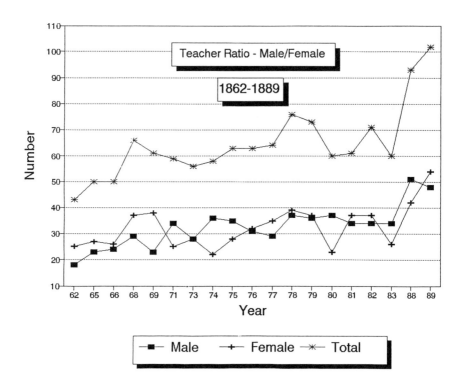

The significant decrease of men in the teaching force in 1869 may be accounted for by increased opportunity for male employment with the coming of the railroad. Similarly the increases in male teachers in 1874 and 1875 may be attributed to local and national economic depression. Apart from these increases and decreases, the most important aspect of these statistics is the indication that in nineteenth century Salt Lake City, as in the nation at large, males played a more significant role in teaching than in the twentieth century.

The new Salt Lake City School District showed a preference for a feminized teacher corp from the beginning. In 1890, for example, 43 percent of teachers were men, 58 percent women. By 1893 the percentage of women had more than doubled and stood at 87 percent. By the end of the decade 90 percent were

---

41. Prior to the establishment of a consolidated school district in Salt Lake City in 1890 statistics for the city schools were included in the Salt Lake County reports. The county figures are used here to show the overall trend of which Salt Lake City was a significant part. As far as total numbers, of course, the twenty-two Salt Lake City school districts were the largest unit in the county.

women, peaking at 95 percent in 1909, reflecting and even exceeding the national trend towards a feminized profession. The difference could be accounted for by Salt Lake City being a more urban region and reflecting the national tendency for urban areas to have a larger percentage of women in their teaching force. Another factor which might help explain the rapid change is the hiring of outside teachers by the new administration, most of whom were women—and non-Mormons at that. There was therefore a dramatic change in the religious and gender complexion of the Salt Lake teaching corps between the 1880s and 1890s: previously the ratio between non-Mormons and Mormon teachers had been 1:11; in 1893 that reversed, 11:1. In the first year of the district's existence there was an influx of 125 non-Mormon female teachers into the state, most of whom came to Salt Lake City. In the state as a whole, however, in 1896 there was almost an even split between male teachers and females, which reflects not only the more rural nature of the state, but also the fact that the Mormons were still in control of the county school systems.[42]

The bias towards viewing men as more capable of dealing with the intellectual content of the schools, while women were perceived as "nurturers" and substitute mothers is reflected in the fact that teachers in the high school in Salt Lake City for most of the 1890s were predominantly males, while in the primary grades (one through three) all teachers were female.[43]

The virulence of the Mormon leaders' responses to imported teachers helps explain why the territory in 1888 supported a mere thirty-five non-Mormon teachers out of a total of 581. However, paralleling the increase in non-Mormons political power, by 1891 the number of non-Mormon teachers had risen to 209 and the Mormon teachers to around 700. By 1895 the gentile contingent in the teacher corps stood at 443, while the Mormons showed only a nominal increase to 750. At this time almost half of the non-Mormons teaching in Utah (around 220) were teaching in the Salt Lake City schools. During the first years of their existence, the Salt Lake City schools had actually gone from being staffed almost entirely by Mormon teachers prior to 1890, to being staffed by 128 non-Mormons and only 10 Mormons in 1892.[44] In response to the accusation that he was biased in his selection of teachers, the Congregationalist Superintendent, Dr. Jesse F. Millspaugh, gave a break-down of teachers based on religious preference. Ten religious groups were represented, but of 128 non-Mormon teachers eighty were from the four main Protestant churches: Methodist, Presbyterian, Congregationalist, and Episcopalian. Only one Catholic was teaching in 1892 and twenty nine teachers had no religious preference.

---

42. Statistics on male and female teachers come from the reports compiled by various territorial and city superintendents. See Moffitt, "Reports of the Superintendents of Schools . . . ," *passim.* Reports for the following years were not available: 1863-64, 1867, 1870, 1872, and 1884-87.

43. *First Annual Report of the Public Schools of Salt Lake City for the Year Ending June 30th, 1891,* 105. Hereafter the annual reports will be cited as *[Number] Annual Report* [School Year]; *Ninth Annual Report* 1898-99, 79.

44. Bane, "The Development of Education in Utah (1870-1896)," 76; *Salt Lake Tribune,* 13 Dec. 1892.

Some in the community saw the paucity of Mormons as evidence that the board was discriminating against local teachers, but the LDS *Deseret News* defended the Board of Education's hiring practices saying that as much consideration was being given to "home talent" as was justified. Apparently, even the Mormons recognized that there were simply few competent local teachers available.[45] The quality of instruction in the ward-district schools was consequently very uneven, but some of them were under capable leadership.

German-educated Karl Maeser served as head teacher in the Budich Institute in Dresden before converting to Mormonism and influencing the quality of education at the Twentieth Ward School (later renamed the Lowell School). Non-Mormon Parley Williams, later the territory's Commissioner of Education, also taught in the Twentieth Ward. Other city schools which seemed to have earned a reputation as the "principal schools" of the city were those in the Seventh, Fourteenth, Sixteenth, and Eighteenth Wards of the LDS church.[46] However, in at least one of these wards, non-Mormon residents were a majority of voters, but according to one of the non-Mormon educators in the Seventh Ward School, A.S. Martin, the "bitterness and rancor" which characterized much of the city's politics was kept out of the school, even to the extent that the non-Mormon majority elected a staunch Mormon (and critic of free schools), David McKenzie, to the board in 1888.[47] Instances such as this indicate sometimes unclear delineation between Mormons and non-Mormons that at times allowed cooperation between the two. But there is also evidence indicating political maneuvering on the part of gentiles to oust Mormon trustees in the district schools. For example, shortly after Horace Cummings returned from his LDS mission in 1887, Salt Lake County Superintendent William Stewart asked him to be principal of the Twentieth Ward School. The decision probably had the support of the all-Mormon, three-man board of education (all of whom were members of the Mormon People's Party). In July 1888, however, the anti-Mormon Liberal Party arranged to pack a meeting called to select new trustees. By the time the representatives of the People's Party arrived at the ward house, the Liberals had approved the selection of a chairman, a secretary, two trustees and motion to adjourn the meeting. The Mormons arrived too late to find that they "had been outwitted, and that their district was in the hands of the Liberals." The new board immediately repudiated Cummings's contract, forcing him to seek employment as principal of the new Eighteenth Ward Seminary.[48]

45. *Deseret News*, 8 Dec. 1893, cited in Karl E. Lingwall, "The History of Educational Administration in Salt Lake City, 1890-1901," M.S. thesis, University of Utah, 1967, 57.

46. For descriptive details of the Salt Lake City schools before they were organized as free public schools, see *Fifty Years of Public Education, passim.*

47. "Fourteen Years in Salt Lake's Schools," *Deseret News*, 4 May 1902.

48. Horace H. Cummings, Autobiography, Chapter XVII, "Teaching Resumed." Photocopy of rough typescript in LDS Historical Department.

"Quite Fair" Salaries

Statistics on teacher salaries in Salt Lake City before the adoption of free public schools cannot be separated from the Salt Lake County Schools as a whole, but given the fact that the city made up a major part of the county population, the overall figures provide a basis for discussing salary ranges in the area of Salt Lake City in the years before public schools became a reality. From these records it appears that the teachers in Salt Lake County in 1861 were receiving an average of $267.00 per year. In 1867 Salt Lake County teachers were earning $320.82 for working a school term of eight and one half months. Salaries paid to male and females are not broken down in terms of monthly averages, but using the total amount spent on males and females and the numbers of males and females teaching in the schools it is possible to get an idea of the yearly differences between the two. For example, males earned an average of $349.00 in 1868 while females earned in the same year an average of $242.00. The annual amounts paid to teachers in Salt Lake County illustrates how large the differential between male and female teachers was and how it fluctuated over the years: from women earning 31 percent less than what men earned in 1868 to them earning 58 percent less in 1882. The sustained decrease in the average of women teachers' salaries as a percentage of men's salaries in the 1870s (women were earning 68 percent less than men) may be accounted for by the fact that there was an economic depression during this period and also an influx of males into the teaching ranks. Simply because they were males (and perhaps heads of households) men had a better chance of being hired and also receiving higher salaries.[49]

During the nineteenth century rhetoric tended to outweigh reality in appraisals of the pioneer commitment to education; comparisons of neighboring school systems between 1873 and 1887 indicate that in terms of teacher salaries, Utah lagged behind every western state and territory with the exception of New Mexico. During this period Utah paid its male and female teachers an average monthly salary of $41.10 and $23.87 respectively. By contrast Nevada paid its teachers $99.69 and $78.37; Arizona, $88.89 and $78.94; California, $81.67 and 64.65; Wyoming, $80.00 and $60.00; Idaho, $65 and $50.00 and Colorado, $53.82 and $54.16. Even with this difference, one 1881 report termed the salaries paid to Utah teachers as "quite fair" and suggested that some teachers were actually being paid more than they were worth.[50]

Pride in School Economy

The pre-1890 schools were supported rather sparingly by local district taxes (for building and maintenance mainly) and tuition fees. This type of funding was inadequate to meet the needs of the growing school population and it differed

---

49. Statistics on salaries paid to Utah teachers are found throughout the reports of the territorial superintendents of common schools published between 1868 and 1882. See Moffitt, "Reports," *passim.*
50. Stanley S. Ivins, "Free Schools Come to Utah," *Utah Historical Quarterly* 22 (1954): 328.

from district to district. Some districts had more financial resources at their command than other districts—even within the confines of Salt Lake City. Given the different property evaluation throughout the city, school patrons certainly must have differed in their ability and willingness to pay tuition fees.

In 1874, an attempt to equalize expenditures was made by aiding local district schools with territorial funds. Modest though the amount was ($15,000 for two years) this law set important precedents in requiring local trustees to maintain a school in each district for at least three months; failure to do this would lead to forfeiture of the territorial appropriation. Over the next six years the appropriation for district schools increased and by 1880 the territorial legislature was making more than $62,000 available for the school districts of the entire territory. In that year too, appropriations for the district schools were made on the basis of the number of children in the district between the ages of six and eighteen. Along with increased appropriations came increased demands from the Territorial Legislature that schools meet some minimal standards.[51]

Still, Utah did not have what could be termed a system of "free public schools" and the Liberal Party, organized in the early 1870s to counter Mormon influence in Utah politics, brought considerable pressure on the territorial legislature to adopt a free public school system. However, the Second Ward School has been claimed as the first "free public school" because in 1888 it became the first school in Utah to be maintained entirely through tax-money rather than a mix of taxes and tuition. Obviously, some LDS wards in Salt Lake City were willing to tax themselves to support adequate institutions, anticipating the kinds of schools established by the School Act of 1890.[52]

By no means was there an absence of schools in Salt Lake City (or in Utah as whole) prior to 1890, but as Mormon historian B. H. Roberts observed in 1913, the Mormons were much too proud of their economy in government to appropriate adequate support for educational purposes. He also acknowledged that they were often spurred into action by the activities of Protestant churches in establishing competitive private schools available at low cost to the public.[53]

---

51. Moffitt, *History*, 111-13.
52. The claim of the Second Ward as Utah's first "free" school was made in a letter of George K. Reese to Oscar Van Cott, [1924?] LDS Historical Department. Other claims have been made for other "firsts" including the Salt Lake Seventh Ward. According to Joseph L. Henriod, his grandfather Eugene A. Henriod, an emigrant from France, was the first teacher in Utah's first free school established in American Fork in 1867. Lorraine Henriod cites the Provo *Herald*, 8 Dec. 1970, as a source for this claim. To confuse matters more the *Salt Lake Tribune* of 6 September 1878 claimed that a "free" school had been established at the Liberal Institute in Salt Lake City. I have made no attempt to determine which school actually was the first "real" free school prior to 1890. Each community apparently had its own definition of what precisely "free" meant; it is clear, however, that there was no widespread system of free public schools prior to 1890. See *Deseret News*, 4 May 1902; Lorraine Henriod to author, 25 May 1993.
53. B. H. Roberts's comment was made in a speech to a session of the National Education Association in Salt Lake City in 1913. See *Deseret News*, 6 July 1913.

"A Good General School Law": Utah Adopts the National Panacea

As part of the federal strategy of the 1880s to abolish the practice of plural marriage, the office of Territorial Superintendent of Schools was put under the control of the Territorial Supreme Court. Latter-day Saint leaders and legislators still opposed efforts to expand the support of public schools through territorial appropriations, while non-Mormon legislators, Commissioners of Education, and territorial governors persisted in their attempts to pass legislation that would make public schools available to all children. An 1888 measure supported by three members of the Liberal Party and two members of the Mormon People's Party was overwhelmingly defeated in the House of Representatives by a vote of seventeen to five. The council then attempted to assure the expansion of an independent and parallel Mormon school system. After caucusing with Mormon apostles they passed a bill "providing for the establishment and support of district and private [including religious] schools . . . in lieu of [C. E. Allen's] original . . . act to establish a public school system and to provide for the maintenance and supervision of public schools in the Territory of Utah, which has been rejected."[54] According to Edward L. Lyman, a number of LDS apostles (including Heber J. Grant, Franklin D. Richards and John Henry Smith) met with legislators to consider a variety of appropriations bills and educational matters. They did not agree with the governor's priorities and "recommended economy in all ways."[55] One gentile proponent of free schools, C. E. Allen, who had attempted to get a free school law passed in 1888, claimed that the LDS church supported and Heber J. Grant "openly fathered" this proposal to give public funds to private schools.[56]

As might have been expected, the non-Mormon Governor, Caleb West, vetoed the proposed legislation. In West's view the provision of public funds for the support of private interests (including denominational schools) would be a "blow at the public school system which prevails in every section of our country." West argued that the act did not include any provisions for public control or supervision, thus allowing the schools to be used to promote particular religious tenets. The outcome, in West's view would, "destroy the imperfect system of district schools already existing."[57]

Allen, a prominent Congregational member of the Territorial Legislature, introduced legislation (for the second time) to establish free schools during the

---

54. *House Journal of the Twenty-Eighth Session of the Legislative Assembly of the Territory of Utah* (Salt Lake City, 1888), 323.

55. Edward Leo Lyman, "The Mormon Quest for Utah Statehood," Ph.D. diss., University of California, Riverside, 1981, 200-1, 246.

56. Allen's comments are recorded in R. N. Baskin, *Reminiscences of Early Utah* (Salt Lake City: Tribune Reporter Publishing Co., 1914), 199. Clark, in "Church and State Relations," 258-59, gives the impression that the bill providing financial aid to *all* private schools was an example of Mormon largesse. On the other hand, non-Mormon C. Merrill Hough interprets it as an attempt to give Mormon private schools a financial advantage. See his "Two School Systems in Conflict: 1867-1890," *Utah Historical Quarterly* 28 (1960): 126. To me, the evidence points more to Mormon self-interest than "largesse."

57. *House Journal of the Twenty-Eighth Session* (1888), 342-43.

1890 legislative session. He was able to negotiate himself into being appointed chairman of the education committee and on 15 January he introduced public school legislation to the House of Representatives. Incidentally, four days later at a meeting of some LDS general authorities, "it was agreed to seek . . . to get a good general school law passed and to have free public schools."[58] However, Abraham H. Cannon, a Mormon apostle present at this meeting, recorded that the majority of the "brethren" and legislators present at this meeting expressed *opposition* to the idea of free schools:

> [B]ut in view of the present perplexing school laws which were enacted contrary to the advice of President Young and other[s], and which are anything but good, it was thought best to go a little further and prepare the very best school law possible and then submit it to this Council. The establishment of free schools by our people it is thought will have a good effect among the people of this nation in proving that we are the friends of education. Free schools will therefore be established.[59]

This journal entry clearly indicates the close relationship between church and state in Utah, and also suggests that this apparent change in the Mormon position, in part motivated by the "good press" it would give the Church, helped C. E. Allen accomplish his ends. From his position as education chair he shepherded a free public school bill through the House of Representative where it received unanimous approval from the sixteen Mormons in the People's Party and six non-Mormons in the Liberal Party. This education bill disappeared in the all-Mormon Council, however, and it appeared as if it would not be acted upon there. However, as a back-up in his efforts to have free schools established in Utah, Allen had made arrangements (should his bills not be acted on) for Senator George F. Edmunds of Vermont to introduce the same Utah bill as federal legislation. The federal government would then establish a school system and provide maintenance and supervision of a public school system in Utah. According to Allen, when the Mormon legislators read in the newspapers that his school proposal was actually being considered in Washington, D.C., as a federal education bill, "all at once the committee on education in the council became very active" and Allen's free school legislation was approved unanimously.[60]

This act created schools which were in large measure free by making them dependent on tax revenue rather than on tuition, giving elected boards of trustees added authority, and eliminating the traditional small districts which had dominated Utah since pioneer times. A localist perspective supported by the Mormon church was giving way to a more centrist one supported largely by non-Mormons.

Under a variety of pressures, Mormon society underwent much change in

---

58. John Henry Smith, Journal, 18 Jan. 1890, Special Collections, Marriott Library, University of Utah. Smith was a member of the Quorum of the Twelve Apostles of the LDS church.

59. Cannon, Journal, 18 Jan. 1890.

60. Allen's account of his role in passing the school law is found in a letter he wrote to R. N. Baskin on 7 December 1911. See Baskin, *Reminiscences*, 198-201.

the late nineteenth century. In these decades a new public Mormonism was being born in which plural marriage was officially banned, cooperative economics was de-emphasized, and in which Mormons began to align themselves politically as either Republicans or Democrats rather than with the "People's Party."

It should be noted, however, that external pressures had produced changes in only "the most visible symbols of Mormon distinctiveness," while the core of the culture remained quite secure from the onslaughts of modern challenges. Some even assert that "many Utahns to this day have successfully and happily eluded 'Americanization.'"[61] Perhaps they changed just enough to pragmatically "get along," a perspective which some historians have termed "creative adjustment."[62] During the development of the public schools in Utah it is evident that Mormons accepted the secular system because they had to. They then proceeded to adjust it to fit their own needs and make it their own. Given the past conflicts some Mormons and gentiles wondered if a publicly supported system could be established in such a divided community. Others accepted the challenge and set about creating a public school district which they hoped could circumvent the conflicts of the past by focusing on the needs of the present and of the future.

61. May, Utah: A People's History, 130.
62. See Arrington and Bitton's discussion of "creative adjustment" in The Mormon Experience, 242-61.

Jesse F. Millspaugh
1890–98

2

"THE DAWN OF A NEW REVOLUTION"

The Administrations of
Jesse F. Millspaugh, 1890–98,
and Frank B. Cooper, 1899–1901

In 1891 the president of the board of education, George M. Scott (who also served as Mayor of Salt Lake City), described the potential difficulty of "welding" twenty-two ward schools into a "non-sectarian" public school system. This task required sensitivity, since at least sixty percent of the pupils in 1891 were children of Mormon parents. Scott's anxiety is understandable, given Utah's political, economic, and social controversies; the Edmunds-Tucker Act of 1887 effectively disenfranchised Mormon men and women, turned local elections over to the federally appointed Utah Commission, disincorporated the LDS church, and put its assets into the hands of a receiver. The anti-polygamy legislation also promoted free public schools by abolishing the office of territorial superintendent of schools (an elected post held by L. John Nuttall, son-in-law of the Mormon president, John Taylor). In his place the Utah Supreme Court appointed a federally approved commissioner of schools.

On 24 September 1890, Taylor's successor as church president, Wilford Woodruff, issued a manifesto that publicly disavowed the practice of plural marriage, allowing the Mormon church to survive institutionally. About ten days before this major turning-point, the city's first free public schools opened their doors, a symbolic reflection of the changes being forced on Utah and the Mormon church by the federal government.[1]

Integrating the Mormon ward schools into a public system was accomplished, in Scott's words, with "less friction than might have been expected,"[2] although, of course, tensions did surface from time to time. This chapter illustrates how, over the next decade, the Mormons worked with their gentile neighbors to build a school system based on elected trustees; to accommodate the large numbers of new "converts" to public schooling; to hire competent (even if "outside") teachers; and to initiate a graded system radically different from the traditional "one size fits all" approach to schooling.

1. Edward Leo Lyman, *Political Deliverance: The Mormon Quest for Utah Statehood* (Urbana: University of Illinois Press, 1986). The legislation creating the public school system in Utah was entitled "An Act to Provide for a Uniform System of Free Schools." It was passed by the territorial legislature on 13 March 1890. *Laws of the Territory of Utah: 29th Session of the Legislative Assembly, 1890-92.*
2. *First Annual Report*, 1890-91, 15.

PORTENT FOR THE FUTURE: THE ELECTION OF JULY 1890

Under the provisions of the new public school law, the first elections for the new school board were held 15 July 1890. The contest was straight-forward, pitting candidates from the Liberal (non-Mormon) Party against those from the Mormon-sponsored People's Party, although newspapers simply listed the contestants as "Mormons" or "Gentiles." The major theme was the polarization of politics between Mormons and non-Mormons, and few educational issues were dealt with. A leader in the fight against the Mormon control was C. E. Allen, the gentile legislator who had forced the Mormon legislature to accept a free school bill less than six months before. Allen and his cohorts in the Liberal Party were convinced that the Mormons might end up controlling the public board of education in the same way as they had controlled the city's three-man boards of the district/ward schools. The trustees of these twenty-one schools were for the most part LDS, although in some wards token gentiles were elected from time to time.

Mormon claims that the schools were non-partisan, even if dominated by Latter-day Saints, rang hollow with non-Mormons. Such schools were among the most exclusive on earth, the *Salt Lake Tribune* averred. Only Mormons were allowed to teach, and the standards required of the teachers was, accordingly, abysmally low. Nor were schools free and available to those who could not pay tuition. Why, the opposition wondered, had so much community resources gone into building the Salt Lake Temple and Mormon meeting houses while "a little, small, uncomfortable, dreadful den, built of adobes, and without one single enlightened attachment [an outhouse?] such as ought to belong to a school house, has been deemed good enough" for the city's schools. Mormons, in gentiles' minds, could not be trusted to build the new public system. Echoing the principal of the Salt Lake Collegiate Institute (later Westminster College), Dr. Jesse F. Millspaugh, gentile critics wanted to overhaul the entire system, and only the non-Mormons could do it to reflect "American ideas."[3] It was the obligation of the "Liberal Grand Army of Freedom" to "benefit the poor, blind dupes who are too steeped in mossbackism and reverence for counsel [from church leaders] to be able to help themselves."[4]

In a sermon preached in the Salt Lake Tabernacle the Sunday before the election, the church's most prominent intellectual, Elder B. H. Roberts, denied the charge that Mormons only flourished where ignorance reigned. He criticized Protestant attempts to wean children away from their parents' faith through the subterfuge of alternative schools. Roberts quoted Mormonism's founder, Joseph Smith, that humans cannot be saved in ignorance, and that Mormons believed that whatever knowledge was gained on earth would be continued in the after life. Gaining an education was part and parcel of being a Mormon, Roberts seemed to be saying. In spite of being refused public lands funds, the Mormons had provided schools for themselves and others without federal assistance.[5]

---

3. "It is not so," *Salt Lake Tribune*, 14 July 1890.
4. "The Question To-Day," *Salt Lake Tribune*, 14 July 1890.
5. "Sunday Services," *Deseret News*, 15 July 1890. Roberts was a member of one of the church's governing bodies, the First Council of Seventy.

Frank B. Cooper
1899–1901

On the same day that Roberts spoke in the Tabernacle, the *Tribune* sent a corps of reporters to visit twelve Mormon ward meetings. They reported that in some wards, speakers "harangued" the congregations about the elections; some made no mention of it and others announced that special "secret meetings" would be held after the regular worship service. In one ward, campaign material for one of the Mormon candidates was reportedly distributed. Expressing satisfaction that there was apparently no official church directives on how to vote, the *Tribune* concluded that "every meeting was conducted according to [the] political zeal or lack of it" in the ward bishop. Still, the paper warned, the only thing that would stem a Mormon tide at the polls would be the "sheer force of numbers" organized by the gentiles.[6]

On election day, each side determined to "get out the vote" with offers of free rides to the polls and the usual hoopla of electioneering. The Liberal Party had wagons on which were emblazoned such slogans as "Free Schools for Free Men" and "Education is the Fall of Superstition." One large "bus" drawn by six horses and carrying sixty five "prettily dressed" school children tugged at voters' hearts and minds with "We Appeal to You Today." The *Tribune* interspersed its partisan commentary with slogans such as "See to it Gentiles, that everyone of you votes, and see that your neighbor votes too" and "Will all Gentiles be sure to see that they vote early today?"

In all likelihood, a significant degree of chicanery was evident in the voting, although neither side would admit to such. As Edward L. Lyman points out in his detailed analysis of politics in Utah during the 1890s, in the municipal elections held the previous February there was widespread importation of voters by both sides. The paving of Salt Lake City sidewalks and developing the public water supply in City Creek Canyon were indeed public works project initiated by the Mormon City council to increase their voting rolls by 200 to 400 men brought in from the outlying areas "until after the election." Some people were even "called" to come and live in Salt Lake City by their church leaders so that they could vote for the People's Party. The importation of miners and other "transients" from Park City helped swell the rolls on the Liberal side.[7]

The same kind of tactics were apparently used in the school election of July 1890. Mormons accused Liberals of paying off their imported voters with whisky, cigars, and "sometimes even women." A "horde of Liberals" was apparently brought into the Second Ward by the railroad. Not needed in that ward, they were shipped to the Twentieth Ward polls. The only ward in which no fraud was detected was the Fifth; no fraud was needed because this municipal ward was seventy-five percent gentile.[8]

The Liberal Party swept to victory. Only three Mormons were elected: George D. Pyper, a Scottish emigrant living in the Fourth Ward, by only 15

---

6. "The Question To-Day," *Salt Lake Tribune*, 14 July 1890.
7. Lyman, *Political Deliverance*, 111-13.
8. "The School Election. Many People's Party Voters Stricken from the Lists," *Deseret News*, 15 July 1890.

votes; William J. Newman, an English emigrant, and John N. Pike, in the Third Precinct. With the exception of George Snow, who apparently had some Mormon roots, all the other board members were non-Mormon, giving the Liberal Party a majority of seven votes on the new board. Of the gentiles elected, two were in the mining industry, one was an engineer, one a grain merchant, one an attorney and one (William Nelson) was actually the editor of the *Salt Lake Tribune*. Four of them were also members of the Scottish Rite Free Masons, beginning a pattern of Masonic representation that endured until the middle of the twentieth century.

The three Mormon People's Party members on the first board were a judge, a retail shoe salesman, and a clerk in the Utah-Idaho Sugar Company.[9] Clearly the Liberals had an edge in terms of socio-economic power. They saw the election as part of the capitalist transformation of Salt Lake City, a shift away from the Mormons' cooperative focus. Not even fasting and praying for divine help in overcoming their opponents, which President Wilford Woodruff pleaded for, could compensate for failure at the polls.[10]

When the voting was tallied the *Tribune* exulted: "THE VICTORIOUS LIBERALS! . . . EDUCATION IN THE HANDS OF FRIENDS" and claimed "[t]he contest was for a free and progressive school system [supported] by the Liberals, against a reactionary and unfriendly feeling towards free schools on the part of the Mormons." The *Tribune* attributed the gentile success to the fact that many of the Mormons who had been brought in to vote in the February municipal elections had decided to leave so that they could tend their crops in Cache Valley. Another reason for the Liberal victory was that "decent and respectable Mormons" had realized that forty years of Church control of education had not produced the good schools "that every American child is entitled to." Gentile victory would, it was claimed, accrue to the "educational, moral and business interests of the city."[11]

Predictably, the Mormons saw the Liberal victory as nothing less than outright fraud. Commenting in his journal, Mormon Apostle Abraham H. Cannon wrote that the non-Mormon "control of school funds and general educational matters . . . had been brought about by [a] great many frauds . . . perpetrated by the 'outsiders' in today's proceedings."[12] Many of the People's Party decided it was no use fighting the Liberal hammerlock, but the *News* urged Mormons not to give up; in the next election they would challenge the "party of chicanery, dishonesty and fraud." Failure to do so would simply give "aid and comfort to our foes."[13]

----

9. "The School Election," *Deseret News*, 15 July 1890.

10. According to Lyman, Mormon leaders recognized in the late 1880s and early 1890s that some things were outside of their control and they asked the members of the church to fast and pray so that "the Lord may interpose in behalf of his people and preserve them from their enemies." Lyman, *Political Deliverance*, 120.

11. "The Victorious Liberals . . . Education in the Hands of Friends," *Salt Lake Tribune*, 15 July 1890; "The Reason Why," *Salt Lake Tribune*, 17 July 1890.

12. Abraham H. Cannon, Journal, 14 July 1890. Photocopy of original in possession of H. Stanley Cannon, Salt Lake City.

13. "A Repetition of 'Liberal' Fraud," *Deseret News*, 15 July 1890.

The Mormons rightly feared the damage from a low turnout: 25 percent fewer People's Party votes were cast in July than in February and out of a total of 4,759 the Liberals garnered 2,893 to the People's Party's 1,866. In almost all wards the Liberal vote increased and the People's decreased. The margin of victory was bolstered by the fact that practicing polygamists were disenfranchised by federal law. Some who had lived at the same address for 20 to 30 years were actually stricken from the rolls. Not to be ignored in explaining the failure at the polls is the reality that Mormons did not always obey their leaders' every whim. For example, a few years earlier there had been considerable resistance to Church demands that all Mormon communities establish academies.[14] The 1890s were difficult, economically, for Utahns. Poor families probably were not enthusiastic for more taxes and the luxury of an expanded school system.

Following the election the board continued working to keep Mormons out of power. At its first meeting on 19 July 1890, three names were placed in nomination for the office of superintendent: Dr. Jesse F. Millspaugh, and two other non-Mormons, E. M. Collins of Salt Lake City and George P. Beard of Vermont. The board decided that to be considered a person must be a registered voter of Salt Lake City, and the meeting adjourned without taking action. Four days later a new slate of candidates was considered and voted on: E. M. Collins received one vote; Professor William M. Stewart (who had beaten Millspaugh in the last election for the superintendency of Salt Lake County) received three, and Millspaugh, with six, was elected. The vote reflected the split along party lines with the Mormon People's Party voting for the only Mormon, Stewart, and the Liberals for Millspaugh and Collins. However, in a show of symbolic public unity, Mormon board member George D. Pyper moved that the choice be made unanimous and Mormons and gentiles gave the new superintendent their endorsement.[15]

In the aftermath of the election, Mormons challenged the seating of one gentile, Parley L. Williams, because some of the votes cast for the People's Party candidate were not counted, and his margin of victory was a mere two votes. The court upheld the challenge and in September, Williams (formerly the federally appointed Commissioner of Territorial Common Schools) was displaced by Richard W. Young, giving the non-Mormons six votes and the Mormons four.[16]

While the words sometimes changed, variations on the first election persisted well into the twentieth century. Much of the conflict over school elections in Salt Lake City can be viewed as a struggle between those who wanted the schools to express the local culture and those who wanted them to reflect national "republican values." It pitted a centralist perspective against a localist perspective, cooperation against competition, and religious community against an increasingly secular society.

---

14. John D. Monnet, "The Mormon Church and its Private School System, The Emergence of the Academies, 1880-1892," Ph.D. diss., University of Utah, 1984, 363-64.

15. Board of Education, Minutes, 19, 23 July 1890.

16. The case of Williams vs. Young is discussed in the Salt Lake Herald, 26 Sept. 1890.

FREE MASONS AND FREE SCHOOLS

Mormons were to be disappointed time and time again as Salt Lake City impaneled boards that reflected "the world" rather than "Zion." One example was the Free Masons, who, given their small numbers, had an inordinately preeminent representation for decades. Next to the Mormons themselves, the Masons were the most cohesive group and could act as a countervailing influence on the board, representing the powerful economic interests of the gentile community.[17]

With fewer than six hundred members in Utah during this period, the fact that the Masons held over 30 percent of the seats gives a sense of how disproportionately strong they were. Masonic involvement was probably tied to their self-perception as defenders of the separation of church and state, and their conviction that free public schools were necessary for the maintenance of that separation. Apparently many voters in Salt Lake City accepted the Masonic perception of the need for an effective bloc to counter Mormon hegemony. In addition, the Masons refused Mormons admission to Masonic lodges because of polygamy, and their suspicion that the Mormons had adapted Masonic ceremonies for use in the LDS temples, exacerbating some of the rivalry between the two groups.[18]

During the 1890s Masons feared that the Mormons would dismantle the free school system or use the public schools to promote Mormon beliefs through the Religion Class movement. This general fear permeated many of the elections in later years, but it was not until the 1940s, when the Masons had enjoyed a long period of dominating the board (15-20 years), that the specific issue of released time seminary became the specific focus of attention in Salt Lake City. But, as will be discussed in Chapter Six, by that time it was too late to fend off what many non-Mormons perceived to be an attack on the principle of separation of church and state: in 1943 the Mormons held an insurmountable majority of 7-3 on the board. The Mormon majority used it then to promote Mormon religious interests, just as the non-Mormons had used their majority in Millspaugh's time to block what they perceived to be Mormon incursions on the integrity of the free public schools.

MORMONS AS "FRIENDS OF EDUCATION"

In spite of their opposition, Mormon leaders were faced with the reality of a free public school system, and rather than boycott it, as some had thought they would, they immediately engaged in a struggle for control of the schools' government. Abraham Cannon reported that at a meeting of the Mormon Quorum of

17. I am indebted to Robert D. Braman, the Grand Secretary of the Masonic Lodge in Salt Lake City, for giving me access to lodge records.

18. Michael Homer, "Masonry and Mormonism in Utah, 1847-1984," *Journal of Mormon History* 18 (Fall 1992): 57-74. Homer deals with charges that the Mormon temple ritual was a plagiarized version of the Masonic ritual in his article, "'Similarity of Priesthood in Masonry': The Relationship between Freemasonry and Mormonism," *Dialogue: A Journal of Mormon Thought* 27 (Fall 1994): 1-113. For background on Masonic promotion of free public schooling, see Henry Wilson Coil, *Coil's Masonic Encyclopedia* (New York: Macoy Publishing and Masonic Supply Co., 1961), 489-90; also Carl F. Kaestle, *Pillars of the Republic: Common Schools and American Society 1780-1860* (New York: Hill & Wang, 1983), 167-71.

Twelve Apostles, the majority, given the newly passed school law, "thought [it] best to go a little further and prepare the very best school law possible and then submit it to the [Legislative] Council. The establishment of free schools by our people it is thought will have a good effect among the people of this nation in proving that we are friends of education. Free schools therefore will be established."[19]

As part of this unabashed public opinion campaign, the Church board of education invited a number of prominent American educators to visit Utah in 1892. Among them was Charles Eliot, president of Harvard University. Seven thousand people converged on the Mormon Tabernacle in March 1892 to hear Eliot discourse on religious liberty. He praised the stalwart Mormon pioneers and drew numerous parallels between them and the original religious colonies of New England. Eliot commended the Mormons for their "interest in the rising generation in education" and of having "already the beginning of two universities" in the state. Referring to Utah as "this most successful of American colonies," Eliot focused on the desirability of "liberty of education by any religious community which desires to bring up its children in its own faith." Identifying three levels of education in America as public, denominational, and private, Eliot hoped that in Utah all of these types would be "amply protected" because "there is room for all, there is work for all." Mormon Church President Wilford Woodruff responded to Eliot's comments saying he was glad he had lived long enough to hear "such gentlemen from abroad express such sentiments." He hoped that they day would soon arrive when Utah, like Massachusetts, would enjoy all the liberties guaranteed by the Constitution.[20]

Even such a prestigious figure as President Eliot could not, however, convince local gentiles that Mormons were "loyal Americans." While the *News* characterized Eliot's comments as "American to the core[.] . . . [H]is utterances breathe the air of liberty and the spirit of education and progress," the *Tribune* denounced Eliot as the "[m]ost profound crank among all the cranks of New England," adding that he had "very little common sense," was "stuffed," and that "a mistake was made when he was given an education at all." When informed of the *Tribune*'s tirade against him, Eliot dismissed it as "untrustworthy." He insisted that given the abandonment of polygamy, Mormonism should be treated as equal to other religions.[21] Included among the platform of "friends and promoters of education in Utah" at Eliot's speech had been numerous Mormon church leaders, Brigham Young Academy's Karl Maeser, James E. Talmage, Rev. Dr. David Utter of the Unitarian church, and Superintendent Jesse Millspaugh. If the *Tribune*'s vitri-

---

19. Cannon, Journal, 18 Jan. 1890.

20. "President Eliot's Address," *Deseret News* 17 Mar. 1892, as cited in Journal History of the Church of Jesus Christ of Latter-day Saints, 16 Mar. 1892, hereafter cited as Journal History. The original is in the LDS Historical Library, Salt Lake City. A microfilm copy is available at the University of Utah.

21. "An Assault on President Eliot," *Deseret News*, 18 Mar. 1892, in Journal History of date. See also *Salt Lake Tribune*, 18 Mar. 1892, and citation from the Boston *Advertizer* in "President Eliot Replies," *Deseret News*, 26 Mar. 1892, in Journal History of date.

olic attack is evidence of continued hostility toward the Mormons, certainly the presence of Utter and Millspaugh on the Tabernacle stand is some evidence of an increased degree of tolerance on both sides—a necessary condition if public schools were to succeed.

Another guest of the Mormon "outreach" campaign in 1892 was Colonel Francis W. Parker, principal of Cook County Normal School in Chicago. Although most of his visit was spent conducting a summer institute for teachers at Brigham Young Academy in Provo, where he "inspired the teachers to a high pitch of enthusiasm," he was also invited to speak in the Tabernacle in Salt Lake. Mormon Apostle Abraham H. Cannon liked what Parker had to say about the care of children and the role that religion and parents should play in developing the "highest interests" of their children. Appealing to the Mormon sense of practical education, Cannon reported that Parker "urged the teaching of children to work, even in preference to the training of the mind." It was all, of course, part and parcel of the "New Education" in which consideration of children's "nature" supplanted the traditional notion of education as dispensing subject matter. One observer, Charles Ellis, claimed that Parker found more sympathy in Utah with his child-centered pedagogy than in many Eastern communities, because "Mormons are in some things a reformatory people, more so in the past perhaps than now. But they have always been full of solicitude for their children. It is a great mistake to accuse them of opposition to education, as has been done for years."[22] Ellis's comments suggest that the Mormons' attempt to cast off their label as anti-education was taking root. If gentiles at home were not convinced by Mormon friendliness to outside educators, some national journalists were seeing them in a more positive light.

"IN HARMONY WITH AMERICAN SENTIMENT AND PROGRESS"

Understanding the culture surrounding the formation of Salt Lake City's schools requires recognizing the efforts of professional educators who were made responsible for organizing the new district. Most notable among these was the new superintendent, Dr. Jesse Fonda Millspaugh, a long-time Utah resident and member of the Congregational church.

The new superintendent was born in New York, reared in Michigan, received a BA from the University of Michigan in 1879, served as principal of a high school in Frankfort, Indiana, for two years, and in 1883 received an MD from the University of Pennsylvania. That year he was appointed principal of the Presbyterian church's Salt Lake Collegiate Institute; he became its superintendent in 1885.[23] He was well-enough known in 1888 to run as a candidate for the position of superintendent of schools of Salt Lake County, garnering a respectable 2,556 votes against 3,305 cast for a popular Mormon educator, Professor Will-

---

22. "Colonel Parker's Visit to Utah the Theme of an Interesting Correspondence," *Deseret News*, 22 Aug. 1892, citing an article by Charles Ellis in the Boston *Transcript*, 10 Aug. 1892. See also Cannon, Journal, 7 Aug. 1892.

23. *Deseret News*, 30 June 1894.

iam Stewart of the University of Deseret.[24] When he took the head of the new public school system in Salt Lake City he was, therefore, no stranger to Utah and was regarded by many as the territory's best educator.[25]

Appointed by the Liberal vote, but with the eventual support of the entire board, Millspaugh set about bringing order out of the seeming chaos of the old LDS ward school systems. Central control, not local autonomy, was the by-word among educators such as Millspaugh. Centralization of school administration was a keystone in building the much-praised "one best system" of public schooling, mirroring the emerging corporate model of business efficiency. Mormon Utah's cooperativism in the nineteenth century was viewed as the antithesis of the new model.[26] In 1887 Millspaugh blasted the old Mormon-controlled system, saying that rather than attempting to rebuild it "we would do more wisely to congratulate ourselves that there is in it so little whose complete annihilation need be lamented." It was not possible to build on top of what was there, he claimed: "Only the complete demotion of the entire fabric and the building upon its ruins of a system that is in harmony with American progress and sentiment" would give Utah the schools it needed.[27]

It would have been impossible for Millspaugh to acknowledge that parts of the old system actually met the local community's needs and may not have been as blighted or as anarchic as his professional eyes viewed it. Millspaugh, a typical progressive administrator of his day, cringed at old community education. The unitary system reflected what progressives perceived to be "best" for a nation increasingly shaped by small committees of "successful men" who made up the boards of directors of modern business corporations. As David Tyack so aptly describes them: "Their social perspective tended to be cosmopolitan yet paternalistic, self-consciously 'modern' in its deference to the expert and its quest for rational efficiency yet at times evangelical in its rhetorical tone."[28] Millspaugh fits perfectly into Tyack's profile; the Mormon community's gradual embrace of new schooling is testimony to his effectiveness as an administrator.

No documentary evidence indicates that Millspaugh openly criticized the "local culture" while superintendent. However, his highly competent supervisor of primary schools, Miss M. Adelaide Holton, ventured during her first few years to comment publicly on the city's schools. In a letter to the new national journal, *Primary Education*, Holton described education in Salt Lake prior to the establishment of public schools. Only a small number of children "received even the rudiments of an education," she wrote, giving educators the opportunity to es-

---

24. James R. Clark, "Church and State Relations in Education in Utah," Ed.D. diss., Utah State University, 1958, 253.

25. Wain Sutton, *Utah, A Centennial History* (New York: Lewis Publishing Co., 1949), 686.

26. For development of the centralization ethic in American schools, see David B. Tyack, *One Best System: A History of American Urban Education* (Cambridge: Harvard University Press, 1974), 126-76.

27. J. F. Millspaugh, "The Education Which Utah Needs," cited in Clark, "Church and State Relations," 263-64

28. Tyack, *One Best System*, 127.

tablish ideal schools "because there were no old ideas to overthrow." The *Deseret News* took issue with Holton's vision of a once "virgin wilderness" that was "lo, now, an educational paradise." In Holton's view, teachers were eager to come to Salt Lake because, in addition to higher wages, they found the children, both Mormon and non-Mormon, so "deprived of the advantages of public schools" as to be eager and anxious to learn: "all craving mental food." The *News* claimed that the schools prior to 1890 were not, as she made them out to be, so "hopelessly pitiful." (Not, it should be added, words that Holton used in her letter.) Holton, the paper concluded, simply did not have enough knowledge about the past to make such an assessment. A few days later the Mormon newspaper published another editorial which gave an account of a meeting with Holton. Holton thought the *News* had misinterpreted her comments, which were not motivated by any prejudice on her part. Indeed, a reading of her letter a century later gives one the impression that her evaluation of the Salt Lake schools was, for a non-Mormon, restrained and relatively objective.[29]

The incident is less significant in content than symbolic of a new willingness on the part of the Mormons to allow a rejoinder to their criticisms. This type of maturity made the work of Millspaugh and Holton possible. More of this kind of dialogue undoubtedly went on between community members and the professional staff. Unfortunately the tendency was for the board conflicts to grab headlines, while the quiet work of educational diplomacy went unnoticed.

"THE NEW ORDER OF THINGS"

Those who for many years had supported the concept of free public schools no doubt agreed with the *Tribune's* comment that 15 September 1890 was a "day among days" and would be remembered as "the dawn of a new revolution for Utah." Even the *Deseret News* recognized the significance of "the new order of things."[30] In any case, the nostalgic "little red school house" nestled in a green meadow may owe more to Currier and Ives lithography than to history or geography. Most early-nineteenth- century, one-room schools were unpainted and situated in the least desirable land in the community. Horace Mann, in his famous *Second Annual Report* of 1838, lamented the fact that in many Massachusetts communities the "children must continue to breathe poisonous air, to sit upon seats, threatening structural derangement, until parents become satisfied that a little money may well be expended to secure to their offspring the blessings of sound health, a good conformation, and a strong, quick-working mind."[31] The connection between an appropriate physical plant and learning was a tenet of what would be known as "Progressive Education." However, in Salt Lake City in

---

29. "We Live and Learn," *Deseret News* 30 Jan. 1894; "Explanations All Around," *Deseret News* 31 Jan. 1894, in Journal History of date; Holton, "The Public Schools of Salt Lake City," *Primary Education*, Jan. 1894, 30-31.

30. "The Public Schools," *Deseret News*, 16 Sept. 1890.

31. Horace Mann, *Second Annual Report Covering the Year 1838* (Facsimile Edition, Washington, D.C.: National Education Association, 1948), 31.

1890 the most immediate problem facing Superintendent Millspaugh was the need for any buildings at all.

When schools opened in September 1890, 8,818 children of school age had to fit into 2,728 seats. Fortunately, only 2,862 appeared for school on the first day.[32] In the Nineteenth Ward school house, 345 pupils were enrolled, but there were only 200 seats; in the Sixteenth Ward, one hundred students were crowded into a single room. The overcrowding was vividly portrayed in the Salt Lake Tribune: "[T]he new primary school building is already so crowded that the teacher has her desk in the fireplace, while the children are roosting in the windows and up the chimney."[33]

Things could have been worse: if all students who were enrolled in the schools had actually attended school in 1891, the teaching load for primary teachers would have been 81.5; intermediate, 57.4; and grammar, 21.2, making an average load of 63.6 per classroom. Fortunately for the teachers, the low attendance lessened the load to *only* 56.2 for primary, 43.1 for intermediate, and 15.7 for grammar, with an actual average classroom load of 45.2.[34]

A number of measures were taken to remedy the problem. The school board negotiated with five LDS wards for use of their church facilities as school rooms. So pressing was the situation that the board agreed to rent the Twenty-First Ward meeting house, even though the school had to be vacated on Thursday morning from ten o'clock until noon so that the Mormons could hold their weekly "fast and testimony" meeting. Hammond Hall, a school established by the Congregational church's New West Education Commission, was also used. Sarah Husband rented her private home for school use at $90 per year and the Lutheran church leased its facilities for $50 to accommodate part of the high school.[35] The *Tribune* and the *Deseret News* put aside their differences and supported a $600,000 bond issue for the construction of needed public school buildings. In the June 1891 referendum on the bond issue, 1,102 citizens voted "Yes" and only 82 voted "No."[36]

As a result of the bond issue, in the next few years the district was able to build new schools—nine being constructed in the 1892-93 school year alone. By the middle of the Salt Lake City School District's first decade of existence, "Eastern observers" praised its buildings, which were "superior to [those of] any city of like population." Given the long struggle antedating the establishment of the public school system, the board can be forgiven its self-congratulatory declaration: "We believe it can now be truly said that the great majority of Salt Lake school children are as well-housed, as well taught and are making as good

---

32. *First Annual Report*, 1890-91, 97; "Public Schools Open," *Salt Lake Tribune*, 15 Sept. 1890.

33. "Education Notes," *Salt Lake Tribune*, 14 Sept. 1890.

34. *Second Annual Report*, 1891-92, 101.

35. *First Annual Report*, 1890-91, 29; "Educational Notes," *Salt Lake Tribune*, 14 Sept. 1890; "Work of the Public Schools," *Salt Lake Tribune*, 18 Sept. 1890.

36. "The Board's Address," *Salt Lake Tribune*, 23 May 1891; "The School Bonds," *Deseret News*, 5 June 1891. Some legal reservations on the issuance of bonds were expressed in "The School Bond Question," *Deseret News*, 28 May 1891.

progress as any children in the whole country."[37]

The system's persistent growth was celebrated by William Nelson, president of the board of education, in 1894. By that year 89 percent of the school-aged population was enrolled and 72 percent were actually attending. Between 1891 and 1893 the school population had increased by 12.5 percent, but enrollment had gone up 58 percent and attendance 109 percent. A 28 percent increase in the school age population was outdone by a 129 percent increase in enrollment and a 170 percent increase in attendance. Nelson summed up the developments with a single word: "Astonishing."[38]

HIRING "PROPER TEACHERS"

With a Liberal majority in control of the board, it should not be surprising that 89 of the 101 teachers hired in 1890 were non-Mormon. Some among the Mormon People's Party worried the board of education would choose teachers to promote its own agenda, namely "to get control of the education of Mormon children [and] turn the public schools into missionary establishments to labor the advancement of the liberal party." The Salt Lake *Tribune*, of course, rejoiced in the hiring of a new corps of teachers, because they were not required to pass "an examination on the cardinal points of the golden plates."[39]

Perhaps Mormon worries were rightly founded, but the new teachers were also competent professionals. Superintendent Millspaugh's main concern was to have a well-trained cadre of teachers in the public school system—Mormon or non-Mormon. During his administration the percentage of Mormon teachers fluctuated from around 12 to 40 percent. In reality, Utah's native teaching corps was simply too small to supply all the teachers required, but in time this changed to the extent that the charge was made in later years that Mormons had flooded the market with their own teachers.

Lack of experience and training also probably accounts for the difference in salaries paid to Mormon and non-Mormon teachers during the first decade. For example, in 1890-91 non-Mormon male teachers were paid an average salary of seventy-eight dollars per month, compared to sixty-eight dollars paid to their Mormon peers. Non-Mormon females received fifty-one dollars compared to Mormon women, who received forty-six. Two years later, Mormon women had achieved parity (sixty-nine dollars) with non-Mormons, but the males received ninety-seven dollars compared to the non-Mormon men, who received one hundred twenty-two. Reflecting a traditional pattern, even Mormon men received significantly more than either Mormon or non-Mormon females.[40]

Perhaps the new teachers were not aware of previous struggles over denominational influence in the schools. In 1891 the *Deseret News* complained that

37. *Fourth Annual Report*, 1893-94, 63.
38. Ibid., 14.
39. "Public School Opened," *Salt Lake Tribune*, 15 Sept. 1890.
40. Salary schedules for Mormon and non-Mormon teachers are found in the *Biennial Reports of the Commissioner of Schools for Utah Territory* for the years 1888-95.

some Protestant teachers included more doctrine in their moral instruction than was warranted by the law. The *News* was adamant in asserting that common schools ought not to be made denominational, although the paper had supported such schools before the passage of the Free School Law.[41] If Mormons couldn't teach their religious beliefs in public school, neither could non-Mormons.

The charge teachers were given the first year sums up the broad moral basis from which they were supposed to operate. Teachers were "on all proper occasions to impress upon the minds of their pupils the principles of morality and virtue, a sacred regard for truth, love of God, love to man, love of country, sobriety, industry and frugality."[42] This was to be done, of course, "apart from the use of any denominational influence." Here was a platform for moral education on which even theologically disparate elements of the community could unite—and they did. Both sides eventually agreed with non-Mormon Professor G. M. Marshall of the University of Utah, that a non-sectarian orientation in public schools was *not* the equivalent (as Cannon had suggested in 1886) of being irreligious or "Godless."[43]

The roster of teachers during the first decade included men and women from Illinois, Missouri, New York, Kansas, Nebraska, Iowa, Indiana, and from Germany, France, and Scotland. Most had been prepared to teach by non-Utah institutions—88 percent in the first year were "outsiders." By 1892 the dependence on outside teachers dropped to 65 percent; by 1894 fully half were graduates of Utah institutions. In reporting this change Millspaugh said it represented an increase "in the numbers of teachers whose interests are most closely identified with the city in which they labor." This, he said, was not brought about by lowering standards, but because the Territorial Normal School at the University of Utah was doing better work in preparing new teachers.[44] In 1895, however, the percentage of local teachers fell to 28 percent, a fact which illustrates the rather unpredictable nature of the early profession, as does the data on the variety of institutions in which the teachers received their own education. In 1893, for example, 11 percent of all teachers in Salt Lake Schools had a "Common School" (elementary) education; 28 percent, high school; 7 percent, seminary and academy; 33 percent, Normal School and 19 percent had graduated from a college or university. The fact that almost all of the city's teachers at this early date had *some* high school preparation speaks well for the commitment to the academic preparation of teachers which the Salt Lake City schools were making.[45]

Notwithstanding this effort, in 1894 Superintendent Millspaugh complained about the lack of stability in the teacher corps citing the fact that 40 percent of the teachers were actually new to the district that year. This turnover he blamed

---

41. "District and Church Schools," *Deseret News*, 10 Sept. 1891.
42. *First Annual Report*, 1890-91, 113.
43. G. M. Marshall, "Public School System in Utah," *Utah Magazine* 9 (Apr. 1893): 267-68.
44. *Fourth Annual Report*, 1893-94, 76
45. *Third Annual Report*, 1892-93, 52.

on the lack of certainty of tenure arising out of the practice of hiring teachers for only one year at a time. Pointing to the example of Germany ("whose schools are the best in the world") he urged that tenure should be granted to all teachers who are not proved incompetent. He also faulted the legal requirement that all Utah teachers must be trained at "our own university" and those from "outside" must submit themselves to regular re-examination at the University. This yearly examination was an "undeserved humiliation" he said, and "drives away those who are well-fitted" by nature and qualification. Even those who had been trained in some of the country's best institutions had to take the prescribed examination.[46] Eventually the legislature dropped the requirement and the new law of 1896 granted lifetime certificates to graduates of the Normal School at the University of Utah and five-year certificates gained by examination.[47]

By 1899, of 217 teachers and principals employed by the District, 44 percent had been trained in Utah institutions, principally at the University of Utah and Utah State Normal School in Logan, with a sprinkling from the Salt Lake High School, Hammond Hall, Rowland Hall, and St. Marks. Only one of the high school teachers (Horace Cummings, who later became a major influence in Mormon educational circles) had been trained locally and all of the principles were trained elsewhere, most of them in the East and Mid-west. The trend, however, leaned toward eliminating the predominance of "outsiders." Certainly Millspaugh acknowledged this when he commented: "As never before, the people of the city have come to realize that the schools are theirs and that their interests in the school are vital."[48] The percentage of locals increased during the early years of the twentieth century so much so that by 1914 Ellwood Cubberley of Stanford University criticized the city's schools for being too provincial.

This same evolutionary development had, of course, been replicated in countless American communities in the 19th century. Centralization of teacher preparation and the standardization of normal schools' curriculum was a national phenomenon. So too was the conflict over whether the local schools should reflect the beliefs of the religious communities that spawned them, or whether they were supposed to reflect the larger system of values known as "the American way of life."

THE ESTABLISHMENT OF GRADED SCHOOLS

Ungraded schools, in which children aged five to late teens shared the same classroom, were the rule in America for much of the nineteenth century, especially in rural areas. Mid-century reformers, however, perceived the lack of a systematic approach to education. As the nation industrialized, urban communities pioneered schools organized around students' ages. Ever seeking ways to make the system more efficient for large numbers of students and increased cultural diversity, school leaders were anxious for some system of categorization. Age

---

46. *Fifth Annual Report*, 1894-95, 75-77.
47. *Salt Lake Tribune*, 12 Sept. 1896.
48. *Ninth Annual Report*, 1898-99, 80-90; *Eighth Annual Report*, 1897-98, 48-53.

seemed the most logical division. As Karl Kaestle has observed:

> Reformers believed that graded schools were not only a great pedagogical inven-
> tion, consistent with principles of efficiency and division of labor, but that they
> spurred industry and were therefore morally sound. Furthermore, they believed
> they were an essential expression of democracy in education.[49]

This "credo" dominated non-Mormon perceptions of the pre-1890 schools
in Salt Lake City. One school singled out in 1885 was described as the "Black
Hole of Calcutta." The same observer also reported "constant disorder and a total
absence of those little refinements which are among the most essential rudiments
of education . . . scarcely elbow room on desks and benches of the crudest form."
The pupils "were bright and promising little people, who, with proper school
room, plenty of air to breathe, an atmosphere regulated on scientific principles,
and a graded course of instruction . . . could not fail to become more useful
members of society than can possibly be the case under the present deplorable
system."[50] Just as the national reformers perceived the future of the Republic at
stake in the ungraded schools, this highly charged description of a "Mormon
School" makes the (gentile) reform of Mormon society dependent on graded
schools.

By the time Dr. Jesse Millspaugh was installed as Salt Lake City's educational
leader in 1890, the movement towards graded schools had almost become part
of the conventional wisdom in the United States. Dr. John R. Park, President of
the University of Deseret, and Dr. Obadiah Riggs, Territorial Superintendent of
Common Schools, had endorsed the notion in the 1870s, but without any widespread effect. The ungraded schools, according to Millspaugh, betrayed a "lack of
definite purpose and goal which in all the classes of graded schools constantly
present themselves before the pupil to arouse his ambition and lend stimulus to
his exertions."[51]

In the first year of the Salt Lake City Public Schools, educators put great effort into classifying students, preparatory to implementing a graded system. According to Millspaugh some resistance to the graded system "as being strange and
arbitrary" was expressed by many school patrons, but in time the change from the
ungraded to the graded system was accepted as satisfactory.[52] When John R. Park
advocated a similar graded system to the Mormon school trustees during a tour of
northern Utah schools, he also took care to distinguish it from "the procrustean
plan of classification, that is an arbitrary grouping of pupils" with no thought
given to how different students are in "capacity, taste, or disposition."[53]

While no mass protest to the graded system seems to have developed among

---

49. Kaestle, *Pillars of the Republic*, 133.
50. "A Mormon School," *Salt Lake Tribune*, 10 Jan. 1885
51. *Second Annual Report*, 1891-92, 109-10.
52. Ibid., 97.
53. John R. Park, in *Biennial Report of the Territorial Superintendent of District Schools . . . 1878-1879*, 9-10.

the Mormon people, initial, subdued objection to the new arrangement may reflect the feeling among Mormons that the co-operative spirit of the ungraded schools was more in accord with Mormon social egalitarianism. The systematic classifying and ordering of how people *should* live, work, or be educated according to some agreed-upon criteria—in this case age—is based on an assumption of inequality.

In his first report Millspaugh referred to the graded system's perceived "defects and limitations": the assumption that "pupils who are classified together are really equal in natural ability and preparation for the work at hand." Such a defect could be removed and the graded system more easily accepted if people would simply recognize that all pupils are "not physically and mentally of the same mould and fibre" and that this fact leads to the need for "sifting and adjustment" of grades. The new system would do this by sorting pupils on the basis of age, but would also provide opportunities in which children with "brighter abilities" would sit "side by side with pupils of duller intellects."[54]

Of course, reorganization of classrooms along graded rather than ungraded lines was promoted because it was more economical in "multiplying the teacher's efficiency many fold" and also because it allowed for better teaching opportunities. No reports mentioned the hidden agenda of the dominant capitalist values which were prevalent in the industrial United States. Accepting such a radical restructuring of schools in Salt Lake City was part of accommodating to the competitive American way. Millspaugh rationalized graded schools by pointing to "wholesome emulation" in which students are urged to "equal or surpass" each other. Furthermore the system was "merely the employment in school administration of the principles of division of labor" which had made American industry so productive.

It would be unfair to Millspaugh to leave the impression that he was no more than a technocrat. He was interested in more than establishing a system for its own sake; he was deeply interested in the child. Millspaugh held that the history of education had been stifling the "childish instinct to force helpless little ones to attend to those things which are devoid alike of enjoyment and interest to them, to compel infant sight to see truth as mature vision beholds it, and to do all in the midst of unattractive surroundings, with the accompaniment of threats and blows." He praised Friedrich Froebel (the initiator of the kindergarten movement) for his emphasis upon enjoyment as a part of learning: "I believe I am clearly within the truth when I say that interest and enjoyment, as a general rule, characterize the work of the school."[55]

Even if all the classrooms did not always reflect the needs of children, Millspaugh was at least trying to go beyond the traditional subject-centered curriculum. And even if the schools were moving away from Mormon cooperative values, the Mormon community itself was changing to accommodate to the economic and social realities of twentieth-century America.

---

54. *First Annual Report*, 1890-91, 109-11
55. *Fourth Annual Report*, 1893-94, 93.

"SENTIMENTS OF GALL AND WORM WOOD": THE ELECTION OF 1898

As late as 1898 elections still reflected the divisiveness of 1890. Like many others, this election was heralded as a non-partisan event, and the nomination of a Jewish Democrat, Simon Bamberger, by Republican C. E. Allen in the Fifth Ward gave it that aura. As in the past, partisan politics and sectarian differences once again played the decisive role in choosing board members. Still, diversity increased among those running: in addition to Bamberger's membership in Salt Lake City's Jewish community, W. B. LaVielle claimed to represent "the laboring element in the city" and came within a few votes of defeating banker M. H. Walker at the nominating convention. Miss Rachel Edwards, nominated by the Democratic Women's Club, was the first woman to make an attempt (unsuccessfully) at gaining a nomination to the board.[56]

However, the persistent division between Mormon and non-Mormon is evident in the last-minute candidature of Mormon C. W. Symons against non-Mormon Critchlow in the First Precinct, *after* the nominating convention had chosen Critchlow as the non-partisan candidate. Similarly, English born, ex-Mormon M. H. Walker found himself opposed by an English Mormon emigrant, John C. Cutler, in the Second Precinct, while the non-partisan choice in the Fourth Precinct, Brigham S. Young, was opposed by non-Mormon H. G. McMillan. Only Mormon Newman in the Third Precinct and Jewish "Gentile" Bamberger in the Fifth were unopposed. In spite of efforts to the contrary, the politics of the Salt Lake board election process could not be channelled into a simple non-partisan, non-sectarian event.

The LDS church did not take official positions at every election. Enough unanimity existed in the culture that individual Mormons usually ended up expressing *a* Mormon if not *the* Mormon perspective. In the opinion of LDS First Presidency member George Q. Cannon, the gentiles would only get what the Mormons allowed them to have. Mormons vigorously resisted Gentile encroachment whenever the occasion warranted it. Sometimes they may have done so because "the Brethren" wanted it done, but frequently they were not acting as much for the Mormon church as for Mormon culture. The lay nature of Mormon ecclesiastical leadership enhanced the perception that every Mormon was carrying out "Church" policies. The *Tribune* may have been overly sensitive to Mormon influence in the elections, but when they reported that former board member, Bishop M. S. Woolley, exhorted his flock to attend the convention and see to it that one of "our people" was nominated, there is no reason to doubt that such a direct appeal to LDS loyalties was made. However, the directive to do so may not have originated with the Quorum of the Twelve. Indeed, given the history of the relationships between Mormons and non-Mormons in Salt Lake City politics it would have been more surprising if no appeal had been made to such cultural and religious loyalty.

---

56. "Democratic Women's Club," *Salt Lake Tribune*, 17 Nov. 1898; "Walker & Young," *Salt Lake Tribune*, 9 Nov. 1898.

According to the *Deseret News*, more votes were cast in the 1898 election than in any previous, and in both precincts the non-Mormons were victorious by a very narrow margin—Critchlow by 62 votes out of almost 2,000 cast and Walker by 95 votes out of over 1,700.[57] The election returned two Mormons and three non-Mormons to the board, maintaining its six non-Mormon, four Mormon composition. It was still 7-3 for board members who were identified as Democrats and Republicans.

The *Tribune* interpreted the 1898 contest as a replay of past years: "a fight of Mormons against gentiles for control of the board of education" with LDS bishops and their councilors in the First and Second Precincts "laboring unceasingly in the interest of [Mormons] Symons and Cutler." According to the *Tribune*, "the class of Mormons known as 'block teachers' also turned out and spared no pains looking toward polling the full strength of their people." Cutler's forces were charged with conducting a smear campaign, spreading rumors that Walker had been nominated by the "saloon element" in the city. After his defeat Symons was reported to have told his opponents that "We [Mormons] will fight you from this on," suggesting that future school elections would see more of the Mormon vs. gentile struggle. In return a gentile was quoted as telling Symons's supporters, "You are laying up wrath for yourself; there are other elections and we will remember you." Although Gentile Critchlow won, after the contest he complained of the role the Mormon church had played in opposing him and sought an official investigation of church and state affairs being united contrary to the Utah Constitution. One observer of the scene, Judge O. W. Powers, noted that he "found the line drawn between Mormons and Gentiles as closely as ever. . . . We are drifting back into the old conditions. In one precinct the Mormons get up and fight the Gentiles. In another the Gentiles inaugurate the trouble."[58]

The Mormon newspaper denied any "Mormon attempt to overpower the non-Mormons." With Mormon voters making up a majority in three of the five municipal wards, if the Mormons had wished to draw an ecclesiastical line they could have done so. As it was, three non-Mormons were elected. This fact, in the eyes of the *News*, demolished the claim that the church had organized a defeat of the gentiles. What the *News* does not say, however, is that in two of the precincts (Third and Fourth) in which Mormons held a majority, Mormon candidates *were* elected; in only one precinct out of five could it really be said that the Mormon majority may have gone to a non-Mormon. In the Second Precinct, which probably had a majority of Mormon voters, the Mormon candidate said he lost because many of the people he had counted on (presumably LDS members) simply did not vote for him. The local situation seems to resist the influence Mormon culture might have wanted to exert. The *News* was both correct and mistaken in its assessment: correct in denying any overall church role in defeating non-Mormons, but mistaken when it ignores the personal Mormon vs non-Mormon na-

57. "The School Election," *Deseret News*, 8 Dec. 1898.
58. "Regular Nominees Win. Hot Fights in the First and Second Precincts," *Salt Lake Tribune*, 8 Dec. 1898.

ture of the campaign. It did claim, however, that Walker may have received a larger Mormon vote if his supporters had not resorted to injecting anti-Mormon "sentiments of gall and wormwood into the campaign."[59] In explaining the defeat of Symons in the First Precinct, the *News* claimed that the results would have been different had the practice of assessing teachers and principals for campaign contributions been made public before the election. Superintendent Millspaugh denied that he or the board had used any intimidation in assessing any of the school personnel, although he admitted that some probably did make contributions to what they viewed as a righteous cause, their prerogative as citizens.[60]

The fact that Millspaugh was repeatedly elected unanimously by the Mormons *and* non-Mormons on the board is another indication that the Mormons were anxious to portray themselves as pluralistic at a time when to be otherwise may have jeopardized the efforts to gain statehood for Utah. Any hint that the hierarchy controlled the political life of the territory was to be shunned. Having a superintendent who was a member of the Congregational church was no-doubt seen as an important element in counteracting the perception (and perhaps the reality) that Mormon power permeated every aspect of public life in Utah.

SALT LAKE HIGH SCHOOL: "THE LIGHT OF OPPORTUNITY"

Most of the growth in school buildings and in enrollment and attendance during the 1890s can be attributed to the development of elementary schools. Not until the second decade of the twentieth century did the secondary school show signs of significant growth in Utah or in the nation. The first public high school in Utah was housed in the Fourteenth Ward Schoolhouse at 153 South 200 West, later known as the Fremont School. One part of the high school was also organized in September 1890 in the basement of the Scandinavian Lutheran Church at 400 East and 200 South. These two units were consolidated into one unit in January 1892 at the Fourteenth Ward building, with a total of fifty students; the high school classes met there until W. R. Malone requested a separate building for the high school. In June 1892 the board leased the second and third floors of the Clayton Building (an unused furniture store) on South Temple for use as a high school beginning in September 1894.[61]

The first graduation for the Salt Lake High School was held at the Salt Lake Theater on 9 June 1893, with six girls and four boys receiving diplomas. In 1895 the principal again complained that the high school needed its own building; students were coming from some of the new schools which are "unsurpassed in attractiveness and sanitary provisions" and were disappointed when they came to high school.[62] In 1897 the high school moved to a building on Pierpont Street where twenty-two classes were conducted in competition with the noise of the

---

59. "The School Election," *Deseret News,* 8 Dec. 1898.
60. "Taxation of Teachers. The Story of the Shameful Practice Raised a Storm of Indignation," *Deseret News,* 8 Dec. 1898.
61. *Fifty Years of Public Education,* 42-3.
62. *Sixth Annual Report,* 1895-96, 77.

nearby factory. In 1901 this facility was destroyed by fire. The lack until 1914 of a building fully devoted to the high school indicates that the secondary curriculum was less of a priority during these early years.

Some of the latent opposition to maintaining and expanding the high school surfaced in the election for the school board in December 1897. As in the past, the *Tribune* and the *News* were fully at odds. The *Tribune* and the *Herald* favored expanding the high school and both criticized the *News* for not being active in supporting the idea. The *News* in response said it did not want to take a position on the issue, but would leave it to the voters. Their editorial claimed that Mormons favored "true education," but wondered if the people should be taxed to support the proposed expansion.[63] In the process of nominating candidates for the school board, the issue of whether candidates would or would not support the high school became a major criteria for gaining support of the "non-partisans," as the faction favoring the high school was designated. Rumors abounded that the high school would be shortened by two years; would be incorporated into the University of Utah Preparatory School, or would be abolished—all because of a shortage of funds and too great a tax burden. According to the *Herald*, the majority of people wanted the elementary schools and the high school to remain, but wanted the school system to be managed more economically.[64]

Two weeks before the election, the *Tribune* charged Elder B. H. Roberts with attacking the city's public school system in a sermon delivered at the LDS College. Roberts responded in the next issue that the article was a "perversion of half-quoted sentences." While admitting that his comments had been misleading, he vigorously denied that he had attacked the public schools. He added that if he lived in Salt Lake City he would "vote to sustain" the city's schools at their "present high level of good work."[65] Given his standing intellectually, one might expect Roberts to support the high school. Although the *News* appears reticent to campaign for high school supporters, no institutional church campaign against expanding the high school seems to have occurred.

There is no doubt, however, that individual leaders, especially at the local level, were not immune to using their church position to influence local elections. At the general level, however, there were no statements indicating the "church" as a whole either opposed or supported the high school's expansion. Indeed, on the eve of the election Apostle John Henry Smith, when asked his opinion, said he favored the board as constituted, which implied his support of those who wished to maintain the high school.[66]

---

63. "Do Not Insult the People," *Deseret News*, 1 Dec. 1897.

64. "Will Represent All. Citizens Plan of a Comprehensive School Ticket," *Salt Lake Tribune*, 17 Nov. 1897; "The Political Arena. Many Discussions Heard Regarding the Coming School Elections," *Salt Lake Herald*, 17 Nov. 1897.

65. "Latter-Day Saint College . . . Lecture by Elder B. H. Roberts on Education," *Deseret News*, 15 Nov. 1897; "Roberts' Attack on Public Schools," *Salt Lake Tribune*, 16 Nov. 1897; "Note from Mr. Roberts," *Salt Lake Tribune*, 17 Nov. 1897.

66. "Movement Ill Advised. Apostle Smith Opposed to New School Ticket," *Salt Lake Tribune*, 1 Dec. 1897.

Individual members of the LDS community did, of course, speak out against the secular schools from time to time. For example, at the beginning of the 1897 election campaign two of Brigham Young's sons, Brigham Jr. and Willard, engaged in a public discussion at a taxpayers' meeting prior to the nominating convention in the Fourth Municipal Ward. The candidates for the board expressed their support of the high school "with economy," but both Youngs spoke in opposition to using taxes for high school support. Brigham Jr., a senior member of the Council of the Twelve Apostles, claimed that his taxes were so high that they threatened to drive him out of his home just as he had been by Illinois mobs in 1846. He said he favored high standards of education, but there was a great need to practice economy and, he reportedly said, "I want to begin economizing by lopping off the high school."

His brother Willard did a *reductio ad absurdum* on the idea of having a free high school by saying that perhaps the community should also have a free university and a free law school. Willard felt the majority of people in the Fourth Ward were opposed to the free high school and that Latter-day Saints would prefer to maintain their own LDS College. He proposed that after the eighth grade students should attend the denominational schools in the city. Probably because of the Youngs' influence, both candidates, J. B. Toronto and M. S. Woolley, were defeated at the nominating convention.[67]

Other Mormons expressed anti-high school sentiments in the church meetings, which probably gave the comments a degree of legitimacy. For instance, the *Tribune* reported one sermon under the headline "Opposes Free Schools—David McKenzie's Startling Utterance." This Scottish immigrant's theme was that "Education is Right, but Free Schools Wrong," a position based on Brigham Young's views. McKenzie was opposed to a tax-supported school system when many (the Mormons) would "prefer to use the money thus diverted in sending their children to some other school."[68] While there may have been religious reasons for opposing the high school, Salt Lake City was sharing in the national economic depression and the Mormons were supporting a private high school and also paying taxes to support the public schools. Undoubtedly some of the opposition in the 1897 election had its roots in these circumstances.

Notwithstanding increasing Mormon diversity, non-Mormons continued to fear that church members wanted to return to church-governed schools. For example, on the same day McKenzie gave his sermon opposing tax-supported schools, the Reverend Adelbert Hudson delivered an impassioned plea at Unity Hall on behalf of the free school system, with special emphasis on the need for a good high school. He linked the availability of high schools to good citizenship and self-government, suggesting that Salt Lake City should consider abolishing the city council and other "expensive luxuries" rather than reducing the high school—"the sheet anchor of the Nation's safety." In a not-so-veiled reference to the "religious motives" that had entered the debate, the Reverend Hudson as-

---

67. "High School Enemies Favor Sectarian Schools," *Salt Lake Tribune*, 18 Nov. 1897.
68. *Salt Lake Tribune*, 22 Nov. 1897.

serted that if "any ecclesiastical authority" should attack the free school system it would be resisted by the people as an attack on self-government by "the interfering of secret councils and all the subtle plottings of ecclesiastical bigotry."[69]

On election day, 2 December, those who opposed the high school expansion distributed a flyer in the Fifth Municipal Ward. It urged the employment of Utah teachers in Utah schools and stated that "Common School Furnish Substantial Mental Food—All Should Receive It Free." This was followed by the downside: "High School Furnish Luxuries for all—who CAN AFFORD IT." The flyer proclaimed "Necessaries First—Luxuries Afterwards," a fair indication that the issues were probably more economic than ideological, although the bounds between these two are difficult to determine.[70]

In spite of a vigorous attempt to unseat the incumbent board members on 2 December, the *Tribune* proclaimed "High School Victory." The *Herald* exulted "Was a Splendid Victory" followed by "The little red school house wiped the earth with the opposition today." In contrast the *News* gave the election a muted headline of "The New School Board" and made no mention of the high school issue whatsoever. Nor did the *News* make any mention of the Mormon-Gentile composition of the board, although it did note that five new members of the board were lawyers. The other newspapers pointed out that the bitter contest had reminded some of the earlier 1890s when Mormons ran against gentiles regularly and openly—"a straight Gentile and Mormon fight," as the *Tribune* described the contest in the First Ward, adding that "Gentile women were strictly in evidence, and they just about stood off the Mormon ladies." It was acknowledged, however, that in some wards the Gentile candidates were elected by Mormons honoring the pledge to support the "non-partisan" candidates elected at the mass meetings, all of whom supported the maintenance of the high school. One of those doing so, James C. Bowen, was disciplined by his ward bishop for having opposed the "Right Ticket." In any event, the high school was saved and the board consisted of six gentiles and four Mormons. It was claimed that one Mormon candidate had been defeated by friends of Superintendent Millspaugh when he proposed replacing Millspaugh after the election with Dr. James E. Talmage of the University of Utah.[71]

Some of the opposition to the high school in the 1897 election may have been a residual from the perception that it was an elitist institution—a perception not lacking in substance. Nationally, high schools in the early 1890s were an uncoordinated melange of Greek and Latin classical studies designed to prepare students (mainly males) for admission to universities and colleges. The wide diversity of quality in the high schools meant, however, that universities were being confronted with little uniformity in student preparation. To correct this the

---

69. "High School Sermon," *Salt Lake Tribune,* 22 Nov. 1897.
70. *Salt Lake Herald,* 1 Dec. 1897.
71. "Altogether Satisfactory," *Salt Lake Tribune,* 2 Dec. 1897; "Bowen is Expelled. Driven from His Teacher's Quorum for Supporting Critchlow," *Salt Lake Tribune,* 4 Dec. 1897; "New Tickets in Fifth," *Salt Lake Herald,* 1 Dec. 1897; "Was Splendid Victory," *Salt Lake Herald,* 2 Dec. 1897; "The New School Board," *Deseret News,* 2 Dec. 1897.

National Education Association invited Charles W. Eliot, President of Harvard, to head a committee (the 1892 Committee of Ten) to propose a reorganization of the nation's high schools. This report ultimately led to standardized high school curriculum, parity for modern languages, and a focus on modern scientific subjects. The other major objective, and perhaps the primary purpose, of Eliot's committee was to make the high school the avenue for non-college bound students to acquire knowledge which would help prepare them for life. Here was an extreme departure from the traditional notion of the high school serving the elite citizenry; American education still grapples with the impact of this radical shift.[72]

In spite of some opposition, the high school grew steadily, if slowly. In 1890-91 there was a minuscule average of 26 students in attendance at the high school: a year later the number had tripled and by 1892-93 had reached 153—a six-fold increase. By the end of the Millspaugh era an average of 492 students attended high school. High school enrollment grew much faster than the total school enrollment. As a percentage of the total school population, the high school students went from making up a mere 0.7 percent of the total attending in 1890 to a little over 5 percent of the total in 1898. Much of this increase may be accounted for by the changes occurring in the high school curriculum and by the economy's inability to "absorb" the large numbers of young people as workers. In 1894 Millspaugh cited the Committee of Ten in a discussion of arithmetic teaching, concluding that the teaching of "cube root, duodecimals," and other unnecessary aspects of arithmetic "serve no useful purpose at the present time" and should be postponed until students are taught algebra. Millspaugh also quoted the U.S. Commissioner of Education as saying the committee's report was the "most important educational document" ever to appear in the United States. It was, of course, only the first of many national reform proposals that would shape how Salt Lake City went about the business of educating its children.[73]

According to W. R. Malone, the principal of Salt Lake High, the publicity surrounding the Committee of Ten had helped bring the high school into public focus. The committee's proposals had been discussed by local teachers and the Salt Lake City High School was judged to be more in line with the report than deviating from it. Malone went even so far as to claim that what was being done in Salt Lake City was even better than what Eliot's committee proposed.[74]

The reports submitted by high school principals during the 1890s claimed the high school was the apex of the public school system. In addition to providing the traditional preparation for the few who wished to attend a university, it also served a wider populous. This broader social purpose was to help those "born to humbler walks of life . . . see the light of opportunity" even though they "may not have the possibilities of profound scholarship or attain to distinction— most men do not." Nevertheless, the very availability of the high school was proposed as a means of helping "every poor boy and girl" widen his or her spheres

---

72. Edward A. Krug, The Shaping of the American High School (Madison, University of Wisconsin Press, 1969), chapters 1-4.
73. Eighth Annual Report, 1897-98, 76; Fourth Annual Report, 1893-94, 97-98.
74. Ibid., 109.

of life and usefulness by providing "a fair chance in life." The high school appears in this view not only to be the apex of the public school system, but a crucial gateway of American meritocracy and a necessary adjunct to the "safety and prosperity of the State."[75]

"STEADY MOVEMENT IN THE DIRECTION OF HIGHER IDEALS"

Although Millspaugh came out of a private, denominational school system to head the Salt Lake City schools, there are no indications either in the official minutes or in newspaper accounts that he failed to discharge his responsibilities in other than a "professional" and relatively unbiased manner. In 1894 the *Deseret News* even included Millspaugh in a series of vignettes about local educators and praised him for the work he had done in crystallizing "into one system" the varied schools of the city. He had done so, the *News* said, "with superior skill and characteristic fidelity."[76]

In 1892 and 1894 Millspaugh was re-elected to the superintendency by the unanimous vote of the board, but in 1896 his salary of $3,000 was cut as part of a retrenchment policy in wake of economic depression. When he was considered for re-election in 1898 a charge was brought against him of "negligence of duty." The board heard the charge, brought by a woman who claimed to have been accepted as a teacher but never called in by the superintendent. In addition she charged that Millspaugh had acceded to a parental demand that a child be promoted when it was not warranted. The *Salt Lake Tribune* reported that Millspaugh "proved himself above all the pettiness of the accusation" and was given the full support of the board, which dismissed the charges. Millspaugh himself said that he had been "placed at a disadvantage in having to fight a woman and the task was a most disagreeable one. I am very glad it is all over."[77]

With the board attempting to reduce his salary and community members picking at his performance as superintendent, Millspaugh began to wonder if he should not move on to other challenges. The next attempt to reduce his salary still further, this time to $2,400 from $2,500, was voted down 5 to 2. Shortly thereafter he was unanimously elected to another two-year term. During this time, reports circulated that while the Salt Lake board was considering his re-election he was actually in Chicago looking at other professional opportunities. On his return to the city he confirmed rumors that Dayton, Ohio, had been interested in him. He also revealed that the year before he had been elected to the superintendency of the New Haven, Connecticut, schools at a salary of $3,500, but had declined for health reasons. In connection with his trip to the East, Millspaugh mentioned that Salt Lake's schools were regarded there as being

---

75. *Second Annual Report*, 1891-92, 110-11; *Seventh Annual Report*, 1896-97, 96-7.

76. "Local Educators," *Deseret News*, 30 June 1894. In this series Millspaugh was singled out for praise along with such local worthies as James E. Talmage of the University of Utah; J. H. Paul of the Agricultural College in Logan; and W. S. Kerr of Brigham Young College.

77. *Salt Lake Tribune*, 5 June 1898, as cited in Karl E. Lingwall, "The History of Educational Administration in Salt Lake City, 1890-1901," M.S. thesis, University of Utah, 1967, 123.

among the best in the United States. He added, in words that seem to have a contemporary ring, that the Dayton schools had not learned to economize: with only a few more students than Salt Lake City they employed 350 more teachers.[78] Millspaugh also let it be known that he would accept the board's election for another two-year term, but added that he reserved the right to resign before his new term expired "if conditions and circumstances" warranted it.

In his 1898 report, Millspaugh mentioned the progress made since 1890: better discipline, better health of students, more attractive surroundings, increased cooperation between home and school, higher standards of scholarship; enrollments and attendance increased so that for "every 100 pupils enrolled during the year, more than 79 were in actual daily attendance." This he compared to the 57 in actual daily attendance in 1890-91. Of course, the endemic complaints of lack of funds, too many students, and too many absences because of infectious illnesses also appeared in his report. He also complained about the neglect of school work because students had been distracted by the patriotic enthusiasm over the training and departure of troops from Fort Douglas for the Spanish-American War. Millspaugh concluded that there was a "steady movement in the direction of higher ideals. . . . It is not by a single leap that higher standards may be attained. Progress in this direction may be slow; most healthful development is evolutionary, not revolutionary. If no retrogression takes place; if no stagnation is permitted; if advancement along all lines remains the watchword, the future of education in this city is assured."[79]

Within only a few months of his election to another two-year term, the superintendent used his escape clause. In December of 1898 he announced that he had accepted the presidency of Winona State Normal School at Winona, Minnesota, which he assumed on 4 January 1899. Because of legal enactments, an attitude of accommodation on the part of the Mormon majority (what one observer has characterized as "clever politics"), rising expectations of parents, the efforts of sensitive and capable "gentile" educational leaders, the increasing commitment of the teachers themselves, and the apparent willingness of students to attend school with minimal coercion, it was obvious by 1898 that public schools in Salt Lake City would be a fixed part of the community as the twentieth century began. Much of the credit for this achievement must go to the Protestant educator, Jesse F. Millspaugh, who led Salt Lake City schools from being a congeries of parochial institutions to becoming a system that received considerable national attention as a showcase of the American public school. In a retrospective assessment of Millspaugh's contributions, D. H. Christensen credited Millspaugh with the adoption of the "new education" espoused by such luminaries as Johann Pestalozzi and Francis Parker; the successful passing of bonds for new school buildings; the increase in attendance figures; and the issuance of free books and supplies. Most importantly he promoted the needs of children for whom the old

---

78. *Salt Lake Herald*, 15 June 1898, as cited in Lingwall, "History of Educational Administration," 124-25.
79. *Eighth Annual Report*, 1897-98, 53.

system of ungraded classes was "an instrument of torture." Millspaugh attracted to the district "a surprisingly large number of well trained and efficient people, despite the fact that salaries were low." While care must be used in accepting all these plaudits uncritically, yet at a purely descriptive level and given the norms of successful schools of the day, Millspaugh had, in the words of one of his early co-workers, Lizbeth Qualtrough, indeed left Salt Lake a legacy reflecting "his zeal, his faith and his power to inspire." Even those who wanted an insider at the helm, conceded that Millspaugh had laid a foundation for future growth and development.[80]

After leaving Utah, Jesse Millspaugh served as president of Winona State Normal School in Minnesota until 1904 when he became president of Los Angeles State Normal School (later the University of California, Los Angeles). He served in this capacity for thirteen years and died in Los Angeles in 1919 at the age of sixty-four.[81]

"NO UTAH MAN NEED APPLY"

Because Millspaugh left before the expiration of his term, the board of education asked Adelaide Holton, Supervisor of the Primary Schools, to act as superintendent (in consultation with Millspaugh's secretary Miss Cox) until a successor could be chosen. As far as can be determined no women applied for the position and Holton served until Millspaugh's successor had been named about six months later. For this she received extra pay of $350.[82] Millspaugh's departure raised the question of whether a local person or an outsider should be appointed to replace him. This in turn reintroduced the religious factionalism that had dominated earlier school politics.

The board of education, in 1898, was evenly balanced for the first time. The following year, though, four seats were held by members of the LDS church and six by non-Mormons. It was this split board of 1899 which had the task of selecting a successor to Millspaugh and prior to the selection there was considerable discussion in the newspapers over the issue of whether a Utah person would even be considered.[83]

As might be expected, the *Tribune* feared that the schools might again come under "sectarian" control. This elicited a response from "A Citizen" in the *Deseret News* who stated that "the Mormon people are not so blind to the fact, that as long as there are Gentile residents there will be Gentile teachers." Admitting that Mormons were partial, the correspondent averred that so too were the Gentiles,

---

80. D. H. Christensen, "Jesse Fonda Millspaugh," *Utah Educational Review* 25 (Feb. 1932): 300-1, 330, 332-33; Qualtrough's tribute is in *Twenty Ninth Annual Report,* 1919-20, 120.

81. "Dr. Jess F. Millspaugh, Former Salt Laker, Dies," *Deseret News,* 13 Dec. 1919.

82. Board of Education, Minutes, 30 Dec. 1898; 23 May 1899. Holton graduated from the Oswego Normal School in New York in 1882 and came to Salt Lake City in 1892. She left Salt Lake District in 1901 to become primary supervisor in Des Moines, Iowa. She authored a number of educational textbooks and is listed in *Who's Who in America,* vol. 9 (Chicago: Marquis and Co., 1916).

83. Assertions about religious affiliations of board members were derived mainly from obituaries in Salt Lake newspapers.

"there being this difference, the latter hang on like grim death." The writer went on to claim that Eastern educators were not all they claimed to be and "have not always covered themselves with glory in the Salt Lake City schools."[84]

The News was highly critical of the manner in which the sub-committee had gone about its business and asserted that two or three of the board "who proclaim their ability to dictate terms" had already decided that they must look beyond the local scene for a suitable candidate. The entire board had not even met to discuss the issue, but already it was apparent that a banner had been hung proclaiming: "No Utah Man Need Apply." As far as can be ascertained only two of the five member sub-committee charged with winnowing down the number of applicants were non-Mormons—E. B. Critchlow and H. P. Henderson—so it is entirely possible that some Mormons on the committee also favored an outsider.

The need to consider a local product was the subject of a formal Deseret News editorial in its first comments on Millspaugh's resignation. There the idea was expressed that while scholarship was a necessary quality of a new superintendent "a man may be a scholar and be a villain still." The News hoped that the majority on the board would give due consideration to "home applicants" concluding that otherwise "it will be difficult to persuade the public that the motive is not some other than a desire to fill the place with the best ability obtainable."[85]

The sub-committee of the board eventually published a list of qualifications which would have inhibited all but the most persistent of the forty people who applied for the position. The person sought must, the committee said, be intelligent, a trained leader, respected by business, teachers and community with a reputation beyond the community, be between 33 and 50 years of age, in good health, "a man of culture and refinement, of broad scholarship, of proved administrative ability and well trained in modern educational methods." The future superintendent should be endowed with much common sense and business judgement, a man of ideas and resources who can lead the schools of Salt Lake City to higher achievement, but not through experimentation. "Other things being equal," it would be best if he were from "our own neighborhood, or from the western or middle states" and be willing to make Salt Lake City his permanent home and identify with the people of the city.[86]

In spite of what appeared to be a great deal of sentiment in favor of a local person, at its meeting of 11 April 1899 the board elected an "outsider," Frank Cooper of Iowa, over a prominent Utah educator, Professor Joshua H. Paul, who had served as President of Brigham Young College in Logan. Jere Frank Bower Cooper was born in 1855 in Mount Morris, Illinois, attended Cornell University for a year in the late 1870s, and served as superintendent of schools at LeMars, Iowa, from 1883 to 1890. After a year as a professor of pedagogy at the State University of Iowa he spent eight years as superintendent of schools at Des

84. "The Public Schools," Deseret News, 28 Dec. 1898; see also letter of H. A. Smith, "A Utah Man Preferred," Deseret News, 16 Dec. 1898.

85. "The Superintendent of Schools," Deseret News, 21 Dec. 1898.

86. Board of Education, Minutes, 2 Feb. 1899; "Give Us A Utah Man," Deseret News, 3 Feb. 1899.

Moines, Iowa, the position he held at the time of his election to head the schools in Salt Lake City. While his religious affiliation was not mentioned during his bid for the superintendency, he appears to have been a member of the Congregational church. Prior to coming to Utah he had joined the Masonic Order in Iowa, but there is no evidence that he was active in the Masonic fraternity while living in Utah.[87] Frank Cooper's Masonic affiliations may have served as a recommendation to the four members of the Masonic order who were on the board when he was appointed—Edward B. Critchlow, Simon Bamberger, H. P. Henderson and M. H. Walker. Such factors, however, never became a matter of public discussion.

The religious overtones surrounding Cooper's appointment are stark reminders that the same old suspicions were still alive under diplomatic facades. In the eyes of one national education journal, Cooper's task was to continue the work begun by Millspaugh of civilizing Mormons through the development of public schools. Salt Lake City, the article said, was "a good place for a superintendent with a missionary zeal [who] is willing to suffer crucifixion if need be." The work of "converting the Mormons" would be no bed of roses for the new superintendent, the article predicted, "or, if it is, the roses will have their thorns."[88]

The board was split on Cooper's appointment, even to the extent that the Mormon minority simply refused to make the vote unanimous after he had been elected by a vote of six to four. The *Deseret News* openly criticized Cooper's appointment as an example of the board's desire to keep Mormons from having a voice in school affairs. Members of the board had "freely declared that 'Mormon' control of school affairs must and shall be prevented." Great effort had been made to keep Mormons in a minority on the board "and to continue the appointing power in that board, instead of vesting in the people where it belonged." The much touted "non-partisanship" of board elections, the *News* declared, was in fact a screen to block Mormons from gaining influence on the board. As far as the Mormon newspaper was concerned, "[t]he only reason Joshua H. Paul was rejected by the six majority as superintendent of schools was because he is a 'Mormon.'" The *News* derided the title of "Dr." given to Cooper by his supporters and denied that he had graduated from Cornell or had even taught at Iowa State University. The acerbic editorial ended with the accusation that the main reason Cooper had been appointed was because he had been recommended by ex-superintendent Jesse Millspaugh and the acting superintendent Adelaide Holton. The implication was that the board was still dominated by anti-Mormon sentiment. The "indignation" aroused by Cooper's appointment, the *News* hoped, would lead to action that would "settle the matter at the first lawful opportunity"—referring probably to the Mormon desire to have the

---

87. A sketch of Cooper's life can be found in Clarence Bagley, *History of Seattle* (Chicago: Clarke Publishing Co., 1916), 446-47.

88. *School and Home Education* (May 1899): 487-88.

superintendent elected by popular vote of a majority of the people.[89] The issue
of popular election of superintendents was not confined to Salt Lake City
schools. In many urban centers throughout the nation progressive reformers
campaigned energetically to remove the "people" (often members of minority
groups) from direct participation in school politics. The reformers believed that
the community was best served if the choice was made by the small boards usually elected at large across the cities rather than allow the masses to meddle in
school affairs.

While Cooper was being considered for the Salt Lake superintendency, Representative Alice Smith Horne, a Mormon teacher and legislator from Salt Lake
City, introduced legislation that would have permitted the direct election of superintendents in Salt Lake City and Ogden. The ensuing debate on the bill's merits raised the old arguments about the "'Mormon plot' to capture the schools and
return them to the chaotic level of pre-1890." On the other side were charges
that school personnel were being hired because they were anti-Mormons.[90] The
boards in Salt Lake and Ogden asked the legislature to drop the bill after bitter
exchange. Eventually it was dropped from consideration; the next election finally
brought a Mormon majority to the board and the need to elect a Mormon superintendent through a popular vote became moot.

In spite of the initial criticism Cooper suffered, the Council of Women's
Clubs organized a "brilliant reception" for Cooper at the Kenyon Hotel, at which
"all classes without regard to sect or party" tendered the community's greetings to
"Professor Cooper." Mormon musician Evan Stephens composed a special song
of welcome and Mrs. A. V. Taylor, President of the Council, gave an address on
the hopes of Salt Lake City mothers that the new superintendent would help
their children to "live nobly in the positions of life in which God has placed
them: that they shall live their own lives unselfishly, sincerely, joyously."

The president of the board, W. A. Nelden, spoke as a businessman in welcoming the new superintendent. Reflecting the *zeitgeist* at the turn of the century,
he described the schools as a "business proposition" that "should be conducted
upon the same principles that every business man conducts his business"—that
is, as an investment. Salt Lake City had invested millions of dollars in the system,
resulting in "a better class of people" being attracted to the city. Professor William
Stewart of the University of Utah said the board had chosen Cooper wisely and
anticipated an expanded curriculum that would include kindergarten, industrial
education, and manual training. In response, the new superintendent underscored his main objective as superintendent: "I stand unalterably for the inalien-
able rights of children and will protest against any interference with these rights,
either from within or without." He viewed his appointment as the launching of a
"little argosy of hope for public schools" and prayed that it would return to the
citizens "full freighted, bearing a burden of blessing for the children of Salt Lake

City."[91]

Following the reception, Cooper was interviewed for the *Deseret News* by Joseph H. Paul, whom he had defeated in the contest for the superintendency. Cooper elaborated manual training as a necessary aspect in the education of the whole individual, from kindergarten through the higher grades. He expressed admiration for Utah's "progressive spirit" and, with respect to the "new education," he laid out his educational philosophy: "Today has demands all its own, heightened and glorified by the excellence of the yesterdays, and the educational system which might have been suitable for a departed day is unworthy of the present because the present is new and contains new issues and new requirements."[92]

Copper continued his progressive tenor in his first talk to the teachers. In Deweyan terms he asserted that school should be a "miniature world in which [the child] can enjoy himself, in which he can improve himself, in which he can enlarge himself and so he can be living" instead of *preparing* for living. Teachers should assist and serve children, and the superintendent should serve teachers.[93] In time the new superintendent made friends on both sides of the cultural spectrum and when he come up for election to a two year term on 13 June 1900 he received a unanimous appointment.[94]

Unfortunately, Cooper did not get much of a chance to implement his new educational perspectives in Salt Lake City. Although the reception at the Kenyon Hotel had made much of the close co-operation between home and school, after Cooper had been in Salt Lake a year he complained of too much parental indifference, a lack of enforced compulsory school laws, and a decline in attendance.[95] Cooper's principal difficulty, however, was smallpox, which closed schools for thirty days. This epidemic precipitated a fracas over whether children who had not been vaccinated against smallpox should be allowed to attend school. The board originally voted to exclude un-vaccinated children in December 1900, but when the Mormon majority was seated on the board they rescinded the decision and allowed un-vaccinated children—40 percent of the students—to attend school.

Predictably, this issue pitted the *Deseret News* against the *Tribune*. The *News* took the position that the Board of Health had no legal right to interfere in school affairs and that vaccination against smallpox had not proved to deter the spread of the disease. The *Tribune* disagreed on all counts. For refusing to heed the Board of Health's order six members of the Board of Education were taken to court. Eventually the Utah Supreme Court ruled in favor of excluding un-vaccinated students, but the issue was made moot by the state legislature's passage of the McMillan Bill, making it legal for parents to refuse vaccination for their children.

91. "Welcome to the Superintendent," *Deseret News*, 12 May 1899.
92. "Interview with Professor F. B. Cooper," *Deseret News*, 13 May 1899.
93. *Salt Lake Tribune*, 14 May 1899, as cited in Lingwall, 140-41.
94. Board of Education, Minutes, 13 June 1900.
95. *Eleventh Annual Report*, 1900-1901, 60-61.

During the heated debate over the vaccination issue, Superintendent Cooper was caught between the contradictory mandates of two legal entities—the Board of Health and the Board of Education. In February, when the superintendent expressed a desire to address the board concerning which board the teachers should obey, Oscar W. Moyle invoked the "gag" rule preventing Cooper from speaking without the unanimous vote of the board. "If we have a superintendent who cannot comprehend our order I am opposed to hearing him," said Moyle. Cooper responded that it was the first time he had ever sat on a board and had not been allowed to ask a question "and I hope never to again." To this Moyle replied, "You might not have the opportunity."[96]

Within a few weeks, Cooper was appointed superintendent of Seattle schools and resigned from his Salt Lake position. He claimed that Seattle had lobbied him throughout the past year, but that he had wanted to stay in Salt Lake for two years. He must also have been aware of the rumors in the press (all denied, of course) that the board's new Mormon majority intended to remove him; Moyle's comment that Cooper "might not have the opportunity" to make any statements to the board was certainly not an empty threat. In the spring of 1901 Salt Lake City was looking for its third superintendent of public schools while Frank Cooper began to make his mark on the public school system of Seattle, Washington, where he left a twenty-nine year legacy of "good schools."[97]

Within a few months, Oscar Moyle invited a young Mormon educator, D. H. Christensen (then in Illinois preparing to enter the University of Chicago's doctoral program) to interview for the superintendency. In June 1901 Christensen became the first of a series of Mormons to direct the development of public schools in Salt Lake City, ending a decade of gentile leadership of the city's schools.

---

96. The issue of small-pox vaccination is covered in detail in Lingwall, "History of Educational Administration," 148-70.

97. For an insightful appraisal of Cooper's role in the development of progressive schools in Seattle, see Bryce E. Nelson, *Good Schools: The Seattle Public Schools, 1901-1930* (Seattle: University of Washington Press, 1988).

3

"HOME ABILITY FOR HOME AFFAIRS"
The Administration of
D. H. Christensen, 1901–16

The sequence of events following Frank Cooper's resignation as superintendent indicates that Oscar Moyle, if not the entire Mormon majority on the school board, wanted D. H. Christensen, a relatively urbane, scholarly administrator from rural Utah, as Cooper's replacement. Christensen's unanimous election as Salt Lake's third superintendent was in no way a portent that the Mormon/gentile antagonisms were at an end. To the contrary, between 1901 and 1916, the elections for the school board were, if anything, more acerbic and divisive than those of the 1890s. They were similar, however, in that the Free Masons of Salt Lake City once again played a major role in representing the interest of non-Mormons. Although non-Mormons held a significant bloc on the board it was not until the end of Christensen's tenure that they once again achieved dominance.

In spite of the struggle between Mormons and non-Mormons, the school district was not made moribund. The city was becoming an economic center of the Mountain West, and with economic growth came population expansion and the enlargement of the school system. The public high school became more a necessity as industry left fewer and fewer jobs for a young work force.

By the end of Christensen's tenure, the two schools that would eventually evolve into two West and East High Schools competed with the private Mormon high school. The public high schools reflected the national concern that some students be prepared for college and others for various "probable destinies." Although considerable energy was put into manual and industrial education, by 1917 Salt Lake lagged behind similar cities in vocational course enrollment. Apparently, among the students at least, the manual arts and domestic science classes were perceived as rounding out one's life rather than as preparation for the world of work.

In 1913 the National Educational Association chose Salt Lake City as the site of its annual convention, a concrete example of the way in which the city's schools were regarded as "regular American" institutions. The visit of Dr. Booker T. Washington of the Tuskeegee Institute in Alabama reinforced the perception that Salt Lake was a progressive educational city. Washington saw great affinity between the histories of African-Americans and Mormons, and his focus on vocational education, reflecting national concerns for a trained work force, dovetailed into the Mormon penchant for practicality.

Other national concerns shaped the programs of the city's schools. The

D. H. Christensen
1901–16

perennial "back to basics" movement belied the common perception that schools were student-centered, activity-oriented, "embryonic communities" of John Dewey's making. Some of this found its way into the Salt Lake schools, but the main focus was still upon teacher-centered, subject-oriented institutions securely insulated from any real concern with the larger world—except perhaps, as they reflected an overweening concern for efficient, scientific management.

In spite of talk about Mormon accommodation to secular society in this period, as late as 1916 there were still considerable degrees of political, social, and cultural tensions. While the Mormon accepted the public schools in a manner unthought of two decades before, they were still anxious to be in full control of their children's schooling. They wanted schools to reflect Mormon culture, if not in teaching religion then certainly in making sure that teachers and administrators upheld Mormon values. Just as strongly, gentiles made sure public schools were independent of the control of the Mormon church.

POLICY FOLLOWS ELECTION RETURNS

During the election campaign of 1898, the Mormons, who had come out on the losing end, warned that future elections would be fought on a clear Mormon/non-Mormon basis. Non-partisan pleas were expressed during the election of 1900, but as in the past, these never went much beyond rhetoric. In the same issue of the *Deseret News* that announced the formation of a nominating committee for "non-partisan" school elections, the editor challenged the old notion that the Church interfered in school politics. When non-Mormon "sectarian religionists" spoke out on issues, according to the editorial, they were not regarded by the non-Mormons as exercising religious interference: "[B]ut let an active 'Mormon' engage in a similar task and the air is rent with cries of horror, and the prejudices of non-'Mormons' are worked upon, and the screws are applied and the lash is [unleashed], until weak people are terrorized and made to believe that something awful is going to happen if they support a 'Mormon' candidate [for] any office."[1] Denying that the Mormons wanted to promote sectarian division, the *News* warned antagonists that should such division occur "it would not be to their profit, they may rest assured." The latter reference seems to say that when, eventually, the Mormons would become a deciding factor on the board, they would promote their own interests in spite of opposition. The editorial concluded that the issue of "home ability" should be given a "free chance" in the upcoming election.[2]

Three precincts during the 1900 election saw very little controversy, partly because they were safe seats for the incumbents: the Second and Third were safe for the Mormons and the Fifth for the gentiles. However, in the First Precinct, which over the years had increased its Mormon vote, the nominating committee pitted the incumbent, Democrat non-Mormon E. W. Wilson (who was also chairman of the Salt Lake County Democratic Party), against Republican Mormon and

1. "Tomorrow's Election," *Deseret News*, 4 Dec. 1900.
2. Ibid.

bishop's counsellor L. Frank Branting, whose nomination was seconded by Mormon educator J. H. Paul. Paul believed that Wilson had been responsible for sabotaging Paul's appointment as superintendent the previous year.

In the Fourth Precinct, Mormons launched a different strategy to defeat incumbent H. P. Henderson, a gentile, Presbyterian, Free Mason. Joseph Geoghegan, a successful Irish Catholic businessman, the father of eleven children who enjoyed good relations with his Mormon neighbors, was nominated by the "nonpartisans" to oppose Henderson. Geoghegan said he was induced into running "as a protest against narrow-mindedness and bigotry" which had led to Mormons and Catholics being denied positions in the schools because of their religious orientation, a rationale denounced by the *Herald* as a smoke screen for "the active agency [i.e., the Mormon church] at work to secure [Geoghegan's] election."[3] He was viewed as a "church" candidate, even though he was a practicing Roman Catholic. Rumors surfaced that Father Dennis Kiely, the Vicar General of the Salt Lake Diocese, was making a house-to-house canvass of Catholics in order to ensure defeat for Henderson and that he knew of specific instances in which Catholics had been denied positions because of their religion. Kiely denied both reports, although he did say that he believed that both Mormons and Catholics were discriminated against in the schools. The *Herald* quoted the Vicar General as saying, "It was not the Catholics who nominated Mr. Geoghegan, but the Mormons."[4]

Some Mormons, however, countered the reports that Geoghegan was the "official" candidate of the Mormon church. Brigham S. Young (Brigham Young's grandson), who was then serving with Henderson as a representative of the Fourth Precinct, stated his unequivocal support of Henderson and vehemently denied that religious discrimination played a part in the selection of teachers. A letter to the *Herald* from another Mormon who planned to vote for Henderson also denied that the election in the Fourth Precinct was actually a Mormon/non-Mormon contest. In the inflammatory rhetoric of turn of the century politics in Salt Lake City this was not likely to persuade many voters. Both sides were already convinced that the election was a clear-cut competition between Mormons and their sympathizers and the anti-Mormon element in the city.

On election day the *Deseret News*'s front page headlines claimed that of twenty-six teacher applicants from the University of Utah, only seven had been hired by the Board of Education. The article lauded Oscar Moyle's long-time policy to increase the proportion of Utah-trained teachers in the city's schools. Conversely, the *News* charged that E. W. Wilson consistently opposed the hiring of Utah teachers.[5] The message to people in the First Precinct was clear: to increase the number of local teachers, Wilson should be replaced by Branting.

Admonishing their readers to "Re-elect the Old Board" (made up of six non-

---

3. Phone conversation with Joseph Geoghegan's daughter, E. M. Geoghegan, Salt Lake City, Jan. 1992; Letter from N.Y.S., "Religion Not In It," *Salt Lake Herald*, 4 Dec. 1900.

4. "Lively Fights Are On," *Salt Lake Herald*, 2 Dec. 1900.

5. "Teachers from University," *Deseret News*, 5 Dec. 1900.

Mormons and four Mormons) the anti-Mormon *Herald* praised board members for their commitment to good education and asserted that the schools would benefit if they were all returned. Geoghegan's candidacy was based on an "airy, unsubstantial fabric of discrimination against Catholics"; they were surprised that a man as "far-sighted and keen-witted" as he would allow himself to be so used. The main issue in the school elections was, for the *Herald*, the domination of politics by the Mormon church. This domination was clearly evident in the Mormon's success in making Utah, normally Democratic, Republican at the last general election. At that time the Church, it was claimed, had influenced the state vote, turning it from supporting Bryan to giving its electoral votes to McKinley by a small margin.[6]

To back up its contention, the *Herald* published accounts of LDS bishops urging their flocks to vote for Branting and claimed that a flyer had been distributed at a Mormon Mutual Improvement Association meeting in the LDS Second Ward publicizing Branting's candidacy on the Sunday before the election. While such activities were not beyond the pale of probability, in this instance the flyer was actually one announcing Professor Evan Stephen's annual Christmas concert and offering a prize of $20 to the Sunday School class which had most members in attendance at the concert. Given the charged atmosphere it was easy, however, for contestants to read ulterior motives into every move.[7]

On 5 December, a rather light turnout of voters (only one twelfth of the electorate) led to both non-Mormon incumbents being defeated by considerable margins. For the first time in the history of the board the non-Mormon majority was clearly waning. Although the Mormons did not have an absolute majority in this election, they did achieve parity through the concerted efforts made to replace Wilson with Mormon Branting. If Catholic Geoghegan was elected, as appears to have been the case, by "churchmen," then the Mormon vote on the board could be considered 6-4.[8] The Mormons now had a block they could use, if they wished, to promote their own agenda, especially if the non-Mormons ever split on an issue.

Friction between Mormons and gentiles was no where near an end. One of many instances following the election came at a board discussion about the naming of a new school (later named Lafayette) at the board meeting of 7 May 1901 when Cooper's resignation was accepted. A number of names were discussed by the board—Utah educators such as John Park and Karl Maeser among them. When the name of "Kimball" was suggested, board member Critchlow asked which Kimball was meant. When told Heber C. Kimball (Brigham Young's counsellor) who had owned the land on which the school stood, Critchlow snorted: "Oh! What in [hell?] did he ever do for education?"[9]

---

6. "Re-Elect Old Board," *Salt Lake Herald*, 4 Dec. 1900.

7. "The Facts in the Case," *Deseret News*, 6 Dec. 1900.

8. "The Reason of Yesterday's Results," *Salt Lake Herald*, 6 Dec. 1900.

9. "Session of the School Board," *Deseret News*, 8 May 1901.

"Home Talent" at Last

The *Herald* accurately complained that the election of 1900 was a victory for those "demanding the employment of more Utah and home-educated teachers." This focus on hiring local teachers coincided with the claim that Cooper's vacated superintendency should go to a competent local person—i.e., a Mormon. Some thirteen persons from across the country applied for the position, but as the *Herald* noted in its headline of 8 May 1901: "No Utah Man Applies."[10] However, a telegram dispatched by Oscar Moyle to D. H. Christensen in Chicago produced a "Utah Man" in very short order.

David Henry Christensen was born in Manti, Utah, in 1869, the son of Danish immigrants. In 1870 his father, Herman J. Christensen, was excommunicated from the LDS church for "selling goods in Manti in opposition to counsel" and consequently young "D. H." attended the Presbyterian Mission School in Manti until the age of twelve. His earliest ambition was to prepare for the Presbyterian ministry, influenced to some degree by his Scottish teacher, Mrs. McMillan, wife of the Rev. Joseph S. McMillan. When he was fourteen he affiliated himself with the LDS faith, but throughout his life he paid tribute to the influence his Presbyterian Mission School experience had on his educational development.

In 1887 Christensen entered the Normal Course at the University of Deseret, graduating in 1890 as a teacher. He later received a BA after the institution became the University of Utah. In 1890 he received an appointment at the age of 21 to be principal and teacher in Payson's schools, a position he held concurrently with the superintendency of the Utah County School District from 1893 to 1897. For approximately a year he also served as a member of the Utah State board of education prior to serving a mission in Germany for the LDS church.

While in Europe he intended to study the educational system of Germany and make comparisons between the American and German schools. Accordingly, at the conclusion of his mission he enrolled at the University of Goettingen, where he attained a "creditable record" in the study of psychology, anatomy, physics and "Ueber das Gedachtnis" (thought processes) between October 1900 and March 1901. In the spring of 1901 he decided to return with his wife Catherine and children to the United States where he immediately made plans to enter the University of Chicago's Ph.D. program in education. While preparing to take the Chicago entrance examination he received Moyle's invitation to accept the superintendency of the Salt Lake City schools.

Christensen travelled to Salt Lake to be interviewed by the board, which questioned him cordially but carefully about his "experience and scholastic training." Recounting the event, Christensen felt that his recently completed mission "was not a contributing factor in my favor." Much to his astonishment, however, the board elected him to the superintendency by a vote of 7 to 2. All of the Mormons on the board voted for Christensen, joined surprisingly by two Free Ma-

---

10. "No Utah Man Applies," *Salt Lake Herald*, 8 May 1901.

sons: Simon Bamberger and Matthew H. Walker. Perhaps the fact that he had been educated in a Presbyterian school, had studied pedagogy at Goettingen, and had an excellent record as a teacher and administrator in Utah County schools, made non-Mormon board members less wary of Christensen's religious affiliation. The board of education on 2 July 1901 made his election unanimous and offered him a salary of $2,800 per year. At age 32 he became the first member of the LDS church to hold the superintendency. He served a year of the unexpired term of Frank Cooper and was subsequently elected to seven two-year terms, ending his tenure in 1916.[11] The Mormons saw his selection as vindicating "home ability for home affairs."[12]

Schools in the Context of Culture and Politics

If J. F. Millspaugh in the 1890s laid the foundation for a modern school system in Salt Lake City, D. H. Christensen built the walls and put on the roof. The history of city school systems since the early decades of the twentieth century has, in the words of David Tyack, "been in large part an unfolding of the organizational consequences of centralization."[13] Christensen and the men and women he appointed to work with him played a major role in the unfolding process as it took place in Salt Lake City in the early years of the twentieth century.

The more society changed from a simple, personalized organization to a complex, depersonalized entity, the more public schools changed and responded to the demands placed upon them. The school in the twentieth century began more and more to assume some functions traditionally placed upon the family, the small community, and the church. These institutions had always played a dominant role in social control. The expectation that schools should play a similar role increased rapidly as the other institutions declined in importance. During the early decades of the twentieth century, school and society became inextricably joined to each other under the banner of "Progressive Education" as more than ever society viewed schools as the "balance wheel of the social mechanism" Horace Mann had envisioned in the 1840s.

In this atmosphere of progress, Utah was integrating into the national political and economic scene. Accommodationism, a survival strategy, came to pervade all aspects of life in the "Beehive State," although there was never a complete disavowal of Mormon values and practices. Consequently, the political, cultural, and religious tensions of the 1890s, although sometimes muted and submerged, certainly did not entirely dissolve. The city might now have a com-

---

11. Biographical data derived from D. H. Christensen Papers, Special Collections, Marriott Library, University of Utah; Oral histories of Dean K. Christensen and Kathleen C. Hall, Spring 1990; also "Transcript of Studies," University of Goettingen, in letter to the author from Dr. Ulrich Hunger, University Archivist, 27 July 1990; "Board Unanimous for Christensen," *Salt Lake Herald*, 3 July 1901; "Unanimous Vote for Christensen," *Deseret News*, 3 July 1901; Board of Education, Minutes, 2 July 1901.

12. "Home Talent Recognized," *Deseret News*, 3 July 1901.

13. David B. Tyack, *One Best System: A History of American Urban Education* (Cambridge: Harvard University Press, 1974), 126-27.

petent Mormon superintendent, but the old antagonisms persisted, including the supposedly non-partisan contests for the board of education. D. H. Christensen fell heir to this community divisiveness. It is something of a tribute to his political skills that he stayed at the helm for as long as he did. Eventually, much tension eased and the overt Mormon/gentile conflict was muted (at least in public debate) towards the end of his tenure.

A major symbol of Christensen's success in building an effective school program was the decision of the National Education Association to hold its annual convention in Salt Lake City in 1913. D. H. Christensen played a major role in Salt Lake's selection and he must have felt honored when thousands of educators converged on Salt Lake to celebrate the Fourth of July and to honor public schools' roles in building America—and Utah.

Welcoming the assembly, Governor William Spry touted the fact that in 1913-14, Utah had used 86 percent of its tax revenues in support of education—a figure so "astounding" that he had it double checked for accuracy. This had led to an even more astounding figure: 88.1 percent of the state's revenue was actually earmarked for education. The other welcome address came from the State Superintendent of Public Instruction, A. C. Nelson. He illustrated the city's "cosmopolitanism," with the fact that the city's teachers came from more than one half of the states. The cordial atmosphere even invited jokes about delegates swimming in the Great Salt Lake, where "you will have all your sins washed away and become fit subjects to dwell in Zion—if you repent." The editor of the *Journal of Education*, A. E. Winship, praised Utah for not only entering the educational mainstream, but for being leaders of educational progress. This stood out in stark contrast to Winship's criticism in 1886 that the Mormons had a stranglehold on educational progress in Utah.[14]

Before such accolades resounded at the NEA convention, however, Salt Lake City's schools had remained the battleground for a continuation of the protracted struggle over control of the public schools. Indeed, as part of the NEA meeting in Salt Lake, Sunday, 5 July, had been declared Educational Sunday, the sermons preached throughout the city still echoing past disputes. One given at Immanuel Baptist Church was entitled: "The Two Bulwarks of Liberty: The Free Church and the Free School." At the Congregational Church, the Reverend Elmer Goshen, an ardent critic D. H. Christensen and of Mormonism in general, preached on "The Cost of Liberty." The city's schools may have been showcases for pragmatic pedagogy at the NEA convention of 1913, but the years leading up to it were characterized by political confrontations between Mormons and gentiles.

Politics kept entering the picture partially because some groups did not believe that Mormons had *really* given up the practice of plural marriage as promised in the Manifesto of 1890; nor had they, it was widely held, given up their

---

14. *Journal of Proceedings of the Fifty-First Annual Meeting of the National Education Association*, Salt Lake City, 5-12 July 1913, 26-29; A. E. Winship, "The Education Cure of Mormonism," *Proceedings of the National Education Association* (1886): 117; see also his comments made during a visit to Salt Lake City in *Utah Educational Review* 4 (Jan. 1911): 24-25.

control over almost all aspects of life in Utah. Local Protestant ministers stopped
Democrat B. H. Roberts from being seated in the U.S. House of Representatives
in 1898 because he was a polygamist. Similar objections were raised about seating Republican Reed Smoot in the U.S. Senate in 1903. There ensued a three
year investigation of Smoot's suitability for membership in the Senate because he
was member of the Quorum of Twelve Apostles and belonged to a church that
embraced polygamy theologically even as it disavowed the practice. In Smoot's
case, however, the Senate ultimately voted to accept him.[15]

These non-educational circumstances were reflected in the schools when the
new American Party appeared on the Utah scene. This party consisted of a "coalition of anti-Mormon ministers, businessmen and professional people" who questioned the loyalty of the LDS people and the legitimacy of the church's claims to
having given up plural marriage. In 1904, the anti-Mormon American Party
elected its first candidate when Joseph Oberndorfer, a Free Mason in the Fifth
Civic Ward, defeated Dr. Gilbert Pfoutz, a fellow Free Mason but also a "non-partisan" candidate, perceived as under the thumb of the Mormon hierarchy. Oberndorfer had only a plurality of 62 in the 1904 board election, but in 1905 the
American party elected the mayor and six of the city's councilmen. As might have
been expected, the dominant theme of the election campaign was that the LDS
church controlled the city's politics. In 1907 the American Party once again
gained control of the city by electing a former Democrat as mayor over the attempts of both Democrat and Republican parties to forestall further American
party gains. In spite of a large Mormon voting bloc among the Salt Lake City
electorate, the American Party exploited the fact that the Mormon vote was split
between Democrat and Republican candidates. Their ability to raise the specter
of church domination worked in their favor for a number of elections. Nevertheless, when the city adopted a commission form of government and elections became (supposedly) non-partisan, they lost their electoral advantage.[16]

In spite of considerable American Party success in the municipal elections
and although they ran complete tickets against the much criticized non-partisan
ticket, the Americans never elected any more than one or two of their candidates
to the school board. Ironically, the reputedly non-partisan Mormons increased
their numbers on the board, finding an ally in the Catholic Church's *Intermountain Catholic*, which denied the Americans' assertion that the Mormon church
controlled the schools. According to the Catholic newspaper, "there are a good
many more Gentiles than Mormons teaching in our public schools." The opposition to the Mormon influence in Salt Lake City's public schools, according to the
Intermountain Catholic, was based on secular prejudice against religion: simply
having a majority in Salt Lake City did not necessarily mean the schools were, as

---

15. Thomas G. Alexander, *Mormonism in Transition: A History of the Latter-Day Saints, 1890-1930*
(Urbana: University of Illinois Press, 1986), 11, 18-26.
16. "One American is Elected," *Salt Lake Tribune*, 8 Dec. 1904; Thomas G. Alexander and James
B. Allen, *Mormons and Gentiles: A History of Salt Lake City* (Boulder, CO: Pruett, 1984), 140-42; and
conversation with Thomas Alexander, 10 Sept. 1990.

charged, sectarian. Some Protestant teachers were using their position to debase the Catholic religion in the eyes of Catholic children.[17]

In the election of December 1906, the *Tribune* inveighed against the "agencies of a corrupt, lecherous, criminal priesthood" and called for an American victory on the school board.[18] Numerous cartoons on the front page of the *Tribune* during this election attacked reputed LDS influence: lecherous looking board members asked a trim young teacher: "Are you prejudiced against polygamy?"; a spindly Joseph F. Smith hurtled a bowling ball of a "non-partisan ticket" down an alley toward the ten pins (the board) saying "I think I'll make a strike this time."[19] The non-partisans listed at the primary conventions, the *Tribune* claimed, "read very much like the roster of a ward priesthood meeting." It warned its readers that if the Mormons gained control of the school board, LDS Religion Education Classes (then a part of many public schools in Utah's rural areas) would be introduced in Salt Lake. It trusted the "enlightened public of Salt Lake" to see through the "malevolent hypocrisy" of the non-partisan ticket and sweep them all from office.[20]

Opponents of the non-partisan approach may have over-reached themselves and created something of a backlash: the election results were reported by the *Herald* as victory for the non-partisans, while the *Tribune* somberly announced that "Mormon Church Controls Schools"—"Six Members of Board Will be Mormon Elders." Including Professor Byron Cummings of the University of Utah, considered a "Jack Mormon" supporter, the Mormon majority on the board could be viewed as 7, while the non-Mormons had 3, two of whom were Free Masons. In the *Tribune's* view the landslide was "attributed to Gentile apathy and to Mormon activity. Every Mormon bishop in Salt Lake, and practically every block teacher, were at work for the non-partisan ticket."[21] The Mormon-supported ticket even overcame the American majority in the First and Second Wards, giving the Mormons their first majority since the public schools were established in 1890. The Mormon bowling ball may not have commanded a "strike," but it had produced something of a "spare" perhaps; the 6-4 status persisted through most of D. H. Christensen's tenure as superintendent.

So too did the *Tribune's* attacks on the Mormon-dominated board. In 1908 the paper expressed keen disappointment that the "fraudulent, 'non-partisan' sectarians will retain control of the schools as heretofore, in the interests of the Mormon Church." Unfortunately, the editorial complained, the majority voting in a very light election were willing to have "Mormon partisanship and Mormon sectarianism in charge of public schools. And as long as they wish it so, there is nothing more to say. But some day the public is liable to have a rude awakening, when it is too late." In this particular election four Mormons were elected, and

17. *Intermountain Catholic*, cited in "As to the Public Schools," *Deseret News*, 8 Oct. 1904.
18. "School Regeneration," *Salt Lake Tribune*, 17 Nov. 1906.
19. These cartoons appeared in the *Salt Lake Tribune*, 4 Dec. and 22 Nov. 1906.
20. "The School Primaries," *Salt Lake Tribune*, 19 Nov. 1906.
21. "Mormon Church Controls Schools," *Salt Lake Tribune*, 6 Dec. 1906; "Non-Partisans Win Election," *Salt Lake Herald*, 6 Dec. 1906.

the composition of the board continued with 6 Mormons and 4 non-Mormons (2 of whom were Masons). The *Deseret News* saw the results as a clear statement that the schools "shall remain without the pale of party politics." The *Intermountain Republican* interpreted the election as repudiating the American party, which it termed "professional agitators exploiting their people with the unworthy gospel of hate, for their own selfish ends." The election had left the Americans where they should be: "standing humiliated and alone," and the newspaper hoped for an end to the use of religion as a determinant of worthiness to serve the community as a member of the board of education.[22]

Once again, cartoons derided the Mormon leadership for interfering in the schools: in the *Tribune* of 30 November 1908, a gargantuan Joseph F. Smith, portrayed as the school board, had his hand firmly wrapped around a public school and was saying: "We must continue to have a 'non-partisan' board." In spite of vigorous warnings about Mormon dominance in the face of American control of the mayor and city council, the American party failed to gain a majority on the school board. Mormons, when not split by party affiliation, were still the largest group of school patrons. In reality, Mormons themselves were divided along a continuum of liberal to conservative (as were the gentiles) and coalitions were as likely to be formed as much on the basis of political as on religious ideology. Also, apparently many people *were* apathetic and simply did not get exercised over the issue of Mormon control of schools. The significant degree of apathy during board elections may simply mean that the schools were satisfactory to most patrons.

MASONS AND MORMONS: A REPRISE OF THE 1890s

Notwithstanding the rhetoric about Mormon control of Utah politics and education, the early decades of the twentieth century witnessed a concerted effort on the part of Mormon leaders to minimize institutional interference in local affairs. This may explain why Salt Lake City public schools did not pray at the beginning of the school day, although this was a common practice in many county schools; nor was there any reading from the Bible. Although the Mormon church adopted its released time seminary program in 1912, this program did not become an accepted part of the Salt Lake City schools until the early 1940s. Obviously, Mormon influence did have some boundaries within which it had to operate.[23] In school affairs, for example, the church's power was effectively checkmated by the existence of a vocal non-Mormon minority with deep economic and social roots in the community—the Free Masons. One of the most co-

---

22. "The School Election," *Salt Lake Tribune*, 3 Dec. 1908; "Non-Partisans Victorious," *Deseret News*, 3 Dec. 1908; "Fairly Easy Lesson," *Intermountain Republican*, 4 Dec. 1908.

23. In a series of interviews with people who attended school in Salt Lake City during the first two decades of the twentieth century, I have made a point to ask about school prayer and Bible reading; all interviewees said that these practices were not part of the school program. See oral history interviews with Wallace F. Bennett, Frances G. Bennett, Lowell L. Bennion, Merle Bennion, Dorothy Snow, and Dortha McDonald, in Special Collections, University of Utah.

hesive groups outside the Mormon church itself, the Masons felt morally obliged to counter the Mormon majority. In the 1890s the Free Masons had made up one third of all persons elected to the board, and in the first two decades of the twentieth century they continued to play a major role.

During D. H. Christensen's years as superintendent, almost fifty percent of the school board belonged to the Salt Lake City Masonic Lodge. Members of the Masonic fraternity also represented mining, banking, mercantile and other business interests—groups that have traditionally dominated school boards throughout the United States. While tension had existed between Mormons and Masons in Utah for years, the persistence of Masons on the board of education was less an expression of anti-Mormon sentiment than an expression that the public schools should be secular. Because of this commitment, from 1890 to the 1960s there was at least one Mason (and usually more) on the board.[24]

The Masons were a persistent reminder that if Mormons were to participate in the emerging pluralistic culture of Utah, they would have to accommodate the values of corporate America. Their support of public schools and their willingness to work with Masons and other non-Mormons indicates that they were able to do this. The success of the schools implies that there must have been considerable mutual respect between the two groups.

While various charges over school politics and religious influence filled the Salt Lake papers in the early twentieth century, it appears that both sides were making a point of principle: on the part of the Mormons that community schools should not be directly antagonistic to Mormon culture, and on the part of non-Mormons that the separation of church and state should be strictly observed. Other than these values, the public schools seemed to have been little influenced by the controversies which captured the headlines between 1900 and 1916. Nor is there evidence that D. H. Christensen became involved in controversial elections campaigns. He instead focused on meeting the needs of the burgeoning population in a new industrial era. A "scientific" administrator, he tried to transcend partisan politics. Realistically, of course, anyone in a position of shaping and implementing public policies can never be fully detached. Although neither board members nor Christensen left any personal account of the election campaigns during his administration, one intriguing personal note has survived. In it a former board member, Professor Byron Cummings of the University of Utah, wrote to Christensen from Germany congratulating Christensen and the board on making progress in the schools. He added that he was also aware of "some of the things you have to nag at and annoy you still; and I hope the Good Lord will some day in the near future be sufficiently merciful to you to relieve you of some of your *sehr hochgeboren, hochgeehrten Mannes* [high born, highly respected men]. For the sake of the boys and girls of Salt Lake, I hope that may come before the fine new $500,000 high school on the east bench is occu-

---

24. This was suggested to me by Mr. Horace A. "Bo" Thomas, Worshipful Master of Research Lodge, Grand Lodge of Utah, in a telephone conversation, 10 July 1991.

pied."[25] Cummings may have referred to Christensen's conflicts in 1911 with board members McMullen and Sullivan, who openly criticized some of his decisions. However, his prayer for relief from the "snob" element was not answered during Christensen's tenure.

"THE MORMONIZING PROCESS" CHALLENGED

In spite of testimonies to the lack of direct Mormon church involvement in the schools, the active presence of such a group made it inevitable that religious bias would be read into almost any action. For example, around 1911-12 D. H. Christensen persuaded the board to fire his Supervisor of Primary Schools, Rosalie Pollock, whom he considered incompetent for the position. Pollock gave the *Tribune* a statement claiming she had been released because of pressure from the "mysterious influence" (i.e., the Mormon church). Her complaint was followed by an editorial claiming the case was an instance of "sectarian management of the public schools." It also accepted Pollock's contention that the six votes cast against her reflected the Mormon alignment on the board.

An indignant Christensen drafted a denial that the board originated the movement to dismiss Pollock, claiming that responsibility for himself. He explained that his decision was based on the reports of teachers and principals who had expressed no confidence in Pollock. Christensen asserted that he had never on any occasion "been approached either directly or indirectly by any person representing any sect or other organization as to my official or personal duty towards such sect or organization or towards any of its members." Nor, he added, had he ever sought, hinted at, or even desired such advice.[26] Pollock was replaced as Supervisor of the Primary Grades by Lizbeth Qualtrough, a non-Mormon educator who had come to Salt Lake in 1890 as one of Millspaugh's competent corps.

Of course, given the fact that many teachers were Mormon, that the board did have a Mormon majority, and that most students were the children of Mormon parents, there was a "Mormon influence" in the schools. However, the extent to which this pervasive cultural influence shaped policies is difficult to ascertain with any degree of precision. One charge levelled often was that Mormons had influence via the curriculum. In 1909 the *Tribune* reviewed Apostle Orson F. Whitney's history text *The Making of a State*, then used in the city's schools. The text, approved by the "Mormon 'non-partisan'" board of education,

---

25. Byron Cummings, Berlin, Germany, to D. H. Christensen, 3 Apr. 1911, Christensen Papers, Special Collections, University of Utah.

26. The incident involving Pollock was apparently publicized in the *Tribune* sometime during the school year 1911-12. I have not been able to locate the exact citation, but Christensen refers to it in the draft of his response. See letter, "To the Public," in Christensen Papers, Special Collections, University of Utah. His view that the public schools should not be instruments of the Mormon church is supported by oral history interviews conducted with his children. See oral histories of Dean K. Christensen, 27 Mar. 1990, and Kathleen Christensen Hall, 10 Apr. 1990, Special Collections, University of Utah. Note: Because the oral histories used in this book were still being processed at the time of publication, no pagination has been used. The table of contents for each interview will assist interested persons in locating topics referred to in the text.

was viewed as a "pretty raw piece of business." Whitney, according to the *Tribune*, ignored the Mormon leadership's failure to abandon polygamy after publicly disavowing the practice. Consequently the paper characterized the book as "[i]ngenious, evasive, smooth and plausible. But utterly ignoring the core of the whole matter." The text proved that Mormons were foisting apologetic and sectarian interpretations of historical events on the public schools. Ironically, the State Textbook Commission took Superintendent Christensen to task four years later for his own negative evaluation of the same text.[27]

Another instance of supposed Mormon domination occurred in 1911 when "D. H." appointed a "ruralite" from Utah County, George N. Child, as the supervisor of Salt Lake's grammar schools. According to the *Tribune*, Child succeeded the late John S. Welch—"an educator of national reputation"—solely because Christensen wanted a Mormon in the position. Christensen had allegedly passed over Salt Lake principals and hurried the appointment through before any opposition could develop. For the *Tribune* such instances resulted from "packing . . . the school board with six Mormons, out of a total of ten members, when the Mormons are in fact a minority in the voting population of this city." This "imposition upon the non-Mormons and upon the schools themselves" led to graft and covering up attempts to investigate such activities. Inquiries had been "hushed up on account of sectarian influence," claimed the *Tribune*. If this "Mormonizing process" persisted, the *Tribune* predicted, voters would rise up and "sweep the whole sectarian gang out of power."[28] Of course, Christensen denied that he had made the appointment on other than educational grounds.

While Superintendent Christensen seemed to have been rather even handed in his appointment of assistants, given the large number of Mormons in the state's normal schools, it would have been something of a miracle if local Mormon influence had not been felt. When Ellwood P. Cubberley examined the city's schools at the end of the Christensen era he not only found too few teachers, but too many who were inexperienced and were from the "immediate neighborhoods, and with purely local outlook and training." In spite of efforts to increase the amount of tax money available for schools, teacher salaries were not enough to attract "the better class of young people" to the profession. This may explain why only local people were being attracted to Salt Lake in 1914 in contrast to trained professionals from other parts of the country, who had flocked to the city in the 1890s. To remedy the situation, Cubberley and his associates recommended that one hundred new teachers should be added to the district and the salaries should be increased by some forty percent.[29]

---

27. "Imposing on the Schools," *Salt Lake Tribune*, 7 May 1909. Christensen criticized Whitney's book in a session of the Text Book Commission, although he had previously approved of the book as a manuscript. See A. M. Buchanan to D. H. Christensen, 13 Dec 1913, in Christensen Papers.

28. "Child Selection Raises Big Row," *Salt Lake Tribune*, 8 Dec. 1910; "Not Good For Schools," *Salt Lake Tribune*, 9 Dec. 1910.

29. *Report of the Survey of the Public School System of Salt Lake City, Utah* (Salt Lake City: Board of Education, 1915), 57-58. Hereafter cited as *Report of Survey*.

"Estimate of Teachers"

If no rigorous system of teacher evaluation was in place in the early years of the twentieth century, neither was evaluation entirely random. Principals and supervisors reported their opinions regularly and on this basis raises or decreases in pay were made. For example, at Riverside School in 1900, Charine P. Moffet was evaluated as "Industrious, judicious, talented, Remarkable improvement. Recommend increase in salary." The following year she received the increase, going from $40 per month to $45. On the other hand, one of her colleagues was evaluated only as a "Fair" teacher because of "lacking in force and judgement. Her manner is affected, not winning. There is a looseness in her teaching." "No increase" was the terse comment added by M. A. Holton, the Primary Supervisor.

While most comments about teachers often fell into routine expressions of minimum praise, one noticeable exception was the evaluation process of Washington School's Lizbeth Qualtrough. Her comments reveal a deep knowledge of her teachers and a keen sensitivity to the value of positive reinforcement. For Helen Burbank she wrote: "Think a raise would encourage [her] for she is trying." Burbank's monthly salary increased from $62.50 to $65.00. A. Z. Woodson had "grown wonderfully during year. Gets excellent results." Her salary increased by $5.00. In fact, it appears all of Qualtrough's teachers received increases. Of Retta Cassady she said, "[Her] services can not be paid for in money." Already getting $70 per month, the following year she received $2.50 more. In a letter to Frank Cooper she praised her teachers as "loyal, faithful, kindly workers" who had borne her shortcomings "patiently and kindly." Describing herself as having "thorns, self-opinionated and over emphatic," she concluded that "when a body of teachers gets along with me without much friction, it speaks well for the teachers."[30]

Cubberley and his associates never thought to discuss the obvious disparity between amounts earned by women teachers compared to men. A cursory examination of teacher rating sheets for this period indicates that female teachers received less than males and elementary teachers of both genders received less than their high school counterparts. According to official tables the average monthly male salary was $101.36 with women receiving an average of $69.62. While some of this difference may be accounted for by the fact that many men had more formal university training, most of it was simply gender discrimination, in spite of the fact that Utah's legal code clearly stated that female teachers with the same level of training and doing the same work should receive the same compensation.[31]

During Christensen's years the forms for evaluating teachers became more precise, requiring teachers to be ranked with points: Excellent=95-100; Very Good= 85-95; Good=75-85; Fair=65-75. Below 65 was considered Unsatisfactory. These "grades" were used to rank the teachers in terms of their knowledge

30. "Estimate of Teachers, 1899-1900," copy in possession of author.
31. For a discussion of a history of gender differences in salary schedules in Utah, see John C. Moffitt, *History of Public Education in Utah* (n.p. 1946), 322-24.

of subject matter, children, methods, discipline and application. These ratings give the impression that most teachers were in the Good to Excellent categories with only an occasional "F" or "U." In 1902, principal David A. Nelson summed up his entire staff at Riverside School by writing across the bottom of the evaluation sheet: "These are the best lot of teachers I have ever known." It was not all sweetness and light, of course: Principal J. O. Cross at Wasatch School evaluated one teacher as "G" and "VG" in all the required categories. However, at the bottom of the sheet he wrote that her "manner is unfortunate, in that she antagonizes pupils and patrons. More complaints come to me concerning her than any other teacher." Needless to say she was recommended for "No increase," as was another teacher who "lacks vigorous personality, and on this account is the weakest teacher in the Wasatch corps."

D. H. Christensen kept close watch on teachers' salaries, making notations in his personnel directory. As Christensen visited schools, which he often did, he could, for example, see at a glance that Rose Howard, typing teacher in Room 90 at West High, was receiving a salary of $700; the principal, L. M. Gillian, was receiving $3,000, while J. Leo Fairbanks, the art teacher, had a salary of $1,400. This personal involvement indicates that salaries were arrived at through personal negotiations with the superintendent. Alga Mills, seventh and eighth grade teacher at Whittier School, wrote Christensen in 1915 thanking him for the "influence exercised on my behalf" in securing her an increase in salary, awarded to her in the middle of the school year. When former acting-superintendent of Salt Lake City schools, Adelaide Holton, asked him to favor the appointment of her niece as a teacher in 1913 she forthrightly requested: "Please give her $700 if possible, because she will be a college graduate."[32]

"SUBSTANTIAL AND MARKED GROWTH"

In his first report as Superintendent, Christensen used a phrase that epitomizes the history of education in the twentieth century: "The past year has been one of substantial and marked growth, viewed from any viewpoint."[33] As the city grew, so too did the schools. The city's population in 1890 was 44,843 and by 1900 it was 53,531, an increase of 20 percent. During this period the number of school children went from 6,368 to 12,979, an increase of 103 percent. By 1910 the city's population had increased to 92,700; by 1930 to 140,267. The city's school population stood at 27,168 in 1920. In addition to natural increase, other factors abetted the school explosion. Among them were enforcement of compulsory education laws; increased parental commitment; a broadened sense of curriculum designed for a diverse population; and the expansion of the common

---

32. See Christensen's salary notations in his copy of district *Directory*, Christensen Papers, Special Collections, University of Utah; also letters: Alga Mills to D. H. Christensen, 18 Jan. 1915; Ida Fitzsimmons to D. H. Christensen, 15 Dec. 1915; M. Adelaide Holton, Hamilton, New York, to D. H. Christensen, 13 May 1913, in Christensen Papers.

33. *Twelfth Annual Report*, 1901-1902, 72.

schools into secondary education.[34] During this period of sustained growth the public high school became a prominent feature of the educational skyline.

As discussed in Chapter Two, the Salt Lake High School was characterized by survival rather than aggressive development at the turn of the century. Visitors were puzzled by the incongruity of Salt Lake City's modern elementary school system compared to the high school, which was "relegated to the middle of a block, on an obscure alley, abutting the back doors of several noisy business concerns." In "a blessing in disguise," the district was released from the ten year lease on the Pierpoint Street property in September 1901 when a fire in the basement of the Oregon Short Line building worked its way into the high school floors. From Pierpoint Street, the high school moved to the old University of Deseret/University of Utah building on Second West and First North.[35] Inadequacies were still present, however; the lack of an assembly hall and laboratories required the board to rent the facilities of the Deseret Museum, a block away.

In spite of much rhetoric about the need for education, Salt Lake citizens were apparently not enthusiastic boosters of expanding the common schools to include the high school. As yet there was no constitutional provision for the public support of secondary schools. Also, the Latter-day Saint University offered a competing high school program. James Clark has estimated that at the turn of the century only eleven percent of Utah's secondary school population attended non-Mormon denominational schools; 41 per cent attended public schools, and 48 percent attended private Mormon secondary schools. Salt Lake City probably reflected a similar configuration. For example, in 1902-03 the public high school had 848 enrolled, while the LDS High School had 1231. In the 1907-08 school year, there were 1,225, while 1,384 were enrolled in the LDS High School.[36] As noted earlier some Mormons, including Brigham Young's sons, opposed expanding the public high school in 1897, citing the existence of a private LDS high school in the city. As late as 1915 the president of the LDS church, Joseph F. Smith, criticized the increased taxation for the high school's expansion. At the church's October Conference he said, "I believe we are running education mad." At the same time, however, another Mormon leader, Anthony Lund, enthusiastically favored expanding the high schools. Pluralism had come to Zion. The waxing and waning of support probably had as much to do with personal dispositions and local economic conditions as it had with a particular religious or political ideological stance.[37]

With or without community boosters, however, population pressures shaped educational policies, and in September 1903 the Salt Lake High School established a branch known as the "East Side High School" at the Bryant School.

---

34. Sources for attendance data are from tables in the *Twenty-ninth and Thirtieth Annual Reports*, 1918-20.

35. *Fifty Years of Public Education*, 138; *Twelfth Annual Report*, 1901-1902, 86-7.

36. James R. Clark, "Church and State Relations in Education in Utah," Ed.D. diss., Utah State University, 1958, 280; *Thirteenth Annual Report*, 1902-1903, 81; *Nineteenth Annual Report*, 1908-1909, 84.

37. Alexander, *Mormonism in Transition*, 162.

With 150 students and six teachers, the curriculum was limited to first-year high school work; students finished their program at what was referred to for convenience as the "West Side High School." In 1904, the principal of the East Side High School, W. J. McCoy, promoted the establishment of a separate high school to serve the needs of students east of Main Street, warning that parents would send their children to "other institutions," probably referring to the LDS High School (also known as the Latter-day Saint University).[38]

George Eaton, principal of the Salt Lake High School initially supported the idea of a branch on the east bench, but later argued against it. His rationale included a lack of continuity between the two schools, the difficulty of supervising two physical plants, segregation of the student body, cost, and the threat of some parents to send their children to LDS High. Paradoxically, the Mormon school was used to support both the establishment and curtailment of an additional public high school. By 1905, Eaton's views prevailed, and in spite of petitions signed by almost 400 parents, the board voted to consolidate the two schools.[39]

Ironically, in the same year the board decided to amalgamate the schools, Superintendent Christensen decided that a city of Salt Lake's size actually required two high schools. The renewed movement was stymied in 1908 when the electorate refused to amend the state constitution to allow a special tax for the support of high schools. However, in 1911 Utah voters approved an amendment allowing the creation of a high school fund, giving "secondary education a remarkable impetus throughout the state."[40] With support from the superintendent, pressure from patrons, a shift in the constitutional status of the high school and the creation of a "high school fund," the goal of two high schools in Salt Lake City was realized in 1915 when East High School was erected on Thirteenth East.

Even though two schools now existed, the long-time principal of the Salt Lake High School, George Eaton, could not bring himself to regard the two schools as separate entities. He hoped the school colors, red and black, would be the common property of both schools or that future distinction "could easily be brought about by the adaption of a different shade of red for each."[41] New principals were appointed for the new East High and the Salt Lake (later West) High and Eaton became "Supervising Principal" of both schools.

"THE PEOPLE'S COLLEGE"

American high schools of the nineteenth century tended toward being rather selective preparatory schools for those students who would be able to attend col-

---

38. *Fourteenth Annual Report*, 1903-1904, 120-21.

39. Details on the establishment of the "East Side High School" can be found in *Thirteenth Annual Report*, 1902-1903, 123; *Fourteenth Annual Report*, 1903-1904, 107-8; *Fifteenth Annual Report*, 1904-1905, 85-6.

40. Moffitt, *History of Education in Utah*, 141, citing A. C. Nelson, State Superintendent of Public Instruction on the benefits that accrued to the state schools as a result of the positive vote in 1911; *Nineteenth Annual Report*, 1908-1909, 181-83.

41. *Twenty Third Annual Report*, 1912-13, 53.

lege. However, some significant changes began to occur in the rationale for the high school in the early years of the twentieth century, preparing the way for the comprehensive American high school that has marked the American educational landscape ever since—viewed as a bane and a blessing by educational commissions and educational reformers.[42]

As the twentieth century progressed, high schools increasingly came to be seen as "the people's college." This role was in large measure shaped by the 1892 "Committee of Ten" (discussed in Chapter 2). In the words of Salt Lake's George Eaton, the new high schools were to teach Americans from age 14 to age 20 "how to live."[43] According to Principal W. J. McCoy of the short-lived "East Side High School" in 1904, when less than half of high school graduates go on to college, the high school should focus on work useful to the "mass of students." McCoy's words identify him as a progressive administrator of the era.

Broadening the curriculum's appeal, then, met the republic's need for good citizens. If America's young people dropped out of the system, the nation would be weakened. Ironically, at the same time the high school was being touted as all-inclusive, questions arose about the problem of standards in a school designed to meet multiple needs. With "fast and slow" students in the same school the need to differentiate between them became more urgent, not simply because "slower" students could not keep up "with the progress made by the strongest and brightest," but also because those unable to keep pace with the fastest would become prime candidates for the league of "drop outs." McCoy recommended, instead of culling out the unfit, that extra time be allowed to prevent students from becoming humiliated or discouraged and subsequently dropping out of school.[44]

Keeping as many students in high school as was possible was a top priority with Salt Lake administrators. Still, a few suspected that high school actually educated some people above their natural station. George Eaton in 1907 said that "many a good farmer or merchant had been spoiled by trying to make a lawyer or engineer out of him" as well as causing problems for the professions they are "forced" into.[45] In spite of such reservations, Eaton believed that those who continued on to high school should realize that education has a dual function: providing courses that would contribute to their occupational pursuits, as well as offering general mental training.

---

42. For positive British views of American education in the early 1900s see Sir Michael Sadler's "Impressions of American Education" and Alfred Mosely's "A British View of American Schools," both published in 1903 and reproduced in Sol Cohen, ed. *Education in the United States: A Documentary History*, 5 vols. (New York: Random House, 1974), 4:2101-08. For adverse criticism of the "comprehensive" nature of much of American public schooling see William C. Bagley, *Determinism in Education* (New York: MacMillan Co., 1939).

43. For a detailed discussion of the work of the Committee of Ten, see Edward A. Krug, *The Shaping of the American High School* (Madison: University of Wisconsin Press, 1969), chapters 1-4. The annual reports of the Salt Lake City schools reflect much of the spirit and expressions of the Committee of Ten; see *Fourth Annual Report*, 1893-94, 97-8; also George Eaton's comments about the aims of the high school in *Eleventh Annual Report*, 1900-1901, 71 and *Fourteenth Annual Report*, 1903-1904, 118.

44. *Fourteenth Annual Report*, 1903-1904, 119.

45. *Seventeenth Annual Report*, 1906-1907, 116.

Perhaps Ellwood Cubberley had these issues in mind when in 1909 he indicated that the changing American schools reflected the social and industrial changes in society at large. "Our city schools," he said, "will soon be forced to give up the exceedingly democratic idea that all are equal, and that our society is devoid of classes." He believed schools would have to "begin a specialization of educational effort along many new lines in an attempt to adapt the school to the needs of the many classes in city life."[46]

MANUAL TRAINING AT THE PEOPLE'S COLLEGE

While there had been emphasis on the work ethic in nineteenth-century American common schools, it was not until the early twentieth century that manual training was identified as the most effective way of transmitting the so-called Protestant ethic to the rising generation. Much as Japan supposedly offered the best educational model in the 1980s, German practices were much admired in the early 1900s. D. H. Christensen had observed German models first hand during his residency at Goettingen in 1900. No doubt he drew on that experience to establish the Manual Training Department in the Salt Lake District in 1902. Such a program, it was believed, would promote the productive power of the nation and dignify manual labor for boys. It would also convince girls of the science in cooking and art in sewing: "[T]he truly cultured woman should know something about each."[47] In addition to fulfilling a social need, manual training attracted a larger, more differentiated student population by appealing to broader interests. Education for George Eaton in 1901 was much more than abstract studies in mathematics and language. He urged more attention to motor and manipulative studies such as biology, geology, physics, and chemistry, and argued for the inclusion of physical education and athletics as part of the school curriculum. These, he complained, had been merely tolerated rather than actively encouraged.[48]

Along with increased attention to manual training came charges that the curriculum was being weakened by "non-academic" subjects, Advocates countered that honed motor skills would make students more well-rounded. The concept even spilled over into the elementary grades. Grace Frost, principal of Onequa Elementary School, said manual training classes captured the interest of boys who had been irregular in attendance, but who now could not be kept away from school.[49] Shop work enjoyed so much popularity that two boys broke into Washington School on a Saturday so they could work.[50]

Of course, proponents claimed manual training was on a par with academic disciplines and was actually an aspect of liberal education. Unfortunately for

---

46. Ellwood P. Cubberley, *Changing Conceptions of Education* (Boston: Houghton Mifflin Co., 1909), 56-7.
47. *Twelfth Annual Report*, 1901-1902, 78.
48. *Eleventh Annual Report*, 1900-1901, 67.
49. *Twenty-second Annual Report*, 1910-11, 88.
50. *Twenty-fourth Annual Report*, 1913-14, 97.

those who saw manual training as a ladder of opportunity, evidence suggests otherwise. Gaining competence in "joinery, carving, lathe work, mechanical drawing" had more to do with future occupations than broadening the horizons of young people.[51] Accordingly, "manual training" eventually became interchangeable with the term "industrial courses."

When the decision finally to establish two high schools was made around 1910, the board of education agreed that the "Westside High School" would specialize in "industrial and commercial courses," while the "Eastside High School" would focus on "general studies." The development of the industrial courses was viewed as an important factor in "determining the future industrial and commercial possibilities" of Salt Lake City.[52] With the new East High School under construction in 1911-13, the "west side High School's" "technical building" added a forge room, a foundry, and a machine shop. J. T. Hammond, President of the Board, reported that the "new high school [East] shall be the classical and the present one [West] the technical school." In other cities, he noted, when "strong manual training, domestic science and commercial courses" were included in high schools, there was a "marked increase in the attendance, showing that many boys and girls had formerly failed to attend high school because its course did not meet their needs." No geographic boundaries divided the two schools. Students could attend either depending on interests or inclinations.[53] Assisting students realize their "probable destinies" seems to be what D. H. Christensen had in mind when he noted in 1915 that the West catered "more and more to the manual and commercial type while the East school will maintain its academic stamp." This, according to the superintendent, was "the ideal outcome."[54]

Whether this was, in fact, "ideal" is problematic. The city's businesses and industries no doubt wanted the greater emphasis on manual training. However, increased attention to manual arts notwithstanding, in 1914 only three students (all boys) graduated from the high school's mechanic arts course, compared with 16 in the classical course, 28 in the scientific course, and 36 in the commercial course (mostly girls).[55] As a practical program, actually preparing young people for the marketplace, manual arts training may not have attracted as many students as was hoped. Still, there can be no doubt that the program grew: at the beginning of Christensen's tenure the district employed no manual arts instructors, while fifteen years later eleven male teachers and two female teachers were employed as full-time instructors in manual training.[56]

Christensen's successor as superintendent, Ernest Smith, complained in 1917 that Salt Lake City lagged behind other areas of the country in the number of students taking "industrial education" classes. In 1917 only 177 out of 1213 boys were enrolled in such work—a mere fourteen percent. The growth in num-

51. *Nineteenth Annual Report*, 1908-1909, 135.
52. *Twelfth Annual Report*, 1901-1902, 86-7.
53. *Twenty-second Annual Report*, 1911-12, 7-8.
54. *Twenty-fifth Annual Report*, 1914-15, 88-9.
55. *Twenty-fourth Annual Report*, 1913-14, 137-39.
56. *Twenty-sixth Annual Report*, 1915-16, 122.

bers of instructors without commensurate numbers of students taking manual training may indicate that the program had become a part of general education rather than a program producing workers. Ironically, this had been manual training's original aim.

Ultimately, in the words of historian Harvey Kantor, manual education's main outcome was to transform "conflicts over the organization of the economy and the nature of American society into policies aimed at proper socializing; and this narrowed debate about the nature and meaning of work, as well as altered educational practices." Given the paucity of evidence that, for most students, industrial training made a significant difference in the work they did, Kantor concluded that "vocational education appears to have been an illusory solution for the economic, social and educational ills that accompanied the industrial transformation of work."[57] For African-Americans and for lower-class white students, vocational education promised them more in the way of economic, social, and educational advancement than it could possibly fulfill. Many were disappointed when their status in the workplace and in society did not materially improve.

The decline in interest in Salt Lake City may have been due to this type of parental class consciousness. One 1919 study observed that many Utah parents "are not anxious that their boys should learn trades." High school, many parents seemed to believe, was to enable boys to be more prepared for "'dressed up' jobs rather than to engage in that pursuit which necessitate the wearing of overalls."[58] Whatever else may be said of them, manual or industrial arts courses were never perceived as a way to increase one's social standing in the community.

Illusory it may have been, but vocational education served as a major rationale for expanding the school programs in Salt Lake City's public schools. Not even the traditional Western and Mormon antipathy towards the federal government prevented expansion of school programs backed by the largesse of Washington, D.C., in the form of financial assistance through the Smith-Hughes Act of 1917. Nor were Mormons immune to adopting the traditional American faith that education could solve problems actually rooted in political, social, and economic conditions. Even in the last decade of the twentieth century it is difficult to accept the fact that in the absence of social and industrial policies that promote the creation of jobs, no amount of tinkering with public school curriculum and slotting students into vocational classes will create employment opportunities.

BOOKER T. WASHINGTON ENDORSES
UTAH'S TECHNICAL AND INDUSTRIAL PROGRAM

An interesting moment in the history of manual education in Salt Lake City

57. Harvey A. Kantor, "Vocationalism in American Education: The Economic and Political Context, 1880-1930," in Harvey Kantor and David Tyack, eds., Work, Youth and Schooling: Historical Perspectives on Vocationalism in American Education (Palo Alto: Stanford University Press, 1982), 43, 36. See also Harvey Kantor, Learning to Earn; School, Work, and Vocational Reform in California, 1880-1930 (Madison: University of Wisconsin Press, 1988).
58. J. H. Tipton, "Methods of Teaching Mechanic Arts," M.S. thesis, University of Utah, 1919, 27.

involved the prominent African-American educator, Booker T. Washington. D. H. Christensen's faith in the manual arts led him to visit Washington at his Tuskeegee Institute in Alabama in February of 1911. For Washington, African-Americans' success in American society lay in becoming indispensable skilled workers. In his famous address at the Atlanta Cotton States and International Exposition in Atlanta, 18 September 1895, Washington said that the "greatest danger" facing former slaves was the failure to recognize "the fact that the masses of us are to live by the productions of our hands" and that they must "keep in mind that we shall prosper in proportion as we learn to dignify and glorify common labor and put brains and skill into the common occupations in life. . . . No race can prosper till it learns that there is as much dignity in tilling a field as in writing a poem."[59] With emphasis on the useful over the ornamental, on physical labor as a means of obtaining recognition, it is no wonder that Washington struck a spark of interest in the Mormon superintendent of Salt Lake City. The Mormons shared more than an ample portion of Dr. Washington's values.

Washington visited Salt Lake City in March of 1913 at Christensen's invitation, where he addressed the ideals behind the Tuskeegee Institute at the First Methodist Church, the Salt Lake High School, and the Latter-day Saint University (actually a high school). His lecture at the University of Utah on the "Industrial Development of the Negro Race" was attended by state education officials and almost all the general authorities of the LDS church.[60] The noted educator was serenaded by University of Utah students singing "old plantation songs," and given a special organ recital in the Mormon Tabernacle. His theme during his visit was the relationship between education and the progress of the "negro race" since the "Emancipation Proclamation." As might be expected, the emphasis was upon practical education.[61]

Commenting on Washington's perspective on education, the *Herald Republican* approvingly noted that he "owns no burning desire to make his race prominent or powerful; his wish is that its members will be useful and self-supporting. The future holds no visions for him of eminent negro doctors, lawyers, judges

---

59. "The Atlanta Compromise," in D. Calhoun, *The Education of Americans: A Documentary History* (Boston: Houghton Mifflin Co., 1969), 349-51.

60. Washington's article appeared in the 17 Apr. 1913 issue of the country's leading African-American newspaper, the *New York Age*. An excerpt appeared in the *Deseret News*, 7 May 1913. See also Louis R. Harlan and Raymond W. Smock, eds., *The Booker T. Washington Papers*, 14 vols. (Urbana: University of Illinois Press, 1972-89), 12:149-53. As a result of his favorable comments about the Mormons, Washington was roundly criticized by a number of prominent Protestant leaders, who claimed he had been used by the Mormons to enhance their national image. One Baptist could not understand how he could speak with favor about a group that believed that blacks were cursed with the "mark of Cain." See Harlan and Smock, *Washington Papers*, 12:182, 195-96. Until 1978 the LDS church prohibited African-American men from ordination to its lay priesthood. See also John M. Whittaker, Journal, 27 Mar. 1913, Special Collections, University of Utah, in which Whittaker refers to "negro blood" as "accursed blood."

61. "Eloquent Defense of 'Colored Brother,'" *Deseret News*, 26 Mar. 1913. See also letter of Booker T. Washington to D. H. Christensen, 31 Mar. 1913 and photograph of Washington with two of Christensen's children taken at Tuskeegee Institute in February 1911, in Christensen Papers.

and scientists. . . . Because the negro character often lacks the practical, he has made it his life work to inculcate that attribute, to educate the young of the race along practical lines."[62] With such a benign (and, for such critics as W. E. B. DuBois, an essentially flawed) social outlook for his race, it is no wonder that Washington was popular among the dominant white majority in America. While much of Washington's theory is rooted in what he perceived to be the needs of former slaves, in a very real sense he also echoed a common notion that many students (of whatever race) should be channelled into practical education rather than academic. As noted above, channelling students into their "probable destinies" was a theme of the so-called progressive era. In retrospect, Washington's focus on vocational education proved to be a chimera. Instead of advancing racial justice it stereotyped African-Americans as only fit for manual skills. Nevertheless, he was widely applauded for his "progressive" views and nowhere more loudly than in Utah.

In reflecting on his visit, Washington drew parallels between the history of African-Americans and Mormons: both had been "inhumanely persecuted" and grossly "misrepresented before the world." He praised Mormons for their health, cleanliness, progressive perspective, and attachment to farming. Like the Negro, "the Mormons are suffering, because the people from the outside, have advertized the worst concerning 'Mormon' life." He praised Mormon schools as "first class" and noted that "they are pushing the matter of technical and industrial education to a stronger degree than we are in the south among the colored people." At the University of Utah he was astounded to see pictures of his own Tuskeegee Institute's industrial departments displayed in one of the classrooms. The university teacher informed him that Tuskeegee was used as a model for their instruction in vocational education. According to Washington, the Mormons told him that they had "learned their methods for the most part from Hampton, Tuskeegee and similar institutions." He spoke at some length with Mormon bishop John M. Whittaker and received from him "some mighty interesting information [about the Mormons] that ought to prove of value to our race."[63] His visit not only gave Mormons much sought after "good press" but also assured D. H. Christensen he was on the right track with his emphasis on vocational education.

CURRICULUM FOR "HOME PROBLEMS"

As might be expected, superintendents' annual reports frequently reflect the masculine gender bias in society at large. However, females were not entirely neglected in the curriculum. Domestic science was promoted as an essential component of the public school program and "cooking, preservation of foods, dietetics, nursing, sanitation, laundering and needlework" were viewed as equal to boys' courses such as "mechanical drawing, carpentry, molding, forging and

---

62. "Booker T. Washington," *Herald Republican*, 29 Mar. 1913, in Journal History, of date.
63. Harlan and Smock, *Washington Papers*, 12:149-53; Whittaker, Journal, 27 Mar. 1913.

machine work."[64] The domestic science curriculum for girls was proposed as a solution to the "home problem," although the term was never precisely explicated. Apparently the American home at the beginning of the twentieth century was adjusting to the new demands of industrial society. Principal George Eaton was positively ebullient as he contemplated the results of girls' instruction in the science of domesticity. "It is," he exulted, "an inspiring sight to see a class of refined American girls in white aprons with sleeves rolled up busily engaged in solving the mysteries of the culinary art."[65]

For Eaton, the courses based on "domestic science" and "manual training" met the needs of females and males respectively in a "natural" manner. Similarly, the scientific courses were dominated by males, while English and "Normal Preparation" (teacher education courses) were dominated by females. In Eaton's words, "[t]he segregation of sex by courses is, after all, natural and logical." Paradoxically, Eaton complained that not enough males were going into teaching: only two males had done so in nine years compared to hundreds of females.[66]

Domestic science also entered the elementary schools. Lizbeth Qualtrough, for instance, used cooking classes as an example of the kind of class that ten-year-old girls found relevant: "Nothing has ever before been introduced which has been so universally and so immediately liked. The cooking hour has been the joyful anticipation of the entire week."[67] A few girls upset expected roles and took manual training classes. Frances Grant Bennett reported that she enjoyed being the only girl in a woodworking class at Whittier School (around 1912) and was proud of having made a breadboard.[68] Nothing indicates, however, that Frances was preparing to become a carpenter. The principal of Jefferson School, W. J. McCoy, argued that boys should not only be taught how to *make* an ironing board, but also to press their trousers.[69] In spite of McCoy's support, no record shows boys enrolling in such a course.

In spite of adjusting the curriculum to meet student needs, schools frequently had a difficult time holding males through to graduation. Oscar VanCott, principal of Wasatch Elementary School, reported that almost 52 percent of his school was male, compared to only 40 percent of the graduating class, a condition he said prevailed also in the high school and university. This arose, he explained, from too much "effeminacy" in the curriculum—water coloring, modelling, and weaving every day—while more "masculine" activities involving saws and planes were only taught once each week. Reflecting a common perspective of the era, VanCott said courses should be gender-differentiated because the aims of education for males and females are essentially different: "I believe that school should render unto the boy the things that are his and unto the girl the things that are hers. In this way only can we provide for the true function of

---

64. *Seventeenth Annual Report*, 1906-1907, 116.
65. *Nineteenth Annual Report*, 1908-1909, 135.
66. Ibid., 133-34.
67. *Twenty-first Annual Report*, 1910-11, 98-99.
68. Oral history, Frances Grant Bennett, Mar. 1990.
69. *Twenty-fourth Annual Report*, 1913-14, 85.

citizenship in manhood and womanhood."[70]

The School as Social Center

Another progressive notion influencing national as well as Salt Lake City schools viewed educational institutions as a social center that would "empower citizens to play a greater part in shaping their own destinies."[71] This was another in the long line of aims at making the public school a panacea for social ills. In Chicago the notion took the form of Jane Addams's "Hull House" in which immigrants were taught how to become a force for the regeneration of their neighborhoods. While Salt Lake City certainly did not have the large scale immigrant population of Chicago and other urban centers, the city's schools began to assume roles beyond the traditional "three Rs" as the curriculum became more inclusive, even under the direction of relatively conservative leaders.

According to Superintendent Christensen, the public school should be the "social center of the community." Evelyn Reilly, principal of the Lincoln School, concurred with his perspective. For her, although some questions had been raised about the paternalistic role of the school, "all thoughtful people are coming to the conclusion that the school must supplement and direct the work of many homes and do anything that the home cannot or will not do."[72] The school should even supplement children's diets, according to Rosalie Pollock, who asked for an appropriation in 1910 to provide bread, butter, jam, and milk for Salt Lake kindergartners. Foreshadowing the social programs of the 1970s, Pollock referred to the kindergartners as "a walking famine": they were ever in need of food. Investing money in food, she claimed, would prevent children from becoming "dull and stupid." She also suggested that cots be supplied so children could take naps.[73]

Taking her cue from what she knew of conditions in large congested urban centers, Pollock's successor as Supervisor of Primary Grades, Lizbeth Qualtrough, continued the theme of attending to the needs of the "whole child." In her first report to Christensen in 1913, according to Qualtrough, the teaching of the three Rs was secondary to attending to children's physical needs. In some places, she said, the "simple laws of sanitation and civilization should precede the laws even of English grammar." Pedagogically and financially, she continued, it makes little sense to pay teachers eighty or ninety dollars a month to "develop the mind of a child whose stomach is calling for food. There are localities where a bath tub and a warm lunch at noon would be vastly more effective in the creation of good citizenship than twice the amount spent on any kind of textbook." Christensen himself drew attention to children who were harmed educationally because they lacked proper nourishment, whether due to "shiftless home condi-

---

70. *Twentieth Annual Report*, 1909-10, 174.
71. Lawrence A. Cremin, *American Education: The Metropolitan Experience* (New York: Harper & Row, 1988), 225.
72. *Twenty-second Annual Report*, 1911-12, 84-5.
73. *Twenty-first Annual Report*, 1910-11, 58-9.

tions or poverty." For Christensen, providing nourishing meals was in the interests of all: "[O]nly those properly fed can successfully cope with the requirements of carefully organized and effectively directed class work." According to Christensen, the problem in some parts of Salt Lake City was greater "than we might wish to believe." Accordingly he recommended to the board of education that a low-cost, or even free, meal for students should be provided.[74]

In the fall of 1914 the Riverside School established a soup counter where students could purchase a bowl of soup and two slices of bread for two cents. The operation was under the direction of the domestic science teacher, Elva Scott, and served as a model for other schools. In this day of efficient management, "receipts covered all expenses," but some parents whose children did not have school lunch options complained that they were subsidizing lunches for the poor. Christensen countered by asserting that all students, "regardless of their station in life, will be better nourished and will work better with a warm lunch at the noon hour."[75]

Another "progressive" innovation saw school children combatting dirty streets, unclean meat shops, and other breeding places for flies and mosquitoes. Clean-up brigades typified the notion that schools should promote an improved social environment. At a Parent-Teacher's Association meeting in Salt Lake City in 1914, George Eaton, Principal of the Salt Lake High School, reiterated the idea that the school should be a "social center, a debating ground for questions involving the welfare of home, school and community—a nonsectarian, nonpartisan meeting place for all."[76]

Such a view, of course, radically departed from the traditional conception of academics, but was a basic ingredient of the progressive vision. Whether schools actually became such social centers is open to question, but there can be no doubt that many educators thought in these terms and that curriculum was modified by these expectations.

Progressive era education dictated that instruction traditionally given in the home was now assumed to be the proper function of the public school. Instruction in "contagious diseases, sanitation, sex physiology, nutrition and first aid to the injured" would become the "new basics" of the twentieth-century school. Correcting "false beliefs and practices" benefitted individuals, homes, and communities. Changes in one aspect of the school inevitably led to others. For example, physical education led to sweaty children, which, in turn, led to showers and expanded facilities to prevent smelly classrooms.[77] Not that all these additions were accepted without question; "hysterical agitation" for and against sex education had, according to George Eaton, an adverse affect on such instruction nationally, but he recommended that it be included in the Salt Lake District's cur-

---

74. *Twenty-fourth Annual Report*, 1913-14, 114-15.

75. Report on the history of Riverside School in *Fiftieth Annual Report*, 1939-40, 87; "May Extend Lunch Plan to all Schools," *Salt Lake Tribune*, 20 Nov. 1914.

76. *Report of Survey*, 296; "Parent-Teacher's League to Meet," *Salt Lake Tribune*, 27 Oct. 1914.

77. *Twenty-third Annual Report*, 1911-12, 42-3.

riculum. He further suggested that the district employ a male and female physician to give instruction in sex hygiene.[78] By 1921 an MD was appointed to supervise the health of the children, but only one was listed as a health instructor.[79]

As is usually the case with changes in the school, the rhetoric of reform loomed larger than the reality. Certainly, the idea of the school taking over parental responsibilities may have been enough for some people to raise questions about expanded curriculum. Ironically, even as progressive measures were being recommended as necessary components of the modern school, there were calls for removing "fads and frills" from the curriculum. In 1915, the slogan of the Utah Education Association was the perennial "Back to the Basics." And a perspicacious observer of public schooling might be forgiven if he or she asked with some incredulity: "What—again?"[80]

"FUNDAMENTAL SUBJECTS" AND AN EXPANDING CURRICULUM

In addition to making school governance supposedly non-partisan, adding manual and vocational education to course offerings, and focusing on the school as a social center of the community, educators of the Progressive period were obsessed with making education "scientific." These educators did not, however, perceive science in narrow technocratic terms; they interpreted it as "the latest authoritative knowledge flowing from philosophy, psychology and pedagogy," which could be used "in the development of more humane and effective instructional methods and more efficient and economical administrative techniques."[81]

For Christensen, efficient schools were means to the end of an effective school experience for children. In spite of expanding the curriculum to include social service and manual arts, Christensen believed school work should focus on the "fundamental subjects." Given this orientation, he could point with some pride to the measured achievements reported by the Cubberley survey, conducted by national experts. The survey found Salt Lake schools successful in teaching the basic skills and ranked "high among cities of her class, in each of the five studies in which tests were given"—spelling, composition, reading, writing, and arithmetic. Spelling in particular was praised as "being 16 per cent above the standard."[82]

Although some criticism concerned the quality of the teaching corps, the success in teaching fundamental skills was attributed to the close supervision by Christensen and his supervisors. In the words of a national school publication, they had "succeeded in making unusually effective use of a corps of teachers which is not very promising in its qualifications." Many principals reported to the Cubberley team that "they felt under constant pressure from the superinten-

---

78. *Twenty-fifth Annual Report*, 1914-15, 92-3.
79. *Thirty-third Annual Report*, 1922-23, 66.
80. "Teachers Present at Great Peace Meeting," *Salt Lake Tribune*, 24 Nov. 1915.
81. Cremin, *American Education: The Metropolitan Experience*, 226.
82. *Report of Survey*, 184.

dent to be efficient principals and to make a success of their work, or else run the risk of being removed from their positions."[83] The Superintendent apparently knew what he wanted accomplished and did not mince words when setting out his priorities. As recounted by his son, Christensen's philosophy was summed up in a statement he made to the Salt Lake City elementary teachers: "I told them, I didn't ask them, I told them, each one of you teachers are going to do four things for each child in your rooms. You are going to teach each child arithmetic, spelling, reading and writing. If you don't teach these things I will put someone in your place who will."[84] The survey of 1915 confirmed the superintendent's emphasis had productive results.

THE BUSINESS OF SCHOOLS

Adding so-called "frills and fads" to the curriculum made demands on teachers and administrators, as well as on the general taxpayer. Salt Lake's education budget had increased markedly since 1890, from $203,594.80 in 1890-91 to $1,143,858.20 in 1915. Educating *all* of the city's children required a significant investment of public funds.[85] Such increases make it understandable that pressures were exerted on boards and superintendents to make the schools more efficient.

As if to forestall any criticism that the schools were wasting public funds, the 1915 Cubberley survey claimed that Salt Lake City schools were being administered very efficiently. However, the experts from Stanford did not ignore the fact that compared to fifteen other Western cities, Salt Lake City was rated second lowest in per capita spending for its children ages five through fifteen. The remedy, of course, was to raise taxes. Cubberley concluded that in 1915 it was "very evident that Salt Lake City can afford large families"; given the city's large per capita wealth, Salt Lake should have been able to support schools more than it was.[86]

Although Salt Lake City had a greater percentage of school age children than any other Western city, it levied a lower tax rate. Unless serious increases were made in the city's investment in its children, Cubberley concluded, "It looks as though even more serious cramping and crowding of the schools, and the employment of more cheap and inexperienced teachers, with little or no development, would be the inevitable result." Much of the blame, however, was laid more on the state legislature than on citizens: "Recent editorials in the leading newspapers regarding the schools and their support would lead one to feel that they, the people, are willing to go even further and support the schools even generously. It is the people of Utah, as represented in the state legislature, who stand in the way." The legislature had imposed on school districts a "maintenance tax-

---

83. "Schools of Salt Lake City," *Elementary School Journal* 16 (Nov. 1915): 118; *Report of Survey*, 44.

84. Dean K. Christensen, Oral history, 27 Mar. 1990.

85. *Twenty-ninth and Thirtieth Annual Reports*, 1918-20, 105.

86. *Report of Survey*, 301-18.

limit so small as to make really good schools for the future entirely out of the question." In Ellwood Cubberley's opinion this was neither "justice nor sound public policy." If a community wanted to tax itself more to improve its schools, it should be allowed to do so.[87] Cubberley suggested that "[t]he people of Salt Lake City as a body scarcely realize how inadequately their schools are supported, or what a handicap they labor under by reason of the restrictions laid upon them by the laws of the state."[88]

Cubberley's recommendation—a model law giving the district much more power over financing—was never enacted. In time, however, legislation did extend the amount of state money flowing to each school district, although there remained a legal limit on how much districts could raise by means of mill levies.[89]

SCIENTIFIC MANAGEMENT

Efficiency was the watchword of early-twentieth-century American society, making the time required to do a task synonymous with success. Taking its cue from innovations in industrial efficiency, American public schools applied Frederick W. Taylor's principles to the burgeoning school "industry."[90] The profession of "educational administration" developed in tandem with the emphasis on scientific measures of child development, curriculum cost, and teacher effectiveness. Once again, Utah's "local culture" fit in with the national drive. In 1903, well-known economist Richard T. Ely asserted that Mormon organization "is the most nearly perfect piece of social mechanism with which I have ever, in any way, come in contact, excepting the German army."[91]

The drive for educational efficiency had another dimension; now administrators were viewed as producible on demand through university training. A major tenet of the new profession was "Centralization of authority and responsibility for effective lay control in the board; *and for professional and business management in the staff.*"[92] The national efficiency movement coincided with D. H. Christensen's tenure as superintendent. His reports indicate not only that he was aware of national trends, but that he focused his considerable energy and leadership skills on making himself and his immediate staff *the* professional team upon which the board was obliged to rely.

This professionalization of administrative roles removed boards of education

---

87. *Report of Survey*, 314.

88. *Report of Survey*, 317-18.

89. Moffitt, *History of Public Education in Utah*, 143-45.

90. Raymond E. Callahan, *Education and the Cult of Efficiency* (Chicago: University of Chicago Press, 1962), 19-41.

91. "Economic Aspects of Mormonism," *Harper's* 56 (Apr. 1903): 668. While Ely further commented that "the social cement of their religion binding them together and bringing about submission to the leadership explain the wonderful achievements of the Mormons," the same characteristics may have prompted the anti-Mormon American Party to attempt control of the board of education.

92. Paul Hanus, "Improving School Systems by Scientific Management," cited in Cohen, *Education in the United States*, 4:2260.

from the influence of local "special interest" groups (often religious and ethnic minorities). Boards were to understand that their election did not give them the necessary expertise to manage day to day school affairs. If education were to be conducted on scientific principles, lay intervention could no more be tolerated, it was argued, than herbalists and folk medicine practitioners could intrude on the scientific physician. A survey of the nation's leading superintendents, conducted by Arthur H. Chamberlain of the University of California, supported this strengthening of the superintendent's authority at the expense of lay boards of education.

Although Christensen seemed in line with most of the nation's superintendents, he differed over whether boards should be elected at large or on a political ward basis. He was one of only two superintendents out of fifty participating in this survey to favor the ward method. In large urban areas superintendents favored at-large elections, which weakened the influence of religious and ethnic minorities. Christensen's position apparently responded to the realities of Salt Lake City politics. The Mormon majority had a vested interest in ensuring significant representation on the school board. Christensen's own appointment reflected that the board, beginning in 1899, had an LDS majority. While Mormons in the early twentieth century were busy accommodating mainstream America, this did not mean they neglected nurturing future generations. They supported public schooling, but did not abrogate thereby their obligation to meet the needs of the Mormon community. Electing board members on a municipal ward basis reflected the Mormon need to have input at the local level and gave some semblance of democratic representation to the board as well.

Christensen showed uncanny ability to manage political affairs during his long tenure. Nothing more aptly describes Christensen's *modus operandi* than his response to the national survey's last question: "Looking toward economy and efficiency, how would you suggest further increasing the superintendent's power?" Christensen responded tersely: "No further power desired. Superintendent must show merit in recommendation, move on conservative ground and keep within available funds." His long tenure as superintendent is one indicator of the degree to which he lived up to these ideals. With a Mormon-dominated board, Christensen had no other choice than to reflect the Mormon community's values. Christensen centralized the power of his office through "[a]bsolute confidence and frankness in dealing with board members, whether favorable or unfavorable to superintendent."[93]

But Christensen's schools, even if serving a population largely Mormon, also served the larger purposes of national unity. Cubberley's use of the term "controlled freedom" in praising the Salt Lake City schools accurately describes what such schools were about. It represents some of the tensions inherent in the "one best system," supposed to promote both initiative and conformity among princi-

---

93. Arthur H. Chamberlain, *The Growth of Responsibility and Enlargement of Power of the City School Superintendent.* University of California Publications, 3 (15 May 1913). See chart of questions and answers in the appendix of the report.

pals, teachers, and students.

The schools of Salt Lake City reflected the foregoing paradox. The 1915 Cubberley survey, conducted as it was by some of the most prestigious (and conservative) progressives in American education, was as much a capstone on the structure which D. H. Christensen had erected as it was a blueprint for reform. More important than a reform blueprint, the Cubberley report clearly legitimated the paradox.

"ANTAGONISM TO AN EFFICIENT SUPERINTENDENT"'

In January 1916, just six months after Cubberley's visit to Salt Lake, Superintendent Christensen stunned the board of education with a terse announcement: "Permit me to advise you that I shall not be a candidate for reappointment to my present position. I expect to devote my time and attention to my business interests after June 30 of this year."[94] For the past three years Christensen had conducted the business affairs of a family-based construction company his brother had managed until his death in 1913, but there appear to have been other circumstances that caused him to leave education at this particular time. In a letter to an inquirer he indicated that it was time to allow a new leader to take the schools into a new phase of their development.

The editor of the influential *Journal of Education*, A. E. Winship, lamented Christensen's retirement, describing him as a master of the "art of city supervision" and praising him for helping principals and teachers work together more effectively. Although one might regard Winship's comment that Christensen "dominated educational situations that have been more complex than . . . those of any other city in America" as somewhat rhetorical, it still shows the esteem in which he was held by the national educational establishment. According to Winship, Christensen said he resigned because he was "tired of the everlasting nagging by a few people."[95] Of course, this sentiment is not evident in the Salt Lake City newspapers of January 1916. There, Christensen simply stated that he felt retirement was propitious: he wanted the Cubberley survey to be the "last word upon that period during which I was actively connected with the work in my present capacity."[96]

However, some evidence also indicates that the relationship between Christensen and the board was not as benign as the official record suggests. Christensen's daughter recalled that one reasons her father resigned was that he was tired of criticism from the Masons. In 1914, one of the two Masons on the board, A. D. McMullen, charged that Christensen had "bought off" opposition to his re-election by offering salary increases, a promotion, and "other favors" to the principal of West Side High School. The board held formal hearings on the charges, but on a 7-2 vote decided that McMullen had failed to prove his assertion. Mc-Mullen and the other Mason on the board, George M. Sullivan, cast the two dis-

94. *Twenty-sixth Annual Report*, 1915-16, 81.
95. *Journal of Education* 83 (10 Feb. 1916): 155-56.
96. "D. H. Christensen to Quit Position," *Salt Lake Tribune*, 12 Jan. 1916.

senting votes. In an "impassioned speech" Christensen said he could "lay his ear to the ground" and come up with rumors about McMullen, but that he did not operate in that manner.[97]

The conflict with the board's Masons was only one irritant Christensen endured during his superintendency. Others have been alluded to earlier—charges of using pay as a means of gaining support from staff, appointing Mormons to administrative posts, and a community dispute over the location of a new school. The reduction of Mormon board influence after December 1912 no doubt influenced his decision. This election witnessed Masons McMullen and Sullivan, who were to become Christensen's nemeses, replace two Mormons on the board. The Masons on the board thereby increased their numbers to five, a configuration that persisted until 1918, when the Mormons ended up with eight of the board seats and the Free Masons with a minority of two.

While these shifts in power were certainly significant to Christensen's resignation, it is difficult to pinpoint exactly why they occurred. The 1910 election was the last in which charges of church influence were aired in the *Tribune*. Then, in contrast to the previous four elections, the 1912 election passed without any hyperbolic rhetoric about Mormon domination of the board. The American party had disappeared from the list of contenders and a "non-partisan" slate was promoted even by the *Tribune*. The same thing happened in the city's 1911 municipal election, which has been described as the "death throes of the previous division of political parties on religious lines." Apparently, economic realities overcame ideology. In 1911 the *Tribune* and *Telegram* were involved in a lawsuit, and evidence from the trial indicated that these newspapers had suffered economically from their staunch support of the American party. When the 1912 school election rolled around, the *Tribune's* tone was muted and, for the first time in any school board elections, the outcry over the danger of Mormon domination was absent. In this benign climate, the once six-member Mormon majority dropped to four.[98]

Other factors may have influenced this low-key election: did the Mormons, in exchange for a toned-down *Tribune*, promote some semblance of political ecumenicism? Was the new Mormon minority related to Salt Lake City having been chosen for the National Education Association annual conference in July 1913? Lack of written records make definitive answers difficult to come by. One thing can be documented, however: in place of the single-issue candidates of the American Party, a new threat appeared on the horizon—the emergence of the Socialists as the only opposition to "non-partisan" Mormons and non-Mormons. In a large front page headline, the *Deseret News* warned its readers that a low non-partisan vote would likely result in a Socialist victory. The fear of Mormon domi-

---

97. Oral history, Kathleen C. Hall, 10 Apr. 1990. Details of the conflict are in "Christensen Probe Started by Board," *Salt Lake Tribune*, 9 Dec. 1914; "School Board Holds Charges Lack Basis," *Salt Lake Tribune*, 11 Dec. 1914; "Darrow Deposed from High School . . . Stormy Session of Board," *Deseret News*, 4 Dec. 1914; "Vindication is Voted By Board," *Deseret News*, 11 Dec. 1914.

98. "School Elections Today," *Salt Lake Tribune*, 4 Dec. 1912; "Non-Partisan Ticket Carries Every Ward," *Salt Lake Tribune*, 5 Dec. 1912; Alexander and Allen, *Mormons and Gentiles*, 146-47.

nation had given way to fear of Socialism. As it happened, in spite of a low vote the Socialists were thoroughly decimated, receiving only 657 of the total 5,274 votes cast and securing no board seats.[99] In the spirit of ecumenicism—or economic and political reality—the new board consisted of five Free Masons, four Mormons and one other non-Mormon. This configuration remained the same for the next two election. Local religious squabbling was crowded off the newspaper headlines by the commencement of the Great European War. Perhaps with war on the horizon it was the Germans' turn to serve as a unifying force in school board elections.

The elections were less aggressive to be sure, but the actions of at least some Masons on the board dispelled any myth that an armistice had been signed. When Christensen tendered his surprise resignation in January 1916 he gave no inkling that he harbored a great deal of suppressed indignation. At the board meeting held to name a successor, M. M. Warner charged that a conspiracy among certain board members had forced Christensen out of office to replace him with someone "more subservient to certain factions" on the board. The assistant city attorney, Moses Davis, spoke for a group of citizens ready to investigate reports of "cabal and conspiracy" on the board. Some suggested that certain board members—Sullivan and McMullen—had sought election on the platform of removing the superintendent. Davis quoted D. H. Christensen as saying that "no red-blooded man could remain as superintendent of this school system while members of the board sit here as the board is now constituted." It was, according to Davis, the "peanut politics and the insinuations going on here and around him" that forced Christensen's resignation. The board received these reports in typical silence, then elected non-Mormon Dr. Ernest A. Smith as the fourth superintendent of Salt Lake City School District.

Immediately following this D. H. Christensen made a statement in which he asserted, after acknowledging his interest in the family business, that Sullivan and McMullen had been a major factor in forcing his decision. Their presence, he asserted, was detrimental to the board, and it would "be best for the school system if Mr. Sullivan and Mr. McMullen withdrew before the expiration of their terms."[100] There was no applause, no questions—only the stifled silence of a board that saw itself as above the confrontation, debate, and rejoinder.

At Christensen's retirement, just past the district's silver anniversary, the schools of Salt Lake City were generally in good shape, the system managed by professionals focused on meeting the needs of all of the city's school children. Christensen and his co-workers had done much to shape the Salt Lake City schools in the image of national educational thought. A steady stream of prominent educators, including John Dewey and Canadian educator James Hughes, at-

---

99. "School Election May Go By Default," *Deseret News*, 4 Dec. 1912; "City Vote Light; Results Decisive," *Deseret News*, 5 Dec. 1912.

100. Detailed accounts of this 13 June meeting are found in "Call on Board Members to Resign," *Deseret News*, 14 June 1916 and "School Board Has Dramatic Session," *Salt Lake Tribune*, 14 June 1916. The minutes of this meeting are parsimoniously recorded as "Mr. Christensen requested to be heard and stated his reasons for resigning." See Board of Education, Minutes, 13 June 1916.

tested to Utah's educational triumphs. Although numerous non-Mormons made significant contributions to the schools of the period, the positive national image of Salt Lake City's schools tended to identify progress with the dominant Mormon presence in the city. Still, in spite of seeming difference from the rest of America, Utah's schools, especially those of Salt Lake City, were accommodating at "all deliberate speed" to the secular, competitive larger society. In the next few decades this would become more and more marked as the LDS church closed its academies, turning some of them over to the state. If Salt Lake society was not yet as pluralistic as the West and East coasts, its schools were beginning to take on an aura of cosmopolitanism rooted in the larger vision of D. H. Christensen and his assistants such as Lizbeth Qualtrough and George Eaton. In spite of fears that Mormon-controlled schools would be creatures of the dominant church, under the administration of Christensen's "home ability" the schools became thoroughly American. Yet the ever-burning issue of church-state relations continued to bubble to the surface of school polity well into the twentieth century.

D. H. Christensen continued his involvement in the education community by serving thirty-one years as a member of the University of Utah's Board of Regents. In 1948 his alma mater acknowledged his contributions to education in the state by bestowing on him an honorary doctoral degree in education—the degree he was working toward when he accepted a call to become the city's superintendent almost fifty years before. He died in Salt Lake in 1956 at the age of 86.[101]

---

101. "Death Ends Long Career of S. L. Education Leader," *Salt Lake Tribune*, 8 Jan. 1956.

Ernest A. Smith
1916–20

4

A COMPROMISE OUTSIDER STAYS THE COURSE

The Administration of
Ernest A. Smith, 1916–20

The task of replacing D. H. Christensen deeply divided the board—no possible candidate garnered sufficient support to win the superintendency. This stalemate benefitted a compromise candidate who successfully welded competing factions into a majority. The new choice, Dr. Ernest A. Smith, an historian late of Allegheny College, Pennsylvania, was the third non-Mormon to occupy the post since 1890. During his tenure the district faced the Great War, a circumstance that affected—shaped, even—the Salt Lake schools as it did schools throughout the nation. At the same time, of course, other circumstances continued to mold the schools, principally the ideology of "administrative progressivism," which seemed compatible with the local culture's continually evolving emphasis on hierarchy, organization, and conformity.

Within a few years of taking the district's helm, Smith would realize that no superintendent has a guaranteed tenure, even at the best of times. Smith would come under fire in the local press for not being able to control the board's factionalism. Then, in 1918, the board make-up, for the first time ever, was eight Mormons and two Masons. Perhaps seeing the writing on the wall, Ernest Smith tendered his resignation to the dominantly Mormon board in 1920.

APATHY, A DIVIDED BOARD, AND A COMPROMISE SUPERINTENDENT

In the Board of Education election of 1916, only 1,072 of a possible 26,000 electors cast ballots. Some credited the poor turnout to inclement weather, but with only five negative votes cast in the entire slate—the lowest negative vote ever cast in a board election—a better case could be made for dampened public enthusiasm, satisfaction with the status quo, or involvement in the national war effort.[1]

The 1914 and 1916 elections not only indicated a profound voter apathy, they also yielded boards evenly balanced between Mormons and non-Mormons (mostly Masons)—a condition similar to that which existed at the turn of the century. In spite of some evidence that Salt Lake City schools were becoming more progressive, the old politics of "insiders" and "outsiders," or Mormons and

---

1. "Vote is Close to Unanimous," *Salt Lake Tribune*, 7 Dec. 1916.

gentiles, persisted. When Christensen resigned, then, the reemergence of this rhetoric hardly surprised the community.

On Christensen's departure the board split over choosing someone already in the system—Mormon George N. Child, the supervisor of the grammar grades, or non-Mormon George A. Eaton, supervising principal of the high school department—or a genuine outsider, such as H. B. Wilson of Topeka, Kansas, or B. B. Jackson of Minneapolis, Minnesota. The president of the board, W. J. Barrette, and board member George Sullivan, both of whom were Christensen nemeses, strongly favored Wilson, while the other three Masons on the board apparently supported Jackson. Given the probability that the four Mormons on the board (Howard, Cutler, Moyle, and Bradford) favored a local appointment, it was numerically impossible for any of the candidates to be selected. When this situation became obvious, a compromise candidate became the unanimous choice of the factious board.

Dr. Ernest A. Smith was a recently married, forty-one year old Methodist Episcopalian from Meadville, Pennsylvania. The professor of history and economics seemed an odd choice, given the movement toward professional educational administration, but Smith had impeccable academic credentials: an A.B. from Ohio Wesleyan and a Ph.D. from Johns Hopkins, with additional studies at Oxford and the University of London. Smith also actively participated in the National Education Association and had served as principal of Valdosta Collegiate Institute from 1890-94; professor of History and Politics at Allegheny College from 1898-1910; and was Albert Shaw Lecturer in Diplomatic History at Johns Hopkins University in 1908. From 1910-13 he was an assistant professor of history at Princeton University, a position, some claimed, secured for him by his friend Woodrow Wilson. Prior to taking the position in Salt Lake, Smith returned to Allegheny College (1913-1916) where he married and also wrote the institution's centennial history: *Allegheny, A Century of Education*. His earlier publications included *The History of the Confederate Treasury* (1901) and *The Diplomatic Contest for the Ohio Valley* (1909). Smith was clearly the most distinguished scholar ever to have served as superintendent of Salt Lake City's public schools, and perhaps remains so. Nineteenth-century Americans viewed such academic credentials as sufficient preparation for an administrator, fitting rather nicely Tyack and Hansot's notion of "aristocracy of character," as opposed to the professional "managers of virtue"—the typical, business and efficiency oriented twentieth-century administrators. By the early twentieth century, such credentials as Smith's were viewed as professionally minimal; formal preparation for administrative leadership was more and more the rule.[2]

Little information exists about the selection process, except that Smith was an acceptable compromise. Some objections to an outsider surfaced in the *Deseret News*, and locals were said to favor the appointment of Child or Eaton. Im-

2. Details on Smith's life and many accomplishments are contained in *Allegheny College Bulletin* (Nov. 1926); David Tyack and Elizabeth Hansot, *Managers of Virtue: Public School Leadership in America, 1820-1980* (New York: Basic Books, 1982).

pressive as Smith's academic record was, the Salt Lake *Herald* attacked the appointment because Smith lacked professional training or experience: He had served only a short time as the superintendent of "an unimportant Georgia community [Valdosta] of 7,656" prior to 1898 and theoretical or academic experience were not deemed good preparation for dealing with the practical problems of the schools. Further, the *Herald* argued, the board had conducted its business too secretively, with "disregard for public opinion." The *Tribune* weighed in with criticism that other outside candidates (Wilson and Jackson) were much better prepared. According to the *Deseret News*, part of the compromise between factions (Mormon/Mason?) on the board was that George Child (a Mormon) would retain his position as grammar school supervisor and speculated that he might even be appointed assistant superintendent. Whatever the private board discussions entailed, once a compromise was reached, the board, in an amazing show of unity, voted unanimously to elect Smith to a two-year term.[3]

SCHOOLS RESPOND TO NATIONAL NEEDS

Although some nationally prominent progressives, such as Randolph Bourne, actively opposed U.S. entry in to the Great War, John Dewey threw his support behind President Wilson. As might be expected, public schools across the nation did the same. In Utah, the Mormon leadership demonstrated considerable pacifist sentiment and called on Mormons to resist U.S. involvement. However, once Wilson committed the nation to "save the world for democracy," the Mormon community and its leaders filled in the ranks. According to historian Thomas Alexander, the alacrity with which they did this "helped in changing the national image of the church."[4] Such support for the war, like their unabashed commitment to public schools, was concrete evidence that the Mormons were truly integrated American citizens.

The war and its aftermath overshadowed Smith's first year as superintendent as well as most local political concerns. In spite of the war, and his lack of experience as a public school administrator, Smith kept the agenda of "progressive" development on track, especially in administration. The Salt Lake District, in the four years of Smith's incumbency, continued to gradually evolve in terms of the centralized, efficient system of D. H. Christensen and his predecessor, Jesse F. Millspaugh.

The barrage of graphic propaganda to "Beat Back the Hun with Liberty Bonds" and the need to preserve civilization from being crushed by the blood-drenched boots of "barbarians" resulted in numerous student enlistments in the armed services and in the cancellation of German as a language taught in the

---

3. "Smith is Appointed as Superintendent," *Salt Lake Tribune*, 25 Apr. 1916; "Salt Lake's New Mystery," *Salt Lake Herald*, 26 Apr. 1916; "E. A. Smith Here to Meet School Board," *Deseret News*, 24 Apr. 1916; "Ernest A. Smith Head of Schools," *Deseret News*, 25 Apr. 1916; "School Board is Criticized," *Deseret News*, 17 May 1916; Board of Education, Minutes, 11 June 1916.

4. Thomas G. Alexander, *Mormonism in Transition: A History of the Latter-day Saints, 1890-1930* (Urbana: University of Illinois Press, 1986), 46-49.

schools. Students also responded to the need for more farm workers and the district promoted "war gardens" at private homes and at the schools. With 200 prizes offered for the best gardens, thousands of gardens sprouted throughout Salt Lake City. Domestic arts programs met the war's needs as suggested by the American Red Cross, as students snipped cloth for pillow fillings, made gun wipes, knitted mufflers, rolled bandages, prepared first aid kits, and raised money for Liberty Bonds, French orphans, and Belgian relief. Even teachers were enrolled by the U.S. War Department to read Selective Service questionnaires from all males 21 to 31 years of age. The teachers composed an index that allowed quick retrieval of the names of persons with particular qualifications and received a commendation from the War Department for their work.[5]

High school principal George Eaton reported that the "abnormal conditions" of war created a deep feeling of unrest in the work of the schools, although he was pleased to report that by the end of 1916 some 88 students had volunteered for service in the armed forces. Salt Lake City schools had offered "cadet training" as part of the curriculum, enabling many students to qualify as officers. By the end of 1917 over 600 high school cadets had joined the armed forces; the war, Superintendent Smith noted, had effectively demonstrated that "school is life." "The war," he continued, "had been carried into the school" and was infusing the traditional curriculum with a "new and engrossing significance" as "the circumstances of the time" touched history, geography, civics, music, and languages. War poems "possessed immediate vital appeal" and arithmetic lessons were constructed around calculating food problems and the collection of thrift stamps. Essay competitions on the themes of "Why Every Family Should Purchase Liberty Bonds" and "Why the United States Entered the War" reinforced political realities. Without even a hint of questions about *whether* the United States should have gone to war, educators claimed, quite frankly, that students benefitted from the broadened perspective forced on the schools. Students seem to have followed W. H. Auden's "Unknown Citizen": "When there was peace, he was for peace; when there was war, he went."[6]

Although the war may have had an invigorating influence on some aspects of the curriculum, Eaton also noted a "very heavy decrease in attendance." Some Utah schools outside the Salt Lake District closed six weeks early because of student withdrawals. Eaton hoped parents would realize that, in spite of the national war crisis, their children belonged in school. After all, he argued, "upon the education of the youth our ultimate strength and advancement as a civilized nation depend."[7]

"Strength" for Eaton meant more than morality and intellect, as indicated by his subsequent plea for increased physical education. Salt Lake City high schools

---

5. *Twenty-sixth and Twenty-seventh Annual Reports*, 1915-17, 138; *Twenty-eighth Annual Report*, 1917-18, 12-19. See Liberty Bond posters published in newspapers at this time in Christensen Papers, Special Collections, University of Utah Library.

6. *Twenty-eighth Annual Report*, 1917-18, 9-21; W. H. Auden, "The Unknown Citizen" in Lawrence Perrine, ed., *Sound and Sense* (New York: Harcourt Brace & Co., 1956), 103.

7. *Twenty-eighth Annual Report*, 1917-18, 154-55

retained only one physical education instructor for every 600 students, and most of their energy went into coaching rather than giving instruction in the theory and practice of physical education. Students, Eaton averred, graduate with "sound bodies as well as trained minds." To this end he proposed "a systematic and scientific" program of "physical training." Again, Eaton's main rationale was that such a program would serve the needs of the country, a common theme in war-time education.

PROGRESSIVE EDUCATION—SALT LAKE STYLE

When, in 1915, Brigham Young's statement that "Education is the power to think clearly; the power to act well in the world's work, and the power to appreciate life" marked the entrance to the official Utah State exhibit at the Panama-Pacific Exposition in San Francisco, Mormon/gentile conflict appeared to be declining. Such a universal definition of education appealed to both Mormons and gentiles. It was also thoroughly American in placing the pragmatic first and "appreciation" last. By 1916 Salt Lake City's schools were well on their way to reflecting, not the parochial interests of one particular group, but what was then called "progressive education."[8] Another symptom of change came in 1917, when Democrat Simon Bamberger, a Jew who had served on the Salt Lake Board of Education between 1898 to 1903, took office as governor of Utah—the first non-Mormon to serve in that capacity since the much disliked federal territorial governors.

In his first message to the legislature, Bamberger noted that "Utah has finally and definitely succeeded in removing the schools from any vestige of partisan political influence."[9] Perhaps he overstated the case slightly, but compared to the wrangling of most of the period from 1890, a greater degree of pluralism was evident as was increased openness to outside influence.

As Allan Payne points out in his study of the Mormon response to progressive ideas, the big names of so-called progressive education—including its "father" Francis W. Parker, John Dewey, G. Stanley Hall, Willard Wirt, and Charles Eliot—visited Utah, as did other progressive luminaries such as James L. Hughes, Liberty Hyde Bailey, and Jacob Riis. University of Utah faculty such as William Stewart and Mosiah Hall were personally acquainted with Parker and Dewey. Milton Bennion of the University of Utah and John A. Widtsoe of the Council of the Twelve Apostles had "studied in the Midwest and East and . . . came under the progressive spell." Payne argues that such contacts with progressive education sustained in Utah schools a relatively progressive environment generally unexpected from such a religiously oriented community. Utah embraced progressivism, according to Payne, because a large degree of congruence

---

8. The quotation attributed to Governor Brigham Young was made in an address to the Regents of the University of Deseret in 1851. "The Utah Educational Exhibit," *Utah Educational Review* 9 (Sept. 1915): 1.

9. Governor's Message to the Legislature of Utah, 18 Jan. 1917, cited in James R. Clark, "Church and State Relationships in Education in Utah," Ed.D. diss, Utah State University, 1958, 286.

existed between some Mormon social ideals and those espoused by progressivism. For example, the Mormon focus on a redemptive earthly community called for such attributes as manual labor, mastery of the environment, and economic stability rooted in agriculture and handicrafts. Such emphases on practical education may have been "unconscious vehicle[s] to preclude critical thinking that might threaten Mormon ideology" at a time when the church was under the pressure of external criticism over the recently abandoned practice of polygamy and the church's long-standing role in Utah's economic and political affairs.

Mormon thinking also seemed congruent with American progressivism's emphasis on "child centeredness." According to Payne, the language of child-centeredness was familiar to Mormon educators. However, Mormons were less inclined to promote individualism in children; under the stress of accommodating to external social and political pressures, extreme individualism was the last thing Mormons needed. Leaders were more interested in obedience than in self-expression. During the 1920s one of the "memory gems" recited by Mormon children at their weekly Primary held that "Obedience is heaven's first law/ And order is its result./ This is a lesson good to learn/ For child and for adult."[10]

One Utahn, Edna Clark Ericksen, who met Jane Addams in Chicago, became a member of the general board of the LDS children's Primary organization in the 1920s. In that capacity, she introduced the "Trailblazer" concept as part of the church's weekday instruction for young boys. This program emphasized activity, including crafts, instead of passive listening for children, again reflecting a commitment to the progressive ideal.[11]

Payne also identifies as progressive the correlation of school and out-of-school experiences. Mormons embraced this notion in building the Kingdom of God as a community enterprise, which had led to the overlapping of church and school functions that many Protestants found so objectionable in the late nineteenth century. Closely related to this was the notion of the school viewed as an instrument of social reform. However, using schools to control social change was probably more attractive to Mormons than active participation in social and political protest movements.[12]

The above examples suggest that Mormonism was not necessarily reactionary to all progressive educational reform, and that a religious, hierarchical community could have public schools reflect at least some aspects of the national progressive mainstream. Although "progressive" education was at this time defined by the national network of professionals (the "administrative progressives" who were closely linked to Ellwood Cubberley and other university based educa-

---

10. This verse was brought to my attention by Martha Stewart of Salt Lake City. She recalled it being used in the Forest Dale Ward in Salt Lake City. The Primary was the LDS weekday religious activity program for young children.

11. Edna Ericksen related her interest in progressive education and its connection with the evolution of the "Trailblazer" program in a conversation with me shortly before her death in 1983.

12. The discussion of the degree to which Mormons were able to use progressive educational ideas is based on Allan Dean Payne, "The American Response to Early Progressive Education, 1892-1920," Ph.D. diss., University of Utah, 1977.

tors), many locals used the "old-fashioned technique of urban politics" to promote their interpretation of a progressive agenda for public schools.[13] In Salt Lake City, D. H. Christensen used the community's unique religious orientation to promote his notion of progressivism. And his successor, Ernest Smith, in spite of being an "outsider," could adeptly size up and meet the local community's needs. Progressivism did not rule out flexibility. Additionally, progressive education, in spite of its liberal aura and claims to the contrary, was a conservative movement. Mormons did not have to change radically to fit the progressive mold, at least as many of America's "administrative progressives" defined it.

In reality, the progressive movement was a rather commodious umbrella under which a multi-faceted array of educators assembled (or more precisely, under which they were *placed* in an attempt to simplify their complexity). They ranged from "child needs" enthusiasts and other social reformers to administrators who emphasized social efficiency, differentiated vocational goals, and centralized control. Nationally, the latter, conservative tendencies overshadowed the child-centered and social-centered variety. In Salt Lake City, in spite of local enthusiasts such as Lizbeth Qualtrough, the same conservativism prevailed. The fact that people as diverse as Charles Eliot of Harvard, Ellwood Cubberley of Stanford, and John Dewey of Columbia could all be accommodated under the "progressive" sobriquet illustrates, even as it complicates, the issue of exactly what progressive education was.[14]

FOCUS ON THE CHILD

In spite of a predominant conservativism that viewed the school as an agent of the state, many Salt Lake educators focused on individual children in the context of a putative democratic society. In 1918 George N. Child, Smith's Assistant Superintendent, plead for removal from the schools of anything extraneous to student progress. For Child, schools were democratic institutions preparing *all* children—not just the "fittest"—to survive in society. Attempting to democratize the schools, Child advocated eliminating "autocratic" school discipline and replacing it with "intelligent and willing obedience to constituted authority." He reported that most grammar school held enlightened views on discipline, but that too many still demanded a "blind, unwilling forced form of obedience," which reduced education to "a suppressed and lifeless thing."[15]

Consistent with Child's "pedagogical progressivism," Lizbeth Qualtrough, Supervisor of the Primary Division, believed, with John Dewey, that children need physical involvement in learning and should creatively express themselves through "tearing, paper-cutting, clay-modelling and the sand-table." Modern

13. Tyack and Hansot, *Managers of Virtue*, 140-44.
14. For discussion of the varieties of progressive education see John and Evelyn Dewey, *Schools for To-Morrow* (New York: S. P. Dutton & Co., 1915); Lawrence A. Cremin, *The Transformation of the School* (New York: Vintage Books, 1964), 127-239, and Tyack and Hansot, *Managers of Virtue*, 105-14.
15. *Twenty-eighth Annual Report*, 1917-18, 41, 46.

classrooms needed to be changed from "listening places" to "doing places" where children can move around freely, unrestrained by stationary desks.[16]

The shift from a subject-matter, rote learning approach toward the progressive, child-centered methods finds illustration in an enforced, eleven-week vacation during the influenza epidemic of 1918. While many bemoaned the loss of learning time, Qualtrough asserted that during the vacation children had continued to mature. In spite of uncovered subject matter, children returned to school, according to Qualtrough, with greater power of concentration and had soon made up for lost time. Qualtrough believed schools spent too much time and effort "in getting ready to function in the social and industrial organism." Reduced school time meant saving money for taxpayers. Over the next decade this notion was put into effect when time devoted to schooling was cut from twelve to eleven years.[17]

Whether Child's democratic measures were successful is open to question. Some oral history interviews indicate the period's dominant theme was strict discipline. Merle Colton Bennion recalled that class work included memorizing much poetry from authors such as Sir Walter Scott. Teachers also persistently emphasized formal grammar. Lowell L. Bennion recalled a similar traditional focus but identified teachers as "moralizers as well as teachers of subject matter." Through personal stories they "humanized the subject matter," which students enjoyed. Bennion held one Irving Junior High mathematics teacher (a Mr. Winward) in high esteem for his ability to relate to the students.[18] What occurred in Salt Lake City classrooms near the end of World War I was probably a mix of traditional and progressive ideas, mediated through the dispositions and training of individual teachers. However, schools certainly became more pleasant places in which to spend time as children's needs increasingly became a component of the modern school curriculum.

Less evident than child-centered classroom activity, in Salt Lake schools at least, was another element crucial to progressivism: the extension of the curriculum beyond school walls into the community's social life and problems.[19] In Salt Lake's schools, progressivism ultimately remained more in written school reports than in actual classroom practices, in spite of teachers and supervisors such as Lizbeth Qualtrough who were more willing to light a candle than curse the darkness. Like so many dedicated teachers, they assumed they could make a positive difference in their students' lives.

DIVERSE STUDENTS AND A DIFFERENTIATED CURRICULUM

As Salt Lake City schools became increasingly mainstream, Superintendent Smith and others continued to advocate progressive postures taken by D. H.

---

16. Ibid., 50.
17. *Twenty-ninth Annual Report*, 1918-19, 76-77.
18. Lowell L. and Merle C. Bennion, Oral History, 29 Mar. 1990.
19. Arthur Zilversmit, *Changing Schools: Progressive Educational Theory and Practice, 1930-1960* (Chicago: University of Chicago Press, 1993), 16-18.

Christensen. War might hinder pedagogical innovation, but it also facilitated programs to meet society's demands, as discussed above. Ironically, lessons learned from the Germans—especially industrial efficiency—were being used to resist Germany's military might.[20] Ironic too, was Cubberley's assertion that America's "city schools will soon be forced to give up the exceedingly democratic notion that all are equal, and that our society is devoid of classes." For Cubberley, diversity of students and too much democracy in the schools led inexorably to a differentiated curriculum: "an attempt better to adapt the school to the needs of the many classes in the city life."[21] Schools met the needs of the individual as a creature of the state, not as a semi-autonomous entity.

However, even such systematic school programs did not necessarily mean that students would be attracted to them. Given increasingly diverse student populations (in age and social class, at least), schools now had a correlative need to "hold" them in place. Apparently a differentiated curriculum did not always succeed in doing that. In 1917 the high schools' failure to retain ninth graders was attributed in part to the schools not being "adapted to the need of the children of the city as they should be." This, as would be expected, was noted by the "progressive" Cubberley team in 1915.

Another factor weakening the high school's holding power was inadequate counselling in junior high school. In this respect Salt Lake City seemed to lag behind other districts in the state. At least as of 1918, Millard County High School, North Sanpete High School and Spanish Fork High School all reported having "departments or bureaus designed to assist young persons in securing employment." In 1917 in Salt Lake's schools only 177 boys out of 1,213 were enrolled in shop work—a meager fourteen percent and a number that put Salt Lake City schools "somewhat behind in the [national] procession." All teachers in all grades should consequently "encourage and advise boys—to pursue the technical course in high school."[22]

One bright spot, however, was West High School's commercial course in which 600 out of 1,200 students were enrolled. Requiring only three years to complete "added incentive to the vocational significance of the work." The growing need for clerical expertise made such courses relevant. By contrast the "mechanic arts course . . . has attracted scarcely a corporal's guard"; in Dr. Smith's opinion, the $150,000 spent in equipment for only fifty students was a "wholly inadequate return upon the investment."[23]

Smith's negative assessment was repeated in other areas of the country. Studying vocational education in California, Harvey Kantor argues that voca-

---

20. Ellwood P. Cubberley, *Changing Conceptions of Education* (Boston: Houghton Mifflin Co., 1909), 53-54.

21. Cubberley, *Changing Conceptions*, 56-57.

22. W. Carson Ryan, Jr., *Vocational Guidance and the Public Schools* (Washington, D.C.: U.S. Bureau of Education, 1919), 137-147; *Twenty-sixth and Twenty-seventh Annual Reports*, 1915-17, 178.

23. Ibid., 138.

tional programs throughout the nation had virtually no "economic relevance."[24] For vocational education, the "fair-haired boy" of the social efficiency administrators, to fail the crucial test of cost-benefit analysis must have been difficult to accept. Educators seemed to follow Robert Frost's advice: "For dear me, why abandon a belief/ Merely because it ceases to be true./ Cling to it long enough, and not a doubt/ It will turn true again."[25] The lines summarize American infatuation with vocational education since it became a staple commodity of educational reform in the first decades of the twentieth Century.

Like the mechanical arts course, the domestic science course, designed to make high school more meaningful for females, drew comparatively few students. Perplexed over the low enrollments, the head of the Department of Domestic Arts, Anna L. Corbett, could find "no sane reason why the matter of patching, darning and other phases of mending should be less dignified than the translating of foreign languages."[26] What Corbett meant by "sane reason" is less clear than the fact that parents and students perceived social class reasons for not making the patching of clothes in school equal to academic work.

When young people rejected "darning" and mechanics over language study, educators assumed the lower grades were at fault and increased the emphasis on industrial education in grammar schools. The Manual Training Supervisor, Milton Clauser, drew attention in 1917 to the inescapable realities of the work place. Eight-Six percent of Salt Lake's boys were being funnelled toward occupations "that are so crowded that only the exceptional man could expect to succeed in them." The solution was to socialize boys—especially in junior high—not to have unrealistic expectations. In junior high school, Clauser held, the "function of all studies . . . should be considered as largely pre-vocational," giving boys a broader view of vocational opportunities. With such a program in place the inevitable result would be that the industrial education "shops at the West High School should not only be filled, but they should be running on double time."[27]

Smith's tenure also saw increased attention to mental measurement in organizing the curriculum. This stemmed from the development of testing instruments designed to identify those fit and unfit for military service. According to Clarence Karier, "Historians generally mark the beginning of the testing movement with the mass testing of 1.7 million men for classification in the armed forces during World War I."[28]

In Salt Lake City prior to 1916, children who did not seem to fit the "normal" range of mental ability were assigned to the "Atypical School" (the old

24. Harvey A. Kantor, *Learning to Earn: School, Work, and Vocational Education in California, 1880-1930* (Madison: University of Wisconsin Press, 1988), 168.
25. Robert Frost, "The Black Cottage," in J. H. Nelson and O. Corgill, eds., *Contemporary Trends: American Literature since 1900* (New York: MacMillan Co., 1949).
26. *Twenty-ninth Annual Report,* 1918-19, 81.
27. *Twenty-sixth and Twenty-seventh Annual Reports,* 1918-17, 178-80.
28. Clarence J. Karier, et al., *Roots of Crisis: American Education in the Twentieth Century* (Chicago: Rand McNally & Co., 1973), 112.

Twelfth Ward School on the corner of First South and Fourth East, and now the site of the district offices). The Atypical School provided special education to fit students' needs, but by 1915 such a "complex variety of mental aptitude and inaptitude" existed that the supervisor of special classes decided that the "scholastically subnormal" or "merely dull normals" needed different instruction from those who were "feeble minded." Mingling types, this administrator believed, cast "a stigma . . . unkindly and unnecessarily upon the majority of those enrolled in school." Subnormal and dull students returned to schools near their homes, where they received special help in subjects in which they were "backward." They also attended the regular classes for other courses, thus benefiting from the stimulation of the brighter students. The transfer reduced the Atypical School by two thirds and led to more efficient use of special education teachers. The district remained responsible for the "feebleminded" at the Atypical until the state later established an institution at American Fork.[29]

According to George Snow Gibbs, head of the Department of Exceptional Children, public schools needed to restructure to better accommodate those "exceptional" children who had particular "fundamental capacities imposed on them by Nature's selective draft." Most of these children, Gibbs felt, "will be compelled by society to assume the responsibilities of normal adulthood." The extent to which schools met the needs of exceptional students is, of course, difficult to determine. Notwithstanding this, educators felt that they were successful in preparing students for their role in life, limited though it might be.

The Utah Plan of 1919

In 1917 the National Education Association, in response to what many were calling "The Emergency in Education," formed the "National Emergency Commission" to investigate ways in which the schools could best serve the nation's needs after the war had ended. According to this commission, the public schools could be at the forefront of efforts to: eradicate illiteracy, Americanize foreigners, equalize educational opportunity, promote physical and health education, and improve the preparation of teachers, especially in rural areas.[30]

Utah's educators responded enthusiastically; early in 1918 they put forward the "Utah Plan," which had four main parts: every student up to the age of eighteen should be enrolled in compulsory and part-time education; all aliens between sixteen and forty-five who could not read or write English at a fifth grade level should attend compulsory Americanization classes; all students between twelve and eighteen should be under school supervision even when not in school; and all children should have a physical examination under the auspices of the school system.[31]

The "Utah Plan" received rave reviews from national educators. Charles

---

29. *Twenty-sixth and Twenty-seventh Annual Reports*, 1915-17, 135-36

30. Catherine J. Rogers, "The Life and Work of George Newport Child," M.A. thesis, University of Utah, 1941, 14.

31. Rogers, "The Life and Work of George Newport Child," 20.

Prosser, the leading exponent of vocational education (and later the promoter of "Life-adjustment Education" of the 1940s) called it a "model, compulsory, part-time education law" and claimed Utah was leading the way in year-round education. The program, he said, represents the idea that the state has the right "to regulate and control not only the education, but the employment of children." A. E. Winship, editor of the *Journal of Education* and one-time critic of the Mormon domination of Utah's educational scene, visited Utah with Prosser to campaign for the new law's acceptance. Claiming that Utah had "made greater strides in the fundamentals of public school education in thirty years than any other state" he praised the 1919 law as the nation's first "which eliminates loafing of young people up to the age of eighteen."[32]

Dr. Ernest Smith observed, as he left his post as Salt Lake's superintendent, that Utah's religious climate was a major reason the plan was so enthusiastically promoted in the state: "the discipline and training of the majority of the Utah people contribute to the favorable acceptance of the new plan. The moral instruction of youth is a cardinal tenet of the dominant church and the close supervision of personal affairs is an accepted practice."[33] The person implementing the Utah Plan was George N. Child, who served as State Superintendent for a short period before succeeding Smith as superintendent of Salt Lake District in 1920. But a variety of reasons kept the plan from ever really taking off: partisan political interference; the war left people wary of change and wanting to return to "normalcy"; reduction in taxes limited experimentation; a lack of organized public support; and a general public impression that the plan was overly "ambitious and pretentious."[34] And it is no wonder. The plan apparently demanded that schools prepare three sets of reports dealing with each student's health, employment, and out-of-school activities. The reports would include details concerning "the use of narcotics, care of person, sleeping habits, and kind and amount of recreation." Perhaps not realizing the amount of time that would be required ("three thousand waking hours they spend out of school"), superintendents throughout the country praised the plan as a "call to civic and moral righteousness for all the youth." The Utah Plan, described by David Tyack as "social uplift with a vengeance,"[35] could not have happened in the 1890s heyday of Mormon/gentile conflict. As it was, however, this Mormon-inspired "social uplift" program was not criticized in the local press; it was readily accepted—in spirit, at least—by all facets of the community. One of its outgrowths—a committee on Americanization and citizenship—had a highly ecumenical profile consisting of,

---

32. Charles A. Prosser, "Utah Educational Program," in "Utah Educational Pamphlets," Special Collections, Brigham Young University; A. E. Winship, "Why Go to Salt Lake City," *Journal of Education* (3 June 1920).

33. Ernest A. Smith, "Compulsory Character Education," in *National Education Association Addresses and Proceedings.* Fifty Eighth Annual Meeting, Salt Lake City, 1920, 473

34. LeRoy E. Cowles, "The Utah Educational Program of 1919 and Factors Conditioning its Operation," Ph.D. diss., University of California, Berkeley, 1926, 5; Rogers, "Life and Work," 37.

35. David B. Tyack, ed., *Turning Points in American Educational History* (Waltham, MA: Blaisdell, 1967), 323.

among others, Adam S. Bennion, superintendent of LDS schools; Bishop J. S. Glass of the Utah Catholic diocese; W. H. Reherd of Westminster College; and John A. Widstoe of the University of Utah. Apparently even these diverse people could agree on the general meaning of citizenship. However, local superintendents were left with the task of initiating the campaign.[36]

While the Utah Plan was not adopted in toto, it represented the direction public schools outside and inside Utah were taking: away from an academic emphasis and toward an individual and social emphasis, expanding the role of school in the child's life and family. It also expressed the progressive faith in school as a panacea for whatever ails society.

In the next few decades this paradigm would play a crucial role in establishing the character and mission of the American comprehensive school—serving, it was claimed, all the needs of all children of all people. Compulsory schooling (including lower socio-economic groups previously excluded), would bring schools under obligation, politically and pedagogically, to fit the practical needs of students into the curriculum.

FRICTION AND FACTION

Unlike the strong support that D. H. Christensen enjoyed throughout most of his fifteen year tenure, the unanimous decision to appoint Smith as superintendent in 1916 began to erode in 1918 when two of the board's prominent Mormons, Oscar Moyle and Arnold Giauque, voted against another two-year term. Board president Moyle explained his vote as a protest against the friction that had plagued the board—presumable between Mormons and non-Mormons—recently and in the past. Because Smith had been a compromise choice, it was perhaps inevitable that the artificial unanimity would begin to fray. A few months later, the board elections reflected a comparative resurgence of interest in the schools (compared at least to 1916)—the numbers voting (2,843) almost tripled the 1916 totals. This was, of course, still less than ten percent of the eligible electorate, prompting the Salt Lake Herald to comment that "[i]f election returns are a criterion, Salt Lake voters take little interest in their schools."[37] In contrast to the previous two elections, voter apathy in 1918 favored the dominant cultural group. A clean sweep, Mormons secured eight of the ten seats on the board.

No direct link between Moyle's complaints against Smith and the 1918 election results can be precisely documented, but Moyle's role in driving off non-Mormon Superintendent Cooper in 1901 makes it reasonable that Moyle helped orchestrate the Mormon landslide. Masons George F. Wasson and Dr. F. S. Bascomb were defeated in normally strong Masonic municipal wards by Mormons I. E. Willes and G. A. Iverson. All this was done, of course, in the spirit of bi-partisanship and non-sectarianism. This time around the newspapers did not frame

36. "Committee in Charge of Better School Work Outlines Observance," Salt Lake Tribune, 20 Nov. 1920.
37. "Willes and Iverson on Education Board," Salt Lake Tribune, 5 Dec. 1918; "Few Citizens Help to Elect School Board," Salt Lake Herald, 5 Dec. 1918.

the election as an issue of church domination, as was commonly done between 1890 and 1910. With eighty percent of the board seats held by Mormons, even the casual observer must have seen such numerical domination, if not as ideological hegemony, then as a fact of life in the City of the Saints.

However, having a Mormon majority on the board did not always mean unanimity, in spite of stereotypes. At least some Mormons on the board were willing to take stances not always endorsed by other Mormons. One such instance occurred in December 1919 when the "Mormon Battalion Memorial Committee" petitioned the school board to set aside the week of 5 January 1920 as a time "devoted to the study of the early Utah pioneers." According to the board minutes, "various opinions" were expressed and the issue was left to the "discretion of the Superintendent."[38] The minutes, however, offer an incomplete account. The request actually asked the board to designate that the story of the "Mormon Battalion"—a group of Mormon pioneers that marched from Council Bluffs, Iowa, to California in 1846-47 as a U.S. Army battalion—be taught as a special history lesson during the first week of 1920.

The discussion included six Mormon board members and two Masonic members; in spite of a clear Mormon majority the proposal was rejected. Most felt it was simply not within the prerogative of the board to designate when the topic should be taught. Mormon board president Oscar Moyle opposed the idea on the grounds that it would open up the school to the influence of other "outside organizations." He did not want the school used for propaganda or for a drive to raise funds for the proposed Mormon Battalion Monument. Moyle's motion to refer the matter to the Committee on Teachers and School Work was approved unanimously; a special Mormon Battalion week apparently never fell within the superintendent's "discretion."[39]

By all indications, Mormons, as a group, did not have a specific, identifiably "Mormon" agenda for "their" public schools. Satisfied with a significant majority on the board, they did not shape the curriculum to exact Mormon specifications. Given the pre-eminence of Mormon culture in Utah, however, the schools would still reflect Mormon community values whether specific lessons were taught or not.

It would be naive to assume that LDS leadership was disinterested in developments that might diminish their influence. The church has always been concerned that in giving up its role in secondary education it would lose an important means of influencing its youth. Consequently, the LDS Church Commissioner of Education, David O. McKay proposed in March 1920 that the church should increase the number of Latter-day Saint students who were training to be teachers. In an address to the Church Education Committee, McKay "pointed out that this was a psychological moment for the L.D.S. Church to move into the field of teacher education. There was, he said, a shortage of trained teachers in the State of Utah. He reasoned that if the L.D.S. Church normal schools were strengthened immediately, in five years these schools could turn out

---

38. Board of Education, Minutes, 9 Dec. 1919.
39. "Battalion Study Request Argued," *Salt Lake Tribune*, 10 Dec. 1919.

enough teachers to dominate the teacher supply situation in the state."[40] McKay also reported conversations with Presidents John A. Widtsoe of the University of Utah, President E. G. Peterson of the State Agricultural College in Logan, and the State Superintendent of Public Instruction, George N. Child (all of whom were members of the LDS church), in which each of these "secular" educational officers was willing to cooperate with the LDS Church Board of Education in implementing its teacher education policy.[41] Ernest Smith was *not* included.

With such far-reaching guarantees of maintaining the Mormon cultural/religious influences, the Mormons on the Salt Lake City Board of Education did not need to concern itself with overtly Mormonizing the schools.

SCHOOL POLITICS AND SMITH'S RETIREMENT

The absence of an account by Ernest Smith of his experience in Salt Lake City, and the paucity of official school board minutes create difficulty in documenting the reasons behind Smith's resignation as superintendent. No public discussion explains why Smith was not even considered for re-election—he was simply described as "retiring from the position." It seems reasonable, given his initial appointment as a compromise between various factions on the board, that he did not enjoy the kind of support necessary for both the board and him to be effective. His departure in 1920 may have been an extension of the factionalism of 1918, which had led Oscar Moyle and Arnold Giauque to cast negative votes for his retention. The Salt Lake *Telegram*, while praising Smith for doing his work in a "conscientious manner," in the same sentence mentioned "school politics" that reduced the schools' effectiveness. The editorial suggested that Smith "permitted" the political issue to develop to "a point that it threatened to be a real disturbing problem in connection with local educational activities."[42] Although the newspapers reported that the board passed "vote of appreciation for services performed" by the outgoing superintendent, the minutes are strangely silent about any such words of appreciation (not even the vote is mentioned) and none of the local papers (except for the *Telegram's* terse and partly critical comment) seem to have taken the opportunity to thank Ernest Smith for four years as the city's superintendent.[43]

Dr. Ernest A. Smith did not stay long enough to make any lasting personal mark on the schools of Salt Lake City. After he left Salt Lake, he became an assistant professor of education at Northwestern University from 1920 to 1925; president of Wisconsin State Teachers' College in LaCrosse, Wisconsin, for one year; and as president of the University of Toledo in Ohio in 1925. He served in this capacity for only a few months before he died of a heart attack, "superinduced by in-

---

40. Extracts from David O. McKay comments in Minutes of the General Board of Education of the Church, 1911-1928, LDS Historical Archives, cited in Clark, "Church and State," 282-83.

41. Clark, "Church and State," 282-83.

42. "School Situation Clarified," *Salt Lake Telegram*, 10 June 1920.

43. "George N. Child Made School Head," *Salt Lake Telegram*, 9 June 1920.

digestion," following a Beta Theta Pi banquet at Troy, Ohio, in December 1926.[44]

NATIONAL POLITICS OF EDUCATION COMES TO SALT LAKE

In spite of the politics involved in Smith's removal as superintendent, he perhaps could feel some satisfaction in having the NEA once again choose Salt Lake City as the location for its annual convention. To have a relatively small city host the NEA twice in seven years was seen as another evidence that Salt Lake was exchanging its image as the Mormon mecca to being a mecca of modern education.

According to the national *Journal of Educational*, American educators who attended the convention would be able to bathe in the Great Salt Lake and partake of Utah's cooperative spirit, aside from observing a model school district: "Utah had made greater strides in the fundamentals of public school education in thirty years than any other state in the Union." Those who came to Salt Lake City would have the opportunity "to study the working of the best public school laws in America."[45]

Some less educationally viable, and unannounced, reasons for meeting in Salt Lake City surrounded the politics of education. If 1920 can be seen as the watershed year when the old religious/political antagonisms faded, it may also be viewed as the year Salt Lake City school teachers became active participants in the politics of national education. They, or at least their rural compeers, were employed to change the very face of the National Education Association. In his opening remarks, delivered in the Mormon Tabernacle, Ernest Smith alluded to the far-reaching implications of the business to be conducted in Salt Lake City. Referring to Brigham Young's statement "This is the place" on his first viewing the Salt Lake Valley, Smith announced that "this is the place" where the crisis in the NEA's governance would finally be resolved through a representative assembly.[46]

Until 1920, annual conventions of the NEA were actually democratic assemblies in which *all* teachers who attended had a vote in the deliberations of the convention. This led to the conventions held in Boston, Chicago, and Milwaukee controlled by radical teacher organizations, much to the discomfiture of the conservative, administrative-oriented NEA leadership. With radicals in the majority of packed assemblies, there had been no chance to change the constitution to allow a "representative assembly," a move that would displace the influence of such radical urban teachers as Margaret Haley of Chicago. No chance, that is, until the decision was announced to hold the 1920 meeting in Salt Lake City.

The NEA leadership (among whom was the nationally recognized educator, Dr. Howard Driggs, professor of English at the University of Utah) had come to the conclusion that the only way to beat the radicals was to pack the assembly in Salt Lake City with teachers who would vote in favor of the constitutional

44. *Allegheny College Bulletin* (Nov. 1926).
45. "Why Go To Salt Lake City?" *Journal of Education* (3 June 1920): 650.
46. Ernest A. Smith, "Introductory Remarks," in National Education Association, *Addresses and Proceedings of the Fifty-Eighth Annual Meeting held at Salt Lake City, Utah, July 4-10, 1920, 29.*

change. Salt Lake City was "far enough away from the great centers of population so as to make it quite impossible to pack the meeting [with radicals]." The NEA leadership's plans ran into opposition at a meeting of the classroom teachers from Salt Lake City School District and a rebellion of Salt Lake City teachers (who like urban teachers elsewhere tended to be more liberal in their thinking) threatened to sidetrack the proposed changes. To counteract this possibility, hundreds of telegrams were sent to the state's rural districts summoning conservative teachers to the convention. The rural Utah teachers (most of whom were Mormon) swarmed into Salt Lake City on command of their supervising officials. Predictably, the motion to change the constitution was approved overwhelmingly.[47]

When Margaret Haley, the feisty Chicago radical, stood in the Tabernacle and protested the "steamroller" tactics she was booed down, in spite of the efforts of Mormon apostles David O. McKay and Richard R. Lyman to allow her a hearing. The event, said Upton Sinclair, reminded him of a story he had read in his childhood, "a fearsome story about an innocent American virgin lured into the clutches of a diabolical Mormon patriarch; and here is the story made real—the victim being the associated school marms of America."[48]

Sinclair, of course, was the dean of American muckrakers, whose literature was not known for its balanced perspective. He claimed direct collusion between the Mormon church and the NEA leadership. Although former superintendent D. H. Christensen favored the changes, he opposed the strong-arm tactics utilized by the NEA in gaining their objectives. He was cited by Sinclair as one of the plot's opponents, but the fact that he was also a committed Mormon was not mentioned.[49]

In the aftermath of the NEA's "democratization," some Utahns feared that the NEA would never meet again in Salt Lake City. Whether for that or other reasons, it never has. There can be no doubt, however, that Salt Lake City's schools, as they began the 1920s under the leadership of George Child, would more and more reflect the shaping and shaking influences that were emerging throughout the United States.

The fact that Smith, an "aristocrat of character," was replaced by George N. Child, a "manager of virtue," at this particular time, indicates the significant changes taking place in the purposes the public schools served. By personal disposition, by professional training, and by cultural/religious orientation, the new superintendent was more aligned with the social focus of the city's schools.[50]

------

47. Upton Sinclair, *The Gosling: A Study of the American Schools* (Pasadena, CA, 1924), 204-57. For a detailed discussion of the NEA meeting in Salt Lake City, see my "Unpacking the NEA: The Role of Utah Teachers at the 1920 Convention," *Utah Historical Quarterly* 41 (1973): 150-61.

48. Sinclair, *The Gosling*, 250-51.

49. Sinclair corresponded with Christensen about the convention and used him as a source. See correspondence, Upton Sinclair to D. H. Christensen, 18 Oct. 1923 and D. H. Christensen to Upton Sinclair, 23 Oct. 1923 in Christensen Papers, Special Collections, University of Utah.

50. Board of Education, Minutes, 11 June 1918; *Deseret News*, 21 Apr. 1920; *Salt Lake Tribune*, 9 June 1920.

George N. Child
1920–32

5

ADMINISTRATIVE PROGRESSIVISM
SHAPES THE SCHOOLS
*The Administration of
George N. Child, 1920–32*

Salt Lake City entered a new phase with the June 1920 election of George N. Child as its fifth district superintendent. Child was elected by a board that had the largest LDS representation in its history (8-2), but the next election returned a non-Mormon majority in a pattern that remained throughout Child's tenure: six non-Mormons (all but one were Masons) and four Mormons. In the past, this ratio had led to factionalism, but Child's administration avoided the Mormon/gentile acrimony of former eras.

As superintendent, Child focused on giving students greater opportunity to succeed in the world of work, in keeping with the era's "administrative progressivism." Child's tenure coincided with the emergence of the "Cardinal Principles" as a blueprint for America's and Utah's schools. With their focus on "fundamental processes" rather than traditional academic content, the Cardinal Principles laid a framework around which Child and his associates constructed a curriculum that reflected the diversity and paradox of progressive education. Ostensibly committed to the needs of children, the programs Child fostered also responded to the persistent public demand for economy.

Child also focused on teacher development. No longer seen as a slots to be filled by just anyone, teaching positions now required higher academic and professional training and teachers were evaluated regularly by supervisors and principals.

When the Great Depression blanketed Utah's economy in 1929, schools quickly fell into line with national retrenchment. In a sense, Child's reforms from 1922 on had helped prepare the schools for the stringent economy of the 1930s. His focus on scientific testing and efficient student placement, the attempt to make schools more economical by reducing the number of years it took to graduate, and the organization of schools using the Platoon System reflect the power of financial realities in determining educational objectives.

During the 1920s the board was dominated by Masons, but with little public dissatisfaction. The relative ideological calm that prevailed may have stemmed from a "gentlemen's agreement" that if Masons could control the board, the Mormons could have the superintendency.

Child continued to promote a highly differentiated curriculum, emphasizing social and economic efficiency and preparing students for vocations: the schools of this era were not, as is commonly assumed, centers in which John Dewey's

pedagogical ideas flowed unchecked. On the other hand, neither were they traditional subject-focused schools of the nineteenth century. Rather, schools had
mixed messages and meanings, shaped most of all by economic exigencies.

FROM ASSISTANT CASHIER TO SUPERINTENDENT

Born in 1869, the son of John J. Child and Elizabeth de St. Jeor in Clover,
Tooele County, Utah, George Child grew up on a ranch before attending Brigham
Young Academy in Provo. Following a course in the Normal Department he returned to a ranch in Lehi, Utah, where friends reportedly greeted him as "His
Highness, Prince of Learning." He worked in a flour mill in Midway for some
time after his 1890 graduation. That fall, after a local teacher at the Midway
School resigned over discipline problems, Child, newly married to Florence Wil-
lis, finished the year as schoolmaster. He relished the opportunity: "The thrill of
succeeding where someone else failed appealed to him." From 1892 to 1900 he
taught at Central School in Lehi and was later made principal and mathematics
teacher for the seventh grade. He also supervised four other schools. In 1902 he
was elected superintendent of Utah County Schools, but failed to win re-election
in 1904. He worked as assistant cashier in the Bank of Lehi until 1909, when he
was chosen as Superintendent of the Alpine District (the offices of which were,
incidentally, in the Bank of Lehi). During this period Florence died, leaving him
with six small children, and in 1908 he married Julia Alleman.[1]

In 1911 Child was appointed Grammar Grade supervisor in the Salt Lake
District. He worked closely with D. H. Christensen, who admired his "educational enthusiasm and policies." When Christensen resigned in 1916, Child
hoped (as did others who favored an "insider") that he might assume the post.
Instead, for three years Child served as Assistant Superintendent to Ernest A.
Smith until he accepted the position of State Superintendent. Child took this position to "progress," which he felt would not come as Smith's assistant. In April
1920, however, when his tenure as State Superintendent had lasted less than one
year, the Salt Lake Board of Education invited him to lead the city's schools. Although Child had not formally applied for the position, he had discussed the
possibilities with board members. No one doubted how he would respond.[2]

A REPRISE OF THE 1890S—WITH A DIFFERENCE

As might be expected, in view of the ideological make-up of the board, the
invitation for him to consider the superintendency came on a split vote. It was a
reprise of the first board meeting in 1890 when the board voted to install Congregationalist Jesse Millspaugh as the district's first superintendent. At that time
the vote was seven gentiles for Millspaugh and three Mormons against; now

1. Catherine J. Rogers, "The Life and Work of George Newport Child," M.A. thesis, University of
Utah, 1941, 4-13; Albert C. Matheson, "George N. Child," *Utah Educational Review* 26 (Sept. 1932):
12-13, 36-38.
2. Rogers, "Life and Work," 4-13; Board of Education, Minutes, 17 Apr. 1920; "Child May Head
Schools of City," *Salt Lake Tribune*, 8 Apr. 1920.

thirty years later the vote was seven Mormons for Child and two Masons against him.[3]

Neither the non-Mormon nor the Mormon press criticized or exulted in Child's appointment. The *Telegram* expected Child to "stamp out every sign of politics in the Salt Lake schools" and "insure to this city its reputation as one of the leading educational centers of the country." The *Deseret News* stressed that Child's long association "with all the details of [Utah's] system" prepared him to "know what is needed for continued success and improvement." In other words, the *Telegram* sounded the note of bipartisan support and the *News* affirmed that local people (i.e., Mormons) could be trusted as professionals.[4]

At the board meeting on 8 June, Oscar Moyle moved that Child replace Smith at a salary of $6,000—a salary equal to the governor's and the highest of any state official. Masons Barrette and Johnson countered with an amendment, that the position be offered to C. E. Hughes, superintendent of Sacramento public schools. Their amendment was defeated five to two, whereupon Moyle's motion supporting Child was approved by the same margin—the Masons casting negative votes. Three Mormon board members were absent—a circumstance the press failed to notice. Perhaps some members stayed away to minimize a public display of the Mormons' political power.[5]

The Mormon majority on the board symbolized for the Mormon community their emergence as a viable political entity in the schools serving their children, a luxury denied them for thirty years. In spite of the majority, however, and whatever the explanation for it, there seems to have been no overt attempt on the board's part to "Mormonize" the secular curriculum.

A residual fear of Mormon domination may have remained, however. A few months after Child's appointment the electorate turned out at the polls in uncharacteristically large numbers: Almost 3,000 more votes were cast than in 1918, the election which gave the Mormons their majority. In 1920, with strong contests in almost every municipal ward, the Mormon majority was reduced by three, providing again a state of equilibrium between Mormons and gentiles. One of the Masons, Harold Fabian, ran up a total of 947 votes in the Fourth Ward, the largest total in the district. Mason Fred Hathaway racked up an impressive 746 in a four way race, while Dr. Clarence Snow, a Mormon physician and educator appointed to the board in 1919, received only 130. In the First Ward, two Mormons vied for a position and H. A. Smith beat a former board member, W. G. Farrell, by 523 to 522. Perhaps most surprising was the ouster of Oscar Moyle, a veteran of two decades on the board, by a fellow Mormon and newcomer, Ray M. Haddock. Haddock's 430 to 130 vote defeating President Moyle may in part be attributed to Haddock's active membership in the Third

---

3. Board of Education, Minutes, 7 Apr. 1920.

4. "George N. Child Made School Head," *Salt Lake Telegram*, 9 June 1920; "School Situation Clarified," *Salt Lake Telegram*, 10 June 1920; "New School Superintendents," *Deseret News*, 1 July 1920.

5. Board of Education, Minutes, 8 June 1920; "G. N. Child Formally Appointed Head of the City School System," *Deseret News*, 9 June 1920.

Ward's reform-oriented Civic Improvement Association.[6] The Association aimed to bring more accountability to city politics; as a member of the old guard, Oscar Moyle may have been suspect, and not without reason.

The leveling effect of the 1920 election did not last long. In December 1922, the Mormons were reduced to four and the Masons increased to six board members. This election also witnessed increased voter participation. A candidate in the Second Ward, Luella Haymond, entered on a write-in ticket the day before the election and received 159 votes against incumbent I. E. Willey's 324. For the remainder of Child's tenure—until 1932—the board consisted of four Mormons and six non-Mormons.

In comparison to elections from the 1890 to 1913, the campaigns of the 1920s were devoid of controversy.[7] No doubt the economic factors influencing the *Salt Lake Tribune* to cool its anti-Mormon rhetoric around 1913 were still operating in the 1920s. On the LDS side of the ledger, the man who became president of the Mormon church in 1918, Heber J. Grant, had many business contacts beyond Utah and was anxious to integrate Utah and the church into the national scene. Grant's predecessor, Joseph F. Smith, had been deeply implicated in the politics of post-polygamy Utah. As noted in Chapter Three, *Tribune* editorial cartoons often portrayed him as a major impediment to the separation of church and state. Grant stirred up less antagonism, hoping to dispel the myth of Mormon domination. Others shared his approach. In the 1930s, Apostle Richard R. Lyman discussed with his family the need for balance on the city's board, to give a "fair shake for everybody." By not controlling the board, he suggested, the church avoided being blamed if things went wrong in the schools.[8] The Mormons were indeed accommodating to new realities.

Demographic changes may also have played a part in reducing the friction between Mormons and non-Mormons. Contrary to the perception of many non-Mormons and the wishes of many Mormons, the city's population in the 1920s was only about forty percent LDS—exactly the percentage of seats Mormons held on the school board through the late 1930s. The relatively enthusiastic adoption of public schools by the Mormon taxpayers and their resignation to the inevitable fact that Salt Lake was no longer a Mormon city must have helped temper the rhetoric of this era.[9]

Change in Salt Lake City politics was evident to the Salt Lake *Tribune*, which asserted in 1924 that "the separation of church and school has been practically achieved." As the *Tribune* perceived them, the schools of the 1920s were "without

---

6. "Members Named on School Board," *Salt Lake Tribune*, 2 Dec. 1920; "Returns of School Election Given Unofficially," *Deseret News*, 2 Dec. 1920; obituary of Ray M. Haddock, *Salt Lake Tribune*, 4 June 1944.

7. "School Election Vote is Heavy," *Salt Lake Tribune*, 7 Dec. 1922.

8. Amy Lyman Engar, Oral History, 30 Apr. 1992.

9. Conversation with Dr. Joseph Lyon, College of Medicine, University of Utah, 23 June 1992; see also Lyon's tables comparing populations, "LDS—Non LDS, 1920-1970."

noticeable overtone of church connections, at least in the city itself."[10] Headlines that had once roundly condemned the inferior teachers and priesthood-ridden, church-dominated schools, now read "Utah Maintains its Lead in Education" and "Salt Lake Schools Rise to High Plane from Humble Start." The *Tribune* even described early pioneer schools and teachers without characterizing them as inferior. No longer were they viewed, as in the 1880s, as agents of LDS domination.[11]

CARDINAL PRINCIPLES AND A BROADENED CURRICULUM

National influences on Utah education were clearly evident as the NEA delegates assembled in the Tabernacle in July of 1920 to hear the official welcome from newly appointed superintendent George N. Child. Child said Utah's educational legislation, praised by national educators, "was designed to meet the new demands of education" occasioned by the war. The conference heard continual talk of the "crises" gripping the nation—always a necessary prelude to educational reform.

Utah's model legislation resonated with the nation's, as well as Utah's, educators. Utah was sensitive to national views in moral, educational, and social affairs, helping the state remain in the educational vanguard. Local culture still held sway, even if in less obvious manifestations, and the public schools of the early 1920s responded almost amoeba-like to the contours of the landscape surrounding them.

Given his involvement with national educators, George Child was undoubtedly aware of a drab little pamphlet issued by the U.S. Bureau of Education in 1918 at the instigation of the NEA. Entitled *Cardinal Principles of Secondary Education: A Report of the Commission on the Reorganization of Secondary Education*, this proposal significantly shaped how educators perceived schools' roles over the next three decade. The pamphlet's preamble identifies it as responding to the "changes [that] have taken place in American life" over the first decades of the twentieth century: Citizens were no longer able to hide from "problems of community life, State and National Governments, and international relationships." The working individual was compelled to "adjust himself to a more complex order." The document also identified the social problem arising from a more efficient industrial machine: individuals have more leisure time. To meet these challenges these changes required a "degree of intelligence and efficiency" firmly rooted in a greatly broadened conception of education—both at the elementary and the secondary level. Other factors exerting pressure on education were the decline in manual labor, increased specialization, breakdown of the apprenticeship system, changing roles of fathers and mothers in homes, increased urbanization, less unified families, and changes in church roles and community organization. "These changes," the report asserted, "call for extensive modifica-

---

10. "Utah Maintains its Lead in Education. Salt Lake Schools Rise to High Plane from Humble Start," *Salt Lake Tribune*, 7 Sept. 1924.
11. "Utah Maintains its Lead in Education."

tions in secondary education."

The demographic changes in the secondary-school population was identified as a major source of needed change in the schools: in 1890 secondary students nationally made up one for every 210 of the total population; in 1915, shortly before *Cardinal Principles* was released, there was one secondary student for every 73 of the general population. Nationally, only about one in nine students actually graduated from high school. In ominous tones the 1918 report warned: "These facts can no longer be safely ignored." The solution? Schools must be changed to meet new social and economic needs.

The report also noted shifts in educational theory that mandated changes in teaching method and content. These included the idea that each student has a hitherto unrealized wide range of capacities and aptitudes. Hence, the value of subjects must be measured against their applicability to the "activities of life," rather than their place as part of an academic discipline. The changes occurring in society, the increased number of secondary students enrolled, and changes in educational theory called for "extensive modifications of secondary education"— resulting in the creation of a uniquely American institution, the comprehensive high school.

Ideologically, *Cardinal Principles* walked a line between criticizing capitalism for exploiting workers and promoting an individualistic social ethic. It claimed that: "Democracy sanctions neither the exploitation of the individual by society, nor the disregard of the interests of society by the individual." More explicitly: "The purpose of democracy is to organize society that each member may develop his personality through activities designed for the well-being of his fellow members and society as a whole." To become an instrument of such a democracy, "education . . . , should develop in each individual the knowledge, interest, ideals, habit, and powers whereby he will find his place to shape both himself and society toward ever nobler ends."

This simple, and in many ways simplistic, list of aims overwhelmed the other thirty pages of the report; in time the complex discussion of the rationale for changing schools was reduced to a slogan that became known as the "Cardinal Principles": "This commission . . . regards the following as the main objectives of education: 1. Health. 2. Command of fundamental processes. 3. Worthy home membership. 4. Vocation. 5. Citizenship. 6. Worthy use of leisure. 7. Ethical character." The phrase was easy to remember and easy to repeat—and it was repeated, by a generation of teachers for whom it became a veritable litany.

When George Child issued his first annual report in 1921, he asserted that schools exist to meet "necessary human and social needs," which change, of course, over time. No talk here of a changeless curriculum rooted in eternal truth. Based on the *Cardinal Principles,* Child laid out the new fundamental aims of education. Schools, he wrote, exist to promote: (1) good health and physical fitness; (2) good, intelligent citizenship; (3) proper use of leisure time; (4) character; (5) good habits of work and study; (6) mastery of essential tools of education; and (6) appreciation of truth and beauty. Child's list mirrors almost word for word the aims that appeared in the original 1918 pamphlet. In this world view, everything related to education: constructing school buildings, developing courses of study, preparing teachers and administering the system "must finally be justified by whether they economically administer toward the realization of one or more of the foregoing purposes." If they do, Child claimed, then public money is being well-spent; if they don't they should be replaced by practices which "will serve the fundamental purposes specified, for they constitute the elements of life that ensure the future safety of the city, the state, and the nation."[12] These ideas became the driving motivation for much of what happened in Salt Lake City during the next decade.

In adapting the "Cardinal Principles" to the needs of city schools, Child made a few minor changes. In this instance "worthy home membership" is deleted from the list. This likely indicates resistance to the notion that schools are *in loco parentis*. Leisure time is described as "proper" rather than "worthy," perhaps reflecting a Mormon sense that leisure must be within bounds of social acceptability. The word "character" in tandem with leisure suggests that leisure can be overdone through self-indulgence or "wasting" one's time. Similarly, the national statement does not mention the classical ideal of "truth" and "beauty," but the Salt Lake version does. These absolutes were probably included by Child as a means of giving to the national aims a local dimension—certainly religious communities have a vested interest in "truth" even if a rising sense of relativism made the term suspect in relation to public schools. The Salt Lake City version translates "fundamental processes" as "essential tools." Apparently, Salt Lake was not about to jettison the notion that the three Rs were a necessary basis for education. In all, the Salt Lake response to the *Cardinal Principles of Education* illustrates yet another accommodation to national norms. As in politics and economics, however, the accommodation revealed a uniquely Utah perspective.

PROGRESSIVISM OF VARIED HUES

In the next few years, Child's modified Cardinal Principles played an important role in shaping the schools' mission. A 1926 letter to patrons listed the Salt Lake version of the Cardinal Principles and informed patrons that the district was implementing these principles "in both theory and practice." The letter also included a new grading system adopted by the district—a five point scale from A through E based on a "normal" distribution of grades: 5-10 percent A; 15-25 percent B; 40-50 percent C; 15-25 percent D; and 5-10 percent E. This was apparently the first time letter grades were attached to these percentages, showing "standards of success" rather than simply a percentage score. Those receiving an "E" were, of course, candidates for repeating the grade or making up the failed work. In his letter Child sent dual messages: the new schools were based on the

12. *Thirty-first Annual Report,* 1920-21, 9.

social ideals implicit in the Cardinal Principles, but also on new methods of grouping children using supposedly scientific, determined normal distributions. In one document we have progressive education's two faces—meeting children's social needs while labeling them on a range from superior to inferior.[13]

In accordance with the progressive era's many faces and contradictory impulses, those who jumped on the Cardinal Principles bandwagon represented a variety of perspectives. Exaggerated as the influence of "pedagogical progressives" may be, there can be no doubt that some educators stressed a child-centered curriculum.[14] However, the detailed studies of historians such as Zilversmit and Cuban challenge the notion that such teachers were a common feature of the era. *Auntie Mame* was more a stage personality than a classroom reality: "A careful look at actual classrooms . . . shows that progressive ideas had little effect on what went on in typical American elementary schools."[15]

The Cardinal Principles, when first introduced, certainly did not take the nation's schools by storm. Indeed, a decade after this reform proposal was published, out of 1,228 high school principles who were asked if they had implemented the "Cardinal Principles," only a little over half responded affirmatively. Two hundred twenty-five surveyed principals had never heard of the Cardinal Principles and nine did not believe in them. In spite of this apathy, however, a generation of prospective teachers memorized them in college courses and they became, in time, the "organizing motif" for American schools.[16]

For example, a limited survey of former Salt Lake students suggests that some progressive practices promoted in the Cardinal Principles made their way into the schools via the curriculum, testing, student and teacher activities, teaching methods, and general classroom environment. Based on the responses to oral interview questions, there was during the 1920s and 1930s: a steady extension of educational opportunities in the elementary schools; a persistent use of intelligence and achievement tests; greater student mobility in "activities" like field trips or ball games; the use of more colorful texts supplemented by newspapers and phonograph records; and a modified physical plant.[17]

Kathleen Christensen Hall, who attended Stewart School in the 1920s, reported that the curriculum was "free and easy," giving her freedom to learn in a variety of subjects. Hall remembered teachers as enthusiastic: "Mrs. Montrose was such a humdinger . . . she just sparked with it." Stewart School was closely aligned with the University of Utah College of Education; prospective teachers

13. *Thirty-seventh Annual Report*, 1926-27, 15-16.

14. Arthur Zilversmit, *Changing Schools: Progressive Educational Theory and Practice, 1930-1960* (Chicago: University of Chicago Press, 1993), 18.

15. Zilversmit, *Changing Schools*, 18; see also Larry Cuban, *How Teachers Taught: Constancy Amid Change in American Classrooms 1880-1990* (Second Edition; New York: Teachers College, 1993).

16. David B. Tyack, ed. *Turning Points in American Educational History* (Waltham, MA: Blaisdell, 1967), 361; Marvin Lazerson, ed., *American Education in the Twentieth Century: A Documentary History* (New York: Teacher College Press, 1987), 12, 79-80.

17. Gail Mladejovsky, "Discussion of the Questionnaire regarding Respondents from the Salt Lake City School District" (1989).

may have been exposed to William Stewart's Deweyan perspectives. Dorothy Higgs Smith recalled teachers who involved students in learning activities. Nature study and sand tables provided "hands on" experiences that left an imprint on her as a student.[18] T. Edgar Lyon recalled hearing Willard Wirt and other progressive educators speak at the University of Utah in the late 1920s on the need to turn schools away from their "old cut and dried routines." Mormon educator Adam S. Bennion, a modern education Ph.D. from Berkeley who taught at the University of Utah, impressed Lyon by involving the students in "doing" maps, charts, and displays.[19]

Lizbeth Qualtrough wrote about and practiced a decidedly progressive policy in her approach to elementary education. As mentioned in Chapter Three, she recognized that student health needs sometimes had to be attended to before education could take place. For her, as for Dewey, the classroom was a "doing place," not a "listening place." From her perspective, Salt Lake's teachers did not lag behind such avant guard systems as Cleveland in implementing the best features of progressive education.

Photographs of elementary classroom activity also demonstrate Lizbeth Qualtrough's progressivism. Typical photographs record student involvement in a variety of creative activities: models of Indian villages and pioneer settlements; free rhythm dance; children gardening at Franklin Kindergarten; and a student orchestra. In Qualtrough's view, the Salt Lake City schools were "blazing a trail through a somewhat new line of work" by promoting student spontaneity and imagination.

Dortha M. McDonald, a teacher in the 1920s, recalled Qualtrough's ability to recognize quickly whether teachers were sensitive to students needs. Qualtrough noted, for example, one teacher's inconsistency in punishing a child. The child responded with: "I did the same thing the other day and she didn't care a bit." Qualtrough thought that was the "saddest thing she ever heard a child say." Following her death in 1935, one of Qualtrough's colleagues recalled that when asked about "the problem child," she would respond that there were no good and bad children, only children whose needs were being met and those ignored: "The bad child doesn't need punishment, he just needs someone to see that he has a better bed and a bigger breakfast."[20] Qualtrough hardly fit the "school marm" image so often caricatured in the history of American education.

Responding to Salt Lake's (modified) adoption of the Cardinal Principles, one *Tribune* report suggested that the new emphasis might be seen by parents as a retreat from the "principles of education"—a sure threat to the status quo. Of

---

18. Kathleen Christensen Hall, Oral History, 10 Apr. 1990; Dorothy Higgs Smith, Oral History, 2 Aug. 1990.

19. T. Edgar Lyon, Oral History, 7 Feb. 1973.

20. Lizbeth Qualtrough's views are reported in *Thirty-third Annual Report*, 1922-23, 24-29; *Thirty-fifth Annual Report*, 1924-25, 17-18; *Thirty-seventh Annual Report*, 1926-27, 18; Dortha Miller McDonald, Oral History, 23 Aug. 1990, 29; also "Funeral Set for S. L. Educator," *Salt Lake Tribune*, 19 Oct. 1935.

course, the Cardinal Principles had been evolving over a number of years; newspaper reports before 1918 indicate that the narrowly focused, classical aims of education were giving way to an expanded conception of the school's mission. One such commentary appeared in the *Deseret News* a few months after George Child took office. The *News* praised the district's forward-looking curriculum that made schools "clinic[s] where not only the mind of the student is given attention, but also his health, habits and morals."[21]

A 1925 federal survey indicates that movement away from the subject-centered curriculum did not harm student performance in traditional subjects. According to this survey the Salt Lake City schools were further ahead educationally than the "county" schools, spending more time on languages, reading, spelling, arithmetic, history, literature, and nature study. Comparing student scores on the Stanford Achievement Test, the survey concluded that the city's students were some 9 to 14.5 months ahead of their rural counterparts. Elementary school tests indicated that city students were 7.6 months above the U.S. norm, while rural schools fell some 4.3 months below. Summarizing the difference between city and rural schools, the report concluded that "the county schools in grades 7 to 9, inclusive, are progressively retarded educationally, while Salt Lake City shows a decided educational acceleration." In the state as a whole 69.4 percent of high school seniors fell *below* the Iowa norms, while in Salt Lake City only 22 percent fell below that standard compared to some 47.7 percent nationally. Salt Lake, the report said, had fewer illiterate citizens than any other city of its size with the exception of Spokane, Washington.

Differences like these were attributed in part to religion. Rural schools in Utah spent a "decidedly smaller amount of time" on the 3 Rs than did the city schools, while they spent more time on "history (especially local history), hygiene and like subjects." According to the report, "followers of the dominant faith" had a "pronounced interest" in these fields. Other factors leading to a greater interest in the "social studies" included the naturally homogeneous nature of the rural schools, the "cooperative community life found among the people," and the preparation of young people for Mormon missionary service.[22]

Part of Salt Lake's testing success may also be attributed to Superintendent Child's balance between patron demands for traditional subject matter and progressive demands for an expanded school program. Child believed the basics could be maintained without forgetting that "effective education calls for a school rich and full in social and civic responsibilities."[23] His beliefs, in time, were challenged, however, by events unrelated to the debates over traditional or progres-

---

21. "Utah Maintains its Lead in Education"; "Salt Lake City Schools Show Progress for Year," *Deseret News*, 18 Dec. 1920; Paul W. Nance, "An Examination of Salt Lake City Schools . . . 1911-14," term paper, University of Utah, June 1991.

22. Department of the Interior, Bureau of Education, *Survey of Education in Utah*, Bulletin, 1926, No. 8 (Washington, D.C., 1926), 135, 177, 178, 358. This raises an interesting question: were LDS missionaries in this era drawn more from the rural wards than city wards? This survey seems to suggest that this was the case.

23. *Thirty-third Annual Report*, 1925-26, 11-14.

sive the schools. Economic conditions shape school aims too.

A few years after the 1925 survey, a claim began to surface in educational circles that Utah students were unprepared for university studies, particularly in writing ability. Dr. Howard R. Driggs, head of the Department of English Teaching at New York University and formerly a Professor of English at the University of Utah, responded by citing research he had conducted on seventh graders in 1922. Driggs tracked the scores in a series of writing exercises conducted in twenty-four cities in sixteen different states. The results revealed that Salt Lake students scored the highest of any schools and that students at the Normal School at the University of Utah were above the median scores. Driggs's follow-up studies indicated that Salt Lake was adequately preparing students for university work. This could indicate that traditional teaching was still conducted in spite of progressive rhetoric, or that new approaches were not as baneful as many supposed. Another perspective, offered by teacher Dortha M. McDonald, saw the two poles as a rigid approach and one stressing student freedom.[24] There was likely a mix of both, dictated as much by the disposition of individual teachers as by any externally mandated reform agenda.

Quite apart from philosophical dimensions, Salt Lake's schools in the 1920s *were* markedly different from those of a previous age. School buildings were no longer "unsafe, poorly lightened and unsanitary," as many had been described in the 1915 Cubberley survey. Now children were housed in forty-one uncrowded, fireproof, well-lighted brick buildings, in which temperatures were kept at scientifically measured levels. Children were taught discipline, health attention, and "books." Whit Burnett, the *Tribune* reporter who surveyed the schools in 1924, probably enclosed "books" in quotes to scotch the impression that modern schools did not focus on basic skills. Students still used books, but, as Burnett observed, they no longer had to wipe their writing slates using spittle and a lot of "elbow action." Corporal punishment had also gone the way of "mutton sleeves and big moustaches."[25]

PROFESSIONALISM OF TEACHERS

Teachers, according to the *Tribune's* historical comparison, had better academic and moral qualifications. Although the article did not detail what "moral qualifications" were, it said that teachers were unlikely to be "off-type" and must have people in the community vouch for their character. The required academic preparation demanded: "all-day assistants" must be "normal graduates" (two years of college); full-time contract elementary teachers must have normal graduation and successful experience as an assistant teacher; junior high school teachers should have a college degree, although sometimes experience would be counted; high school teachers had to be college graduates with teaching experi-

---

24. Howard R. Driggs, "Utah Schools—A Comparison," *Deseret News*, 17 June 1928; McDonald, Oral History, 29.
25. "Utah Maintains its Lead in Education," *Salt Lake Tribune*.

ence.[26] The professionalization of teaching was on the rise. When Dorothy Snow attempted to teach elementary school after graduating in arts and sciences at the University of Utah, she was refused a position "Because I didn't have hygiene. Of course, I grew up in a doctor's family. I didn't have the history of education, although I had the history of Europe and the United States. . . . I was a good student [but] I couldn't get a job . . . they wouldn't have me."[27]

Each year, the principals forwarded to the superintendent a standardized form summarizing each teacher's performance. In the early 1920s teachers were judged on the basis of personality, teaching power, results, and professional spirit. In each category the principal graded the teacher as Excellent, Good, Ordinary, or Unsatisfactory, followed by a personal evaluation. Teachers who had undertaken special study during the year were marked with a star. The superintendent would accordingly award pay increases (or perhaps decreases as the case might be). Frequently principals asked that certain teachers receive special consideration. In the case of Ivey Van Cott, her principal, Gertrude Arbuckle, gave her an Excellent rating in every category and appended the following: "Miss Van Cott is an exceptional teacher. She must receive recognition or I am sure she will leave the system. Los Angeles has offered her a position at $1600 for next year. She would have gone this semester, but loyalty to the schools here held her to her duty." In contrast, Principal Elizabeth Bond of Washington School rated one of her teachers "Excellent" in personality and "Good" in professional spirit, but "Fair" in all other categories. In the margin she added: "Self satisfied. I do not believe she will ever make a wonderful teacher." Of another teacher (who received more than adequate ratings) Bond wrote: "I do not want her in the building with me next year." Personal feelings could sometimes intrude on "objective" professional ratings.

Later in Child's administration evaluation processes became more complex. Principals were expected to rate their teachers (Excellent, Good, Fair, or Poor) on "Professional and Personal Qualities," including Scholarship, Means and Methods, Discipline, Growth, Professional Spirit, Comity, Pupils' Scholarship, Conduct, Appearance and Attitude, and Advisorship. Marginal comments often tell more than the formal ratings and give a sense of the human dimension of evaluating professional teachers. At Lafayette School the principal noted that "Miss — — not yet acquired the ability to work with a steadiness every day." Edith Kendell of Longfellow School had rated one teacher Fair, but wrote the superintendent a long explanatory note that at the beginning of the year "the girl was just impossible, but she is very anxious to succeed." Her personality apparently made discipline a problem, but the principle seemed to be trying to help her develop such skills. Two months before the school year ended Kendell asked to make another evaluation before a dismissal decision was made. However, the teacher was not rehired.

In 1929 Bruce Millikin of East High was concerned about a teacher who had

26. Ibid.
27. Dorothy Snow, Oral History, 22 Oct. 1990.

difficulty controlling her class because of her age: "[S]he is young enough that the [older] boys take delight in teasing her and she does not know how to handle them." Millikin had suspended one boy and removed others from her class. He suggested that she be transferred to another lower grade school "where she will seem older and less a pretty girl." Another teacher at the same school could not be fairly evaluated, according to Millikin, because "he goes to pieces as soon as I step into the room." Yet another troubled the principal because "he has never admitted to me that he has made a mistake when I am quite convinced he has." However, the principal, "who saw many good qualities in the fellow," wanted an outside evaluation, for fear that "I am misjudging him."[28]

These attempts at rating teachers, however inadequate they may have been, reveal a profession facing the reality of accountability to a tax-paying public. A perusal of these ratings shows few if any teachers who were marked Poor; a few were marked Fair while the vast majority were marked Excellent and Good (with a Very Good added by a few indecisive principals). In the eyes of the principals, the teachers of Salt Lake City were better than average. Principals were also attempting to help teachers who needed improvement. However, when the evidence warranted dismissal, principals apparently acted accordingly. In 1928 Superintendent Child responded to the annual ratings by asking his assistant superintendent, George Eaton, for more information on seven secondary teachers whose ratings were low enough to "jeopardize their reelection." By 1930 five of the seven had not been re-hired.

Progressive directions notwithstanding, some traditions still held sway: a female teacher who married lost her contract, "although she may continue her work at the discretion of the superintendent"; if the school needed the teacher or the teacher needed the income badly enough, the termination could be waived. Child preferred to engage women who were self-sufficient, especially with an oversupply of applicants. Still, the abundance of applicants and the academic requirements did not discourage many women from entering the profession.[29]

Is the Public Getting Its Money's Worth?

The rapid increase in numbers of school children, the need for better equipped schools, and the increased professional qualifications of teachers all added to the total cost of public schooling in the first quarter of the twentieth century. When schools performed "poorly," the public asked: "Why, given the money being spent, aren't we getting better results?" And conversely, when schools did "well" the public asked: "Why, if we are doing this well, do we have to spend more?"

The man who tried to answer these questions for American public schools was none other than Stanford's Ellwood P. Cubberley, who had praised the efficient Salt Lake schools in 1915. Cubberley saw schools mirroring the industrial

28. "Teacher Ratings," 1919-20.
29. "Utah Maintains its Lead in Education."

order in his influential 1916 book *Public School Administration*. In it he claimed that efficient schools were rooted in the "public demand for a more intelligent accounting by school officers of the money expended for public education." A few pages later he laid out his model for school organization, linking it closely to the notion that efficiency experts produce better returns to the owners through "larger and better" outputs. He continued:

> Our schools are, in a sense, factories in which the raw products (children) are to be shaped and fashioned into products to meet the various demands of life. The specifications for manufacturing come from the demands of twentieth-century civilization, and it is the business of the school to build its pupils according to the specifications laid down. This demands good tools, specialized machinery, continuous measurement of production to see it is according to specifications, the elimination of waste in manufacture, and a large variety in the output.[30]

The school factory should minimize cost and maximize productivity. The idea caught on quickly; Cubberley's factory metaphor may have influenced modern schools more than any formal reform proposal. Soon "bureaus of efficiency" were appearing in larger school districts throughout the nation, largely devoted to constructing efficiency tests and rating scales. The bottom line, as it is in all accounting measures, was "Are we getting our money's worth?"

Child had no sooner begun to build on the Cardinal Principles when a national financial crisis took charge of the schools. In contrast to the idealistic and forward looking spirit of his first report in 1921, he began his third report in a somber fashion: "That which can be accomplished in education, as in most other lines of endeavor, bears a close relationship to, and is largely dependent on, the financial ability and willingness of a community to pay."[31] The district was, he said, "in a peculiar financial situation"; citizens were willing to pay taxes but the nation's economic depression had caused property values to fall several millions of dollars, "thereby reducing the available revenue for school purposes until the tax rate is increased." The board, consequently, had reduced the budget by one quarter of a million dollars. Child heeded the board's directive to increase class loads and eliminate special activities. However, he opined that further reductions might prove to be "false economy."

Some continued to complain about increased school costs. Child blamed inflation, which reduced the purchasing power of the dollar. At the same time schools had to keep pace with larger enrollments *and* patron demand for improved education. Child prophesied that it "is not likely that any one of these important factors will change in the near future so as to affect materially school budgets."[32] With the Great Depression capping his tenure, Child was quite aware of the economic realities in operating public schools.

---

30. Cubberley's book *Public School Administration* (Boston, 1916) is cited in Raymond E. Callahan, *Education and the Cult of Efficiency* (Chicago: University of Chicago Press, 1962), 96-7.
31. *Thirty-third Annual Report*, 1922-23, 9.
32. *Thirty-third Annual Report*, 1922-23, 9-10.

TESTING TO THE RESCUE

Salt Lake City did not have an official "bureau of efficiency," although it did eventually have committees to study "Tests and Measurements," as well as the board's long-standing "Finance Committee." The "Test and Measurements" committee aimed to make "conservative use" of "objective tests and measurements," a plan introduced in September 1929. While cautious of overdependence on such instruments, Superintendent Child noted that no superintendent could know his schools well enough without "considerable knowledge and use of scientific objective tests."[33]

These tests formed the core of the scientific and efficient management of the nation's burgeoning public school systems. In 1920 Child said that the nation's economic needs meant that every student could not be interested in academics. Most public school students needed training in industry at schools that "entertain a favorable attitude toward work that must be done." For Child, the junior high school had a particularly important role to play in this vocational preparation—foreshadowing his later commitment to the Platoon System and the eleven-year plan.[34]

A 1922 *Deseret News* editorial paid glowing tributes to the "increased efficiency" of the Salt Lake City schools, citing a special report prepared by the Assistant Superintendent. The use of a new "classification and promotion system" had led to over 5,000 students being one year further ahead in school; the old promotion system (based apparently on age) hampered pupils of superior ability. The new system, based on "the theory of the average child" and the notion that there is a "general regularity among pupils without respect to the matter of age," not only enabled students to advance based on their ability, but led to a savings "to taxpayers" of $75 per child per year. For 5,082 students this "represented the magnificent sum of $381,150 for one year."

While reflecting the general feeling of taxpayers that "too much money was being spent for educational purposes," the editorial also tried to deflect that criticism by recognizing unmistakable signs of progress; the schools of 1922 gave children greater advantages than did those of the 1880s.[35]

Child continued to focus on efficiency. Classes would achieve most if organized on the "homogeneous plan," in which students of like capacities would be grouped together. Child claimed this was done in a "modest, conservative way."[36] Separating children on the basis of ability even seemed antithetical to the egalitarian impulse in American and Mormon culture. In the mid-1920s, however, with burgeoning school populations, formal tracking became an essential part of the "standard curriculum design of the American school."

---

33. *Fortieth Annual Report*, 1929-30, 16-18.
34. "Salt Lake City Schools Show Progress for Year, Already in Front Ranks Among the Country's Educational Systems, Innovations Adopted Strengthen Claims to Leadership," *Deseret News*, 18 Dec. 1920.
35. *Deseret News*, 18 Dec. 1920.
36. *Thirty-fifth Annual Report,* 1924-25, 13.

Lewis M. Terman, the educational psychologist who pioneered ability grouping, believed that focusing on the needs of each child in a homogenous environment best served "educational democracy." He labelled critics who considered his
plan undemocratic, as "educational sentimentalists."[37] Child, in adopting a
"modest, conservative" approach to tracking, no doubt reflected Mormon com-
munitarian values that might balk at Terman's secular elitism. However, the
adoption of tracking in Salt Lake in the 1920s indicates how well-integrated the
Salt Lake City schools were into the norms of the national educational establishment.

Paralleling homogeneous groups was increased attention to "educational
guidance." Principals and teachers were "gradually adjusting courses, standards and requirements" to enable classes to "meet individual [students']
needs and capacities." According to Child, the school was to "adjust students
to classes and courses in which their success is most pleasing and which mean
most to [student] vocational aptitudes." Teachers could no longer be concerned with student academic achievement; they must now guide the students
to acquire knowledge directly pertinent to their later employment. Schools became gatekeepers of economic opportunity, channeling students into jobs determined by aptitude testing. Guidance ultimately reduced free choice in
student programs.

The Eleven-year Plan

The savings praised in the foregoing *Deseret News* editorial did not allay
public fears that schools were spending too much money. The persistent calls for
cutbacks and pressure to get students into the work place earlier forced Child to
investigate other approaches to saving money. Kansas City schools had around
1922 introduced a unique plan that advanced students more rapidly and reduced the number of years spent in public schools from twelve to eleven—six in
elementary, three in junior high, and two in high school—without any detrimental effects on students. The conclusion was compelling: "If one year of training
was not necessary to the pupils, then the public should not have to pay for
it."[38]

Child studied the Kansas City plan and by 1924 had presented an eleven-
year program to the board. Despite opposition, Child convinced the board and
the public of the plan's viability. He laid out the steps and procedures to be followed in the *Thirty-Fifth Annual Report* (1925), arguing that the plan would allow

---

37. A critical discussion of Terman's role in creating the tracking system in the American school
can be found in Clarence J. Karier, Paul Violas, and Joel Spring, *Roots of Crisis: American Education in
the Twentieth Century* (Chicago: Rand McNally & Co., 1973), 118-30. Other educational "scientists"
did not agree with Terman and held that studies of homogenous groups in contrast with heterogenous
groups "proved" that students in homogenous settings did not make better grades, did not learn more,
did not put out more effort and were not insulated from the fear of failure. See "Scientific Studies of
the Value of Homogenous Grouping," *School Life* 12 (Nov. 1926), 52.

38. Rogers, "Life and Work," 72.

students to be ready for "college or practical life" at age 17 or 18; that all essential subjects would be as thoroughly mastered in the shorter course as in the longer one; and that "much dawdling can be prevented as well as loss of time from giving attention to irrelevant or useless subject matter." Child further mentioned that some of the "best school systems in the country" were operating similar programs and had been declared a "success both from the standpoint of educational results and of financial economy."[39]

The plan approved by the board also included new buildings to accommodate the new plan and increased growth in the city's eastern and southern sections. The upper grades and high schools had experienced a "marked increase" in attendance, "out of proportion to the general increase in pupil enrollment." High school enrollment since 1913 had increased some 157 percent compared to the 25-30 percent increase for the population at large.[40]

For a conservative community, this plan was rather bold. Within a few years of its approval, Salt Lake City schools were being featured in national publications as models of what should be done to improve schools and have them cost less. School Life published Child's proposals with George Eaton's comments under the eye-catching title: "A Year of School Life Saved to Children of Salt Lake City." The last line of Eaton's evaluation repeats the familiar litany of savings: "In community expense it would result in the saving of a whole school year, at an age when per capita cost of instruction is highest."[41] The journal praised "Salt Lake City's Significant Experiment," noting that there would be no reduction in the high school instruction: the focus of the 6-3-2 plan was to strengthen the offerings in what were at one time the upper grades of the elementary schools. The plan also increased kindergarten's role; a good foundation there, it was believed, would carry over into the later grades.

The Salt Lake City approach, while following experiments done at the University of Chicago and in the Kansas City schools, differed significantly in that it was the first time a large city had attempted to actually reduce the course of study. Kansas City and most Southern cities never had more than eleven years to begin with. Referring to the early arguments of Charles W. Eliot and Charles H. Judd that school time could be reduced without injury to students the editorial ended by suggesting: "Perhaps the action in Salt Lake City is an indication that the arguments of the elder statesmen are at last having an effect."[42]

Child continued to receive national publicity. In the September 1927 issue of School Life he drew on European experiences to bolster the eleven-year program. Germans, for example, prepared their young people earlier; they were two years ahead of American students. Americans, he asserted, had become too traditional in emphasizing school as a preparation for college. Doing so, Child argued, neglected vocational education for the masses. If ignored, such students

---

39. *Thirty-fifth Annual Report*, 1924-25, 9-11.
40. Ibid., 11-12.
41. "A Year of School Life Saved to Children of Salt Lake City," *School Life* 12 (Apr. 1927): 153.
42. Ibid., 150.

would lose interest in school. Using the new plan, however, students could finish their general education earlier, freeing up time to focus on vocational courses. Child also suggested that students who did not want a full-scale college experience would be well-served vocationally by spending some time in a junior college.[43]

National visibility encouraged the district to proceed with the experiment. By 1929 the plan was introduced into the school system in its entirety. Its implementation included establishing kindergarten classes in all elementary schools; revising the course of study to focus on essentials and on student ability; organizing students homogeneously according to abilities and tastes; and teaching according to the "laws of learning." The fear that students might regress was answered by tests indicating that the eighth graders of 1929 were as well prepared as ninth graders had been formerly.[44]

The era's stress on the Cardinal Principles is clearly indicated in one observer's realization that there was nothing in the adoption of the eleven-year plan that would not make the "seven objectives" fully realizable—even with a reduction of school time. "Economy of time" did not preclude the essentials.[45] Superintendent Child believed this as well. He began the report for 1928-29 with "Economy of Time," referring to the many national reports that cited Salt Lake City as a prime example of efficient management.[46] But not everyone on his staff was willing to make time the essence of education. Lizbeth Qualtrough, who for so many years had carried the banner of progressivism in the district, took advantage of her impending retirement to question the whole notion of compressing education in the name of efficiency. In what was apparently her last published statement as Assistant Superintendent, she appealed for a let-up on the "Economy of Time" fetish: "Life in the classroom is too hurried. The best things in life can not be assembled on the Ford plan, and it is the best things in life that these young people should learn to assemble. Time is valuable, but the Youth of America is its greatest asset and should not be sacrificed to time."[47] It is doubtful that anyone heard her. Certainly those who controlled the purse strings were not likely to turn their backs on efficiency, especially if it promised to save money and not damage students.

In April 1930, after a full year of the eleven-year plan, Child reported to the Salt Lake Rotary Club that the experiment was working well. A study had just been completed at the University of Utah which bore this out: six groups of eleven-year students had been compared with a similar group of twelve-year students; the eleven-year students were ahead of the twelve-year students in five of

43. George N. Child, "Salt Lake City's Revised Program is Working Out Smoothly" *School Life* 13 (Sept. 1927): 7; see also Child's "Economy of Time as Practiced in the Salt Lake City Schools," in Department of Superintendence of the National Education Association, *The Seventh Yearbook: The Articulation of the Units of American Education* (Washington, D.C., 1929), 225-26.
44. Rogers, "Life and Work," 81-2.
45. Joseph S. Stewart, ed., "Southern Experience Shows Eleven Year Course is Enough," *High School Quarterly* (University of Georgia), as cited in *School Life* 13 (March 1928): 130.
46. *Thirty-ninth Annual Report*, 1928-29, 11-12.
47. Ibid., 50.

the six. Plus, over the past year some $125,000 had been saved in school expenses. This news, coming only six months after the economic crash of October 1929, must have been music to the Rotarians' ears. Child informed them that the reduction in expenditures had captured the attention of James Wood of Stephens Preparatory College in Missouri and that Wood had conferred with President George Thomas of the University of Utah and with Superintendent Child. Wood believed that "it will be only a few years before the city schools further cut their preparatory courses to 10 years."[48]

In the next annual report Child's assistant, George Eaton, speculated that without the eleven-year plan the district would have lacked resources during "this period of economic stress"; a thousand students had already been moved through the schools faster.[49] As depression took hold on the nation, Salt Lake City's schools were contributing to the common good in a concrete and tangible fashion.

One part of the original eleven-year plan—the creation of a junior college system—was not implemented, in part because of the economic depression. If the junior colleges had been established, the "chaos" of large numbers of eleven-year students descending on the University of Utah, Utah State Agricultural College, and Brigham Young University would have been avoided.[50] As it was, the increase put additional financial strain on these institutions during the economic depression. Saving money in the public school sector caused higher costs for higher education.

Marching Onward by Platoons

The eleven-year plan was not Salt Lake City's only progressive-era innovation. An educational reform known as the "Platoon Plan" or the "Gary Plan" (after its highest development in Gary, Indiana) was introduced to the upper elementary grades at about the same time. The Platoon Plan divided a school into two groups. While Platoon A was instructed in the basic three Rs, Platoon B was studying art, shop, and gymnastics. At a predetermined time the groups changed places, marching as platoons. The arrangement aimed to "achieve a balance between academic work and social creative activities. It also increased pupil capacity by about 40 percent without requiring extra staff."[51]

According to one proponent, Roscoe Case, the Gary Plan was in keeping with current theories of child nature; it gave students training in citizenship by presenting them with problems to be solved in the school; it was an efficient use of the school plant; and it provided the opportunity to experiment, develop, and test new approaches to education. As with most new approaches, a cadre of

---

48. "Supt. Child Says Eleven-year Course Proves Popular, Check Shows Shorter Term Scholars Excel," *Deseret News*, 8 Apr. 1930.

49. *Forty-first Annual Report*, 1930-31, 18-19.

50. Rogers, "Life and Work," 83.

51. Edward L. Dejnozka and David E. Kapel, *American Educator's Encyclopedia* (Westport, CT: Greenwood Press, 1982), 401-402.

boosters testified that it providing meaningful educational experiences at minimal cost. Randolph Bourne, the darling of social liberals in the early 1920s, saw the approach as manifest in Gary as the "most complete and admirable application yet attempted, a synthesis of the best aspects of the progressive 'schools of tomorrow.'" In his foreword to Case's book, Ellwood P. Cubberley invoked Dewey, claiming the Gary Plan was "an application of the Dewey educational philosophy in a new and an original manner." Dewey himself included the Gary schools in his collection of exemplary school practices, *Schools of Tomorrow*.

Some two hundred districts in the nation adopted the Gary Plan. In Gary there was general agreement on the enlarged curriculum and the services designed to meet the changes occurring in the school's constituency, but large urban centers such as New York witnessed explosive reactions to the system. Labor unions, Jewish groups, and immigrants perceived it as an attempt to offer "cheapened public education" to working-class children. Riots doomed the plan's further development.[52]

No uprisings occurred in Salt Lake City, however, and by the fall of 1930 every elementary school had at least one platoon organized, mainly in the upper grades. A memoir of the "early days" at Oquirrh School describes much marching about "as pupils entered or left buildings. . . . [L]ined up four abreast pupils marched and counter marched in perfect step to piano music or to the school orchestra." Although it was one of the last cities with more than 14,000 students to do so, Salt Lake implemented the plan at a faster rate than any other city. After initial praise, toward the end of Child's administration this much touted innovation was criticized for lack of unity and difficulty correlating subject matter. Consequently, the Platoon Plan became a "Coordinating Group Plan." By 1938 it had been modified into small "'cooperative' groups for the purpose of integrating the experience of the children." A decade later a formal study of the Platoon Plan concluded that the self-contained classroom was a better means of educating children and "contributed more to the growth and development of the entire child than did the departmentalized organization."[53] And so another significant experiment disappeared from Salt Lake City's educational landscape.

THE SCHOOLS AND ECONOMIC HARD TIMES

Just when a compelling case could have been made for promoting reform as a means of improving education, the "crash" of October 1929 forced a shift in priorities. Child was faced with keeping the schools on an even keel during a period of severe financial retrenchment. The depression brought "despair to all

---

52. For discussion of the Platoon System as operated in Gary, Indiana, see R. Cohen and R. Mohl, *The Paradox of Progressive Education: the Gary Plan and Urban Schooling* (Port Washington, New York: Kennikat Press, 1979); Bourne's assessment is found in Lawrence A. Cremin, *American Education: The Metropolitan Experience, 1876-1980* (New York: Harper & Row, 1988), 236-37. Cubberley is cited in John E. Ord, "The Platoon School in Utah," M.A. thesis, University of Utah, 1949, 8.

53. Ord, "The Platoon School in Utah," 33-4, 36-7; *Fortieth Annual Report*, 1930-31, 12, 27; *Fiftieth Annual Report*, 1939-40, 74.

classes" and resulted in "bewildered, resentful, doubtful people" who questioned the continued spending on schools.[54]

Although at the national level the depression was "slow to effect the political economy of public schools," particularly in urban centers, in less prosperous areas the depression's effects were immediately recognizable.[55] Given Utah's relatively weak economy, it should not be surprising that the depression hit the state much harder than the nation as a whole. Utah's unemployment was 35 percent in the winter of 1932-33 compared to 25 percent nationally. Even before the crash the state's per capita income was only 80 percent of the national average—in the next few years it fell by 45 percent. By 1932 the wage level in the city had dropped by one-third of what it had been in 1929 and by 1933 some 12,000 persons were receiving some kind of government-sponsored relief. In spite of a common perception that Utahns have always resisted government "handouts," in 1934, of every 1,000 Utah residents, 206 were on government relief programs—the fourth highest total in the nation.[56]

The spirit of the times is poignantly caught in John McCormick's description of the human dimension of the depression in Salt Lake City:

> Long lines of hungry men, their shoulders hunched against the cold wind, edged along sidewalks to get a bowl of broth from private-charity soup kitchens or city-operated transient shelters. Apple sellers abounded on the city sidewalks. So did shoeshine "boys," ranging in age from teenagers who should have been in school to men past retirement age. An army of new salesmen appeared on Salt Lake streets, peddling everything from large rubber balls to cheap neckties.[57]

These sidewalk entrepreneurs could not make up lost tax revenues or jobs; as income levels dropped, so too did tax receipts, and "school budgets were slashed" along with other human services.

In his first "depression" report, Superintendent Child noted that the schools in the past year had aimed to "inspire and guide every school child into a richer life of understanding, sympathy and action. The score is not a perfect one but justifies a feeling of satisfaction and optimism." Child was not alone in his optimism; public officials from President Herbert Hoover to business leaders and city politicians accentuated the positive, believing that good times were just around the corner. Maintaining a balanced budget would, it was believed, help restore financial stability.[58]

Child noted that tax rates had risen along with enrollments, and that the

---

54. Rogers, "Life and Work," 1-2.

55. For a detailed treatment of the effect of the depression on public schools in the United States see David Tyack, Robert Lowe, and Elisabeth Hansot, *Public Schools in Hard Times: The Great Depression and Recent Years* (Cambridge: Harvard University Press, 1984).

56. For an overview of the depression's effect on Salt Lake City, see Thomas G. Alexander and James B. Allen, *Mormons and Gentiles* (Boulder, CO: Pruett Publishing Co., 1984), 197-229; the statistics cited are based on their discussion on pages 201-202.

57. John S. McCormick, *Salt Lake City: The Gathering Place* (Woodland Hills, CA: Windsor Publications, 1980), 99.

58. Alexander and Allen, *Mormons and Gentiles*, 203.

"per capita" cost of operating the schools during these years had actually declined. "Expenditures for education have been guarded and curtailed" without damaging the school program. Child warned, however, that any "further curtailment" of school support would have serious effects on school morale.[59]

Child's fears were in part realized the following year when the board issued all teachers with temporary ten percent salary reductions—contracts had the regular salary spelled out, but included an agreement that "ten percent should be deducted at the time of payment, to balance the budget."[60]

As a good will gesture at Thanksgiving 1932, many Salt Lake workers contributed to a public fund to benefit the city's thousands unable to get work. The mayor, Louis Marcus, pledged ten percent of his salary, state employees pledged four percent over the next four months, and in response to an appeal from the Salt Lake Chamber of Commerce, Salt Lake teachers agreed to have two percent deducted during January, February, and March of 1932. Other teachers held special late afternoon classes designed to increase the vocational skills of the unemployed. The schools also arranged to hire 100 unemployed persons as census enumerators for the annual public school census.[61]

In addition to the decrease in public funds, the closing of the private LDS High School—due to the church's financial difficulties—in June 1931 added 1,000 students to district's rolls. Fortunately, the board had foreseen this possibility; just as the depression got under way the new South High School opened with 1,552 students in September 1931, surely an act of faith in public education as the depression gathered strength.

SUMMING UP A RATIONAL PROGRESSIVE

The report announcing salary reductions and the opening of South High was Child's last report to the Board of Education. The nature of the problems resolved made him feel that "we shall be more hesitant about applying the term 'impossible' to distressing situations than we formerly were." Personally, however, he did not fare as well; the stress of managing a large school system at the depths of economic depression took its toll on him physically. On 9 July 1932, shortly after completing his last report, George N. Child died at the age of 63 while recovering from an operation at the LDS Hospital.

The first Salt Lake superintendent to die in office, Child was lauded at his funeral in the LDS Assembly Hall as "a big brother" to his neighbors, a "real champion" of teachers, a supporter of student "welfare, vocational guidance and recreational activities," and an advocate of "sound and far sighted" educational policies. Governor George Dern, a member of the Congregational church and a Free Mason, and George Albert Smith, a member of the LDS church's Quorum of Twelve Apostles, paid tribute to Child as "one of Utah's foremost citizens."

A *Tribune* editorial praised Child for his educational insights and "sound

---

59. *Forty-first Annual Report*, 1930-31, 11.
60. *Forty-second Annual Report*, 1931-32, 13.
61. Alexander and Allen, *Mormons and Gentiles*, 204-205.

business judgements." Of course some had disagreed with him, but to his "balancing influence" was attributed the lack of open discord and friction that had plagued some of his predecessors. News reports of his death noted that his ability to work in "harmony with the board marked his administration."

The term progressive was used frequently in eulogies; one tribute even referred to him as "rationally progressive," a description that sums up his perspective quite well. Interested as he was in the needs of children, Child was still conscious of the demand for "proper" use of public resources. As the *Tribune* noted, his educational structure was "erected with infinite consideration of what the foundation would bear." His "business sagacity" kept any latent pedagogical progressive impulses from going beyond practical realities.[62]

Ironically, many of the specific programs Child advocated (including the Platoon Plan and the eleven-year program) were abandoned in the next decade, not because they were inimical to the interests of children—they often simply did not fit new sets of social and economic realities. Other changes, such as the junior high school idea, persisted much longer, but even it gave way to the middle school concept, which was seen, of course, as better serving students. Even at the best of times it is difficult to disentangle economics from the directions schools take. During times of extreme financial stringency it became even more of an issue, and Child's successor would pick up where Child left off—trying to make schools serve the needs of children in an era of conservative financial retrenchment.

---

62. "George N. Child," *Salt Lake Tribune*, 10 July 1932; "Dern to Speak at Final Rites for G. N. Child," *Salt Lake Tribune*, 11 July 1932; "City, State, Church Honor School Head," *Deseret News*, 12 July 1932. See also collection of clippings on Child in Utah Biographies, Special Collections, University of Utah.

L. John Nuttall, Jr.
1932–44

6

STABILITY AND CHANGE

The Administration of
L. John Nuttall, Jr., 1932–44

Just as previous Salt Lake City superintendents had each faced problems unique to his particular tenure, the sixth superintendent, L. John Nuttall, Jr., faced the full impact of the Great Depression and World War II. According to his biographer, the fact that Nuttall's administration fell between these two cataclysmic events required him to make unpopular decisions and provoked hard feelings among his staff, teachers, and the public.[1]

Nuttall's extensive professional training in the economics of education qualified him, however, to handle the crises schools faced as they approached mid-century. Although Nuttall won a unanimous appointment, tension arose and persisted for years over his methods of teacher evaluation. He also won little popularity for his belief that schools simply were not able to correct what was not a failure of education, but a breakdown in the economic system.

For Nuttall, it was not the schools' role to heighten expectations that "opportunity was just around the corner," although the Salt Lake district did become involved in a federally sponsored Program of Occupational Adjustments. Nuttall was honored for his leadership in this enterprise.

As they had been since the 1890s, the schools under Nuttall were exposed to some progressive programs. Nuttall, as a former director of the University's Laboratory School—the Stewart School —was very much steeped in "whole child" philosophy and saw the school as a moderate agent of social reform. Dr. Nuttall was in part responsible for keeping the schools in touch with some ideals, which, if never completely realized, kept public schooling from retrogressing.

Toward the end of Nuttall's tenure, Mormon/gentile antipathy returned. The Masonic majority on the board was whittled away until, by 1942, the Mormons commanded a majority. In 1943 the board approved a released time program so students could study religion as part of the school day. Even this most Mormon of changes, as with almost every other change in Salt Lake schools, had significant national precedent.

L. John Nuttall, Jr., led the schools through the depression, the war, and the last major clash over secular and Mormon values. He died just as the schools be-

---

1. George B. Robinson, "The Educational Contributions of Leonard John Nuttall, Jr.," M.A. thesis, University of Utah, 1951, 13.

gan to turn toward the challenges of the post war era. John Moffitt's assessment of him as "progressive and conservative" aptly describes a superintendent who faced the dual dilemma of maintaining stability while promoting change.

AN INSIDER WITH OUTSIDER CREDENTIALS

Nuttall was born in Salt Lake City in 1887, the son of L. John Nuttall, Sr., and Christina Little Nuttall. His father was described as "a philosopher by temperament and a farmer through circumstance," and his mother "a brainy, quick witted woman." His paternal grandfather, also named L. John Nuttall, played a significant role in the 1880s as secretary to Mormon president John Taylor and as Superintendent of Utah Territory's Common Schools—a position he held until ousted by federal anti-polygamy legislation around 1885.

Educated in the public schools at Lake View, Utah, he attended Brigham Young University High School and normal school and received a teaching certificate in 1906. After a few years as a principal and teacher in Linden, Utah, he studied at Columbia University and the University of Chicago. In 1911 he received a Bachelor of Science and in 1912, a Master's degree from Teacher's College of Columbia University. He taught at Payson High School, was principal of Spanish Fork High School, served as superintendent of Iron County schools and from 1919 through 1922 was superintendent of Nebo School District. From public school administration he moved to a professorship of elementary and secondary teaching at BYU where he also served as director of the training school until 1924. Additional graduate studies led to a doctorate from Columbia in 1930, after which he was appointed professor of elementary education and director of the William Stewart Training School at the University of Utah.

Nuttall was serving in the latter capacity when the Salt Lake City Board of Education unanimously elected him to the fill the position made vacant by the death of George N. Child. In addition to numerous articles for local journals, Nuttall produced thirteen articles listed in the national *Education Index* and three books dealing with education. He and his wife, Fannie Burns, whom he married in 1911, were the parents of twelve children.[2]

The third Utahn to occupy the superintendent's position, he was also the third to come to Salt Lake City after something of an apprenticeship in rural, Southern Utah schools. No evidence indicates that the old "outsider/insider" problem arose surrounding Nuttall's appointment. He had the strong support of the educational establishment and was recommended to the board by George Thomas, President of the University of Utah, Milton Bennion, Dean of the College of Education, and LeRoy Cowles, Professor of Educational Administration at the University of Utah. About six weeks after Child's death, Nuttall was installed as the district's sixth superintendent.[3]

---

2. Robinson, "Educational Contributions," 5-16; Christian Jeppeson, *History of the Lake View Ward* (Provo: J. G. Stevenson, 1969), 108; "Board Votes University Director in Unanimously," *Deseret News*, 26 Aug. 1932.

3. Robinson, "Educational Contributions," 32-33.

THE WORTH OF A TEACHER

Nuttall's appointment in August 1932 coincided with the deepening of the national economic depression. His recognition as an expert in school finance surely played a role in his appointment. According to A. E. Eberhardt, president of the Board of Education in 1932, Nuttall was a "business man type of school-man" who knew more about financing public schools than "all the board members put together."[4]

With financial difficulties at the forefront, Nuttall looked for a way to measure teachers' "worth." Teachers' salaries were reduced a second time by ten percent in 1932-33.[5] By 1934, however, there was some easing of the financial crunch and by the end of 1936 the maintenance deficit of almost $31,000, incurred during the first year of the depression, had been erased. Some small increases in teacher and other employee salaries were made.

In the 1933-34 school year a new salary schedule was drawn up, withholding any increase and mandating that reductions should be made depending on a teacher's rating. Those teachers in the top 60 percent were supposed to be decreased no more than $120 per year; those in the bottom 40 percent were to receive a reduction no greater than $180 per year, while those holding a "probationary appointment" would not be reduced more than $240 per year.[6] Nuttall was confident that a rating plan could be devised that would make the public feel that salaries actually represented the "educational worth" of the teachers. Nuttall's policy met with stiff resistance from teachers and administrators.[7]

The highly subjective means of evaluating teachers and setting salaries common in previous administrations was a far cry from the impersonal, systematic, and "objective" policy Nuttall wanted. According to James Worlton, his assistant superintendent, Nuttall worked out a "sound salary schedule and tied it up with teacher rating, training and service." Nuttall's secretary recalled that the new schedule was to bring fairness to the distribution of salaries.[8] However, in spite of claims that the new system would be fair or objective, the new superintendent's efforts ran afoul of those most directly affected—the teachers.

Nuttall's system consisted of simply ranking all teachers in the district. If there were thirty-five teachers in a given school, the principal was expected to rank all the teachers from one through thirty-five—with "#1" being the best teacher and "#35" the poorest. Paralleling the rating was a salary schedule, with the highest pay going to #1 with decreasing amounts down to #35. When this "scientific" attempt at rating teachers was put into effect for the 1933-34 school year it immediately ran into opposition. Quite apart from the trauma induced when some found their salaries reduced by some $900, it is probable that the

---

4. Cited in Robinson, "Educational Contributions," 35.
5. *Forty-third Annual Report*, 1932-33, 26.
6. Ibid., 18-19.
7. Ibid.
8. Interviews with Worlton and Ann Critchlow Walden, cited in Robinson, "Educational Contributions," 37.

plan was derailed, as similar "merit pay" plans had been derailed in other parts of the United States, due to its inherent lack of precision and fairness. Wayne Urban points out that "the implacable opposition of teacher groups" doomed such proposals nationwide in the 1960s; there is probably warrant for assuming that the Salt Lake Teachers Association—the local affiliate of the Utah Education Association—undermined Nuttall's system. Before the scheme was abandoned some teachers suffered "emotional breakdowns" from which they never fully recovered. Teachers found the system an attack on their personal integrity and classroom autonomy and some administrators objected to its inherent injustice.

The district attempted to modify the reform by classifying teachers into five different categories, but with no better results. Under pressure from teachers and administrators the district returned to the single salary schedule based on experience and training. The attempted innovation did not make it into the national educational press. The episode illustrates the resistance possible when teachers simply refuse to be subservient and tractable employees.[9]

Without Jobs, Can Schools Promote Opportunity?

Nuttall, his economic background notwithstanding, believed that education's aim was not simply to save money or to make schools efficient. His doctoral dissertation at Columbia University, completed one year before his appointment to the superintendency, progressively approached the issue of educational opportunity: a major thesis of administrative progressives was that increasing the number of students was an essential part of educational progress.

Nuttall's dissertation compared ways that Utah's and Maryland's county school systems increased the "amount of educational opportunity" available. He concluded that Utah's centralized county schools promoted greater equality of educational opportunity. However, Maryland had made greater progress than Utah in equalizing teacher salaries. Although his first attempt at salary reform died young, Nuttall spent much of the remainder of his administration promoting a relatively progressive agenda—at least as compared with the social, political, and economic parameters of the times. In the depression era, economic retrenchment was paralleled by a similar educational conservatism. Nevertheless, a perusal of Nuttall's depression-era reports reveals some attempts to move beyond traditional curriculum. Nuttall's major task as superintendent was to provide students with equality of educational opportunity—a daunting task made all the more onerous by the stringent economic situation of the 1930s.[10]

Recent revisionist historians have questioned the schools' efficacy as a pana-

---

9. Robinson, "Educational Contributions," 35-38; Dorothy Higgs Smith, Oral History, 2 Aug. 1990; Wayne J. Urban, "Teacher Activism," in Donald Warren, ed., American Teachers: Histories of a Profession at Work (New York: MacMillan, 1989), 191.

10. Nuttall's dissertation was published as Progress in Adjusting Differences of Amount of Educational Opportunity Offered Under the County Unit Systems of Maryland and Utah, Teachers College, Columbia University Contributions to Education, No. 431 (New York: Bureau of Publications, Teachers College, Columbia University, 1931). See pages 49, 60, 62, 75 and 76-95.

cea for lack of opportunity. Similarly, the depression spawned considerable debate about public schooling's ability to curb widespread economic dislocation. On one side was the traditional claim that the federal government should increase spending on public schools, allowing local systems to determine how to alleviate economic problems. Many non-educational New Dealers rejected this "trickle down" approach as ineffective. They favored direct intervention through federally sponsored agencies such as the Civilian Conservation Corp and the National Youth Administration. Even Charles Judd, Dean of the School of Education at the University of Chicago, expressed serious reservations about expecting the schools to correct massive social and economic problems. In his estimation the real problem facing the nation lay not in schools but in "structural causes, in the connections between industry, government and labor." According to Judd, to think that expanded public education could solve the nation's cataclysmic problems "may be a credit to one's imagination but certainly not to one's sober, objective thinking."[11]

The American schools during the first third of the twentieth century took on missions as broad as the population they were called upon to serve. In John Nuttall's view, while this breadth did not preclude attention to reading, writing, and arithmetic; it meant that schools had continually to accommodate their programs and purposes to the changing economic, social, and technological realities of a given period.

In 1935 Nuttall expressed the need for schools to broaden their base in order to accommodate so many different children. He then enumerated the ways in which the Salt Lake schools were already doing this: the Pupil Personnel Department helped "maladjusted children" through "visiting-teacher service"; more students were retained through graduation due to a program centered on the "articulating unit" between sixth grade and the first year of high school; graduation requirements were being made more "elastic"; high schools initiated physical education for handicapped students and a "general shop" class at West High was meeting the needs of "low ability boys." Other indicators of "individualized" schooling included increased attention to the "mentally subnormal"; allowing part-time students the same status as full-time students; the "sane, conservative use of diagnostic tests and remedial work"; and general attention to the "peculiarities" as well as the "common elements of growth" of all children. Nuttall's direction can be seen as a continual refinement of elements of administrative progressivism that D. H. Christensen and even Jesse Millspaugh had initiated thirty years earlier.

In 1920 only one student in seven remained in school long enough to enroll as a senior in high school. Large numbers of young people left school after the fifth grade; available work did not require school preparation. As Nuttall pointed out: "The lure of the professions and skilled crafts and business work was the motive which held young people in school." In 1935 practically all students re-

---

11. David Tyack, Robert Lowe, and Elisabeth Hansot, *Public Schools in Hard Times: The Great Depression and Recent Years* (Cambridge: Harvard University Press, 1984), 137.

ceived *some* high school experience and eighty percent were graduating. According to Nuttall, the "pressure of unemployment" unfortunately lead young people to expect that they would get better work if they graduated from high school. In reality, however, six out of every seven high school graduates would take work performing "common, simpler tasks." In words that obscure his commitment to equal educational opportunity, Nuttall developed a case for increased school guidance to help them adjust to economic realities.

> School must be motivated by other attractions than preferred vocational placement. Young people must be taught that it is honorable to perform common labor even though the worker has a complete public school or even college education. He must be taught that vocational selection will take place and, if he is not chosen for the restricted fields of employment requiring advanced training, he is not necessarily a failure. He must be taught that success is measured by citizenship participation, by enjoyment of a rich field of understanding and appreciation, and by happy human relationships. All these may be had regardless of the kind of job one has. All of these are dependent in part on school training. In school the program must be adapted and motivated in harmony with this unselected group of pupils, all of whom have complete lives to live and personalities worthy of the most sympathetic culture.[12]

Operating in the midst of the nation's greatest economic depression may have weakened Nuttall's former faith in schools as a means of equalizing opportunity. Perhaps schools do this for some populations during periods of economic expansion, but when no jobs are available, schooling is a limited lever of opportunity, especially in the short term.

Nuttall reflected in his policies and pronouncements dominant themes echoing through the nation. His familiarity with the national network is measured by tendencies mentioned in his 1934-34 report: elimination of pupil failure, individualization, social promotion, differentiated curriculum, and the use of IQ test scores to group homogeneously. These tendencies helped schools accommodate more students and reduce costs by lowering the number of students required to repeat a grade. If a practice could be shown to be both educationally *and* economically effective, the public would certainly respond positively.[13]

Nuttall's assessment of the schools at the depth of the depression mixed the traditional rhetoric of boosterism with a more sober, realistic estimate of schools' limitations. As an active Democrat he supported the federal government's efforts to deal directly with the lack of jobs for those leaving high school. As a schoolman, however, he also envisioned the schools playing a significant role in promoting national economic recovery.

From the outset of his administration, Nuttall enacted policies that would unify "the stratified classes in America" by providing unemployed adults with general and vocational education, including principles of government, idealism,

---

12. *Forty-fifth Annual Report*, 1934-35, 15-18.
13. Tyack, Lowe, and Hansot, *Public Schools in Hard Times*, 38.

and morality. Schools, in Nuttall's view, helped maintain not only an equitable society but a secure and safe one. This rationale led to the establishment of an adult education program in Utah's capital city in 1934. During its first year this program attracted some four thousand adults, attending one hundred and seventy-seven classes, dealing with thirty-seven different subjects. Aside from actually helping unemployed adults cope with the depression, these classes provided some income for unemployed teachers.[14]

As a cooperative effort, the schools provided facilities and textbooks and the federal government's Emergency Education Program paid salaries of $13,634 for the 141 teachers involved in the project during its first year. Nationally, there was some reluctance on the part of boards of education to accept federal money for fear that it would undercut local control, but of $168,500 spent on repairs to Salt Lake City school buildings in 1933-34, $107,600 was provided by the federal government as a means of aiding the unemployed.[15]

SCHOOL AS SOURCE OF HOPE AND LIMITED OPPORTUNITY

Nuttall's speeches and school reports place him among those who believed that the schools were one part of the issue of equality of opportunity. He believed schools must be modified to meet the new demands placed on them. Shortly after becoming superintendent he held the view that the "present chief difficulty in education may be attributed to a lack of definite hope and opportunity ahead which would direct the plans and motivate the work of older children." After eight years in office his opinion was essentially the same, although he seemed to be more critical of the overall economic system.

In a speech entitled "Becoming an Adult; A Social Problem of American Life," Nuttall spelled out some of his concerns: industry and business were not recruiting young workers and the social and psychological problems of unemployment could only be solved if direct action was taken. Schools can play a part, he said, but "faith in an economic system comes only from its ability to serve all of the people," which he implied was not happening. He referred to a letter from a 1938 graduate of a Salt Lake City high school. He was not attending school, not working, and not married—but not because of lack of effort:

> As to future plans, I have not enough financial backing to make any. My life— my career? are at a standstill because of the economic stress of present times. My case is not unique. I regret to express the opinion (which is well-founded) that there are vast numbers of like instances. I am discouraged, disillusioned, downhearted. . . . Suicide I regard as the coward's way out, although the thought of peace without further worry is undeniably sweet. I can but hope. For truly, both my faith and works have been dead—of no slightest avail.

Nuttall used this emotionally charged letter, written eleven years after the depression began, to call for a cooperative effort involving employers, labor organiza-

---

14. *Forty-fourth Annual Report*, 1932-34, 15, 18; *Forty-fifth Annual Report*, 1934-35, 24.
15. *Forty-fourth Annual Report*, 1933-34, 17-18.

tions, press, radio, religious organizations, and schools. Such an effort would make "the industrial and economic system serve the people and thus make them loyal to it. There would be a change from that point of view which would make people fit an economic system regardless of its ability or its leaders' willingness to serve the people who have created the system and whose welfare is dependent on it." In many respects Nuttall sounds like a liberal social critic, but then his ideas on the schools' role take on a decidedly traditional tone. The schools would cooperate with businesses to determine "occupational opportunities." Guidance would help students develop interests in a variety of work, indoctrinating them that a "delay in employment" was "an adjustment of labor supply to technological development." Nuttall assumed that some unemployment was due to students' reticence to do "common" work. While the school can do much to help prepare youth for the gap between school and work, eventually the nation must give "all these young people an opportunity. And that political and economic system will survive which gives this opportunity."[16]

In spite of Nuttall's criticism cited above, much of what happened during these years reflected the traditional faith that with a little bit of tinkering schools would indeed help resolve the nation's problems. Harry Hopkins, one of President Roosevelt's advisors and a promoter of the National Youth Administration, did not agree. More direct federal action was necessary: "That is the crux of the whole thing; to decide once and for all this business of getting an education and going to law school and medical and dental school and going to college is not to be confined to the people who have an economic status at home that permits them to do it."[17]

A PROGRAM OF OCCUPATIONAL ADJUSTMENTS

In the fall of 1934 the Salt Lake Board of Education assigned two coordinators to identify problems young people encountered in their efforts to get work. Many young people did not know how to contact potential employers and many employers didn't know where to find skilled workers. Although these early efforts were stymied by social pressure to employ only men with families, under Nuttall's leadership and with financial aid afforded by the George-Deen Act of 1936, a Vocational Center was established at West High with the explicit purpose of providing unemployed youths with a "program of occupational adjustment." Part of the process was to link industry, business, and the schools, without flooding the market with unneeded workers or failing to train prospective workers adequately. The school had to "chart a middle course and to be assured of the support of both employer and employee."[18]

Nuttall enlisted the Kiwanis Club of Salt Lake to help provide vocational

---

16. Robinson cites this speech as dated 13 Apr. 1940. See Robinson, "Educational Contributions," 45-46.

17. Cited in Tyack, Lowe, and Hansot, *Public Schools in Hard Times*, 126-27.

18. An overview of the beginning of the vocational center can be found in *Fifty second Annual Report*, 1941-42, 51-2; see also *Salt Lake Tribune*, 4 June 1937, cited in Robinson, 49.

guidance to the city's three high schools. He told the Kiwanis that cooperation between industry and the schools would help provide opportunity, but that an elaborate program with no results would harm the morale of the young. Industry would work best with schools "by suggesting specific training needed for employment in their line of work and by drawing attention to fields which may be expanded to provide more employment."[19]

The exact impact these programs had on the unemployment rates is difficult to determine, but 116 boys were started as apprentices in part-time jobs during 1935-36. In the same year over 1,500 students (718 of whom were high school graduates) enlisted in the adult education program at the evening high school. Of these, 908 studied commercial subjects, 266 occupational trades, and 337 general education subjects. Fifty-three people received their high school diplomas in this way. The number participating represented about 75 percent of the number graduating from high school in the previous year (2,009). By 1938 the Evening High School at West High was Utah's largest educational institution; it was meeting the needs of the two-thirds of Salt Lake's students who did not go to college.[20]

Nuttall received extensive recognition for his occupational work in the Salt Lake City schools. The "National Occupation Conference," funded in part by a grant from the Carnegie Corporation, chose him in 1937 to be part of a team to study occupational work in midwestern and eastern cities. He was also selected as a member of the committee that produced the 1938 yearbook of the Department of Superintendence of the National Education Association. When he was chosen to contribute an article on "Employment of Post High School Youth" in the yearbook, the *Salt Lake Tribune* saw it as "recognition of the successful experiments carried out here under his supervision." According to the superintendent, by 1937 the Salt Lake City school district was one of the "foremost" leaders of the "Occupational Adjustment Program" in the nation. Since the program's inception in 1934, "literally hundred of young people, men and women have been aided." When the American Association of School Administrators met in St. Louis, Missouri, in February 1940, Nuttall led the section entitled "Adopting the Training Program to the Needs of Your Community."[21]

Of course, as much good as Nuttall's programs did, the nation's economic problems were not fully relieved until the U.S. entered the Second World War, when the armed forces absorbed many young people who otherwise would have been unemployed. As is the case with many educational innovations, larger issues crowd out the significance of educational reform. The economic depression did it during the thirties—now the war machine was ready for a turn.

---

19. *Salt Lake Tribune*, 10 Mar. 1939, as cited in Robinson, "Educational Contributions," 50-1.

20. *Forty-sixth Annual Report*, 1935-36, 45-46; *Forty-fifth Annual Report*, 1935-36, 111; *Salt Lake Tribune*, 16 Apr. 1937, 10 Nov. 1938, as cited in Robinson, "Educational Contributions," 55.

21. Information on the recognition given to Nuttall was gleaned from articles appearing originally in the *Salt Lake Tribune*, 28 Mar., 6 Apr., 18 May 1937, and 27 Feb. 1940. These are quoted extensively in Robinson, "Educational Contributions," 51-2.

PROGRESSIVE EDUCATION—RHETORIC OR REALITY?

In spite of conventional wisdom that equates the 1930s with progressive education, students of depression-era progressivism claim that innovation in the curriculum was, unfortunately, the exception rather than the rule: "We suspect that actual changes in instruction were modest [during the depression era] and that the traditional teacher-centered mode of drill and recitation remained by far the most common pattern."[22]

In the absence of actual descriptions of classroom activities in say, 1920, with those of 1940, it is difficult to offer a precise analysis of what changes, if any, occurred. However, there are some rough indicators that might serve to gauge the degree to which a few Salt Lake City's schools during this era were at least "mainstream progressive," although "drill and recitation" probably dominated most schools.

One indicator of the extent to which some Salt Lake City schools attempted to move beyond tradition is an experimental curriculum developed and implemented between 1933 and 1938. Conducted by James T. Worlton, Assistant Superintendent of Schools, and Arthur E. Arnesen, Supervisor of Curriculum and Research, this study had "the desire to provide children with enriched and meaningful educational experiences; to democratize classroom practices; and to devise methods and techniques of practical classroom application for an increased emphasis on the personality development of pupils."[23] The experiment was one of a number of studies organized in various parts of the country under the general direction of Professor William A. McCall of Columbia University's Teachers College. McCall, a psychometrician, believed in 1937 that the time was ripe for the "scientific" measurement of experiments in progressive education. By 1939, six studies had been reported in the pages of Teachers College Record; Salt Lake City was the seventh.

The second semester of the 1936-37 school year marked the commencement of the experiment. Three of the district's best "conservative" schools were designated as control schools along with four comparable "experimental" schools. The latter were following the "new curriculum, with its philosophy, methods and techniques," while the control schools followed the traditional curriculum. The experimental curriculum was K through the "articulating unit" (grade 7) core curriculum, based on "the nine individual and social functions selected as the basic things that people do." These functions included, for example, "Health and protection of life and conservation of natural resources"; Socializing the individual—intergroup relations"; and "Consumption of goods and services." Four of the nine, according to Worlton and Arnesen, had never been part of the traditional school curriculum: "Enrichment of life through leisure activities; Expression of spiritual and aesthetic impulses; Conservation and improvement of race culture"; and "Education as a means of achieving individual and social goals." Obviously the "Cardinal Principles" of 1918 had influenced the educators

22. Tyack, Lowe, and Hansot, Public Schools in Hard Times, 152, 163.
23. James T. Worlton and Arthur E. Arnesen, "Salt Lake City Experiments with Curriculum Development," Teachers College Record 41 (Nov. 1939): 136.

who identified these basic social functions of public schools.

Sophisticated measurement tests determined student progress and at the end of the experiment, in May 1938, the observers concluded that the experimental schools more successfully put into practice a democratic way of living. Typical of many attempts to test progressive practices, the control groups did somewhat better on the basics. However, as far as social and personality gains were concerned (the summum bonum of education for progressive educators), the experimental schools made greater gains. Teachers involved in the experimental schools were also convinced that the approaches used in their schools were more successful than the approaches of the standard curriculum.[24]

Perhaps not coincidentally, the Progressive Education Association held its Utah Regional Conference at the University of Utah only a few months after the curriculum experiment was concluded. The conference theme was "Education Moves Ahead" and the program reads like a "who's who" roster for progressive education: William Heard Kilpatrick and Lois Hayden Meek of Teacher's College; Paul Hanna of Stanford; Elsie Ripley Clapp of the Progressive Education Association; Louis Raths of Ohio State; C. L. Cushman and M. R. Ahrens of the Denver Public Schools. L. John Nuttall served with Clapp, Hanna, and others on a panel to consider questions like: "What are the promising movements in education today?" and "What are the responsibilities of schools? Of the home? Of the community?" At the conference's conclusion, William Heard Kilpatrick, the father of the "project method," took to the pulpit of the Mormon Tabernacle and, suitably backed up by the Mormon Tabernacle Choir, "preached" on the subject "Education for Today."[25]

If "progressive" is defined as a broadening of the curriculum to accommodate a wide range of student abilities and needs, it can with some justification be claimed that Salt Lake's schools in the 1930s offered a more progressive menu than had been adhered to in the first two decades of the twentieth century. Evidence of change via such broad principles is likely to be less radical in appearance than if narrowly conceived practices had been adopted. This may be why some historians have labelled American education during the depression as "short-term dislocation and long-term continuity." It may also explain why the broader and more conservative "Cardinal Principles" played such a dominant role in shaping the curriculum (and some school practices) during the 1930s.[26]

"LEARNING BY DOING"

A few examples of "progressive" changes will illustrate the conservative nature of school change and also show the connection between community and the school—a dominant feature of progressive thought. The traditional Halloween

---

24. Worlton and Arnesen, "Salt Lake City Experiments," 135-56.

25. Other guest speakers gave "sermons" on the same topic along the Wasatch Front including Paul Hanna in Provo, C. L. Cushman in the Logan Tabernacle, and Elsie Ripley Clapp in the First Ward Chapel in Cedar City. "Progressive Education Association, Program for the Utah Regional Conference, April 22, 23, 24, 1938, Salt Lake City."

26. Tyack, Lowe, and Hansot, *Public Schools in Hard Times*, 190-94.

celebration had become a problem as vandalism increased. In response, the Uintah School organized an official Halloween Parade as a means of preventing mischief. Also at Uintah, the whole school was transformed into a Ute Indian village in the spring of 1935, the "Indian ceremonies and rituals portrayed, rival[ing] those of the Red Man himself." Using the school in this way departed from the sterility of text book instruction about Native American life. In 1936 the Onequa School instituted a curriculum in which students helped plan and work out real-life "problems." In addition to improved visual aids the program used excursions and outside speakers to involve students. Such approaches, mild as they may be, give some credence to the claim that progressive education existed in Utah's capital city.[27]

Local school initiatives to clean up the physical environment might also be seen as progressive. At Jordan Junior High School, under the leadership civic-minded Principal D. R. Coombs, teachers and students transformed an eye-sore on the banks of the Jordan River into a campus quite unlike any other in Salt Lake City. The beautification project included cleaning up the river bank that skirted the school, planting lawns, flowers, and willow trees, and constructing a bridle path along the river bank. Student twins Harry and Larry Blundell supervised other students in constructing a copper and concrete sundial for the school grounds. The sundial project had grown out of geometry, art, and civics classes. A boat house was built and students constructed boats for use on the river. Juanita Barclay Wheelwright recalls that her own interest in artistic expression was a direct result of the natural environment of the Jordan School campus, where students were encouraged to observe nature closely rather than paint "all tree trunks brown and all leaves green."[28]

The Jordan River beautification project was entered in a national competition sponsored by *Current Events* magazine and in 1941 was the subject of an article in the *Reader's Digest*. The writer, Frances K. Rummell, saw the project not only as a way of cleaning up the community, but as having educational benefits. Perhaps most importantly, in the view of adults who see every generation but their own as lacking a work ethic, the project had channeled "their storming energy, their yearning for accomplishment" and prevented the "inane frittering" away of these priceless assets of youth.[29]

Another "progressive" practice may be seen in Nuttall and Eaton's 1933 movement to reorganize the school athletic program to promote intra-city competition and to allow many more students to be involved in athletics. Withdrawing the city schools from the Utah High School Athletic Association, George

27. *Fifty Years: Fiftieth Annual Report*, 1939-40, 112, 101.

28. "Jordan Junior High School Scrapbook," Special Collections, University of Utah; conversation with Juanita Barclay Wheelwright, 16 July 1991.

29. Frances V. Rummell, "After-School Work for Softies," *Readers' Digest* (Jan. 1941): 19-21. This article appeared originally in *The Kiwanis Magazine* of January 1941. In spite of a deep sense of pride in this project in the 1940s, a later generation did not continue the tradition of involving students in civic projects and in time the river, which gave the school its unique setting, was actually covered over in the interest of safety.

Eaton claimed that the boys would be able to compete with others of the same age and maturity and "more time would be given to encourage and to develop athletic participation within the school." Within three years the program was hailed a success and the slogan "Every Boy An Athlete" was being realized. Nuttall wanted to maximize the active participation of all students; the change brought not only an increase in those playing, but also in those attending the games (including, presumably, girls—as spectators).[30]

Although the new athletic philosophy, at least in theory, fostered cooperation over competition, Nuttall said the "only reason" for withdrawing from the state association was a very practical one: Salt Lake City schools, since 1928, had allowed students to graduate at the end of the eleventh year in school, and its teams were put at a "distinct disadvantage, and even in some danger" when competing with teams whose senior players were more mature. Quite frankly, the competition was uneven and the eleven-year schools were not racking up the wins every community expects. In spite of the proclaimed success of the intra-district athletic program, in 1942 the schools rejoined the association against Nuttall's will.[31] In time the Eleven Year Program was also abandoned.

Just as Nuttall suffered some criticism for his alleged tendency to be undemocratic—evident in his attempts to force a merit pay system on the teachers—neither did his espousal of progressive ideas always win acceptance. One former board member, highly critical of Nuttall's progressive philosophy, described him as a

"very Academic person," brought up in the Columbia University "philosophy," not advocating grades or marks but rather a curve. He didn't believe students should compete against each other, so poor students wouldn't get inferior feelings. . . . I could never agree; it was tried and proved unfeasible. . . . [P]eople should be encouraged, not held down to a level of mediocrity just for less depressed students . . . they don't do that in Russia . . . they just weed them out. . . . [T]hey don't have unemployment, those who fail, they sweep the streets. We try to bring everybody along . . . we've missed.[32]

No doubt this evaluation contains more than a little personal bias. Nevertheless, this description of Nuttall's focus on using schools to meet the needs of individual students says something about Nuttall's progressive philosophy of education.

SCHOOLS AS A BASTION OF DEMOCRACY

The onset of war brought some disruption of enrollments and some school personnel were drafted into military service. But Nuttall, socially aware educator that he was, saw the war as a challenge to the schools to preserve the nation's

---

30. *Forty-third Annual Report*, 1932-33, 14, 35-6; *Forty-fourth Annual Report*, 1933-34, 23.

31. *Fifty-second Annual Report*, 1941-42, 16; Letter of L. John Nuttall to Jesse N. Smith, Chairman, Committee on Teachers and School Work, Board of Education, Minutes, 8 May 1933.

32. Al Church, "The Controversy of Mormons and Masons, Reflected in the Salt Lake City School System, as Recalled by M. Lynn Bennion, Lawrence Schroeder, R. Y. Gray, Paul B. Cannon [and] Newell Dayton," Term Paper, University of Utah, 1973, 13-14.

"political, cultural, and spiritual traditions." In Nuttall's words, "the social setting" of the times shape the aims of the society's schools. The war was, of course,
viewed as a struggle between good and evil, and few doubted that schools were an
important agency in promoting the good of democracy against the evils of totali-
tarianism. While the focus of the report issued on the eve of World War II could
very easily have been one which stressed nationalism or played on a fear of "foreign" influences, it was significantly entitled *Children in a Democratic American City*,
and its major focus was the principle of "respect for and the recognition of the significance of each person as an individual." District staff prepared statements on
how individual differences could be met across the curriculum, including the special needs of gifted students, remedial students, those with physical impairments
and those who had behavior problems. Each school outlined ways they were
meeting individual differences and, naturally, there was no one way to do this. The
headings of these presentation give some sense of what was being attempted: "The
Transient Child," from Emerson School; "The Ego of Adolescents," from West
High, while Irving Junior High proclaimed: "The School Exists for the Pupils."[33]

Included were case studies of how children had been helped as individuals.
For example Irmgard, a fourteen-year-old student at Jordan Junior High, was recognized as a bright student who was being affected by the war: her natural parents were in Germany and other students apparently harassed her over her
language and national origin. This in turn caused her to keep to herself: "[She]
broods considerably about her real parents and the war." Her advisor, however,
kept in close touch with her legal guardians and made considerable progress
with her happiness: "She likes art and sewing and does well in all subjects for
which she is enrolled. Our job is to improve the social outlook and make her
more content with her environment."

John, an eighteen-year old at East High School, moved to Salt Lake City
from Nebraska and was unable to complete the agricultural course he had started
in. Discouraged and dissatisfied, he and his mother, who thought he should attend college, met with his counsellor and "the three of us analyzed his previous
high school work and it developed that he was interested in mechanics but very
much disliked mathematics. He was not interested in college but in aero-me-
chanics. I recommended that he be accepted in the defense training course in
mechanics and requested that credit for this might apply towards his high school
graduation. He did take the training suggested and is very happy in his work."[34]

One fifth grader's mother wrote to the principal of Douglas School that she
appreciated

> very much the efforts you are making to help Sally in her adjustment program. I
> feel that she is improving. She enjoys the marble tournament very much and is
> happy in her work with her teachers. . . . Right now she is interested in a little
> play she is writing for Miss ——— 's work. I wish you could help her avoid talking
> too rapidly, or do you think this would make her self-conscious? The doctor says

---

33. *Children in a Democratic American City: Fifty-First Annual Report*, 1940-41, 91, 93, 95-6.
34. *Fifty-first Annual Report*, 1940-41, 108-109.

her skin condition has cleared up very well.[35]

These examples illustrate the focus on individual needs characteristic of the schools of the early 1940s, although one has to keep in mind that the rhetoric of annual reports may differ from the actual situation in schools. Of course, not every student's needs could be met by the schools, but a humaneness in the statements above suggests that the needs of children were an important part of schools in American society, even during war.

When the war actually became an American reality in December 1941 the schools played a supportive role. School buildings were designated as emergency centers and teachers helped distribute rationing books, registering the entire population for sugar rationing. As in World War I, children were encouraged to sacrifice their own dollars and cents as relief funds for America's British, Polish, Greek, and Russian allies. Also as part of the "war service expected of schools," Salt Lake's schools were among the nation's first to use the public school curriculum as a vehicle for training workers for the defence industries. Vocational education, put in place at the height of the depression, was now "one of the [schools'] gifts to victory," supplying the demands of the defence industries that rapidly mushroomed in Salt Lake City. And, once again, Superintendent Nuttall focused on adult education as an aspect of vocational programs.

In an official statement, "Schools in Wartime," which spelled out the role schools should play during the war, Nuttall devoted considerable space to raising money for the war through increased taxes, direct contributions to agencies such as the Red Cross, and lending money to the government through war bond drives. He cautioned, however, that in promoting bond drives teachers should not create dissension in families without means through "instruction, propaganda or school pressure." To use "institutional embarrassment and pressure," he feared, "may create sentiments of class struggle and ill will as an educational product."[36]

The war directly affected the classrooms in various ways. Teachers warned children of the gravity of "talking too much," and classrooms bore ominous banners which cautioned: "A slip of the lip can sink a ship," although no evidence indicates that a Japanese landing in the Great Salt Lake was imminent. (The fear of a Japanese air attack actually led to the cancellation of an annual music festival in the Mormon Tabernacle; it was instead spread over five nights at the South High auditorium.) Teachers were given air raid warden duties and instructed how to deal with incendiary bombs and air raids. Boy Scouts in city schools were recruited as first aid workers in case of an air raid. Eventually a teacher shortage brought about by the draft and the addition of 1,378 children (as of 1942) of defence workers, led Nuttall to relax the policy against married women teaching. These circumstances also raised the possibility that some federal funds would be made available to help the district hire additional teachers.[37]

---

35. Ibid., 104.
36. *Years of Challenge, Highlights of Public Education in Salt Lake City 1890-1965: Seventy-fourth and Seventy-fifth Annual Reports*, 1963-65, 14.

For all the energy that went into making the schools serve a nation at war, Nuttall reminded readers of the *Fifty-second Annual Report* that the schools had a more long-lasting and significant role to play: the education of eleven grades of children, the oldest of whom would probably be involved in the war, but most of whom "must be brought through to maturity for service in postwar days." War aims must be supported by the schools, he said, but teaching fundamental learning skills, maintaining a healthy way of life, developing tolerance, conserving sound emotional status and basic loyalty to American ideals of freedom— these could not be ignored. Nor did he believe the school should become "the agent of special groups" who apparently wanted to make the war effort the schools' major aim. In spite of efforts to do "business as usual," the schools were shaped by the war; indeed Nuttall went as far as to say, without elaborating, that if the war lasted long it would require "the sacrificing of part of the school program."[38]

THE POLITICS OF RELEASED-TIME SEMINARY

Depression economics, progressive ideology, and the war effort all brought changes in the Salt Lake schools during L. John Nuttall's superintendency, but one thing had not changed: the makeup of the board of education. For nearly all his tenure the Free Masons maintained their majority on the board. Over the years, however, there had been an overt lessening of tensions between Mormons and persons of other or no religion, as Mormons continued to accommodate themselves to public schooling and as non-Mormons became teachers and educational leaders beside their former antagonists. By the 1920s and 1930s, old antagonisms seem to have disappeared in a climate of cordiality, tolerance, and good will.

One issue, however, threatened to return the district to the "bad old days"— the issue of released-time seminary for high school students. Released-time had been allowed by policy everywhere in the state except in Salt Lake City, from seminary's beginnings in 1912 through its growth in the 1920s and 1930s. Masons, who had dominated the school board with rare exceptions since 1890, had successfully thwarted Mormon efforts to institute a released-time policy in the Salt Lake district.[39]

Probably stimulated by the war's focus on freedom and moral courage, the attention of Salt Lake's patrons was drawn to the issue of released-time religious education programs. It could not have escaped the attention of LDS general authorities living in the city that their children lacked a privilege available to every

---

37. Conversation with Ann Curtis, 15 July 1991. Curtis attended school in Salt Lake during the war years; *Fifty-second Annual Report*, 1941-42, 15-17; "City School Board Okehs Care of Job Orphans," *Salt Lake Tribune*, 14 Oct. 1942.

38. *Fifty-second Annual Report*, 1941-42, 13-14, 2.

39. James B. Allen and Glen M. Leonard, *The Story of the Latter-day Saints* (Salt Lake City: Deseret Book Co., 1976), 482-83.

other Mormon student in the state; 10 percent of the LDS students in Salt Lake's school district took seminary compared with 70 percent elsewhere.[40]

For Nuttall, facing as he was a deepening economic crisis, the seminary issue in the early 1930s was a luxury; however, he was very supportive of character education and, given his Mormon roots, would no doubt have encouraged religion as a basis for moral education. In undated personal notes, he wrote that students should ideally spend an hour each day pursuing religious training, either provided by their respective churches or, more practically, by using the Bible in the public schools as an instructional text: "I see no logical reason why we shall not some day teach 'Bible Literature' as part of the 'English Curriculum,' as well as a course in Bible stories; likewise teach Old Testament History and New Testament History in the 'History' curriculum. . . . I know of nothing better adapted for the development of worthy home life and citizenship than Bible study when led by a teacher who genuinely loves the Bible and believes the same."[41]

Nuttall's views may have encouraged the LDS Commissioner of Education, Dr. Franklin West, to ask the Mormon law firm of Bagley, Judd, and Ray in March of 1936 to determine whether the board of education could be "forced to grant released time" to junior and senior high school students in Salt Lake City. Robert L. Judd informed West that because the board had immense discretionary legal authority to make whatever school policies it wished, it was unlikely that it could be forced to act.[42] In 1938 LDS First Presidency member J. Reuben Clark, Jr., had spoken out about the need for parents to have a say in what children were taught; he also encouraged the adoption of policies allowing for released time seminary.[43]

Before the December 1938 school board election, one of the six Masons on the school board, D. E. Hammond, told a *Tribune* reporter that the board had "never discussed released time," but that the issue was clearly "in the air." The *Tribune* warned against a "drift" in sentiment about "the advisability of teaching religion during school hours." The *Telegram* identified "religious study during school hours," as an issue needing to be resolved.[44]

Although only ten percent of the electorate voted, it was a watershed election. Mormon attorney, bishop, and past mission president LeGrand P. Backman defeated Masonic incumbent Harvey Gustin in the first precinct. Nephi Morris, insurance executive and former president of the LDS Salt Lake Stake,

---

40. Allen and Leonard, *The Story of the Latter-day Saints*, 502-503. These figures are for the 1920s.

41. In Robinson, "Educational Contributions," 80-1.

42. Robert L. Judd to Franklin L. West, 11 Mar. 1936, M. Lynn Bennion Papers, Special Collections, University of Utah.

43. "Schools Need Control, P.T.A. Meet Hears," *Salt Lake Tribune*, 19 May 1938; "First Presidency Sets Standards for Church Educators," *Deseret News Church Section*, 13 Aug. 1938.

44. "School Board Policy Change to be Sought," *Salt Lake Telegram* 8 Dec. 1938; "School Board Election Nonsectarian, Non Political," *Salt Lake Tribune*, 7 Dec. 1938; "School Board Election," *Salt Lake Telegram*, 9 Dec. 1938.

won by a landslide over his opponent in the third precinct. It was the first time Masons and Mormons had faced each other in equal numbers in two decades.

Nationally, many supported increased activism for religious education. The character development movement, begun in 1920, had intensified steadily. By 1940, 455 schools systems throughout the United States offered classes or released time for religious education programs.[45] The outbreak of World War II in Europe and the likelihood that the United States would be drawn into the conflict brought new attention to the topic; and the 1940 White House Conference on Children in Democracy included a session on "Religion in the Lives of Children," which reported that an estimated half of American children and youth "receive no religious instruction outside the home."[46] The session urged schools to meet these needs.

In the October LDS General Conference that year, Elder John A. Widtsoe of the Quorum of the Twelve Apostles pointedly appealed for public schools to have "eager cooperation with every project such as our LDS Seminaries and Institutes to supply religious instruction outside the school."[47]

The city's Mormon population was rising as war industry drew Mormons from Utah's rural communities and stood at about 50 percent in 1940.[48] At the first election for the enlarged board of 12, in December 1940, Mormons held their own, maintaining technical parity with the Masons but actually achieving a substantial gain. Four new board members were chosen: one Mason and three Mormons. The Mason was H. J. Plumhof, Congregationalist, former general superintendent of the Union Pacific Railroad, and member of Mount Moriah Lodge since 1908.

The Mormons were Albert G. Zenger, chief bookkeeper for Walker Bank and former member of the Twenty-fifth Ward bishopric; George L. Crowther, editor and publisher of the Salt Lake *Times* and later bishop of the Mt. Olympus Ward; and Genevieve R. Curtis, a former teacher and Relief Society president in Parley's Ward, the first woman to penetrate this circle of Mormon, Mason, and male interests. Mother of eight and wife of prominent coal merchant A. R. Curtis of Sugarhouse, she was a teacher, founding president of the Irving Junior High School PTA, and president of the Salt Lake City PTA Council. Her son Lindsay R. Curtis believed that, as part of the over-all Mormon political strategy, she was "invited" to run for one of the newly created positions. She beat her male opponent, Leo Rusk, two-to-one.

_____

45. Mary Dabney Davis, *Weekday Classes in Religious Education Conducted on Released Time for Public-School Pupils* (Washington, D.C.: United States Office of Education, 1941), 23.

46. Davis, *Weekday Classes*, 1.

47. *Proceedings of the One Hundred and Eleventh Semi-Annual Conference of the Church of Jesus Christ of Latter-day Saints, October 1940* (Salt Lake City: Church of Jesus Christ of Latter-day Saints, [1941?]), 63.

48. Conversation with Dr. Joseph Lyon, College of Medicine, University of Utah, 23 June 1992; see also Lyon's tables comparing populations, "LDS—Non LDS, 1920-1970."

Mormon John B. Matheson, city commissioner and president of the newly created Riverside Stake, was reelected as were two Masons: dentist D. D. Stockman, a Congregationalist and past grand master of the Grand Lodge of Utah; and Frederick C. Loofbourow, past president of the Salt Lake Unitarian Society, former jurist, and Republican representative from Utah (1930-33). Not up for reelection that term were two Mormons (Nephi Morris and LeGrand P. Backman) and three Masons: D. E. Hammond, executive of the Salt Lake Council of the Boy Scouts of America, Fisher Harris, the city attorney, and Seymour L. Billings, trust company executive.[49]

Mormons clearly saw the achievement of equality on the board as a victory. In fact, Franklin West was a bit too exuberant and mistakenly told the LDS Board of Education in January 1941 that the Salt Lake Board of Education was "now composed of eight LDS members and five non-LDS members."[50] The seats were still divided six and six.[51]

Some sense of the anticipation with which Mormons faced the next election in 1942 comes from Mormon school board president Nephi Morris, who reportedly told his non-Mormon colleagues, "We have the advantage and we'll use it." While no evidence exists of official encouragement for Mormons to vote a particular way, Stanley Cannon recalled hearing his father, George J. Cannon of the Ensign Stake presidency, discuss the issue of Mormon representation on the school board around 1938 with his family "and the need for Church members to vote for LDS candidates so as to balance out the Masonic influence on the board." Similarly, Oscar W. McConkie recalled that the bishop of Twentieth Ward in 1942 encouraged ward members to vote in the school elections (the polls were in their meetinghouse) because the "time had come in Salt Lake City when we didn't want the Salt Lake Board of Education controlled by Masons."[52]

Unquestionably, the Masons, as Salt Lake's most viable political minority, feared Mormon bloc voting. Newell B. Dayton, a Mason and former board member, once commented with a certain amount of hyperbole: "The Mormons are organized. The night before election, they can roll 'em in by the thousands. . . . A lot of the people are like sheep and will do whatever the bishop says. . . . He can dominate the whole membership."[53]

For Salt Lake's Mormons, released-time religious education was more and more coming to represent a major issue. And clearly a Mormon majority on the

---

49. "Nineteen Aspire to S.L. School Board Posts," *Salt Lake Tribune*, 1 Dec. 1940; "Voters Elect Seven to Membership on Salt Lake City School Board," *Salt Lake Tribune*, 5 December 1940; Lindsay R. Curtis, *Mother's Footsteps* (Salt Lake City: privately printed, 1962), 68; "'57 Mother of Year Succumbs," *Salt Lake Tribune*, 22 July 1968.

50. Church Board of Education, abstracts of minutes, 8 Jan. 1941, Adam S. Bennion Papers, Special Collections, Brigham Young University. Hereafter cited as Church Board, by date.

51. Amy L. Engar reported that her grandfather, Apostle Richard R. Lyman, believed that the Salt Lake City board of education should be balanced between Mormons and non-Mormons to give "a fair shake for everybody" and that, in fact, the Church did not want to dominate the school board for fear of being blamed if things went wrong. Engar, Oral History, 30 Apr. 1992.

52. Church, "Controversy of Mormons and Masons," 9-10; conversations with H. Stanley Cannon, 8 Nov. 1992, and Oscar W. McConkie, 9 Nov. 1992.

53. Church, "Controversy of Mormons and Masons," 15.

school board would serve the Church Board of Education's interests. Franklin West, as Church Commissioner of Education, appears to have helped plan the strategies followed in making released-time a reality: the first priority was to gain a Mormon majority on the board.[54]

When the 1941-42 school year opened, Nephi Morris, the president of the board and also president of the LDS Salt Lake Stake, informed the board's legal advisors that parents of Mormon high school students would soon petition for released time. He wanted a ruling on whether the board could "legally grant release[d] time during school hours for the purpose of taking classes in religious education." A. M. Cheney responded with an eleven-page summary of legal precedents and problems involving released time in other areas of the United States, concluding that "We do not feel that there exists a proper basis for the expression of an opinion of even substantial certainty." If the board refused to grant the petition, it would be within its legal rights. On the other hand, if they granted released time "probably the courts would be called upon to decide it."[55]

Apparently LDS patrons were willing to risk litigation. On 10 February 1942, a petition bearing some 3,500 signatures was presented to the board asking for a released-time program and graduation credit for Bible classes. Such a program, the petition said, would promote "good citizenship" and combat "the excessive amount of juvenile delinquency and crime which prevails in our community." Safeguarding civilization required the "acquiring of deep religious convictions through careful guidance in the field of religion." The petitioners urged the board to act "immediately" on the matter.[56]

A few days before the election of December 1942, the *Tribune* editorialized that voting in this election was crucial because of the role schools must play in "post-war reconstruction." It hoped that "sectarian exclusiveness" would vanish and appealed to voters to select board members who were "selfless and who put national needs above advantage for self, party or denomination."[57]

---

54. Marian West Wilkinson, interview, 25 June 1992. This brief interview gave me a useful sense of Franklin West's involvement in the released-time debate. A transcript of a taped interview dealing with the life of Franklin L. West by Roy West at the LDS Historical Department deals with the issue of released time, but I was not permitted to examine this document.

55. A. M. Cheney, Letter to the Board of Education of Salt Lake City, 18 Dec. 1941, School District Files.

56. R. Y. Gray, Clerk, Letter to Members of the Board of Education, 19 Feb. 1942, in Salt Lake City Board of Education, Minutes, 10-24 Feb. 1942. No trace of the signed petition could be found but a copy of the wording dated 20 Feb. 1942 is in the files.

57. "Boards of Education Take on New Importance," *Salt Lake Tribune*, 1 Dec. 1942. Historically, *Tribune* warnings against "sectarian exclusiveness" and "denominational" advantage had been code words for "Mormon domination." This occasion was probably no exception, but the rhetoric was muted compared, for example, to 1906, when the anti-Mormon American Party failed to gain control of the Salt Lake board. Then, the *Tribune* headline had trumpeted: "MORMON CHURCH CONTROLS SCHOOLS" (6-7 Dec. 1906), and the paper attributed the Mormon victory to gentile apathy, stuffing the ballot boxes, and intense Mormon efforts to "get out the vote." The new board consisted, the *Tribune* reported, of one Mormon bishop, one bishop's counselor, four Mormon elders, one jack Mormon, one Catholic, and two members of the American Party.

But in that election, the balance tipped by a crucial seat. Dr. Rowland Merrill, a prominent ophthalmologist and son of Joseph F. Merrill unseated Fisher Harris, a Mason, in the fourth precinct. For the first time since 1920 the Mormons held a majority. When the board convened in January 1943 it consisted of seven Mormons, four Masons, and Hubert Cochrane, an employee of the City Water Department and a member of the Loyal Order of the Moose. The Masons averaged six years of service on the board, and the Mormons 4.5.[58] The seven Mormons were prominent in business and ecclesiastical circles, the kind of people whose presence constituted an automatic stamp of approval among hierarchically conscious Latter-day Saints.

With a Mormon majority on the board, it was time for LDS leaders to act. On 8 June 1943, a delegation of prominent LDS citizens, headed by attorney Lynn S. Richards, son of Apostle Stephen L Richards, attended the board meeting. Richards's main law partners were Henry D. Moyle, who in 1947 would be appointed to the Quorum of the Twelve Apostles, and David Lawrence McKay, son of David O. McKay, then second counselor in the LDS First Presidency. Other members of the group were D. Crawford Houston, Director of Communications for the Kennecott Copper Company; Lester F. Hewlett, businessman; attorney Perris S. Jensen and his wife, Gwen Williams Jensen; Justice Martin M. Larson of the Utah Supreme Court; and E. J. Steinfeldt, a lieutenant (and later chief) in the Salt Lake police force.[59]

Richards petitioned the board to release students for seminary during what would otherwise be a study period. He claimed to represent many parents who felt a need for "character education, plus religious and spiritual values [as] part of our City school's educational system." Released time, Richards affirmed, would not disrupt the school schedule nor conflict with either the state or federal constitutions.[60]

Board members who opposed the petition, all of them non-Mormon, questioned the difficulty of administering the arrangement, feared that eventually credit would be requested, expressed doubts about the measure's constitutional-

---

58. All of the Mormons, with the exception of Merrill, had at least two years of service on the board, a total of twenty-seven years of service. Matheson had served continuously since 1933. The three Masons elected prior to 1943 totaled twenty years of service among them; Stockman had been first elected in 1931. In summary, 42 percent had been elected in the 1930s, 33 percent had won their seats in the previous election, and 25 percent were new.

59. Five of the petitioners were members of the Edgehill Ward of the Sugarhouse Stake. Ironically, the board of education was leasing Edgehill's meetinghouse, along with two others, for $200 a month from the LDS church to alleviate overcrowded schools. School Board, Minutes, 10 Aug. 1943.

60. School Board, Minutes, 8 June 1943. Jensen told me that he circulated the petition in the Edgehill Ward, probably in his adult Sunday School class. Telephone interview with Perris S. Jensen, 30 Dec. 1991. In his reminiscences, William E. Berrett, later director of seminaries, claims that the school board first granted a 1942 petition but revoked it in 1943 when the non-Mormons gained a majority and passed a policy requiring students to have eighteen units to graduate. See his *A Miracle of Weekday Religious Education* (Salt Lake City: Salt Lake Printing Center, 1988), 29. My research does not corroborate Berrett's claims; however, the school board did increase the graduation requirements during the mid-1940s, presumably after the 1943 election. This development would have seriously hampered released-time seminary attendance.

ity, and expressed concern about the lack of prior notice and, hence, public discussion of the issue. Richards asked that the board act immediately and assured
them that credit would not be requested. After the delegation left, Backman
moved to summarily adopt a released-time policy. Non-Mormons Plumhof, Cochrane, and Woolley, requested that the motion be held over "until a later meeting so that other citizens could be heard from." The issue was scheduled for
reconsideration two weeks later.[61]

On 22 June the board met to debate and decide the issue. The *Deseret News*
was relatively restrained though supportive of released time, while the *Tribune*
and *Telegram* opposed the idea with vigor as did the Salt Lake Ministerial Association and other groups.[62] If the newspaper reports are accurate, most of those
who spoke at the meeting were vehemently opposed to the idea and were
greeted with applause and cheering. When a Mrs. E. P. Evans supported the proposal because it would give "the spiritual protection each of us needs in these
catastrophic times," her remarks were "all but drowned in the flood of boos,"
hisses, and jeers.

Stockman feared that the proposal was not in the best interests of the education of children. A second Mason on the board, Plumhof, cast doubt on the va-
lidity of the original petition which he (probably correctly) claimed had been
circulated only in LDS wards. He proposed that a petition should be circulated
city-wide for a correct reading of the community's sentiments. Eighty-year-old
Oscar VanCott, a veteran Utah educator who had reputedly produced the first
draft of Utah's 1890 first free-school law and who had vehemently criticized the
seminary idea in the 1930s, brought the meeting to a climax by proposing that
the people at the meeting hold a standing vote directly on the motion. This was
not allowed, but "a spontaneous standing vote showed [that] the audience was
almost unanimously against the adoption of the motion."[63] After VanCott's
grandstand gesture, Backman moved that the board adopt the released-time proposal as petitioned by the parents' delegation. Predictably, the seven "Yeas" were
Mormons, and the five "Nays" were four Masons and a Moose.[64]

Although some talk after the meeting hinted at legal action against the
board, reaction seems to have died down quickly. Interviewed for the *Deseret
News* two days later, the Episcopal Bishop of Utah, Reverend Arthur W. Moulton,
actually praised the board's decision as an aid to religious education in general,
adding that "some of our people have been too quick on the trigger in criticizing
this proposal." He was willing to allow time for the experiment to be tried and

---

61. Board of Education, Minutes, 8 June 1943; also "Seminary Hour Asked," *Deseret News*, 9
June 1943; "Religion Class Action Deferred," *Salt Lake Tribune*, 9 June 1943.
62. "Sponsor Defends Religious Classes at High School," *Salt Lake Tribune*, 22 June 1943;
"School Board Okeys Religious Classes: Court Fight Looms," *Salt Lake Tribune*, 23 June 1943.
63. "S. L. School Board Votes Religion Classes by 7 to 5," *Salt Lake Telegram*, 23 June 1943.
64. Board of Education, Minutes, 22 June 1943. These minutes are extremely terse and neutral,
hence my reliance on the much more detailed newspaper accounts. For a more detailed account of this
dispute see my "Masons and Mormons: Released-Time Politics in Salt Lake City, 1930-1956," *Journal
of Mormon History* 19 (Spring 1993): 67-114.

hoped to make use of facilities (presumably LDS) for Episcopalian religious education. The Superintendent of Catholic Schools in Salt Lake City, the Reverend Dr. Robert J. Dwyer, said that released time had been useful where it had been tried and that it would remain to be seen how the Salt Lake plan worked out.

Nothing would have been more natural than for the issue to have become a rallying cry in the 1944 board election, in which seven members were up for reelection. But in a remarkably "light vote," four incumbents were returned and three new members were elected. Wilford Beesley, a Mormon, and George Keyser, a Mason, were returned unopposed. When the board organized in January 1945, the composition was nine Mormons, two Masons, and one who was neither—the first time the Mormons had ever achieved such a decided majority. No editorials exhorted citizens about the dangers of "sectarianism." Even the *Tribune* had limited its preelection rhetoric to a simple reminder that voting in board elections was one way of ensuring "the quality of intelligence and citizenship of tomorrow's men and women." The divisiveness of 1943 was left behind and the Mormons had assumed responsibility for the direction schools would take.[65]

By August 1943, the guidelines for implementing the released-time policy were approved by the board. In addition to stating unequivocally that no credit would be given for these religion classes, the policy declared that no change in graduation requirements would be made to accommodate students. Principals were also cautioned about hindering parent requests or making it difficult for students to take seminary if they wished.[66]

The LDS seminary case remains an example of local church/education/political interests in tension. As George S. Counts pointed out in his classic 1929 study, a school board functions primarily in the realm of political power. A liberal, progressive educator who urged schools to become direct agents of social change, Counts termed as a "pious fraud" the view that bankers, merchants, lawyers, etc., could represent disinterestedly the best educational interests of the community. On the contrary, "the content, spirit, and purpose of public education must reflect the bias, the limitations and the experience of the membership of this board."[67]

Board president T. Quintin Cannon suggested that the tension between the Masons and the Mormons on the board was, rather than primarily over religion, over power in the community—especially money power. He claimed that when the Masons were in power, most of the school district's tax receipts would be deposited in gentile banks such as Tracy-Collins Trust, Walker Bank, and Continental Bank. Conversely, when Mormons were in control of the board, the money

---

65. "4 Incumbents Retain Posts in School Elections," *Salt Lake Tribune*, 7 Dec. 1944; "School Board Election Scheduled," *Salt Lake Tribune*, 5 Dec. 1944.

66. *Plans for Administering Released Time for Religious Study in Salt Lake City Schools,* copy in School District Files. This plan was transmitted to the board on 10 August and by 1 September, a form for parents to sign had been produced and apparently approved by the board. Board of Education, Minutes, 10 Aug. 1943.

67. George S. Counts, *The Social Composition of Boards of Education: A Study in the Social Control of Public Education* (Chicago: University of Chicago Press, 1927), 96, 1.

was deposited in Mormon banks like Zion's First National and Utah National Bank.[68] Certainly the Salt Lake board of education members represented the business, professional, managerial, and commercial interests that dominated public boards nationwide, while simultaneously lacking representatives of what Counts terms "the laboring classes."[69] However, in Utah class and social considerations are often overridden by religion, so that many issues which might be interpreted as economic or political elsewhere are reduced in Utah to a matter of Mormon vs. non-Mormon, or as in the issue of released time, Mormon vs. Mason.[70]

The Legacy of a Conservative Progressive

The released-time question was the last major issue Superintendent Nuttall faced. For some time he had suffered from diabetes, and within a year of the adoption of the guidelines governing the program Nuttall died of a heart attack at age 57. One of his former students, J. C. Moffitt, superintendent of Provo City School District, claimed Nuttall had influenced the educational thinking of more Utahns than any other educational leader. Another put him in the same category as A. C. Nelson, William Stewart, Joseph Kingsbury, and Karl Maeser. Under Nuttall's leadership Salt Lake City's public school system withstood the turmoil of the depression and the onset of World War II. He never let the public and teachers forget that the primary aim of the schools was to meet the changes forced on them by the larger society, at the same time keeping individual students' needs at the forefront. If there was sufficient evidence to support a course of action, he would be progressive and adopt and promote the idea, but in the absence of warrant for change he remained conservative. Milton Bennion assessed him as an educator who was critical of the status quo and anxious to make changes. However, he was no radical and had a basic commitment to "fundamentals and thoroughness."[71]

The schools of Salt Lake City at mid-century gave the impression of being relatively humane institutions. Nuttall helped shape the schools to this end. The progressive education he espoused and tried to implement provided continual challenge to future generations who might be tempted promote special interests or favor the status quo rather than recognizing broad-gauged interests and ever-expanding needs of the human community continually calling for new insights and change. Nuttall's schools tried to do both.

---

68. T. Quintin Cannon, telephone interview, 27 June 1992. This view merits further study.

69. Counts, *The Social Composition of Boards of Education*, 60.

70. Counts claimed that clergymen "were practically without representation" on national public school boards in the twentieth century, although in the nineteenth century they played a sometimes dominant role. He attributed this change to the church's decline as a social institution or to the increasingly social heterogeneity of the population. *The Social Composition of Boards of Education*, 56-7.

71. See Robinson, "Life and Work," 1-2, 65-7, 76-7.

7

MANAGING AN EXPANDING SYSTEM

*The Administrations of
Howard S. McDonald, 1944–45,
and M. Lynn Bennion, 1945–69*

In April 1944, a few weeks before D-Day and sixteen months before World War II would come to an end, Salt Lake City's board of education was searching for its seventh superintendent since 1890. In the interim, a veteran Utah educator and Assistant Superintendent, James T. Worlton, assumed the role of Acting Superintendent. Worlton was responsible for developing a social studies curriculum to replace the traditional emphasis on history. He also promoted the use of standardized tests to classify students and spearheaded the movement to make sure each elementary teacher had "special training in her subject matter field," and was not expected to be an expert in every area. Coordinating Units were organized in which a small number of teachers coordinated their efforts and expertise in teaching several classes. Toward the end of his tenure as Assistant Superintendent he also produced two books: *Moral Primer for Democracy* and *Community Life in Salt Lake City and Utah*, which were used in the district schools.[1]

With the exception of George Child, all past superintendents had come to Salt Lake City without prior involvement in the district. This precedent was established perhaps in an effort to promote diversity of perspective and to downplay any charge of parochialism if the board limited itself to local people. A Mormon-dominated board, such as existed in 1944, would have been especially anxious not to raise suspicion that they were afraid of outsiders. The ideal candidate would be someone with significant "outside" academic and professionals and "inside" sensitivity to the local culture.

In March 1944, Howard S. McDonald, a native Utahn then serving as Deputy Superintendent of San Francisco Schools, was invited to apply for the Salt Lake position. The unanimous choice to fill the Nuttall vacancy, he held the position for only one year. In 1945 he accepted a "call" to become president of Brigham Young University.

For the second time in less than a year, the board set about to choose a new superintendent, ultimately choosing something of a dark horse candidate in the person of a Mormon Church employee, Dr. M. Lynn Bennion. Bennion decen-

---

1. I am indebted to James T. Worlton, Jr., of Colorado Springs, Colorado, for a photocopy of his father's "Autobiography," privately published c. 1952.

Howard S. McDonald
1944–45

M. Lynn Bennion
1945–69

tralized the administration, involving more teachers and principals in governing the district. He diluted the micro-management of district affairs by involving himself, to the point of exhaustion, in as many committees as the board was directly involved in. The old Mormon/Mason tension continued for a time, but the Masons eventually disappeared as a political entity and those who did serve on the board came to trust Bennion as a fair and competent administrator.

Bennion faced the challenge of a growing district that required more teachers, school buildings, and more money. But the 1950s saw a blooming of the American economy and full public support for bond issues to expand schools to meet the needs of the post-war baby boom. When human relations, self worth, and cooperation were seen as essential to the survival of "democracy," the schools obliged accordingly, as they did when the "Sputnik" syndrome made schools the locus of technological supremacy over the Soviets.

Lynn Bennion's retirement in 1969, after almost a quarter of a century of leadership, marked a milestone in the district's history. Bennion had presided over a period of growth. Now his successor was on the verge of presiding over the very opposite of what had made Bennion's years unique, and in some sense easier to manage. The school district was in decline, having crested in school population at 42,323 a decade before; by 1965 it had fallen to 39,416 and the slide continued. New issues of race, ethnicity, and class were making their way into the schools. It is tempting to speculate what Bennion—trained at Berkeley in the thought of John Dewey—would have done had he continued as superintendent. He would perhaps have asked how children figure into such changes. Are they being helped to face this brave, and terrifying, new world? Are the schools serving all of the children of all of the people the best they can?

A SHORT, DYNAMIC INTERIM

The seventh superintendent of the Salt Lake City schools was born of Scottish and English emigrant parents, Francis McDonald and Emily Stevenson, in Holladay, Utah, in 1894. Howard McDonald received a BS degree in Irrigation and Drainage Engineering from Utah State Agricultural College in 1921. After teaching mathematics at Logan he received a part-time appointment as a physical education teacher in San Francisco. This enabled him to pursue a Master's degree in school administration at Berkeley. From his 1925 graduation until 1944 he occupied a number of educational positions, culminating in a ten-year term as Deputy Superintendent of San Francisco public schools. In 1941 he was appointed President of the LDS San Francisco Stake and hoped to become superintendent in San Francisco when Joseph Nourse retired. Perhaps because he was seen as something of a teacher advocate, McDonald did not get the San Francisco superintendency.

On John Nuttall's death in Salt Lake, however, McDonald was invited to interview for that superintendency in May 1944. He had been visited often in California by board member Genevieve Curtis, who was mother to his First Counsellor in the stake presidency, Ray T. Curtis. Curtis likely convinced the board to invite McDonald to apply for the position. Preparatory to meeting the board he studied the latest reports and concluded that the district "had gone in the red for the past couple of years, that teachers salaries were very poor, and that the system as a whole could stand much improvement." He talked to the board about such difficulties and left feeling he would not be appointed. Two of his conditions were that his salary be increased (from $6,000 to $8,500) and that his appointment be unanimous. He did not think they would accept his conditions and told board president Stockman that they should hire one of the other able applicants. Surprisingly, the board met both demands and McDonald became superintendent 1 July 1944.[2]

McDonald's one-year tenure was plagued with controversies over control of finances and personal health problems; he really had no opportunity to put his mark on the system. He immediately faced the district's lack of resources with a firm determination to improve the lot of teachers, whose morale and salaries, in the aftermath of the depression and the war, were abysmally low. He lobbied the Utah legislature to change laws governing school finances and personally took on the Utah Tax Payer's Association, the Apartment House Association, and assorted mining interests over the need to increase funding for the schools. McDonald even took the campaign to the floor of the legislature and, with united pressure from a coalition of other school districts, an education bill was enacted that greatly enhanced school funds. He also pushed the board to abandon George Child's eleven-year program in favor of a traditional twelve years.[3]

With less than a year in as superintendent, in March 1945 McDonald received a call from President J. Reuben Clark, Jr., of the LDS First Presidency, asking him to accept the presidency of the church's Brigham Young University. McDonald obtained a "reluctant release" from the Salt Lake Board of Education and embarked on another phase of his educational career on 1 July 1945.[4] His departure suited a young Mormon educator, M. Lynn Bennion, who had come to a point of decision respecting his job as supervisor of the LDS seminary system.

MAKING RELIGIOUS EDUCATION FUNCTIONAL

During the 1943 debate at Bryant Junior High School on the issue of released time, Lynn Bennion sat in the back of the auditorium, listening intently but not participating actively. As Supervisor of Seminaries for the LDS Church Education System, however, he had more than a casual interest in the debate. He watched as the board's Mormon majority approved released-time for religious instruction, bringing the Salt Lake School District into line with other Utah schools

---

2. Howard S. McDonald, *Brief Autobiography* (Privately published, c. 1970), 36-37. Copy in Brigham Young University Library. McDonald had begun work on an Ed.D. degree at Berkeley in 1925, but did not complete the work for the degree until 1949, shortly before leaving BYU. See McDonald, *Brief Autobiography*, 65.

3. McDonald, *Brief Autobiography*, 54.

4. McDonald, *Brief Autobiography*, 57. McDonald served at BYU until 1949 when he left to assume the joint presidency of Los Angeles State College of Applied Arts and Sciences and Los Angeles City College, positions he held until 1958. Subsequently he was a Regional Representative for the U.S. Commissioner of Education from 1962 until 1964. He died in 1986.

after years of resistance. Overtly, the LDS church kept a low profile during the debate, but it had much at stake in changing the public school policy, and LDS leaders were involved covertly to achieve that aim. Given the makeup of the board, few doubted how the board would vote. But the young Supervisor of Seminaries had no idea that within two years he would be under the board's scrutiny as one of a number of educators being considered for the superintendency of the Salt Lake School District.

Milton Lindsay Bennion was born in Salt Lake City on 4 October 1902, the son of Milton and Cora Lindsay Bennion. The grandson of Mormon pioneer and school booster, John Bennion, M. Lynn (as he renamed himself) grew up surrounded by educational concerns. His father was a Professor of Philosophy at the University of Utah, and during much of Lynn's youth had served as Dean of the University's School of Education. In 1918 Lynn graduated from the LDS High School, spent a year at Utah State, then from 1921 to 1923 served an LDS mission in Missouri and Oklahoma. Entering the University of Utah in 1923 he served an apprenticeship as an assistant teacher and researcher under the liberal Mormon philosopher E. E. Ericksen. In 1926 he received a BS degree in history and political science, with a teaching certificate in history. Encouraged by his father, a friend, J. Willard Marriott, and by his cousin, Adam S. Bennion, Superintendent of the LDS Church Schools, young Bennion signed on to teach seminary in the LDS Church Education System that same year. He also continued his education, in 1932 receiving an MS degree in history and political science from the University of Utah.

While teaching seminary, Bennion was exposed to the thinking of prominent Biblical scholars who were brought to Utah to stimulate the intellectual interests of the Church Education System. Bennion was introduced, at these summer institutes, to such scholars as Edgar J. Goodspeed and John T. McNeill of the University of Chicago, stirring in him an interest in the intellectual study of religion. This exposure also raised "questions about Mormon orthodoxy and the conventional concepts that we were teaching to our [seminary] students." Reflecting on these experiences some years later, Bennion recalled the visiting scholars' approaches as "universal . . . broader [in] outlook than the conventional Mormon orthodoxy by far."[5] Between 1932 and 1935 Bennion pursued a doctoral program at Berkeley. Apostle Joseph Merrill, a guiding force behind the summer institutes, helped financially by arranging for Bennion's wife, Katherine, to teach his seminary classes (although at a reduced salary) while he was in California taking graduate courses in educational administration, educational psychology, philosophy of education, and secondary education. His dissertation, "The Origin, Growth and Extension of the Educational Program of the Mormon Church in Utah," was published in 1939 by the LDS Church Department of Education as *Mormonism and Education.*

---

5. M. Lynn Bennion, Oral History, 15 May 1973. I conducted these oral history interviews. The transcripts are in the Frederick S. Buchanan Papers, Special Collections, Marriott Library, University of Utah. They are in a rough draft form and consequently no pagination has been assigned to them.

In a 1934 letter from Berkeley, Bennion confided to his wife his conviction that the traditional authoritarian approach to teaching seminary was not adequate to meet the problems of modern youth. Influenced by character education studies which challenged the assumption of traditional religious education that verbalizing high moral values led inexorably to high moral behaviour, he had concluded that the *study of values* rather than the *promulgation of dogma* should be the keystone of the seminary program, and that a need existed for a more practical, problems-oriented approach. If the ideas of modern scholars could be utilized, he wondered, "think what could be accomplished" in the seminaries. The books he was reading included John Dewey's *The Quest for Certainty* and Herbert Spengler's *Decline of the West*.[6]

After a year as a general agent for the publishing firm of Ginn and Company, in 1936 Bennion was invited by the church's Commissioner of Education, Dr. Franklin West, to become the Supervisor of Seminaries for the LDS church. Commissioner West gave him free reign to revolutionize the seminaries by implementing "progressive" ideas he had been exposed to at Berkeley, through his membership in the Progressive Education Association, and through his contacts with progressive educators. Bennion wanted to make the Bible meaningful to students by organizing the seminary curriculum around problems youth faced. Neither Dr. Bennion nor his associates saw this approach as undermining LDS teachings—they simply wanted to make the study of religion academically oriented and of functional value to LDS youth.

Unfortunately for Bennion, his revision of seminary teaching coincided with a retrenchment movement among LDS leaders. Following the 1934 death of a relatively liberal member of the First Presidency, Antoine R. Ivins, who had supported bringing outside scholars to Utah, a staunch conservative, J. Reuben Clark, Jr., began to exert a strong influence in LDS education circles. This influence culminated in a 1938 address to Mormon educators at a summer institute in Aspen Grove, Utah, in which Clark clearly spelled out what he thought of the "newest fangled ideas" in education: he reiterated the traditional view that religious truth was revealed by God, not created by human discussion and reflection. Consequently, the primary mission of the LDS education system was to indoctrinate what was already revealed, not to search for new "truths." Scholarship in this schema was subordinate to faith; seminary was to build the faith rather than the intellects of the "youth of Zion."[7]

Bennion was present when Clark delivered his discourse at Aspen Grove. Given his progressive orientation it is not surprising that he viewed these comments as alarming. Dr. Franklin West was not as disturbed, and saw the issue as a

---

6. *Recollections of a Schoolman: The Autobiography of M. Lynn Bennion* (Salt Lake City: Western Epics, 1987), 89-90; H. Hartshorne and M.A. May, "A Summary of the Work of Character Education Inquiry," *Religious Education*, 25 (Sept. 1930), 607-19; 754-62.

7. "First Presidency Sets Standards for Church Educators," *Deseret News Church Section*, 13 Aug. 1938; reprinted by the LDS church as "The Charted Course of the Church in Education," Aspen Grove, Utah, 8 Aug. 1939. Frequently reprinted it has become something of a standard for determining the content and method of LDS education.

matter of differences over methods. However, time would bear out Bennion's fears. For Clark, the good Latter-day Saint was a conformist, not a critical thinker. Doubts could only be answered by the revelations vouchsafed to the church.[8]

Although Bennion's curriculum was relatively successful, especially with younger and less-traditional faculty, over the next few years suspicions were raised about Bennion's approach. Clark once asked him why none of Joseph Smith's revelations were used in the seminaries' Bible curriculum. Bennion informed him that the Bible courses—outside of Salt Lake City—received high school credit and could not, therefore, promote a particular Mormon point of view. Other reports filtered back to President Clark, perhaps through his son, who taught in the Church Education System, about various positions Bennion had taken that might offend Clark.

On the other hand, Bennion received indirect encouragement from David O. McKay on numerous occasions, and a Presiding Bishopric member, Marvin O. Ashton, admonished him to "be yourself" in directing the seminary programs. In spite of such support, around 1944 Bennion was convinced that Clark was not satisfied with him. As overseer of the Church Education System and using his considerable influence with enfeebled LDS church President, Heber J. Grant, Clark began to ease Bennion out of his position, without ever directly approaching him about the issues.[9]

To counteract some of the negative effects of Clark's criticism, Grant's Second Counselor, David O. McKay, who supervised the church's missionary work and who had informed Bennion confidentially of Clark's displeasure, arranged for a church mission call for Bennion, first to Texas and then to California. Family considerations intervened, however, and the mission calls never materialized. But Bennion took some satisfaction in McKay's vote of confidence. When the mission calls could not be arranged, President McKay encouraged Bennion to pursue his career as an educator in the public domain. The opportunity to do just that opened up in the spring of 1945, when Howard McDonald resigned the superintendency to accept the presidency of Brigham Young University.

A SUPERINTENDENT "ACCEPTABLE TO THE WHOLE COMMUNITY"

In spite of his long affiliation with the Church Education System and his lack of experience in public schools, Bennion applied for the superintendency of Salt Lake City's public schools on 22 March 1945. In his letter to board president LeGrand P. Backman, he laid out in some detail his educational experience as a seminary teacher, seminary principal, teacher at Brigham Young University, and even his membership on the Mormon "Deseret Sunday School Union Board." In addition to supervising the seminaries, he added, he had assisted Franklin West in the administration of all LDS schools, from BYU to the Juarez Stake Academy in Mexico.

Bennion identified some of his most important work as selecting qualified

---

8. Bennion, *Recollections*, 106.
9. The details of Bennion's experience as supervisor of seminaries are derived from Bennion, Oral History, 15 May 1973 and 4 Apr. 1974. Also conversation with M. Lynn Bennion, 14 Nov. 1991.

teachers, directing in-service training programs, creating salary schedules and welfare programs for teachers, revising curriculum, and inaugurating guidance programs. He also listed his experience with budgets, buildings, and public relations.[10]

Given his lack of experience in public schools, Bennion thought that his chances of being appointed were minimal. He was, in fact, up against some of the foremost public educators in the state: Aldous Dixon, superintendent at Provo; E. Allen Bateman, Utah State Superintendent; and Roald Campbell, a Professor of Education and director of the University of Utah's Stewart Training School. In addition, Nuttall's assistant superintendents, James T. Worlton and Arthur Arnesen, had also applied.

Armed with strong letters of recommendation from President George Thomas of the University of Utah and President Franklin Harris of BYU, Bennion met with the board, making a brief formal presentation and answering questions. The board did not ask about his church education experiences, nor about his philosophy of education. They liked his sense of humor and that he only took fifteen minutes for his formal presentation. He later recalled that they were pleased when he emphasized decentralized administration.[11]

According to Bennion's recollections, he was elected by a narrow margin of 5-4. The "yeas," he said, were all LDS while the "nays" were three Masons and one Mormon. The latter was probably LeGrand Backman, who did not think Bennion's experience in Mormon education was sufficient for the superintendent's job. One member, Dr. Rowland Merrill, apparently absented himself because he was related to another candidate. If Bennion is correct on the vote count, four members stayed away from the meeting. As in the 1920 election of George Child, some Mormons may have stayed away to downplay the impression of a powerful Mormon majority. Whatever the case, whether elected by a narrow 5-4 vote or a wider 7-4 margin, as indicated in the minutes, Dr. M. Lynn Bennion became the district's eighth superintendent on 1 July 1945.[12]

Bennion regarded his selection as "a near miraculous event." He received numerous letters from associates in the seminary system, some of whom expressed shock and regret that he would no longer be leading the church system. Others acknowledged the considerable institutional pressure and "educational trials" under which he had worked. T. Edgar Lyon, of the LDS Salt Lake Institute of Religion, was confident that Bennion would finally be able to implement educational ideas that had been forced to remain in the realm of theory. Sterling McMurrin of the LDS Tucson, Arizona, Institute said that without Bennion leading the church system, McMurrin would find it difficult to keep up his own interest in the work. Sterling Larson, principal of the LDS St. Anthony, Idaho, Seminary, said Bennion

<hr>

10. M. Lynn Bennion to LeGrand P. Backman, 22 Mar. 1945. M. Lynn Bennion Papers, Special Collections, University of Utah.
11. Bennion, Oral History, 4 Apr. 1974.
12. Bennion, *Recollections*, 128; Board of Education, Minutes of Special Meeting, 26 Apr. 1945. For list of members on the board as of 3 Apr. 1945 see Minutes, 10 Apr. 1945; conversation with M. Lynn Bennion, 14 Apr. 1992.

would enjoy "independence and freedom" in developing the ideas and plans that "you have longed for." Larson added that after working with the "many and varied boards and factions" in the Church Education System "only one city school board would be pie." Lilian H. Whelan, who had taught a younger Bennion at Forest Dale School, was pleased that "one of her boys" had been chosen as superintendent, congratulating him for his "high standards, wholesome attitude, broad vision and great industry."[13]

However, some of the staff at the Salt Lake district headquarters expressed doubt that Bennion could measure up as an effective leader in a public system. Arthur Arnesen, the Supervisor of Curriculum and Research and a candidate for the position, told him: "Frankly, I was surprised in your being named as the executive head of our school system," then listed all the responsibilities that would now be Bennion's. Arnesen did, however, give him a reserved pledge of support.[14]

Some in the community at large, especially among non-Mormons, thought Bennion's appointment may have been "an unfortunate choice" in light of the 1943 released-time seminary controversy. Others, including the Rev. Dr. J. R. Cope of the Salt Lake City Unitarian Church, wholeheartedly supported him. Cope had worked with Bennion for a number of years. The new superintendent, he said, could be depended on to avoid partisan bias, and "under his leadership the whole community will become more thoroughly united." Bennion credited Cope with helping convince many non-Mormons that he was a person who could be "acceptable to the whole community."[15]

The appointment of Bennion, former supervisor of the church's seminaries, as superintendent of a secular public school system may be seen as representative of shifting attitudes as Salt Lake City faced post-war challenges. Given the tensions he experienced in his seminary position, he certainly was not appointed to the superintendency because of his religious orthodoxy. Rather, it was his secular orientation *within* a general context of Mormon community values that made his appointment a sign of the times. In addition to a changing Mormon/non-Mormon configuration, other factors worked on the schools, including a movement to a more open conception of governance; rapid growth in school population; federal involvement in local schools; the perceived threat of Communism (internally and externally); increased militancy among teachers; the shift away from traditional values; and the beginnings of an increasingly complex domestic social environment.

---

13. See letters in Bennion Papers, especially those of Edith and Charles Shepherd, 28 Apr.; Heber C. Snell, 1 May; T. Edgar Lyon, 27 Apr.; Sterling McMurrin, 5 May; Sterling Larson, 27 Apr.; Feramorz Y. Fox, 2 May; Lillian H. Whelan, 3 May 1945.

14. Arthur E. Arnesen to M. Lynn Bennion, 28 Apr. 1945, Bennion Papers.

15. A copy of Cope's statement of support, which appeared in the Unitarian church's newsletter, under the date of 9 May 1945 can be found in Bennion Papers

THE NEED FOR HEALING AND IMPROVEMENT

Shortly after his appointment, Bennion learned about the much-rumored "gentlemen's agreement" between the Masons and Mormons on the board. As he understood it, the agreement was that the Masons would control the appointments made to the powerful clerk-treasurer's office and the Mormons would be allowed to control the superintendency. A perusal of the lists of clerk-treasurers and superintendents from 1901 through the 1940s supports the contention. During this period Masons or other non-Mormons did indeed hold the clerk-treasurer's post and only Mormons were appointed (with one exception, Ernest Smith in 1916) to the superintendency. According to R. Y. Gray, the clerk-treasurer at the time Bennion was appointed, the issue was not really over religion; rather it was a matter of balancing political power. Gray recalled that one former president of the board (a Mormon) had told him that "we have the advantage [as a majority] and we'll use it."[16] This disposition was what the agreement was meant to negate.

Masons on the board took a special interest in seeing that public funds were not squandered. Clerk-Treasurer Gray was apparently in continual conflict with Superintendent Nuttall—described by Bennion as "a very serious and abrasive relationship." One former president of the board told Bennion that a Mason's job on the board during Nuttall's tenure was to "check on Nuttall and his expenditures and keep him in line."[17] Sally Mason, the secretary of the board during the 1940s, used the term "watchdog" to describe the clerk-treasurer's relationship with Nuttall. She recalled an early clerk-treasurer, L. P. Judd, as saying frequently that "We are paid by the citizens and you must never offend the public," while he had a cigar hanging out of his mouth—hardly an inoffensive gesture in Mormon Utah.[18]

Although Bennion was able to improve this relationship, he still faced challenges in dealings with the current clerk-treasurer, R. Y. Gray. Gray's office controlled the disbursal of funds, thus becoming involved in almost every aspect of school affairs, including policy making (by controlling expenditures). Within a year of taking office Bennion resisted Gray's attempts to derail a policy implementation by the Supervisor of Curriculum, Arthur Arnesen. Bennion came down on the side of the educational interests of the schools, but he could not directly oppose the powerful Gray. At the same time he realized the disadvantage in his failure to control the budget.

This conflict resurfaced again and again over the next twelve years. Bennion's staff would make plans only to find that Gray had reduced the amounts needed to accomplish the work. Indeed, the clerk-treasurer had a dominant influence on all the standing committees—he had the final say on expenditures for

---

16. Al Church, "The Controversy of Mormons and Masons, Reflected in the Salt Lake School Board as recalled by M. Lynn Bennion, Lawrence Schroeder, Sally Mason, R. Y. Gray, Paul B. Cannon [and] Newell Dayton," Term Paper, University of Utah, March 1973, 9-10.

17. Bennion, Oral History, 4 Apr. 1974.

18. Church, "Controversy of Mormons and Masons," 7-8.

curriculum *and* for buildings.

As clerk-treasurer, Gray felt directly responsible to the Board of Education *and* to the city's business community. According to Bennion, Gray took great pride in his "honest and meticulous accounting" and in the district's "modest pupil expenditures." On the other hand, Bennion's enthusiasm for educational innovation quickly got him the "reputation of being a spender." This challenged Gray's firm conviction that his role was to keep expenditures as low as possible, even in the face of an expanding system in the post-war years.

In a 1973 interview Gray recalled no real difficulties with Superintendent Bennion, and said that he, as clerk-treasurer, only gave the board his opinion on fiscal matters. However, even after his retirement, Gray was contacted by former board members who were concerned about "wasteful activities." Given his "watchdog" orientation, Gray did his job well as he understood it, even if it caused Bennion some distress.[19] In 1956 Bennion was influential in limiting the new clerk-treasurer, Robert L. Bridge, to financial matters. Bridge, was the first Mormon to hold this post in the history of the district, a symbol of the waning Masonic influence on the board.

In spite of such tensions, Bennion built rapport with the board and gained their backing during his long tenure. In this he was assisted by such board members as George Keyser, a Mason who served as the board's vice-president during the early years of Bennion's tenure. After initial resistance to Bennion's appointment, Keyser helped Bennion make a successful transition from supervising the LDS seminaries to being superintendent of public schools. He admired Bennion's views on the significance of "spiritual values," assuring his fellow non-Mormon board members that Bennion would "serve all of the children of all of the people effectively without any racial or religious bias." Recognizing the realities of operating public schools in a heavily Mormon area, Keysor encouraged Bennion to "keep in touch with 47 East South Temple" (LDS Church Headquarters) and with other religious organizations in the city.[20]

Keysor's advice illustrates once again the changes occurring in Salt Lake's religio-political climate. Perhaps both sides were moderating their stance, as Masons became less suspicious of Mormon intentions and Mormons became less ethnocentric. Also, by the early 1940s Mormon citizens took the position that if the Masons were in any way inclined to influence schools in an anti-Mormon way, then it was necessary and proper that the church members should use religious cohesion to their advantage. This strategy led ultimately to the Masons' decline as an active influence on the board.[21]

With the 1943 Mormon victory over released-time seminary and Bennion's appointment in 1945, the Masons may have decided they could no longer stem the tide of "Mormon influence." Perhaps, in the words of political scientist G. Homer Durham, they had concluded "you can't lick the Mormon Church in

---

19. Bennion, Oral History, 4 Apr. 1974; Church, "Controversy of Mormons and Masons," 9-10.
20. Bennion, Oral History, 4 Apr. 1974.
21. Ibid., 10 April 1974.

Utah" and that cooperation, in the long run, was best for the public schools.[22]At least people like Bennion and George Keyser were aware of the need to cooperate.

TOWARD MORE OPEN GOVERNANCE

Since its inception in 1890, the board had run on a system of standing committees divided up among the board members. In 1937 the four standing committees were Teachers and School Work; Buildings and Grounds; Finance; Rules and School Law. In 1915 Ellwood P. Cubberley's report had criticized this system for its inefficiency; it persisted probably because it gave board members a check against a powerful superintendent, and may have been one strategy to dilute Mormon influence. The system was also fairly common nationwide. Under this system, members of the board dealt with the day to day operations of the schools. The committees were "almost like separate operations," with each committee keeping even separate financial records. According to Bennion, "It was cumbersome . . . divisive in effect . . . and brought about inevitable conflicts."[23]

Not only did the committee system dilute the superintendent's influence on educational matters, it left teachers out entirely. Proponents argued that the board represented taxpayers and had a vested interest in keeping tab of what was being done in and to schools. Bennion believed that, while the business community ought to have some say in the governance of schools, an inordinate degree of outside control was being exercised. Bennion held that the board should restrict itself to policy making and leave the implementation of policy to the professional staff.

Bennion brought his diplomatic skills into play when he decided that he must find a way to influence the standing committees. He knew a frontal attack on the traditional system would not be tolerated, so at the cost of much time and energy he personally became involved, as an *ad hoc* member, in the regular deliberations of each of the standing committees. In this way he was able to help shape each committee's decision so that they would reflect the "priorities that I thought were essential to have a good school system." This structure persisted throughout his administration, but when the board was reduced from twelve to seven members in 1972, Bennion, as executive secretary of the Society of Superintendents, successfully lobbied for the abolition of the board committees.[24]

Bennion also wanted improved relations between the superintendent's office and the staff. In 1946 he organized the Superintendent's Advisory Council, consisting of thirty people chosen by the elected officers of the professional associations affiliated with the instructional staff, buildings and grounds, the superintendent's office and the secretaries. The district's low teacher morale influenced Bennion to organize the Council so that the majority of its members were

---

22. Durham's comment was made to Allan West. See Allan M. West, *My Life as an Advocate for Utah Schools, 1942-1961* (Salt Lake City, privately published, 1988), 86.

23. Bennion, Oral History, 4 Apr. 1974.

24. Bennion, Oral History, 4 Apr., 10 Apr. 1974; Conversation, 21 Nov. 1991.

taken from the teacher corp. At a much later date, when the board agreed to negotiate with teachers over salaries, teachers who had served on the Superintendent's Advisory Council played a major role in making the conflict over negotiations less confrontational than it might have been. Even when teachers went on strike in the 1960s, channels of communication were still relatively open. Such open communication Bennion regarded as among his most significant accomplishments as superintendent.[25]

Bennion's diplomacy, tact, and democratic orientation contributed to a cooperative relationship necessary if he were to provide the kind of leadership he believed the schools needed. Almost any problem can be resolved, he held, if the superintendent has the "board back of [him] and a certain degree of support from the community." Without these preconditions the work of being a superintendent is "almost more than a man can take."[26]

PRESIDING OVER A GROWTH INDUSTRY

The war had delayed the upkeep and expansion of the physical plant, adding to Bennion's pressure to accommodate the "baby boom," the natural increase in population that came as reunited families grew. Projections in 1948 indicated that Utah's population would expand 15 percent in the following decade, while Salt Lake City's school population would increase by some 69 percent. By 1956 the district would need fifteen new elementary schools, four new junior high schools, and one new high school—all at a total cost of over $15,000,000.[27] Shortly after these projections were made, Salt Lake City's voters approved a bond issue that taxed residents to the legal limit. By 1951 the district was rushing to complete a $12,000,000-plus building program, just in time to accommodate the advance of "a tidal wave of post-war babies" who would become first graders around 1953.[28] When Bennion began his tenure, enrollment stood at 30,000; by 1951 it had grown to 35,555. By the end of the 1950s the enrollment peaked at some 42,323 students and thereafter it began to decline. Bennion acknowledged the exhilarating nature of leading when so many positive things were happening in the district, even though it meant that for some "ten years [Bennion] was in the business of building" schools, rather than spending time on pedagogical issues.[29]

Given the LDS cultural value placed on large families and the church's abandonment of its private schools in the 1920s, more schools financed by public funds were an absolute necessity. In the early years of Bennion's tenure the board had to rent temporary facilities, such as LDS chapels, to meet the needs of the burgeoning student population. The district also faced busing children from the new suburbs to parts of the city that were losing population and whose schools

25. Bennion, Oral History, 10 Apr. 1974.
26. Ibid., 4 Apr. 1974.
27. "School Needs Most Acute in Salt Lake," *Salt Lake Tribune*, 2 Aug. 1948.
28. *Sixty-second and Sixty-third Annual Reports*, 1951-53, iv, 5-6.
29. Bennion, *Recollections*, 147.

were under utilized. Meetings to discuss such measures were always well-attended: as Bennion observed, "Whenever you're going to do anything to significantly alter the life pattern, the life style of a family, or a child you have no trouble getting an audience." For example, parents at a mass meeting rejected a proposal to bus children from the Uintah School on Fifteenth East to the Lowell School on the avenues. Local patrons argued that renting a local LDS building would suit their needs; they were not persuaded when Bennion pointed out that such a building was not built for schools in terms of lighting, space, and toilet facilities. Parents wanted to retain the neighborhood school because busing children twelve blocks across Salt Lake City in 1950 was considered too dangerous; childhood patterns of friendship would be dislocated and the children sent among strangers might be picked on. Bennion noted that some social-class biases surfaced during discussions he had with school committees. East Bench parents did not want their children mingling with children from less affluent areas.[30] Some parents even worried that their children would be interacting with children who were members of "other" LDS wards instead of their "own" ward; if busing were prolonged, they would end up going to other ward dances, dating kids from other wards, and even end up marrying kids from the "foreign" wards. ("Oh, boy, how provincial can you get?" responded one non-Mormon board member.) Such attitudes, however, were merely an extension of the sacrosanct neighborhood schools that have formed the core of American public education for over 150 years.[31]

Bennion believed that informed people can together resolve even the most difficult problems, but on numerous occasions the negative of that idea seemed true: that people stirred up emotionally will not be convinced by logic or statistics, and that achieving consensus in a mass meeting is virtually impossible. After one stormy meeting over busing, building new schools, and increased taxes, Bennion attempted to inject some humor into the tense evening by remarking that "the cure for this kind of problem is to have birth control and make it retroactive for ten years." When the press reported the comment the next day, Bennion recalled, some parents "hired an attorney to try to get me fired; they argued that I was not fit to be superintendent of schools."[32]

Other tensions, as mentioned previously, came from the board. One board president who thought Bennion was not moving fast enough in the right direction took it upon himself to give principals direct instructions on how they should do their work. He took charge of the remodelling program for the older schools and even began to tell the other board members what they should be doing. All this violated Bennion's sense of boundaries. This particular board president may have helped speed up some of the remodelling of schools, but he also created conflict and resentment among the board members, who were not able to counteract his interference. He was an aggressive leader—some described him as

30. Bennion, *Recollections*, 144-45; Bennion, Oral History, 4 Apr. 1974.
31. Esther Landa, Oral History, 17 May 1991.
32. Bennion, *Recollections*, 148.

a "hyperactive president"—who wanted things done fast, and seems to have had the schools' interests at heart. Even so, he gave Bennion much grief, on one occasion actually interviewing University of Utah faculty to replace the superintendent. Fortunately for Bennion, the problem was solved in a time-honored Utah manner; his nemesis was called on a mission for the LDS church.[33]

When LDS mission calls couldn't relieve him of meddling board members, Bennion did find some solace in buying a small pasture in the south east section of the Salt Lake Valley. There on his horse, "Consultation," he found some relief from the pressures of his office. With his wry sense of humor he instructed his secretary to tell persistent callers that he was not available because he was "out on consultation."[34]

FEDERAL AID

As often happens in implementing new procedures, the board's busing policy produced another unwanted situation: children out of walking distance from their homes could not go home for lunch. While some schools had lunch programs as early as 1915, most did not provide hot lunches for the students, and certainly not with public funds. The board traditionally held that parents, not schools, were responsible for feeding children. In 1944 the Board even rejected a check for $638.60 from the State of Utah's education department as "an allocation for school lunch" at Edison School (operated by the school's PTA). The board felt that to do so would commit the Salt Lake schools to a permanent lunch program "and may open the way for entrance into other City schools of the State lunch program."[35]

Many people throughout the nation had similar attitudes, but in Salt Lake City such resistance came with a peculiarly Mormon twist. Although no official statement came from church leaders, editorials in the *Deseret News* in the late 1940s and early 1950s expressed decided opposition to federal aid—for anything. In spite of this, every school districts in the Utah, except for Salt Lake, had accepted the federal funds for hot-lunch programs. The Salt Lake board was evenly split on the issue; opponents predicted that accepting federal aid—even for school lunches—would erode local control. In spite of support from parents, health authorities, and the superintendent, it was not until the early 1970s that the board finally accepted federal support for school lunch program. However, at least one board member, Esther Landa, was elected to the board in the interim *because* of her support of federal aid.[36]

Such resistance was hardly new. In 1949 the board passed a unanimous resolution opposing proposals then before Congress that would authorize

---

33. Bennion, Oral History, 10 Apr. 1974; Esther Landa, Oral History, 17 May 1991. Landa (the only Jewish board member) told me that just before this mission call was issued, she had commented to her husband that the problem could, in fact, be solved with a mission call.
34. Bennion, *Recollections*, 149-50.
35. R. Y. Gray, Letter to Committee on Finance, Board of Education, Minutes, 11 Jan. 1944.
36. Bennion, Oral History, 10 Apr. 1974.

$300,000,000 in federal aid to states. They sent a copy of their position to Utah's Democratic Senator, Elbert D. Thomas, who since the mid-thirties had been championing a Federal Aid to Education Bill in the U.S. Senate. President LeGrand Backman said the board saw the bill as a step toward socialism's invasion of "the American way of life": "[Only] local autonomy and complete supervision, control and administration of our own schools . . . will preserve our national heritage and keep our children unhampered from regimentation, and will act as a bulwark against the aggression of foreign influences and ideologies that are contrary to our God-given right of free agency, and the desires and hopes of the founders of our great nation."[37] Although in 1920 the *Deseret News* had actually come out in favor of federal aid, saying that "No effort is too difficult and no investment too costly if it will enable the public schools to turn out young men and women of mental, moral and physical strength," in the early days of the Cold War the *News* took a more conservative tack, and praised the board of education for its stand. The 1949 editorial criticized Senator Thomas as not "hitting it off well with the Salt Lake City Board of Education." Thomas, for his part, told LeGrand Backman that Salt Lake's district didn't have to accept federal funds; but "for Salt Lake City to be opposed to this legislation because they do not need it where the rest of the country needs it so badly seems to me to a little inconsiderate." Thomas cited historical evidence about federal funding to Utah's institutions of higher education and also the massive infusion of federal aid in the form of the G.I. Bill of Rights, which he had helped sponsor. Thomas asserted that no legislation would benefit future generations more than the National Science Foundation Bill, the Federal Aid to Education Bill, and the National School Services Bill. To refuse cooperation with these proposed bills would hurt the children of Salt Lake City.[38]

The Salt Lake *Tribune*, in contrast, wholeheartedly supported the concept of federal aid and singled out Senator Thomas as commendable, along with some Republicans. "[W]here the kids are the money ain't," the *Tribune* claimed, arguing that federal aid would equalize educational opportunity. The editorial compared federal aid to Utah's long-standing practice of poorer districts receiving aid from wealthier districts. Aid would eliminate the "dangerous educational 'slums'" appearing in many parts of the country, and would "insure that no future citizen of the United States is denied an adequate education."[39]

The Utah Educational Association formally criticized the way in which the *News* had "unfairly" handled the difference of opinion between the Board and Senator Thomas, including unwarranted "inferences concerning the loyalty to American ideals of the supporters of Federal aid legislation." The UEA deplored "the unfair and unbecoming methods of the editors of the *DESERET NEWS* and

---

37. "Senator Thomas vs. School Board," *Deseret News*, 19 Apr. 1949.

38. *Deseret News*, 5 June 1920, as cited in A. I. Champlin, "Editorial Policies of the Deseret News and Salt Lake Tribune Newspapers Towards Education in Utah," M.A. thesis, University of Utah, 1963, 58-59; Elbert D. Thomas to LeGrand Backman, 9 Apr. 1949.

39. *Salt Lake Tribune*, 1 May 1949 as cited in Champlin, "Editorial Policies," 59-61; also see *Salt Lake Tribune*, 17 May 1949, for a follow-up article on Senator Thomas.

members of the Salt Lake City Board of Education," while endorsing federal aid as a "means of strengthening America through the improvement of the literacy and civic competence of its citizens."[40] The following year Elbert D. Thomas was unexpectedly defeated by Utah businessman Wallace Bennett. Certainly his support of "socialistic" federal aid did not endear him to conservatives who saw federal aid to education as an alien, foreign ideology.[41]

The largely male twelve-member board had to be prodded and cajoled into looking beyond their own cultural experience. In board member Esther Landa's view, board members often viewed the problems of the poor in the schools as capable of being resolved through the Mormon-style Welfare Plan, in which families do all they can before calling on external aid, a tendency that desensitized many affluent male board members to the poverty in Salt Lake's (largely non-Mormon) Central City area. A growing awareness among the electorate, however, brought three women with a deep commitment to social consciousness to the board in the 1960s: Esther Landa, a long-time social activist; Ada Burton, a public health nurse; and June Orme, a registered nurse. Together they pushed for recognition of Salt Lake City's social problems and for federal aid to help alleviate them. According to Landa, a board meeting held in the Central City created something akin to culture shock for many on the board; they had never been exposed to the conditions that existed among the city's poor.[42] Eventually, in the 1960s, innovations such as "Headstart" were accepted as part of the city's educational program, although not until the 1970s could it be announced that "Lunch is served"—with federal assistance.

COLD WAR CURRICULUM AND THE CYCLE OF REFORM

During Lynn Bennion's Cold War tenure, hardly anything happened in the schools that could not be connected to a national pre-occupation with the Soviet threat. The "great fear," as anthropologist Jules Henry has characterized it, influenced everything about the schools—from the practice of having students scramble under desks during simulated atomic bomb attacks to the increased time spent on the study of mathematics and science as a means of enhancing the nation's response to foreign attack.

In a memo to parents following the Soviet development of an atomic bomb, Bennion explained that schools must "be ready in case of bombing by enemies." A pamphlet was distributed detailing the drills and practice to be followed to prepare for an atomic attack. The program tried to minimize alarm among pupils and avoid "giving them exaggerated ideas concerning the danger that threatens." The memo concluded that "as destructive as we know the atomic bomb is, there

---

40. Alan M. West to Utah Education Association members, 3 May 1949.

41. Republican campaign literature explicitly tagged Thomas as a "communist." During a round-table discussion of federal aid at the UEA convention, he was booed by the educators assembled in the Mormon Tabernacle. Rulon R. Garfield, "An Approach to the Politics of Elbert D. Thomas," M.A. thesis, University of Utah, 1956, chapter 1.

42. Bennion, Oral History, 10 Apr. 1974; Esther Landa, Oral History, 17 May 1991.

is no evidence to justify a feeling of hopelessness or helplessness in the event of such a bombing."[43] In what later seemed "an outrageous" situation, Robert Bullough remembered crawling under fixed desks in his classroom, when the atomic attack signal was sounded and crouching up in the hallway of Garfield School with his head between his legs waiting for the "all clear" signal. As if, given the nature of atomic radiation, there really could be an "all clear."[44]

Eventually, such practice drills became passe, not because atomic bombs were less threatening, but because a new Soviet challenge—Sputnik—was seen as a direct commentary on America's public schools. Few national commissions and few educational reports ever had as much effect as this small Soviet satellite, the first ever, on the American educational establishment. As educational historian Lawrence Cremin described it, "a shocked and humbled nation embarked on a bitter orgy of pedagogical soul searching."[45]

Soviet success, in the thinking of many people, was due to the favorite whipping boy of the American experience: the public school. Admiral Hyman Rickover, the father of the American nuclear submarine, berated the schools for low standards and despised "the theory of John Dewey's adherents that the purpose of education is to prepare the child for life adjustment." Schools, Rickover believed, exist to "train the mind in the arts and sciences," not to focus on "citizenship, group living and apprentice garage mechanicship." The Admiral averred that the school year should be lengthened, a national standard of excellence should be established—not by professional "pedagogues," but by nationally recognized scholars—and special attention should be paid to talented children.[46] Never mind that John Dewey was *not* a proponent of Life Adjustment Education of the 1940s and that most public schools had never embraced Progressive Education, the criticisms of high profile individuals like Rickover was cause for introspection. Some said that Rickover's view was limited by his own interests in national defense—"perspective by periscope"—but there can be no doubt that Sputnik and its accompanying critics had unloosed an avalanche of curriculum change, which eventually rumbled into the Salt Lake Valley.

Prior to the Sputnik-induced reforms, and under Bennion's leadership, in 1954 a committee consisting of ten teachers, principals, and Assistant Superintendent for Curriculum and Instruction Arthur E. Arnesen produced a curriculum report that focused on perceived needs of students. Some impetus for the report came from a 1950-51 decision to reintroduce the traditional twelve-year program for which more courses were needed. (Although students who went through the eleven-year program did as well in university studies as did others, reasons for abandoning the program included: a belief that students were missing out on some of the social experiences of high school and that the Salt Lake

43. M. Lynn Bennion, Memo to The Parents of Pupils in Salt Lake City Schools, 16 Nov. 1951. Washington School PTA Scrapbook, Special Collections, University of Utah.

44. Robert V. Bullough, Jr., Oral History, 11 Apr. 1990.

45. Lawrence A. Cremin, *The Transformation of the School* (New York: Vantage Books, 1964), 346.

46. Robert Wallace, "A Deluge of Honors for an Exasperating Admiral," *Life* (8 Sept. 1958): 114.

City football teams were not doing as well as they might have with twelfth graders on their teams.[47]) The curriculum committee reorganized the curriculum
with a typically progressive rationale—the schools need to be changed "in light
of new times and changed needs." In a prepared text, *Curriculum Foundations for
the Public Schools of Salt Lake City (Revised)*, the committee, aided by teachers and
parents, spelled out essential purposes the schools should serve.

The seven essential purposes identified would have made Admiral Rickover
cringe. Designed to guide the development of the curriculum in Salt Lake City
"now and in the years immediately ahead," the report said schools should: "develop an understanding of, and an abiding faith in democracy; promote physical
and mental health; cultivate a wholesome philosophy of life; develop an effective
command of basic skills; develop aesthetic insights and satisfactions; promote
appropriate use of man's resources and environment; [and] build a foundation
for vocational competency."[48]

These aims recalled the "Cardinal Principles" of 1918—discussed in Chapter
Five. The early 1950s in Salt Lake seemed to exude an expansionist mood, viewing the curriculum as designed to meet a multiplicity of needs rather than the
"training the mind" ideology favored by those who wanted a purely intellectual
curriculum.

This progressive, student-needs theme continued to dominate the talk about
schools. If a photographic essay on school activities—included in the superintendent's report on the eve of Sputnik—indicates accurately what was happening, it
appears as if schools had broken out of the traditional row on row of passive students being drilled by information-dispensing teachers. Pictures showed students "learning by doing": brushing teeth, dressing up, painting, recording
experiments, reading class rules, making maps, and writing poetry. Another segment, entitled "At school I have good friends," showed students attending student council and deciding "what our class should do." The high school section
mentioned "hard study" as crucial to high school, of course, but placed decided
emphasis on "social living."

The report presented the traditional basics as a means to an end: to increase
the enjoyment of literature, the ability to compute grocery bills, and even lay a
foundation for technical careers. Science instruction was vital because of its increasing role in modern society and social studies and health education were designed to help students live healthy, "successful lives in a rapidly changing
world." In addition, Dr. Bennion highlighted the non-traditional aspects of the
curriculum:

Of commanding importance is our responsibility to lift the eyes of children
above the sordid aspects of living to which they are daily exposed. This we at-

---

47. Orvil C. England, "Cooperative University Achievement of Students Having Eleven Years
and Twelve Years Elementary-Secondary Preparation," Ed.D. diss., Leland Stanford Junior University,
1947; Bennion, Oral History, 3 June 1991.
48. *Curriculum Foundations for the Public Schools of Salt Lake City, Revised* (Salt Lake City: Board
of Education, 1953).

tempt to do by giving them an appreciation of beauty and by showing them the constructive side of life. Every child needs daily contacts with great art, music and literature. Every child needs to see and to feel the beauty in commonplace things that can add enjoyment, tone, feeling and warmth to life.[49]

In 1960, when the next school report was published, the schools showed Sputnik's effects: the content and cover showed not the happy faces of children "having fun at school," but a stark line drawing of a rocket and a very factory-like representation of the new Highland High School under the caption: "Facing the Challenge." The pictures inside showed serious students studying the hard sciences and illustrating their work at the Annual Science Fair—annual, that is, since 1958. Students were motivated by awards of $50 and $100 Savings Certificates. The winners were chosen not by professional educators, but by "a core of well-known scientists from the universities, colleges and industries of Utah." Bennion acknowledged that "the stimulating effect of Sputnik is reflected throughout this biennial report." Although Bennion held that the school could not abandon its social functions and ignore the needs of individual students, the nation's perceived lack of scientists and mathematicians shaped definition of what was educationally important.[50]

As historian Joel Spring has suggested, during the Cold War the aims of American foreign policy had more to do with shaping American schools than did the deliberations of educators. Even foreign language instruction received federal funding; the State Department during the Eisenhower administration perceived fluency in foreign languages as a need of national security. This national priority led Salt Lake schools to offer Latin, German, French, Spanish, Russian and Arabic. The Salt Lake District's innovative Russian program at Highland High School won recognition in a *Life* magazine article. The early 1960s was the heyday of TV's promise to revolutionize the schools; in 1959, a pilot project for teaching Russian by television to fifth graders in eleven schools was initiated, and a similar French program was initiated in seventeen elementary schools in Salt Lake City. Not all students were eligible for this experimental program; it tended to favor those identified as having "high intelligence." According to Spring, focusing on academically talented students was a common characteristic of Cold War reforms. However, as far as can be determined, these innovations did not have long-term effects on the district's foreign language programs.[51]

Given the varied and sometimes conflicting nature of the demands placed on them, the schools of Salt Lake City probably did as good a job as could be expected. There is little to indicate that schools anywhere in the country resisted the encroachments of federally promoted science and mathematics curricula or

---

49. *Sixty-sixth and Sixty-seventh Annual Reports*, 1955-57, iii.
50. *Facing the Challenge: Sixty-eighth and Sixty-ninth Annual Reports*, 1957-59, 3-11.
51. Joel Spring, *The Sorting Machine Revisited* (New York: Longman, 1989), 64, 69; "Salt Lake Adds Russian to 3Rs," *Life* (6 Oct. 1958): 113-16; *Salt Lake Tribune*, 12 Aug., 3 Oct., 22 Oct. 1959; Shawn H. Ford, "Salt Lake City's Curriculum and Implementation, 1943-1972" Term Paper, University of Utah, 1990.

questioned the priorities which the national market dictated. The public schools' resilience to quick change, in spite of frequent criticism, recalls Colm Brogan's definition of democracy: It's like a raft that can survive being tossed around on the ocean; in contrast to large totalitarian ships that sink when they hit a storm, democracy never quite sinks, but "dammit, your feet are always wet." After more than a century of efforts to perfect what cannot be perfected, educators should have been used to sloshing around in the waters of reform.

SUBVERSIVES IN THE SCHOOLS

The Cold War not only affected the curriculum, but spilled over into how teachers were regarded in the classroom. Any hint of criticizing or questioning American policies by a school teacher would raise the hackles of patrons. The early 1950s witnessed national debates over Communists in the government and other public institutions, stimulated by the antics of Wisconsin's Senator Joseph McCarthy. While not much "red-baiting" appears to have gone on in Utah schools, teachers who tried to stimulate critical thinking in students were sometimes labelled as "Communists," simply for seeking to increase student awareness. Around 1951 a history teacher at West High School, Joe Curtis, was accused by some students and their parents of being a member of the Communist Party. The vice-principal, Elva Cotterell, asked if he were and he denied any connection. He was, she recalled, a very good teacher, though quite radical in his views of Washington policies. Parental pressure prompted his being reassigned to East High, but his reputation followed him. He became known as "that Communist social studies teacher" and negative student response undermined his effectiveness as a teacher. He was eventually declared unfit to teach by the administration and left the school system.[52]

Given Salt Lake's conservative religious orientation and the election of a conservative governor, J. Bracken Lee, during the 1950s, the "great fear" of communism was a frequent topic of public discourse. Numerous LDS general conference addresses during this period inveighed against "Godless communism" and its handmaiden, socialism. Bennion's name turned up with respect to communism when Elder Mark E. Peterson of the LDS Quorum of Twelve Apostles spoke to the Salt Lake Kiwanis Club. Speaking on the evils of communism, he lambasted Bennion for recommending the communist *Daily Worker* on a reading list sent to Salt Lake City teachers. Bennion was chagrined that Peterson had misread the reading list: the *Daily Worker* had been included on a "not recommended" list. Bennion confronted Elder Peterson with the facts in the case, upon which Peterson admitted having become emotional about the communist menace and that he indeed had been misinformed. He accompanied Bennion to the office of the *Salt Lake Tribune* and there wrote out an apology, printed the next day under the headline: "Apostle Makes Retraction."[53] In retrospect, one might

---

52. Earl Harmer, Oral History, 27 Aug. 1990; telephone conversation with Earl Harmer and Elva Cotterell, 24 Feb. 1992.

53. Bennion, *Recollections*, 161.

wonder why Bennion, with his liberal commitment to examining all aspects of controversial issues, would recommend that teachers not read such basic information about the "enemy." The answer lies imbedded in Apostle Peterson's public response. If Lynn Bennion had followed his intellectual bent for reflective examination of all issues, even communism, there is no doubt that his tenure as superintendent would have been curtailed. As a superintendent under the aegis of a publicly elected school board, Bennion had to moderate his intellectual perspective with a pragmatic need to survive.

Another "subversive" issue surfaced in the last year of Lynn Bennion's administration, when he was compelled to mediate between patron demands that a teacher be fired and the constitutional guarantees on freedom of speech. In 1968 the U.S. Attorney General, Ramsey Clark, at the behest of Senator Everett Dirksen, requested the Subversive Activities Control Board to declare seven persons as bonafide members of a subversive organization, namely the Communist Party of the United States of America. Among the seven were Wayne D. Holley of Mapleton, Utah, and Robert Archuleta of Salt Lake City, who were identified respectively as chairman and secretary-treasurer of the Communist Party of Utah.[54] When word spread to Utah, a delegation of parents from the Riverside School area, including the bishop of the LDS ward, wrote Superintendent Bennion demanding that Archuleta, who had been teaching in Salt Lake City since 1953, be suspended and that an investigation be conducted into the allegation.

Archuleta, who on constitutional grounds and on the advice of his lawyer refused to admit membership in the Party, met for three hours with the president of the board, George A. Christensen. Christensen concluded that Archuleta was a loyal American and that he could not be dismissed. Bennion concluded that the issue should be studied by legal experts, a position many parents interpreted as Bennion's attempt to stone-wall them. The controversy led to telephone threats against Archuleta and his family, and at a public meeting called by the Riverside School PTA he heard comments such as "Kill the dirty son-of-a-bitch." No evidence was ever presented at this meeting that he had taught communism to his students. But Archuleta noticed that children were apt to be more combative after weekends at home. At the PTA "hearing" he pointedly refused to answer questions of "Are you or aren't you?" an attitude that didn't sit well with the parents and local LDS leaders. Noting that Archuleta had never done anything wrong, one speaker at the meeting surmised that Archuleta must have been a very good teacher, because "they [the Russians] would never send us one of their worst people." Others claimed that at times he had omitted the words "under God" from the daily pledge of allegiance in his classroom.[55]

Two petitions were circulated in the community: one to keep him and one to fire him from the Riverside School, but according to Archuleta, the latter petition had many more signatures. The PTA meeting passed a resolution that he

---

54. "Subversive Board Asked to Cite 7 as Communists," *New York Times*, 2 July 1968.
55. The discussion of this incident is based on Robert Archuleta, Oral History, 18 Feb. 1992, and Bennion, *Recollections*, 160-61.

be removed, but the board attorney handed down an opinion that to remove a teacher for having political beliefs without evidence of attempts to undermine the government would open up the board to a law suit. Consequently, in February 1969 Archuleta was appointed to head a new adult school program funded by the federal government, designed to help dropouts get their high school diplomas. In December 1969 the U.S. Court of Appeals reversed the decision of the Subversive Activities Control Board, saying that Holley's and Archuleta's constitutional right of free speech had been violated by the board's findings and the following year the U.S. Supreme Court upheld the Court of Appeals decision.[56]

A NEW KIND OF TEACHER CORPS

When a district supervisor approached veteran teacher Louise Benz at Irving Junior High School in Sugarhouse, circa 1950s, about the need to modify her approach to teaching English through formal "grammar, diagramming and all the things that later were absolutely forbidden," she stood up to the pressure to modernize her approach: "Look here, dearie, I was teaching this when you were in diapers and I am not going to change." A staunch Presbyterian who started off her first class of every day with silent prayer, Benz was feared and liked for the selfsame attributes of strictness and unyielding discipline. Her approach to classroom management she encapsulated in her advice to a new teacher: "Dearie, that first six weeks is hell. Then I just sit back and coast." She was thoroughly organized, taught her students how to write, and knew precisely what she was about from the opening bell.[57]

Although national affairs shaped the curriculum of the Cold War era, it is important to recognize that teachers were by no means inconsequential; Louise Benz's perspective and attitude captures the essence of the traditional teacher's role: that of a knowledgeable professional, in charge and knowing exactly where she was going with her students. In sharp contrast to Benz's approach to teaching English, a new teacher at West High, Earl Harmer, during the same period was successfully minimizing formal grammar instruction, emphasizing student writing and using *Life* and *Time* magazines in the classroom. His classes put together their own reference library and he emphasized themes in literature such as propaganda, prejudice, or the problems of growing up, but to satisfy the demands of the formal curriculum he also had his classes study one Shakespeare play each year. On one occasion he was criticized by the superintendent for requiring too much knowledge of a play's content on examinations. Dr. Bennion would apparently have preferred more attention to meaning and process, but Harmer felt he

---

56. "Informers Tag 2 Utahns as Commies," *Deseret News*, 4 Oct. 1968; "Court Calls Halt to Red Disclosure," *Deseret News*, 13 Dec. 1969; "Justices Let Ruling Stand against Subversive Control," *Deseret News*, Apr. 1970. I am indebted to Robert Archuleta for newspaper clippings dealing with this issue.

57. Dorothy Smith, Oral History, 2 Aug. 1990. The comment was made to Dorothy Smith's daughter, Ann Curtis.

was giving adequate attention to both aspects of teaching.[58] Both Benz and Harmer can probably be described as successful teachers, although one was very traditional and the other flexible and open-ended. However, both were subject-matter oriented and did not involve students to any great degree in the development of classroom materials. At the other end of the subject matter—student spectrum was Dortha McDonald, a student-centered and socially aware teacher who recalled: "I really didn't have to know much to teach first grade, but I had to know and love children." She perceived students as "having a good sense of humor and a deep understanding of the problems of life"; that perspective shaped her own handling of classroom process and discipline.[59]

When Lynn Bennion became superintendent in 1945, he faced a general teacher shortage, exacerbated by the war taking many male teachers into the armed forces and by attracting others to war industries. The ban on married women teachers had been relaxed, as had certification requirements. With increased class sizes clearly in the wings as service personnel returned home and continued to establish families, the district needed more teachers. However, according to a 1948 national survey, 94 percent of the people surveyed considered teaching as an unacceptable choice of careers; among the major reasons for this was the abysmally low reward for a life-time of service in the classrooms. In the post war era teachers made relatively less than persons involved in manufacturing, let alone the much larger salary gap between teachers and other "professionals." This was a continuation of an historic pattern in which teacher salaries have always tended to be lower than wages in manufacturing and other professional occupations, even as the requirements to become a teacher have increased.[60]

According to Dean John Wahlquist, a salary increase in Salt Lake City around 1947 led to a substantial 200 percent increase in students deciding to enter the education program at the University of Utah. But even this increase, which made the beginning salary $2280, was still low compared with many other similar cities and was, according to Wahlquist, "not enough to hold a large majority of graduating teachers in the profession."[61]

Teachers were generally subservient to the board and to the administration. They simply had nothing to do with establishing salary schedules, and the paternalistic perspective the Salt Lake board displayed toward teachers was not untypical of conservative cities in the nation at large. Although Bennion wanted to improve the standing of teachers in the community, he was himself saddled with a powerful board that let him know negotiation was out of the question when dealing with teachers' salaries. Dorothy Smith, secretary of the Salt Lake City Teacher's Association in 1947, recalled sitting in on many "bitter meetings" in

58. Earl Harmer, Oral History, 3 Aug., 27 Aug. 1990.
59. Dortha McDonald, Oral History, 23 Aug. 1990.
60. Susan B. Carter, "Incentives and Rewards to Teaching," in Donald Warren, ed., *American Teachers: Histories of a Profession at Work* (New York: MacMillan, 1969), 54-55.
61. "94% of High School Youths Shun Teaching Career," *Salt Lake Tribune*, 14 Feb. 1948; "S. L. Students 'Face' 82 New School Teachers," *Salt Lake Tribune*, 19 July 1948.

which the president of the board, LeGrand Backman, would assert that "We are the Board of Education"—meaning "we are in control and you do just as we say." Disputes of this kind were regular occurrences, "just not nice at all," and stood out in stark contrast to the chummy relationship that existed in earlier years.

Trying to mediate between the board and the teachers who pushed for negotiation was probably Bennion's most trying and difficult task as superintendent. When the board gave the president of the Salt Lake Teacher's Association a mere two to three minutes to make his case for a salary increase, Bennion thought it degrading, and he supported the move to have a professional spokesman appointed by the Teacher's Association.[62] Attorney John S. Boyden was the first person appointed to this job; many board members resented his presence as a negotiator. In Bennion's view, much of the hostility grew out of the fact that some members of the board were bishops and stake presidents in the Mormon church, used to a top-down relationship with subordinates. Now they were forced by another faithful Mormon, Boyden, to deal with their subordinates as equals.

In 1947 the Teachers Association, with Boyden as its executive secretary, demanded that the board set a pay schedule of from $2,220 to $3,840. The teachers were not satisfied, even when the board adjusted their offer upwards; for the first time in the history of the district the teachers refused to sign their contracts. The board stalled until pressure was exerted by groups such as the Junior Chamber of Commerce, the Salt Lake Council of the PTA, and the Salt Lake Council of Veterans of World War II to meet the last teacher offer, which they finally did by a vote of seven to five. A strike was averted.[63] Eventually Bennion set up a "professional relations committee" consisting of four board members, four teachers and their executive secretary, the superintendent, and the president of the administrators' association. In time this group developed a negotiating process for salary concerns.[64]

However, in 1951-52 the negotiating process broke down and teachers once again gave their unsigned contracts to Boyden. Bennion played a mediating role, but his tendency to empathize with the teachers wore thin; he became frustrated "and emotionally very distressed" by what he perceived as teacher intransigence and their refusal to see that the board did not have unlimited resources. The teacher negotiators simply said that resources were Bennion's and the board's problem—they just wanted to teach and to be paid decently to do it. According to Earl Harmer, on one occasion the board agreed to meet the teachers' demands for an increase in dollar support to Blue Cross and Blue Shield Insurance plus a twenty-five dollar annual salary increase.[65] The board may not have wanted to "negotiate," but results indicate that they were dealing directly with an increasingly aggressive teacher association.

---

62. Bennion, Oral History, 4 Apr. 1974; Dorothy Smith, Oral History, 2 Aug. 1990.

63. Bennion, Oral History, 3 June 1991, 24-25; Leonard D. Carter, "The Development of an Adversarial Employment Relationship between Teachers and Boards of Education in Utah, 1940-1970," Ph.D. diss., University of Utah, 1985, 55-65.

64. Bennion, Oral History, 4 Apr. 1974.

65. Harmer, Oral History, 3 Aug., 27 Aug. 1990.

In the last decade of Bennion's tenure teacher salaries became more an issue involving the Utah Education Association and the state legislature and governor. More and more of the budget was coming from statewide sources and local involvement was reduced accordingly. In the early 1950s conservative Governor J. Bracken Lee consistently blocked larger state appropriations for education, aided in large measure by fiscally conservative Mormon legislators and church leaders, particularly J. Reuben Clark, Jr., of the First Presidency. With the accession of former educator David O. McKay to the presidency of the LDS church in 1951, there was a shift toward church support of teacher demands. That and continued pressure from the teacher organizations led to increased state aid to public schools and for a few years there was a lull in the conflict. However, during George D. Clyde's tenure as governor the issue of increased appropriations rose again. Teachers were more militant, the governor was obdurate, and this time considerable church opposition was evident. The fragile alliance built during the 1950s between the church hierarchy and the teachers came apart. Eventually teachers throughout Utah went on strike in 1964 and the National Education Association imposed sanctions on the state. Utah teachers, a large number from the Sale Lake District, had become examples of the new assertiveness gripping the teaching profession nationwide.[66]

When Lynn Bennion addressed the teacher's institute in September 1964 he may have had the controversy in mind as he counselled teachers about the need to enlarge perspectives. At least for the *Deseret News* editor, Bennion provided in his comments some guidelines which it thought might be useful in avoiding what went wrong "on both sides—in the summer's unpleasantness and what must be avoided in future school controversies." Good will and a sense of self-esteem were necessary for differing points of view to be reconciled: "It is not necessary to have the same points of view. It is necessary to be understood, appreciated, and respected. To create a good human climate, we must have relative freedom from fears and from prejudice, and the ability to dispassionately analyze information from many sources. If we can rid ourselves of biases, prejudices, and fears, there is hope that we can understand and appreciate others."[67] This reflects Bennion's persistent liberal, reasoned, non-confrontational perspective. Within the decade of the 1960s, when protests over Vietnam and racism became ever more strident, many would raise questions as to whether it was possible or even desirable to be so detached in decision making. However, Bennion strove to implement some sense of detachment in his administration of Salt Lake City's public schools. It pained him when the press of events and political, economic, and ideological tensions simply did not allow his ideals to be fully realized.

In the aftermath of these years, a new governor was elected, Democrat Calvin Rampton, whose platforms had included "adequate school finance programs." His administration and the new legislature, in which Democrats had a

66. West, *My Life as an Advocate*, 82-96, 123-30; for the development of unionism among Utah teachers, see W. Dale Rees, "The Professional Education Association Movement in Utah: An Interpretive History," Ph.D. diss., University of Utah, 1977.

67. "RX for School Ills," *Deseret News*, 15 Sept. 1964, as cited in Bennion, *Recollections*, 182-84.

majority in both houses, enacted a "considerably expanded finance program," which Rampton hoped would give Utah's elementary and secondary teachers "not only a living wage, but a wage with which they could live in dignity."[68]

A new phase of teacher participation in the political process had been reached. The U.E.A. was now a bonafide union. As Leonard Carter notes: "The change [in the period 1947 to 1964] was from the traditional 'master-servant' model of employment relationship to one of legal equals in negotiations." As John Evans reflected on the events of 1963-64 he said that the relationship changed precisely when the teachers called their two day "recess" and some boards actually docked teachers for being absent: "[T]he old paternalistic attitude toward teachers just wasn't going to work anymore . . . those days were gone."[69]

RELEASED TIME (REPRISE)

According to M. Lynn Bennion, the LDS church never pressured him on any school issue. In a sense, the church *per se* did not have to exert pressure: LDS members of the community were more than assertive in seeing their values represented in school matters. Mormons were in the majority and, consequently, for most of his term in office the board was almost entirely Mormon.[70] Stereotypes aside, however, Mormons do not agree on every public issue, as illustrated in 1956 when the seminary issue again became the focus of concern.

At a regular board meeting on 12 June some two hundred and fifty people turned up. The meeting had to be adjourned, as in 1943, to the auditorium of Bryant Junior High School. The LDS church Board of Education, through its representatives, Ernest L. Wilkinson and William E. Berrett, planned to request that high school graduation credit, up to one unit, should be given for Bible courses taught in "private schools" (i.e., LDS seminaries). The president of the board, LeGrand Backman, at the outset of the meeting had announced that the board would not make a decision on the issue that night, but would take it under advisement and "come to their own conclusions."

William Berrett argued that granting credit would make seminary students "more Moral, God-fearing and Honorable." He claimed that the course of study would be submitted to the board of education and the staff to "demonstrate it is non-sectarian."[71] Ernest L. Wilkinson, head of the LDS Church Education System and president of Brigham Young University, claimed such credit would be constitutional, citing recent Supreme Court decisions.[72]

In response, at least seven individuals, including representatives of the Religious Liberty Association, the Committee for Religious Freedom, the Salt Lake

---

68. Calvin L. Rampton, *As I Recall*, Floyd A. O'Neil and Gregory C. Thompson, eds. (Salt Lake City: University of Utah Press, 1989), 122-23, 134.

69. Carter, "The Development of an Adversarial Employment," 221-22.

70. Bennion, Oral History, 10 Apr. 1974.

71. Board of Education, Minutes, 12 June 1956. For a detailed treatment of this request for credit, see my "Masons and Mormons: Released-Time Politics in Salt Lake City, 1930-1956," *Journal of Mormon History* 19 (Spring 1993): 104-14.

72. Kern Alexander, *School Law* (St. Paul: West Publishing Co., 1980), 235 37.

Ministerial Association, and the Nevada-Utah Conference of Seventh Day Adventists voiced their strong opposition to the proposal on the grounds that it was an indirect support of religion, that it went contrary to national and the Utah constitutions, that it violated separation of church and state, and put churches not able to afford such a program at a distinct disadvantage. Dr. D. D. Stockman, who had presided at the 1943 seminary debate, reiterated his opposition to the entire practice, but indicated that while in 1943 there had been evidence that many people wanted released time, he was not aware that a large number of people was requesting credit in 1956.[73]

Unlike the 1943 debate, the credit proposal was put on hold by the board, and they referred the issue to the Teacher and School Work Committee for study and recommendation. The board's lawyers concluded that credit would be constitutional as long as the content could be evaluated "using the same standard of scholarship as used in other courses." The course would also have to be as free "from religious instruction and sectarian control as any class in literature, history or mathematics."[74]

While Superintendent Bennion did not get involved in the public debate, it was his personal and professional opinion that such Bible courses could not be non-sectarian. They were designed to indoctrinate students with LDS views and would not bear up under close scrutiny.[75] Perhaps the requirement of having seminary courses scrutinized by professional educators dissuaded Wilkinson from persisting with the plan; in the fall of 1956, Berrett withdrew the proposal. According to a New York *Times* article, two days before the board meeting a number of board members (all of whom were LDS) were quoted as wishing "it hadn't come up."[76]

The Salt Lake School District's historic refusal to give credit for released-time religious instruction was vindicated by the decision of the Tenth Circuit Court of Appeals in 1981. The Appeals Court upheld the 1978 ruling of a federal judge that the granting credit for LDS seminary courses in the Logan City School District was an unwarranted intermingling of church and state. In the same breath, however, it reaffirmed the ruling of *Zorach vs Clawson*, upholding the concept of released-time religious instruction.[77]

One final postscript indicates that the tension over released-time seminary was still alive in the 1960s, but also illustrates the changes occurring in the Mormon community and its relationship to its public schools. Esther Landa, a prominent member of the Jewish congregation in Salt Lake City, was elected to the board of education in 1958. After a successful term she sought re-election in the

73. Board of Education, Minutes, 12 June 1956.
74. See letters of Paul B. Cannon to Judge Rulon W. Clark, 23 Aug. 1956; Rulon W. Clark and Paul F. Royall to LeGrand P. Backman and Members of Salt Lake Board of Education, 4 Dec. 1956, in appendix to Church, "Controversy of Mormons and Masons."
75. Bennion, Oral History, 10 Apr. 1974.
76. "Credit is Sought for Bible Studies," New York Times, 10 June 1956.
77. Elizabeth A. Shaw, "New Rewards for Released-Time: Lanner vs Wimmer Expands Constitutional Church-State Involvement," Utah Law Review 4 (1982): 972-75.

1960s and seemed to be assured a win. Her assurance was, however, rudely shattered on the Sunday before the election, when she was told by a Mormon friend and school teacher that at his priesthood meeting that morning, claims were made that Landa planned to use her influence to abolish the system of released-time seminary classes. Sensing certain defeat if this were accepted as fact, she mobilized her resources and the day before the election distributed to the electorate a statement categorically denying that the elimination of the released time policy was part of her educational platform. She was re-elected.[78]

THE END OF AN ERA

In the fall of 1967 M. Lynn Bennion turned 65, the traditional age for retirement, and shortly thereafter he proffered his retirement to the board, effective July 1968. He had been elected to the superintendency twelve times since 1945, a remarkable record even in the days of long-term superintendents. A special board meeting was called and President George Christensen expressed the board's opinion that Bennion should continue for another year to tie up loose ends, help prepare programs for the upcoming legislative session, and continue the professional negotiations with teachers. It was, in Bennion's words, "too interesting and exciting a time to withdraw," and he stayed on at the board's behest. At the same time, the board decided that his Assistant Superintendent, Dr. Arthur C. Wiscombe, would succeed him on 1 July 1969. In accepting his last election as superintendent, Bennion expressed the hope that the district would be able "to retain a climate where our teachers feel free to speak and will avoid discontinuing services to our students."[79]

In reporting Bennion's retirement the following year, John Cummins, the Salt Lake *Tribune's* education writer, summarized Bennion's educational credo: "It is paramount that we meet the human needs. Somehow this must come first." While acknowledging immense technological and academic growth in the schools, the former student of progressive education at Berkeley and the person who had tried to make religious education respond to people here and now was still convinced that schools must serve a social function: "Most of our problems are people problems. . . . [M]eeting social problems has always been a part of our purpose in education, but the factor of rapid social change makes this a time of stress and challenge for the educator." Revealing his basic sense that ultimately human beings are what public education should be about, Bennion was quoted as believing that

> [p]arents and teachers can cause failures because of wrong assumptions—the assumption that the child's cognitive learning is more important than the child—that this learning must take place on schedule, that all first graders must read no matter what the effort to teach them does to their personalities and their self-concepts. . . . Another false assumption is that we can do all this in school. Many

---

78. Esther Landa, Oral History, 17 May 1991.
79. Bennion, *Recollections*, 176-77.

of our present schools are giving most children academic success, college success and middle class status. But we are not adequately giving their people a sense of social responsibility and compassion. We must change our ways—get out of the school house and bring children and young adults together around great ideals and give them a chance to meet and work with people of other races and economic positions—give them a chance to act and to give of themselves in the improvement of the life of others.[80]

These words describe in large measure the posture some educators attempted to take in the ensuing decade as racism, the problems of poverty, and the issues of war and peace began to reshape the aims and purposes of schools. Perhaps Bennion saw what was on the horizon, but his successor inherited the revolution.

As he concluded his autobiography some eighteen years after his retirement, eighty-six year old M. Lynn Bennion recalled the words of John Dewey when he defined education as the "continuous reconstruction of experience," adding that only in perceiving education in this way "can one have a zest for venturing and exploring in the never ending search for constructive solutions to conditions that need improvement."[81]

Bennion's many years of service to the community was publicly recognized in 1980 when a new school was named the "M. Lynn Bennion Elementary School"—the first Salt Lake City superintendent to be so honored.

---

80. "Program will Honor Long Service of Dr. M. Lynn Bennion," *Salt Lake Tribune*, 26 May 1969.
81. Bennion, *Recollections*, 218.

Arthur C. Wiscombe
1969–73

8

"CAUGHT UP IN A WHIRLWIND"
The Administration of
Arthur C. Wiscombe, 1969–73

Lynn Bennion's quarter-century at the helm of the Salt Lake City school district typified the social calmness, stability, and upward mobility of the post-war years. The brief, tumultuous, four-year tenure of his successor, Arthur Wiscombe, reflected another national reality; the Wasatch Mountains were no barrier to the urban issues that surfaced nationally with the civil rights movement and protests generated by the Vietnam War.[1]

While Salt Lake City did not have the urban underclass of Chicago or New York, it was changing socially and economically. Between 1950 and 1960 the overall population grew by four percent to 189,000 and the schools experienced rapid enrollment increases peaking at more than 42,000 in 1959. During this period some 20 new schools were built. In contrast to this "age of expansion," after 1960 the city's population began to decline. By 1980 it had dropped by fourteen percent to a low of 163,000 with a corresponding decline in school enrollments.[2] Between 1950 and 1970 the district lost 6,000 students and a dozen schools closed—seven in Wiscombe's first year as superintendent. In addition to the overall decline in enrollments was the realization that Salt Lake's population was becoming increasingly heterogenous.

In contrast to the bedroom communities that sprang up around it, Salt Lake City had a higher percentage of people of color and citizens living below the poverty line. Although the numerical decline and ethnic and social change in the city's population had begun during Bennion's years, it did not become a matter of public debate in the schools until after he retired. The stirrings of unrest barely visible in the early sixties, became more and more pronounced as Arthur Wiscombe began to carve out his own niche in the history of the Salt Lake City School District.

THE SOCIAL CONSCIENCE OF AN INTELLECTUAL

Like his three immediate predecessors in the Salt Lake superintendency, Arthur Clark Wiscombe had his roots in the soil of rural "Mormon Country."

---

1. "Troubles of America's Major Cities Showing up in Salt Lake City," *Salt Lake Tribune*, 2 May 1972.

2. Thomas G. Alexander and James B. Allen, *Mormons and Gentiles: A History of Salt Lake City* (Boulder, CO: Pruett, 1984), 278.

Born in Roosevelt, Duchesne County, where his father was a farmer, a justice of the peace, and the bishop of the local LDS ward, Wiscombe graduated from Alterra High School, Uintah County, in 1946. Following high school, he studied social studies education at Brigham Young University where he received a Bachelor's degree in 1952. His first professional position was teaching American history and other subjects at Piute High School. In 1953 he began a Masters in Educational Administration at Columbia University. To say the least, the difference between Circleville, Utah, and Manhattan Island required an enormous adjustment for Wiscombe, his wife, and five children. Living at Harlem's edge, exposed to a large African-American population, probably helped shape the responses he would later make to minority issues in Salt Lake City.

Continuing his quest for knowledge, Wiscombe received a Master's degree in the historical and philosophical foundations of education from Harvard University in 1955. Over the next few years he taught history and philosophy of education at Brigham Young University, served as principal at Uintah High School, and also was assistant superintendent of Uintah School District. Between 1958 and 1961 he was Secondary Curriculum Consultant in the Los Angeles County Schools, followed by a one-year appointment as assistant professor of philosophy and history of education at the University of Utah. In 1962 he was appointed assistant superintendent of the Salt Lake City schools. The following year he completed an Ed.D. dissertation at the University of Colorado, entitled: "Eternalism: the Philosophical Basis of Mormon Education."[3]

Wiscombe has attributed his interest in education to his life-long involvement in the Mormon community. Public speaking, involvement in community affairs, seeking an education, and even the development of a rational perspective were actively encouraged as part of Mormon youth. He did not see any incongruity between his interests in philosophy and his commitment to the LDS church. Nevertheless, his philosophical disposition may have heightened the tensions with the board of education and some school patrons, many of whom were his co-religionists. He freely acknowledged his basic interest in philosophy of education, rather than in the details of administration. He did not actively seek the position as superintendent; when Bennion first offered his resignation in 1968, the board designated Wiscombe as his heir. On Bennion's recommendation, Wiscombe was appointed as the city's ninth superintendent, beginning 1 July 1969.[4]

THE SYSTEM CONTRACTS: SCHOOLS FOR SALE

In the early 1960s, Salt Lake's city council recognized the problems the city would face as its population dwindled. Addressing the physical and economic deterioration of the city's west side and central city areas, a program of urban renewal and revitalization was proposed. By making the central city area more attractive to residents and requiring property owners to take care of their

---

3. Arthur C. Wiscombe, Oral History, 28 June 1973.
4. Ibid., 28 June 1973.

buildings, the council hoped to stave off the uncontrolled urban sprawl that had become endemic in the nation's larger cities. By 1965, "a majority of the city commission and most representatives of the business community favored urban renewal under federal grants," but other businesses and politicians opposed the proposal. Among the latter was J. Bracken Lee, mayor of Salt Lake City, who formed a coalition with some business leaders and forced the commission to submit the issue to a citizen's referendum. A "scare campaign" that pitted traditional Mormon values of personal liberty against the oppressive power of federal funding helped defeat the revitalization proposal by a margin of six to one.[5]

While other efforts at revitalization did succeed (a new city library and new city courts were built) the city lacked an overall "master plan," and Mayor Lee continued to resist all attempts to produce one. By the time "Jake" Garn became mayor in 1972, a report on the city's condition concluded that Salt Lake "had changed from a planned community to a metropolis of blighted neighborhoods." The report identified three major reasons for this: complacency in enforcing municipal codes; denial on the part of citizens that a problem existed; and the LDS church's hesitation to "take a lead in the urban improvement movement for fear of being accused of interfering in the affairs of the community."[6]

Art Wiscombe did not need a special report to convince him that the city, including its schools, was changing for the worse. Many schools had been built during the post-war years as the city expanded. Now, as the city contracted, Wiscombe faced conditions over which he had no control. As he identified them, the major issues he had to confront were: the continuing depopulation of the central city area; the rise of de facto race- and class-based segregation in central city schools; the lack of an overarching plan for the city's schools; and the need to adjust the curriculum to benefit children of a new age. Some have characterized Superintendent Wiscombe as distant and abstract in handling school affairs. However, he was also a person of astute social insight and considerable personal courage in refusing to ignore the situation he had inherited. Wiscombe later reflected that the issues he faced were "agonizing and painful and the setting to make any superintendent quite lonely."[7]

Wiscombe's first concern was to balance the money being spent on schools with declining populations and the lack of funds for ongoing programs. This required closing certain schools. Unfortunately, the board had no firm policy on how to go about this, although it had fully supported Bennion in closing some ten schools during his superintendency, seven during his last five years. Four of these were closed because of declining population and two were replaced with new buildings.[8]

Bennion's success in closing schools without public protest may be attrib-

---

5. Alexander and Allen, *Mormons and Gentiles*, 279.

6. Ibid., 279-80.

7. Wiscombe, Oral History, 28 June 1973. In addition to the oral history, I have used information gleaned during an informal conversation with Arthur Wiscombe in May 1992.

8. Data based on table of school closures since 1953 in files of Salt Lake City School District Office.

uted to the fact that the closures were spread over a longer period, located in politically weak areas of the city (i.e., *not* on the East Bench), and at least two
closures were accompanied by building replacements. In addition, the pace of
depopulation had been not as great during the early '60s and the mood of "public protest" less strident. Bennion also had long, personable relationship with the
board and the public to back him up. In contrast, Wiscombe was new and still
had to prove himself. His personal detached manner and analytical style, making
him able to articulate the issues very clearly, also alienated him from the board
and patrons.

In the early months of his tenure, Wiscombe sought the advice of "prestigious community leaders" on the issues facing the schools, including school closures and the plight of minority students. His advisers warned that, as pertinent
as these issues were, he could deal with them only at great political risk. He
would do best, he was counselled, to inform the community about issues and
wait for power pressures in the community to "emerge and force an accommodation" to one alternative or another. This meant that teachers, demanding higher
salaries while money was wasted on empty schools, would be forced to strike.
The board, in turn, would have to give up some schools to satisfy teacher demands. Wiscombe refused to sit back idly and watch the situation deteriorate.
Other people, some of the "most powerful people" in the Utah legislature, reas-
sured him that he could do nothing to prevent the closing of schools. Still, if he
attempted to get ahead of public sentiment he would end up out on a limb.

In spite of the risks, Wiscombe took what he considered a "statesmanlike"
approach, refusing to be "indifferent to the improper expenditure of hundreds of
thousands of hard-to-come-by taxes and [to] what's happening to the children
through this process."[9] By December 1969, the district's school population had
dropped to 34,000 (7,000 fewer than its peak in 1958) while the operational
costs mounted. By 1984, it was predicted, enrollment would dip to 28,000. Wiscombe reported that the district was planning to consolidate some twelve
schools. He began to educate the community about the schools' problems. Barely
six months into his term, Wiscombe spoke to the Salt Lake Kiwanis Club and
outlined his plan to improve the district, including the need to close more
schools. In addition to declining population and deteriorating buildings—some
from the 1890s and early 1900s—was the escalating cost of running the system,
which had risen from $200 per pupil in 1960 to $2,100 in 1970.

By closing six elementary schools, Wiscombe told the Kiwanis, between
$270,000 to $395,000 could benefit other schools in the district; failure to close
schools would eventually bankrupt the whole system. Other proposals included
the possibility of shifting the sixth grade into "middle schools" and the ninth
grade out of junior high schools. These middle schools would ring the central
city area and busing would make most efficient use of the schools —transporting
students into and out of the central city area. School boundaries would be set in
a pie shape so that each would have an equal mix of central city populations and

---

9. Wiscombe, Oral History, 20 June 1973.

those from other geographic areas in the city. This arrangement, he believed, would prevent the city's black and Hispanic students from being segregated in central city schools.[10] A week later Wiscombe reminded the board that "people cannot have their cake and eat it too." With the district facing teacher demands for higher salaries and parent demands for better programs, Wiscombe reaffirmed the need to close six schools: Hamilton, Longfellow, Garfield, Onequa, Curtis and Grandview.

By a margin of one vote (6-5), a divided board approved the Superintendent's recommendation to close the schools. Immediately citizens called meetings to protest the decision. Two hundred irate parents met at Curtis Elementary School, one of the smallest and newest schools, situated on the East Side around Fourteenth South and Twenty-Second East. Wiscombe bluntly reminded parents that this was only the beginning of the long-term project to close many schools. Eight had been closed in the past ten years, he said, but it would be necessary to close three each year for the district to break even. The information was hardly the kind to endear the superintendent to his listeners.[11]

Some parents argued that move-ins would replenish the Curtis area shortly, but others acknowledged that the district had, in the past, given in to pressures from neighborhood groups and had built unneeded schools. At an ensuing board meeting parents argued against the closures, claiming they had not been properly informed. They said the wrong schools were being closed and that revised boundaries would help some schools have larger populations. Wiscombe was accused of not answering questions adequately. His claims that larger schools and team-teaching should be implemented were challenged as unrealistic.

The protest meeting at Curtis Elementary School was the beginning of the end for Arthur Wiscombe's superintendency. In the audience of patrons was a Salt Lake attorney, John Crawford. He had not intended to attend the meeting, and was convinced, with Wiscombe, that declining populations would cause schools to close. He attended mainly to support his wife, Marilyn, who had organized the meeting. Although he agreed with Wiscombe's arguments, as the meeting continued Crawford became increasingly disturbed by Wiscombe's and board members' responses to questions from patrons. They seemed, in Crawford's view, arrogant and unresponsive. Wiscombe especially seemed insecure and defensive, and his responses did not satisfy attorney Crawford. That night John Crawford woke from his sleep, told his wife that he hadn't liked what he had seen at the meeting, and decided at that moment to run for a position on the school board. His election later that year was in fact a referendum on Arthur Wiscombe's superintendency.[12]

At another board meeting, before a group of angry petition-bearing parents,

---

10. "Wiscombe Cites 'Renewal' for S.L. School System," *Salt Lake Tribune*, 24 Dec. 1969; "S.L. Eyes Plans to Close Six Grade Schools," *Salt Lake Tribune*, 16 Jan. 1970; "Chief of S. L. Schools, Dr. A. Wiscombe, Presses Merger Plan," *Salt Lake Tribune*, 22 Jan. 1970.

11. "Board Acts to Close 5 Schools," *Salt Lake Tribune*, 18 Mar. 1970.

12. John Crawford, Oral History, 26 May 1992.

the board voted to close five of the six schools. Those opposed to consolidation, the board said, had not come up with any alternatives. One defensive board member said his colleagues would not capitulate to threats or be intimidated by teacher, staff, or parental demands. However, one dissenting board member expressed the view that what was needed was an educational philosophy that would favor smaller rather than larger schools.[13] In spite of the protests, the schools were closed, a decision the *Tribune* praised as the best alternative, although the editorial criticized the lack of communication between the board and the patrons.[14]

In August, John Crawford was one of a number of people who put themselves forward for the following November's election. In his platform Crawford focused on what he perceived to be the district's major problems. He took issue with excessive use of funds for non-teaching functions, with closing schools, and with busing children to consolidated schools. These things were being implemented under the "thin veil of economy," but Crawford believed they secretly reflected a desire to correct racial or social imbalance through social engineering. He wanted to "use his energies in charting the future course of our school system."[15] In November he got his wish, although his vision of the future collided head-on with the superintendent's.

THE EXPANSION OF DIVERSITY

As Crawford suspected, Wiscombe's plans to close costly, unnecessary schools were related to his belief that racial minorities in the central city were not being well-served by the schools. Wiscombe was convinced that something should be done to give Hispanic, African-American, and disadvantaged white students the same opportunities offered in more affluent schools. The East/West dichotomy was not new to Salt Lake, but by the 1970s it had rigidified. The board's twelve members tended to represent the interests of small, privileged enclaves rather than a broad spectrum of city interests. The board was also entirely Mormon and highly representative of east side interests.

Historically, Salt Lake City was primarily composed of persons with roots in New England and in Scandinavia, Germany, and Great Britain. At the turn of the century only 61 black students attended Salt Lake City's schools—a minuscule number compared to over 15,000 Caucasian students. Eighty years later in the state as a whole, African-Americans formed only 0.6 percent and Hispanics only 4.1 percent of the entire state population, although Salt Lake City had 44 percent of all blacks in the state, 52 percent of all Hispanics, and 23 percent of the state's Native Americans, the "highest concentration in the state of those groups traditionally most discriminated against and with the least training for available, well-

---

13. John Cummins, "School Officials Defend Closure as 'Start,'" *Salt Lake Tribune*, 3 Feb. 1970; "Panel to Investigate Complaint About Horace Mann, Jr. High Curriculum," *Salt Lake Tribune*, 6 Mar. 1970; "Board Acts to Close 5 Schools," *Salt Lake Tribune*, 18 Mar. 1970.
14. "Dealing With Realities Cause School Closings," *Salt Lake Tribune*, 19 Mar. 1970.
15. "Four More Candidates Seek School Positions," *Salt Lake Tribune*, 8 Aug. 1970.

paying jobs."[16]

As Art Wiscombe prepared to assume office in 1968, the Salt Lake Board of Education published a survey entitled *The Urban Picture*, which squarely faced the fact that Salt Lake City was not impervious to the urban crises gripping other parts of the nation. Quoting John H. Fischer of Teachers' College of Columbia University, showing that someone in the district was serious about racial issues, the preface argued that it was not enough that equal education be provided to enable everyone an equal chance in the race of life; many runners were not equally matched, and "equal treatment of unequals produces neither equality nor justice." Schools, therefore, must, in Fischer's words, provide "unequal, exceptional education as a matter of deliberate public policy to every child who needs it."[17]

The Urban Picture noted that Sputnik had promptly focused America's attention on deficits in science and mathematics education. Now civil rights protests had brought attention to problems faced by minority children, but the response was slower coming. Among the factors the report identified as contributing to this were prejudice, inertia, lack of community interest and the fact that "insights, attitudes and types of competence" required to deal with the human issues were all too often simply lacking in the community. Salt Lake's problems of "depopulation, deprivation and other peculiarities" led to a special "urban factor" that would have to be addressed.[18]

Uppermost in the minds of those who prepared the report was the inescapable fact that finances were thin. With the population shrinkage came an absolute loss of its resource base. The high overhead of small, unoccupied schools was costing $1.7 million; poor attendance in central city areas led to a loss of some $25,000 in state funds; dropouts cost the district $280,000. Paradoxically, the highly trained teacher corps, which required some $800,000, added to the problem. The district required almost one-half million dollars "just to offset the anticipated loss in students." "[T]he financial picture is bleak," the report warned.[19]

In addition to financial problems, human issues regarding the city's poorer children were of great concern. The basics in most middle-class communities, such as regular health check-ups, were for a large segment of the central city inhabitants non-existent. Only 37 percent of central city children had such care compared to 64 percent in the city at large. The central city had 35 percent of its people on welfare, compared to 11 percent for Salt Lake. Test scores for children in the central city schools were much lower than the city norms. For example, IQ scores in central city were 95.6 compared to 105.4 for the district; achievement scores in standardized tests were also lower. Although the central city schools made up less than ten percent of the overall school population, they ac-

16. Alexander and Allen, *Mormons and Gentiles*, 298.
17. Cited in *The Urban Picture* (Salt Lake City: Board of Education, 1968), i.
18. *The Urban Picture*, 2.
19. Ibid., 19.

counted for 23 percent of children who did not attend school. The same ten percent also experienced a much greater degree of instability; children changed
address one to two times each year, compared to the city average of one every
five years. Only half of the children lived in homes with both parents, compared
to 80 percent in the city. Over 10 percent used other than English as their primary tongue. Fourteen out of twenty-seven new cases of TB *in the state* were central city residents and some schools contained more than 50 percent minorities
(principally Hispanics).[20]

These realities made Wiscombe want to reorder the system to address the
problems faced by the city's minority and poverty-stricken students. When he
suggested to the board that he start dealing openly with the issue, Wiscombe reported that he met resistance. The board did vote to authorize him to deal with
the issue, but only by a margin of one vote. That five members of the board were
unwilling to authorize the formulation of a policy distressed Wiscombe. In his
view, these members were in denial that Salt Lake City had any race problems,
and even those who saw a problem did not think the time was right to deal with
it. The large minority on the board seemed to think that the community would
not tolerate the board stirring the waters of racial unrest. The publication of *The
Urban Picture*, just cited, should have been a warning that the issues facing central city schools were a problem that would affect the entire district.[21] Apparently
the board did not take the warning seriously—a common fate of educational reports that convey unwanted conclusions.

AN ONGOING PROBLEM: RACISM IN SALT LAKE CITY

To keep things in proper perspective, it is important to recognize that Salt
Lake City was not free from intolerance and racism. In 1945 M. Lynn Bennion
had encountered the problem as supervisor of LDS seminaries. He had arranged
to have a number of young Mormon girls who worked in the Church Office
Building help at a USO canteen serving soldiers stationed in Salt Lake City.
When President J. Reuben Clark, Jr., of the church's First Presidency heard of the
arrangement he ordered Bennion to cancel it because he considered it inappropriate for the LDS women to serve black soldiers.[22]

In 1949 Allan M. West, Executive Secretary of the Utah Education Association, invited a distinguished black educator from the University of Chicago to
address the UEA annual meetings in the Salt Lake Tabernacle on the topic of IQ
tests and discrimination against minority children. The professor accepted the
invitation, but wondered out loud if he could fill the assignment when there was
a policy against blacks speaking in the Tabernacle. West did not believe that this
was the case, but agreed to check with Presiding Bishop Thorpe B. Isaacson on
the matter. Much to his chagrin, Isaacson told him that there was such a policy

---

20. Ibid., 4-5.
21. Wiscombe, Oral History, 28 June 1973.
22. *Recollections of a Schoolman: The Autobiography of M. Lynn Bennion* (Salt Lake City: Western
Epics, 1987), 117-20.

and that a black speaker should not be invited. In a follow-up letter Isaacson said: "I feel very confident that you will be able to get an outstanding educator to speak to you instead of the Negro speaker you had previously mentioned to me. I am confident that we have many great educators in this country from which you can choose."[23]

In another instance, West had made arrangements for a black high school student in the business program at one of the local high schools to assist at the Hotel Utah in registering UEA members. The assistant manager at the hotel called West, demanding that the young woman be released from her work because "[s]he is black and black people are not welcome in this hotel and the management wants her expelled at once." West refused to dismiss the student and threatened to re-locate the UEA in another city hotel; the management backed down.[24]

Before Lynn Bennion left office, a shop teacher at Horace Mann Junior High, who operated a printing press in his home, printed a derogatory poem about blacks for another person. When the order was not paid for, the teacher sold the poems to students to recoup his losses. The local NAACP organized a march on the board of education offices, demanding that the teacher be fired. Bennion suspended him, and the teacher apologized to the faculty and student body as he "wept with shame and remorse." He later transferred out of the district. In reflecting on the incident, Bennion commented that the teacher was probably not intentionally racist, but, like many others in the valley he was "simply naive . . . [as are many] provincial people. They are victims of their own environmental training and lack exposure [to] and lack association" with diverse peoples.[25]

Bennion's assessment also describes what Art Wiscombe encountered when he attempted to get the board to confront minority issues. Some board members were apparently oblivious to racial issues in Utah. One member, however, manifested more intense racism when, in response to Wiscombe's suggestion that a certain school be closed, he said that the school should be kept open because the children attending it would be future community leaders. If a school had to be closed, he told Wiscombe, it should be one serving black and Hispanic children, "because they will never become community leaders."[26]

In the midst of Wiscombe's campaign to address the plight of minority students, an incident at West High sparked minority community protests that overshadowed, for a time, the controversy induced by closing schools. A highly respected West High music teacher, James D. Maher, had an altercation with four black students in April 1970 that led to a mutual exchange of insults in which the teacher called the students "niggers." The local NAACP, headed by James Dooley, demanded that the board dismiss the teacher. The prejudiced attitudes of teachers, Dooley claimed, helped explain why so many black, Mexican-American

---

23. Allan M. West, *My Life As An Advocate for Utah Schools* (Privately published, 1988), 151-53.
24. West, *My Life As An Advocate*, 153-54.
25. Bennion, Oral History, 10 Apr. 1974.
26. Conversation with Arthur C. Wiscombe, 22 May 1992.

and poverty-level white children dropped out of school.

More confrontational in his approach to the board was Dr. Charles Nabors of the University of Utah, who represented the Utah Non-Violent Action Committee. Nabors argued that the board had ignored its own established policies against teachers using derogatory comments to students. The plan to investigate the issue was insulting to the minorities in the community, who were once again put off by "another round of promises, committee meetings and administrative paper shuffling." When board president Waldo Anderson pledged a study of both sides of the issue, Nabors retorted that Anderson probably did not know both sides. In an emotional response to the board one person, Tallie Cavaness, charged that if a white child had been called a "honkie" by a black teacher maybe the board would understand how serious the issue was. Cavaness told the board that a new day had arrived for minorities in Salt Lake City: "We're not going to beg you one more time to be nice to us."[27]

Wiscombe, during this heated exchange, tried to be as dispassionate as possible and to convince the protesters that something concrete would be done. He refused the NAACP request that the teacher be dismissed—to do so would simply exacerbate the situation. He also suggested that there may have been provocation on both sides. For Wiscombe, the best resolution would come from a sixteen member task force, headed by Robert Freed, Utah Chairman of the U.S. Commission on Civil Rights, which had the responsibility to investigate the issue and report to the board. While Wiscombe was sensitive to the issues being raised by the black community, he did not hesitate to challenge wrong assumptions, such as one black student's charge that he had been kept out of a sports activity because of his race. In reality, the district policy was that a student had to be in the district for at least a semester before he could play on a school team. Wiscombe also worked closely with the NAACP and took seriously their recommendations that: teachers who insult students be punished; a study of overt and covert racism in the Salt Lake schools be made; sensitivity classes for teachers be mandated; more black personnel be hired and schools be informed that derogatory comments would not be tolerated.[28]

The *Tribune* saw the incident at West as a means of turning an unfortunate occurrence into a "positive gain." Reminding its readers of the difficulties blacks face in a community in which whites hold all the power, the editorial said that "in an era of increased social justice and awareness . . . old patterns can no longer prevail, white officials cannot ignore minority complaints." At the same time, it rejected the call from the Utah Non-Violent Action Committee that the board should "fire and fire summarily" the West high teacher—both sides in the dispute must be examined before a judgement is rendered.[29] The editorial ended

---

27. John R. Cummins, "Blacks Charge Racism in S.L. School System," *Salt Lake Tribune*, 22 Apr. 1970.

28. John R. Cummins, "S.L. Hopes for 'Positive Gains' in Racial Situation in Schools," *Salt Lake Tribune*, 23 Apr. 1970.

29. "Gain from Bitterness," *Salt Lake Tribune*, 24 Apr. 1970.

praising Art Wiscombe and James Dooley for a good example of resolving difficult issues.

Already some of the NAACP's suggestions were being implemented in the school district. The special task force met for the first time on Friday at 4:30 pm and continued in session until 2:30 am Saturday. Later that day the board of education announced that the music teacher would be temporarily suspended with pay. The four students would also be suspended from school (although they would be tutored at the district offices) pending the outcome of the task force's investigation.[30]

Also during this period, police were called to quell a disturbance at West High, after a special meeting with the school's thirty-five black students, parents, administrators, the superintendent and the president of the board. This altercation, involving shouts and obscenities, pushing and threats of violence between police and two young men (who were not students at the school), had nothing to do with the original incident. But as a result, police were stationed at the schools in Salt Lake City as they were in other urban centers. During the week in which these events took place, reports from throughout the nation of bombings, boycotts, sit-ins, and destruction of college bookstores appeared in the Salt Lake newspapers.[31] Many citizens assumed that the real problem was one of outside agitation.

When Superintendent Wiscombe arrived at his office on Monday morning, 27 April, he was met by 100 white school patrons with a petition demanding that "uniform rules of discipline for all students" regardless of race be adopted. Complaints were made about a general lack of order at West and that black student infractions carried no consequences, although white students had been punished for breaking the same rules. They also demanded that Maher be allowed to continue as vocal instructor, some parents even insisting on his immediate reinstatement.[32]

Two days later, some seventy people representing the minority communities met in the Central City Community Center and drew up a list of demands they wanted the board to hear at a special meeting to be held in the central city. In addition to calling for Maher's dismissal (as well as that of any teacher committing a similar offense), the group specified general areas that needed attention in the district. The representatives demanded that suspended or expelled students be permitted to return when they wanted to; that all grading procedures be abandoned; that regular meetings be held between students and principals for airing grievances; and that graduation be guaranteed to every student. In addition the group demanded more leisure time in school, relaxation of truancy laws, more leeway for principals in organizing the curriculum, and longer class periods and

---

30. "Parents of West High Pupils Ask Teacher Return, Single Policy," and "Board Faces Challenge over Schools," *Salt Lake Tribune*, 28 Apr. 1970.

31. "Both Non-Students: 1 Youth Flees; 1 Arrested in West High Altercation," *Salt Lake Tribune*, 25 Apr. 1970.

32. "Parents of West High Pupils Ask Teacher's Return, Single Policy," *Salt Lake Tribune*, 28 Apr. 1970.

lunch breaks. They also called for a recognition that the West High incident was *not* caused by outside agitators.

On 31 April nine members of the board attended a meeting at the Central City Community Center. Originally called to discuss more minority representation in the schools, the meeting boiled over into a "scalding attack" on the schools in general, the suspended teacher at West, and on the teachings of the LDS church with respect to race, including a ban that prohibited black male members from ordination to its lay priesthood. There was free use of four- and twelve-letter obscenities, board members were referred to as "pigs," and one speaker said that if Salt Lake were Chicago the Tabernacle would be in flames; and perhaps it should still be burned down: "Salt Lake is way past due for a riot." The board was criticized for not implementing a Black Studies curriculum and not increasing the number of black personnel in the schools.

When someone suggested that a black be seated on the board, Jesse Sawaya responded that he had tried to get elected to the board a few years before but only 25 people supported his attempt. One black woman, Ruth Ross, promised to run in the fall election (she did, but lost). Mary Adams called herself a conservative and said she had sent her children to private schools so they would not be confronted with the "Mormon syndrome." Many Utah teachers, she claimed, were influenced by the Mormon belief about black inferiority. They had therefore, no compunctions in using the term "nigger" when referring to blacks. This religious doctrine, she claimed, shaped the responses of local residents towards non-whites.[33]

Whether indeed citizens who were members of the LDS church were more biased because of their church's teachings about blacks and the priesthood would be difficult to prove. The fact remains, however, that many minority citizens perceived that to be the case, contributing to community tensions. Superintendent Wiscombe himself felt a special responsibility to make sure that his church's teachings on race, with which he found himself at variance, did not interfere with his professional, civic, and moral responsibility to promote equal educational opportunity. After leaving Salt Lake City, when he was being considered for an appointment in a mid-western school district, Wiscombe told those who wondered if he were "encased in the Church's position" on race that for him it was not a theological issue at all. His purpose as an educational leader was to transcend the biases and prejudices he had been taught and give all people "a higher sense of dignity and worth." He was disappointed that the Mormon church as an institution, and so many community leaders who were LDS, shied away from the issue of race. If they had wanted to, Wiscombe believed, they could have taken the lead and used the church's moral and political "power [and] influence in this valley to create a model racial program that [could have] been held up as an ideal to any city in this nation." Many were "aware and sensitive to the problems," but very few were willing to run the risk of appearing to side with

---

33. "Minority Ire Boils Over at School Meet," *Salt Lake Tribune*, 1 May 1970.

those who were critical of the community and its value structure.[34]

Wiscombe was not, however, unwilling to risk himself in such a cause. He was convinced that a coalition of groups such as school PTAs and LDS ward Relief Societies (the Mormon women's auxiliary) in the central city could help provide services to impoverished children and thus help schools do their work more effectively. In an effort to explore such cooperative possibilities, he sought a meeting with a younger member of the Quorum of Twelve Apostles, Gordon B. Hinckley, as he had been advised that he would get nowhere with older members of the church hierarchy. He met with Hinckley on 21 January 1972 to review the possibility of some sort of church-school alliance to combat the growing racism in the community and plight of central city school children. He did not get the extended discussion of the issue that he wished, however. The church leader gave him only fifteen minutes and told him that he had not yet had lunch. Before terminating the meeting, Elder Hinckley told Wiscombe that the Mormon church "never gets involved in political issues." According to Superintendent Wiscombe, Elder Hinckley saw no way in which the Church leadership would want to become involved with the Salt Lake City School Board in dealing with, in Wiscombe's words, the "challenge of racial segregation in our schools and in our city."[35]

Through the efforts of Preston Robinson, managing editor of the *Deseret News*, a few weeks later Wiscombe succeeded in meeting with Belle Spafford, the head of the church-wide Relief Society. He presented to her his concerns and raised questions about how the Relief Society and the schools might work together to secure clothing for children or in tutoring needy students. President Spafford, while apparently sympathetic to the need, concluded her response to the Superintendent with "regret that the membership of the LDS Relief Society units are not composed of socially conscious women." Besides, any such cooperative venture would have to be approved by the Church's First Presidency— something, she implied, that would not likely be forthcoming. Ironically, as Wiscombe left the Relief Society building he noticed a plaque quoting Joseph Smith's words at the founding of the Relief Society in Nauvoo, Illinois, in 1842: "This is the beginning of better days to the poor and the needy . . . [.]" He felt defeated and saddened; the institution that had nurtured in him empathy and concern for children now seemed unwilling to face the issues of the day with "moral resolve, courage, and vision."[36]

His analytical skills and understanding of modern education aside, Wiscombe was still in many ways a Mormon romantic. It perplexed him that the people of Utah who had built strong communities under adverse circumstances could not or would not apply their same skills to the problems of the twentieth-century cities. As the foregoing instances attest, he made a considerable effort to mobilize the "power elites" of the valley to resolve the issues the city was begin-

---

34. Wiscombe, Oral History, 28 June 1973.
35. Arthur C. Wiscombe to Frederick S. Buchanan, 14 May 1992.
36. Ibid.

ning to face as its minority populations increased. By interviewing between 150-200 of the "most prestigious people in this valley" (including an LDS Apostle, bankers, educators, and politicians) he hoped to come up with some concrete plans for dealing with the issues of race, minority relations, and equality of educational opportunity. He delivered hundreds of speeches to church groups, civic organizations, school groups, and TV boards of directors in an attempt to "represent the case for educational improvement, to build community understanding and support for . . . our schools, and to communicate effectively, with the public at large, the challenges and hopes of urban education."[37] However, his efforts were submarined because the board of education itself seemed unwilling to move aggressively in the needed direction—unwilling, that is, until confronted with the reality of racial hostility and frustration directed at the board at the Central City meeting.

Racial hostility was by no means limited to minorities; eventually a white backlash developed at West High. When Wiscombe attended a special assembly, ostensibly to hear student points of view, some 600 students walked out, to protest his refusal to reinstate immediately the suspended music teacher. The student body president of West High, Clayton Christensen, claimed black students were using this one incident to level general charges of discrimination against the school. In Christensen's eyes, "no discrimination exists in the school." Black students, he claimed, were welcome to participate in school functions, but most of them chose not to. His response was typical of the white majority—racism did not really exist, and what problems did arise were due to minorities refusing to become involved.

Over the next month or so the task force, headed by Robert Freed, met in several "secret" sessions. By mid-June the group had issued its report on the incident at West High, concluding that the teacher and the students had been deeply affected by the event and that no purpose would be served in punishing them further. The task force reinstated the teacher and the students and announced that the teacher had apologized personally to the students. For their part, the students acknowledged that they had used offensive epithets when they reacted to the teacher. Prior to the incident the board had put itself on record as favoring improvements in the instruction and treatment of minorities. The altercation simply underscored the need to proceed in that direction. The board also began consideration of new policies designed to govern the relationship between teachers and students, insisting that it would not condone "disparaging racial remarks" on the part of teachers. Nor would it countenance student use of obscene language, intimidation, baiting, or threats against teachers.[38]

The Salt Lake City board was not alone in its unwillingness or inability to face the realities of the day—prior to the West High episode, the State Board of Education issued the report of a survey requested by the city board as a means of

---

37. Ibid.
38. "School Board Approves Budget, Reinstates Teacher, 4 Students," *Salt Lake Tribune*, 17 June 1970.

identifying problems in the schools. Based on interviews of 1,237 teachers, 84 administrators, 5,000 parents, 9,200 students, business, civic and legislative leaders, this April 1970 report concluded that the city's schools were on a par with national norms in terms of achievement scores, enjoyed considerable public support, and had a high level of parental satisfaction. On the negative side, very slow and very fast learners were being ignored; costs per pupil were higher than in surrounding districts; a lack of relationship existed between vocational programs and the jobs students took (an old issue); teachers needed to be more involved in planning the curriculum; some complaints had resurfaced about LDS doctrine being introduced into classroom teaching of Utah history; and school leaders suffered a lack of positive communication with the public. The state report hoped that the district would use the survey to develop "a district wide system of measurable, accountable objectives" which apparently did not include any measures of minority dissatisfaction. Nowhere was there any specific reference to minority issues—the district had to learn about that through direct experience.[39]

Coming as it did during Wiscombe's first year, no doubt he may have viewed this report as a valuable resource. However, the cultural revolution outlined above did not allow him this luxury. By the fall of 1970 new members had been added to the board, bringing new challenges to the superintendent's plans. The revolution took on an added urgency with the rise in awareness of the city's largest ethnic minority—Hispanic peoples.

ETHNIC CONFRONTATION: PRECURSOR TO CHANGE

Responding to the suggestion that the public should be more informed and involved in shaping the aims and purposes of the schools, Wiscombe in the fall of 1970 initiated a series of public forums, involving him and his staff in open exchanges with patrons, students, and the general public.[40] Designed to obtain input on the best ways to handle the many problems the schools faced, these forums also increased the sense among many that the schools might not be able to cope with the flood of change that threatened to engulf them. Having been denied so much of the traditional American dream for so long, minorities became increasingly furious when their consciousness had been raised and they realized how much had been denied to them. It appeared to him, in retrospect at least, that the more he worked with minorities, the less they seemed to appreciate what was being done to change the situations they complained of.[41]

Under these circumstances, even policies that might have been seen as neutral with respect to ethnic origins or race took on more sinister denotations. For example, discipline of rowdy students, appearing time and time again in the history of education, resurfaced in the 1960s and '70s with a more than normal degree of deviance from social standards. In Salt Lake City, school dress codes were

---

39. John R. Cummins, "State School Study Advises City Goals," *Salt Lake Tribune*, 3 April 1970.
40. "Forum, Quiz Slated on School Views," *Salt Lake Tribune*, 4 Nov. 1970; "Students to Quiz SL Schools Chief," *Salt Lake Tribune*, 1 Dec. 1970.
41. Wiscombe, Oral History, 28 June 1973.

challenged in 1969 when 126 girls were suspended from Northwest Junior High for wearing pants to school and were not permitted to return to school until they had dressed "properly." The principal, who according to district policy, had the authority to set dress codes, said he refused to "go along with the trend to do away with standards and I cannot go along with the idea you have to give in every time someone protests."[42] These years witnessed an increase in reports of students smoking in schools, loitering in the halls, assaulting teachers, and in general reflecting the age of which they were a part.[43] Predictably, the more challenges to authority that arose, the more school boards adopted regulations to deal with the challenges. In 1971 the board adopted a policy on discipline designed to bring order to disputes between teachers and students. Under the new policy, a teacher might inflict "reasonable corporal punishment"—excluding paddling—but even then it was to be used only as a last resort.[44]

In response to the discipline policy, a group of west side parents appeared before the board to protest what they saw as a plan that would be used more against minority children. The delegation demanded that the board rescind the policy, remove all vestiges of racism from the schools, and remove police patrols from all schools. The parents refused to give way to the board's need to consider budget items at this particular meeting and forced them to adjourn to another room.

The debate continued in a special meeting convened a few weeks later. Some one hundred parents voiced their disapproval of the discipline policy by making specific charges of brutality against three of the city's teachers. The board responded that while the policy in general did not forbid corporal punishment entirely, it did discourage paddling and that teachers guilty of abusing disciplinary measures would be dismissed. Until charges could be substantiated, the policy would be maintained.[45]

While the issue of discipline caught the headlines, in the long term it was complaints about how poorly the schools were serving the minority students that began to stimulate change. Hispanic citizens organized their own lobbying group entitled the Spanish Speaking Organization for Community Integrity and Opportunity (S[S]OCIO). In January 1970 this group presented Superintendent Wiscombe with a list of recommendations for improving the education of Mexican-Americans in the Salt Lake City schools. The main problems were, in S(S)OCIO's view, an "astonishingly high" drop-out rate, sixth graders who were two to three years below national norms, and the trivialization of Spanish language and Hispanic culture, as well as the problems of poverty in general. Given that Mexican-Americans made up a large portion of the students in Salt Lake City, special programs to meet the needs of this substantial minority were justified.

---

42. *Salt Lake Tribune*, 12 Dec. 1969.
43. *Salt Lake Tribune*, 25 Sept., 3 Oct. 1969; Board of Education, Minutes, 25 Mar., 30 Mar. 1971.
44. Board of Education, Minutes, 4 May 1971; "Corporal Punishment Protest Disrupts Board Meet," *Salt Lake Tribune*, 2 June 1971; "Salt Lake Board Votes to Continue Policy on Corporal Punishment in Schools," *Salt Lake Tribune*, 23 June 1971.
45. *Salt Lake Tribune*, 2, 23, 25 June 1971.

Richard Gomez, the chair of S(S)OCIO, went on to list specific recommendations, including: the formation of a Coordinating Council on Mexican-American Education; the appointment of a recognized Mexican-American educator to serve as a consultant to the schools on establishing bilingual-bicultural programs; and an increased attention to research on the needs of Mexican-American students. Gomez also asked that no schools serving Mexican-Americans be closed before S(S)OCIO was consulted; that special in-service training be given to teachers who deal with minority students; that teachers unable to work with Mexican-American students be transferred; and that the University of Utah and the district should work together to identify and support Mexican-American students who might wish to follow a career in education. Gomez concluded by asking that Wiscombe's staff develop a response to the recommendations that should be "presented to [S(S)OCIO] as soon as practical."[46]

S(S)OCIO also met with the State Board of Education in early 1972 to explore ways in which the board's "educational philosophy might be modified to meet the needs of Chicanos, the state's largest minority." As a result of this meeting, arrangements were made to schedule regular meetings between S(S)OCIO and the State Board. Impetus was also given to the appointment of native Spanish speakers to key positions in the Utah educational agency so that the Hispanic community could have input on the development of educational programs.[47]

Dr. Lionel A. Maldonado of the University of Utah explained why the Hispanic community believed the schools were not working for them: half of all Chicano students were dropping out, not necessarily in proportion to the educational achievement of their parents. Chicanos who got a negative response from the school tended to drop out earlier. Contrary to the notion that language was the problem, Maldonado pointed out that most Hispanic homes in Salt Lake were in fact bilingual. While Hispanics made up some ten percent of the total elementary population, they only accounted for two percent of graduates. The major cause of the failure to meet the needs of minority students lay, he said, in the "reliance on an outmoded assumption inherent in the concept of the 'melting pot' that only a monolingual monocultural society is acceptable." Such an assumption, Maldonado claimed, led inevitably to a loss of talent in society at large—a loss that was unacceptable either pragmatically or philosophically.[48]

The issue of dropouts was longstanding, and part of the problem was the inability to determine the exact number of students dropping out of school. (Indeed an accurate assessment did not become part of the district's student accounting procedures until the late 1980s.) Some felt that the district was even dishonest in reporting statistics to protect its public image. However, the minority community had an almost intuitive sense that they were losing more of their young people than the schools were willing to acknowledge.

46. Richard Gomez to Dr. Arthur C. Wiscombe, 9 Jan. 1970.
47. "Chicano Needs Cry Out for Educational Program Expansion," *Salt Lake City* (10 Sept. 1972).
48. Ibid.

The dropout rate may have ranged anywhere from three to twelve percent of the minority population—depending on how the problem was defined. For example, those students who married or joined the army were not included in calculating the dropout rate, but they nevertheless were real school "dropouts." Whatever the precise attendance and dropout figures, it is evident that minorities perceived the board of education to be dysfunctional with regard to minority communities. Most glaring of all was the absence of African-American and Hispanics teachers, administrators, or central office personnel. One of the first—if not *the* first—Hispanics to teach in the district was Robert "Archie" Archuletta. Reflecting on the issues confronting the community in the early 1970s, Archuletta concluded that the board's inabilities were a major reason for the large number of minority children who failed, were suspended, or were classified as in need of Special Education. Archuletta acknowledged some dysfunctional aspects to minority families (single parent, low income), but he attributed the disproportionate numbers to the schools' built-in tendency toward bureaucracy, sexism, classism, and racism.

For Archuletta the solution was to individualize instruction, something often talked about, but seldom implemented. The school was more inclined to see itself as a socializing agency to promote conformity rather than individual worth. The tragedy, in Archuletta's view, was that teachers who could teach well invariably had jobs in affluent areas—they failed when it came to dealing with the "culturally different" learner, including the children of poor white families. Too many teachers wanted to wipe their hands clean of the children of poverty and minorities, more interested in keeping them quiet than in preparing them for life.[49]

The protests, confrontations, and meetings between minority representatives and educational leaders did not take place in vain. During Wiscombe's superintendency, schools responded to the needs of minority and poor children with the appointment of some 20 Hispanic teachers and administrators. African-Americans increased from one to ten. Immediately after the West High fracas, a noticeable increase in the school system's commitment to education for and about minorities was evident: texts were improved, cultural awareness classes were organized under district auspices; the historical experience of African-Americans was integrated into history courses and electives in minority history were offered for the first time.

Dr. Darlene Ball, Assistant Superintendent, has been credited with much of the groundbreaking work in minority education in the district. In June 1970 she reported that establishment of federally funded Title I programs was well under way and that Salt Lake City was estimated to have about 12 percent of its children entitled to receive such assistance. At the classroom level, the Head Start Program was probably the most successful, partly because it provided additional teaching supplies. Some evidence indicates that the money made available for lunches, educational experiences, and recreational activities did make a differ-

---

49. Robert Archuletta, Oral History, 11 Feb. 1992.

ence in the lives of children. Targeted to help low income families, the program began at the Matheson School in the fall of 1970 and lived up to its name in giving Salt Lake City's disadvantaged children a "head start."[50]

BOARD ELECTIONS AS REFERENDA ON THE SUPERINTENDENT

Wiscombe's attempts to get community support for his innovations in minority issues met with, if not outright resistance, then a disturbing degree of apathy. This, as noted earlier, was coupled with the warning that if he persisted in closing schools, he might end up out on a limb. One sign that the superintendent's base was about to be eroded was the election in 1970 of John Crawford, who had made his platform a refutation of many of the things that Wiscombe was staking his future course on.[51]

By June 1972, it was clear that Wiscombe did not enjoy the necessary support of the board. An executive board session met until midnight, apparently unable to reach a consensus as to whether Wiscombe should be retained as superintendent. The only public indication that there had been a problem came from a brief mention in the *Tribune* that after a long session Wiscombe had been retained by a vote of 6-4, with two members absent. Leading the "nay" vote was John Crawford, who would campaign for his second term on the board in November 1972. He began that campaign saying that he favored more accountability in management of schools and supported a reduction in the number of board members from twelve to seven. Crawford also wanted to develop a long-range master plan for the district, including rebuilding East High School, which had burned the previous spring. He did not mention Wiscombe by name in his statement, but made it clear that he was opposed to "the indiscriminate closing of schools, the busing of students to accomplish a social and economic mix and to any wholesale experimentation with the curriculum in the schools."[52]

The election of a new seven-member board meant that the entire board had to seek reelection. This meant that Wiscombe could no longer be sure of support from at least half of the old board. It appears that the issues of school closing, minority affairs, and teacher relations with the central administration played a major role in the campaign. The old, twelve-member board was seen by one candidate as deeply divided along political lines: between those who supported Wiscombe and those who opposed him, although all of them were Mormons.

The decision to rebuild East High added fuel to the conflict between East and West. According to the candidates, East was rebuilt not because of educational needs, but because of East side political domination of the board. Unlike Crawford, most candidates did not "take on" the superintendent's tenure as an issue of the election. Those who did not make it an issue favored a slower, less

---

50. John R. Cummins, "S.L. School Panel Pledges to Meet More Needs of Minority Students," *Salt Lake Tribune*, 10 June 1970; Wiscombe, Oral History, 28 June, 1973; Archuletta, Oral History, 11 Feb. 1992.

51. "Four More Candidates Seek School Positions," *Salt Lake Tribune*, 8 Aug. 1970.

52. "School Aide Seeking 2d Term," *Salt Lake Tribune*, 26 Aug. 1972.

confrontational approach to resolving the issues with which the superintendent had become identified. Another candidate, June Chapman (a district school teacher) reportedly challenged her opponent, Mervin Jones, to taking a position with respect to the removal of Wiscombe, which he refused to do on grounds that he was not privy to all the facts in the case. Chapman had campaigned with the support of the Salt Lake Teacher's Association, which interviewed all candidates for the board on the issue facing the schools, reportedly asking where candidates fell on the issue of retaining Wiscombe. Without detailed information on the election campaign speeches or literature it is difficult to determine the exact role played by the teachers in ousting the superintendent. Mervin Jones, however, attributed his loss to Chapman (300 votes out of almost 11,000 cast) and to organized teacher opposition to the continuance of Art Wiscombe as superintendent.[53]

Not only did this election turn out to be a referendum on the superintendent, it also made history in another way: it was the first time in the politics of Salt Lake City that an African-American and a Mexican-American ran for public office, although in the 1890s a number of European and British immigrants had been elected to the board. Ruth C. Ross lost in the primary election, but Dr. Eugene Garcia survived it and went on to defeat incumbent Glen A. Lloyd by fewer than 90 votes. Garcia's election was certainly a sign that no longer could the white majority assume that the board would reflect only their complexion and ideology.

In a late-1971 meeting with other members of the Mexican-American community, including veteran teacher Robert Archuletta, a decision was made to organize a campaign to give the minority community a voice on the board. While Archuletta was discussed as a possibility, he felt that the group needed someone with more credibility in the community; Garcia, a Ph.D. who taught at the University of Utah, was chosen because he would appeal to many Mormon voters whose support was essential if the campaign were to succeed.

Early in the campaign religion became an issue when rumors began to circulate that a local LDS stake president had commented that "Mormon Chicanos" supporting Garcia were not "good" members of the church. Orlando Rivera, an active Mormon and social activist, arranged a meeting with Garcia, the stake president, and a number of Mexican-American Latter-day Saints, including local leaders in the west side wards. The stake president agreed to send out a letter to all bishops in his stake requesting that anti-Chicano discussion should cease, which it apparently did.

For probably the first time in Salt Lake school politics, spot announcements on rock and roll radio stations took campaign messages into the homes of the

---

53. I am indebted to the following persons (who agreed to be interviewed over the phone on the 12 and 13 Mar. 1992) for insights into the dynamics of the 1972 election: C. R. Child, Wayne Evans, Mervin Jones and R. C. Wheeler. Some people who ran could not be contacted, others did not respond to my request for information. See also Lavor Chaffin, "Enrollment Dip Hurts Whole City, Wiscombe Says," *Deseret News*, 14 Nov. 1972; "S I Must Face up to School Problems," *Deseret News*, 15 Nov. 1972.

people, as Garcia spoke to the need for minority representation. Another strategy, an "under-the-table" coalition with the Wayne Owens campaign, gave financial support to the Garcia campaign so Mexican-Americans would register to vote (most would also vote for Owens, a Democrat). Massachusetts Senator Edward Kennedy arrived by helicopter at a rally of 2,000 people at St. Patrick's Catholic Church on the West side, announcing his support for Garcia's election to the board of education, as well as Wayne Owens's bid for Congress.

Until the results were announced, few on Garcia's staff thought they would win. Before the election Garcia had found out through a poll that 90 percent of the residents did not even know who the superintendent was, quite apart from what he did. They were more interested in what was happening to their children in the schools than in school politics. Garcia felt that his campaign had raised awareness that could change schools regardless of election results. Eventually Garcia was declared the victor by some 84 votes out of 10,000 cast, making him the first ethnic minority to sit on the Salt Lake City Board of Education.[54]

Garcia was not opposed to the kinds of initiatives Wiscombe was trying to implement. Wiscombe's tenure was not part of his campaign, although he thought most other candidates had made this one of their major themes, and the new, streamlined board seemed decidedly against Wiscombe, who certainly was aware that he was at the center of the election storm. After the election Wiscombe renewed efforts to gain support from influential figures in the community. For instance, one of his admirers, E. C. Zajac, a retired employee of Mountain Fuel Supply Company and later Director of Computers for the State of Utah, saw Wiscombe as standing apart from other Utah educational leaders, with their "muddled morass of theory and gobble-de-gook," because he made decisions for the schools on "the basis of sound business principles." Zajac wrote to former governor J. Bracken Lee asking him to use his influence to prevent Wiscombe from "being relieved of his duties by a group of economic illiterates"—the newly elected board. Lee responded that he would do what he could to see that their "mutual friend Arthur C. Wiscombe . . . is retained in his present position." However, in a recognition of his much reduced role as an opinion maker in the city and state, the former feisty, conservative governor of the 1950s reluctantly admitted that he didn't know what he could do apart from speaking to some of the board members he was acquainted with. The strange alliance between the academically oriented superintendent and the nemesis of Utah educators, J. Bracken Lee, illustrates how pressured Wiscombe was at this particular time.[55] Wiscombe also received support from the Board of Governors of the Salt Lake City Chamber of Commerce.

A few days before the newly elected board was scheduled to meet, the chamber issued a statement urging them to "delay any decision affecting Dr. Arthur C.

---

54. Information on Eugene Garcia's campaign was obtained in a telephone interview with him on 5 Mar. 1992. Garcia was then Dean of the Social Science Division of the University of California, Santa Cruz.
55. E. C. Zajac to J. Bracken Lee, 24 Nov. 1972; Lee to Zajac, 29 Nov. 1972.

Wiscombe" and become thoroughly familiar with the problems facing the district. The president of the chamber, Warren Pugh, who was also president of the Utah Senate, cautioned the board of education that it should not assume that the replacement of an administrator would automatically solve the district's financial problems.[56] L. H. Curtis, president of KSL, the Mormon church-owned radio station, weighed in with an editorial urging the new board to stop "squeezing the Superintendent, whoever he may be, between a Board which sets policy on the one hand and a public which may not like that policy on the other." Hardly an endorsement for Wiscombe, it was still a pointed reminder to the new board that the district's problems were not all of Wiscombe's doing. As the year drew to a close, both the *Deseret News* and the *Tribune* ran lengthy editorials recommending a cautious approach to change. The real issue, said the *News*, ran much deeper than the question of retaining the superintendent; the board had to face up to the difficult financial problems as school enrollment continued to plummet along with revenues. The patrons of the schools should forget the campaign promises (apparently to get rid of Wiscombe), opined the *Tribune* and get behind the superintendent and the board in their efforts to get the schools out of the "financial doldrums."[57]

In spite of such high-powered support, immediately following the election John Crawford made Wiscombe's continuance an issue the new board had to face. After being elected as chairman of the board he set the agenda for ridding themselves of Wiscombe. The first private executive meeting of the board Eugene Garcia attended focused on the inevitable question: "How do we get Superintendent Wiscombe out?" Crawford had apparently already been negotiating with Wiscombe. He proposed that if Wiscombe would agree to step down as of 1 July 1973 the board would pay him one year's salary plus insurance premiums. Wiscombe had no alternative but to accept the offer.

On 6 February the board went through the formality of accepting Wiscombe's "forced" resignation and the president of the board, John Crawford, announced that it was based on a compromise over the differences of opinion that had risen between Wiscombe and the majority of the board. The vote to accept the resignation was 6-1, with Dan Bushnell (who had challenged Crawford for the presidency of the board and favored a slower approach to dealing with the issues) casting the lone dissenting vote.

"All My Energies Are Burned Up"

John Cummins, education writer for the *Tribune*, asserted that although it had "been almost common knowledge" that Wiscombe and the board had been having recent troubles, the problems reached back to the superintendent's first

---

56. Douglas D. Palmer, "S.L. Board Asked to Delay Changes in Administration," *Deseret News*, 27 Dec. 1972.

57. L. H. Curtis, "School Boards," KSL Editorial, November 12/13 1972; "Additional School Closing Only Sensible as Population Drops," *Salt Lake Tribune*, 17 Dec. 1972; "Why S. L. Should Close More Schools," *Deseret News*, 30 Dec. 1972.

year, when he was given a mandate from the board "to develop a plan aimed at revitalizing and revamping the city school district." This led to the campaign to consolidate schools so that money could be used where it was most needed: special programs to address minority needs, the reorganization of fifth through eighth grade students on a non-graded basis, and other "innovative programs." These departures from traditional schooling drew intense fire from many sectors of the community, but the closure of six elementary schools in 1970 and a junior high in 1972 was more than the board and community would tolerate—even if all the evidence pointed to the inescapable conclusion that there really was no financially sound alternative.[58]

In a sense, Wiscombe was a victim of the very revolution he had championed and which was engulfing America's urban school systems in the 1970s. It exacted a tremendous toll personally and professionally on those charged with leading education in a society that seemed, to many, to have lost its moorings. Art Wiscombe visualized himself as "caught up in a whirlwind of so many deep negatives that are so volatile, so political that virtually all [my] energies are burned up just dealing with fires and emergencies and the politics involved in these kind of situations."[59]

Although the president of the board, John Crawford, had easy access to Wiscombe and had negotiated his resignation, he never gave the superintendent a precise reason for not being satisfied with his professional leadership of the district. Other members of the board, however, told Wiscombe that Crawford felt that he did not communicate clearly and that the superintendent's "excessive liberality . . . was too much for him." Lacking any specific details, Wiscombe interpreted this to mean that "I have some views on race that he does not share." Ultimately, Wiscombe felt that the board president simply saw him as "the wrong man for the job" and that the harping on Wiscombe's lack of communication skills was an example of "people who don't like the message, will attack the messenger."[60]

Wiscombe ended his tenure disappointed that he could not carry through to fruition his many plans. At the same time he felt some satisfaction in bringing a greater awareness of the need for equity and justice in Salt Lake City's schools. He was confident that he had "worked long hours [and] served as well as any man could be expected to serve. I'm willing to let the future determine whether or not these issues that we have underscored are indeed real issues that could better have been met a long time ago for a better future of this city."[61]

Of course, they were real issues; it is precisely because they were real that they led to friction within the community. As of the first week in February, Arthur Wiscombe was effectively no longer superintendent, but the melody to

---

58. Eugene Garcia, telephone interview, 5 Mar. 1992; John Cummins, "Wiscombe Quits S. L. School Helm," *Salt Lake Tribune*, 7 Feb. 1973; "A New School Chief, Old School Problems," *Deseret News*, 7 Feb. 1973.
59. Wiscombe, Oral History, 28 June 1973.
60. Ibid.
61. Ibid.

which he had danced lingered on. Within a few weeks of submitting his resignation, Wiscombe listened as the board in solemn session declared that Salt Lake City schools had a problem: there were too many buildings with too few students. The "lame-duck" superintendent simply lowered his head as those who had criticized him for closing schools, now considered it a real problem. John Crawford congratulated the board for doing what the old board refused to do—close schools.

More importantly, however, Crawford also announced criteria that would be used in closing more schools: keeping them as close to the community as economically possible; consideration for the safety of children; minimum travel for students; and retention of new buildings over old. Crawford was, of course, doing what some observers felt Wiscombe should have done all along: he was making the board define the issues instead of making the closing of schools his own personal crusade. The *Tribune's* John Cummins could not resist pointing out that the board's new policy contradicted one of the reasons given for Wiscombe's forced resignation—the disagreement over the need to close schools.[62] In May 1973 the Salt Lake Board of Education proceeded to close four elementary schools, with hardly a murmur of protest in the community.

After leaving Salt Lake City, Arthur Wiscombe was appointed superintendent of public schools in Downers Grove, Illinois. He served there until 1979, when he became president of the Robert Crown Center, a private education institution in Hinsdale, Illinois. He retired in 1983 and now resides in Bountiful, Utah.

---

62. John Cummins, "S. L. Board Okeys Plan to Close More Schools," *Salt Lake Tribune*, 21 Feb. 1973; "4 More Schools to Close," *Salt Lake Tribune*, 2 May 1973.

9

SCHOOLS AS PARTICIPATORY DEMOCRACY
The Administration of
M. Donald Thomas, 1973–84

———

The election of November 1972 had put a young, energetic board in place, which, having secured Wiscombe's resignation, turned its attention to finding a new superintendent. The search for a new administrator should not, a *News* editorial noted, be confined to local professionals; but neither should it yield someone unfamiliar with the "problems and circumstances which are unique to Utah," adding that there are certainly "plenty of former Utahns who have gone on to achieve high levels of responsibility in other school systems who may be eager to return here."[1] It sounded like a replay of the late 1890s when the board was charged with favoring "outsiders" over "insiders." However, the new board, consisting entirely of members of the LDS church, while it gave due consideration to the applications of a number of insiders, chose an outsider's outsider—an Italian-born, former Catholic, now Methodist, who had extensive experience administering schools in the mid-west, the East, and in California— as Salt Lake City's tenth superintendent. M. Donald Thomas was the fourth Protestant since 1890 to lead the district and the first non-Mormon since Ernest Smith in 1920.

Thomas was new wine in a new bottle. During the next decade the district, if not quite inebriated with his infectious enthusiasm, certainly achieved new highs in how its schools were governed, how and what students should be taught, and how teachers and administrators should relate to the central office and to patrons. In time a distinct tone of financial and political stability began to pervade district affairs. In large measure this was due to the expert fiscal management of the new district Business Administrator, Gary Harmer, as well as the agreement between the board and Thomas that they would give him maximum freedom to do his job and not involve themselves in the day-to-day affairs of the district schools.

The new superintendent took as his highest priority the need to continue the process of decentralization that had begun under Bennion and Wiscombe. Thomas pushed ahead with his own interpretation of participatory democracy, which he called "shared governance." In time the district was identified nationally as a showcase for involving a large segment of hitherto silent community members as active participants in *their* schools.

———

1. "A New School Chief, Old School Problems," *Deseret News*, 7 Feb. 1973.

M. Donald Thomas
1973–84

Although boosters claimed it as a success, studies indicated less power sharing than claimed. The traditional "top down" authority relationships had not changed—those who had been denied a voice before shared governance, i.e., minorities, were still without one. One study even suggested that shared governance seemed to work in Salt Lake because it fit rather neatly into the Mormon idea of lay involvement in church government—an involvement that does not include, of course, making any real policy decisions. Nevertheless, implementing the concept gave many people a greater sense of involvement than they had previously had.

Thomas encouraged teachers to experiment with new approaches. He was especially concerned that far too many underprivileged children were not getting the learning opportunities they needed to raise their aspirations. He earned the praise and esteem of Salt Lake's minority populations for his insistence that the students learn not only about their ethnic culture, but also what it would take to function in the larger society.

Pluralism gone mad, Thomas believed, would only end in disaster for those who needed basic skills most: the urban underclass. Because he insisted on more than symbolic integration, Thomas increased greatly the number of minority teachers in the district, contributing to a more diverse and cosmopolitan teacher corps.

With John Crawford's departure from the board in 1979, Thomas began to feel less support from the board, and some board members again began to interfere in the daily work of the schools—not something he relished.

When declining enrollments in the high schools became an issue that could not be ignored, Thomas was warned by the board that none of them could be closed without political and social turmoil. Thomas urged the board to allow the market place of open enrollment to determine which school should close—he felt it would be West—but conflicts with the board, the uncertainty over shared governance, and perhaps just the fact that he had been in his position for ten years, led to a close vote of re-appointment. He resigned in July 1984 and accepted a position to implement the educational reforms mandated by the South Carolina legislature.

M. Donald Thomas was a "respected and colorful, but controversial" superintendent. Those characteristics defined him and his administration. He left the district with a very definite vacuum to be filled. While his exuberant personality sometimes was seen as manipulative, even those who knew they were being manipulated had profound admiration for this human dynamo who made everything he came in contact with hum in sync with his enthusiasm.

THE SEARCH FOR A CONFLICT MANAGER

With Wiscombe reduced to a mere figurehead between February and June 1973, the man who had become his nemesis, attorney John Crawford, took over the day-to-day management of the school system and set in motion the search for a replacement. The board received dozens of applications and eventually winnowed them down to four finalists; three of these were: Raymond Arvison, superintendent of Hayward Unified School System, California; Wayne Carle, the controversial superintendent of Dayton, Ohio, schools; and M. Donald Thomas, superintendent of the Newark School District in California.

Because no records are available documenting the deliberations of the board when it chooses a superintendent, there is no way of describing the process very precisely. However, after interviewing the top four candidates the board chose M. Donald Thomas. In doing so they broke a long-standing practice and informal policy of appointing a Mormon educator to the post. According to John Crawford, religion was never discussed in the meetings leading up to Thomas's appointment. Afterwards, when community members expressed surprise that the board had chosen an "outsider," Crawford responded that they had picked the best person for the position, regardless of religion. Although Thomas was the fourth non-Mormon to be elected to the position, he was the first to serve as superintendent since Ernest Smith's tenure from 1916 to 1920. Of the finalists in 1973 only Carle was a member of the LDS church. Ironically, he had been fired that spring from his position as superintendent of Dayton schools for promoting racial integration too aggressively. He had also just been excommunicated from the LDS church for publicly taking issue with the church's refusal to ordain African-American males to the Mormon priesthood. Some saw the latter as a factor in denying him the superintendency, and it is unlikely that his stance on integration would have endeared him to a board that had already gone through a struggle with Wiscombe on similar issues.[2]

John Crawford played an important role in choosing the new superintendent and had made inquiries of members of the Department of Educational Administration at the University of Utah regarding possible candidates. Crawford told Professor Lloyd McCleary that the board would like someone with experience in conflict management; McCleary responded that Don Thomas had just published an article dealing with that topic. Eventually McCleary met Thomas in Denver and recommended that he apply for the position. Reluctant to do so because he had just taken the superintendency in Newark, California, the previous year, Thomas did not think that the Mormon board in Salt Lake City would want to appoint an Italian born Methodist. McCleary convinced him that he had a chance, and eventually Thomas applied and was invited to visit Salt Lake City. The board liked his frankness in the initial interview, and after investigating his work in Newark voted unanimously to offer him the superintendency. He accepted the appointment on condition that the board would approve a "memorandum of agreement" which spelled out his working conditions. Thomas asked for free time to pursue what he wanted to do, freedom to travel as much as possible without having to notify the board, and an annual salary equal to that of the governor, who was then receiving $30,000. The board agreed to almost everything but felt he should accept something short of the governor's salary. They set-

---

2. Telephone conversation with Don Thomas, 27 Apr. 1972; interview with Wayne Carle, c. 15 June 1973, Dayton, Ohio; Frederick S. Buchanan, Journal, 26 June, 5 July 1973.

tled on $29,500.[3]

Although by the 1970s the religious issue was essentially dormant in governing the public schools, given the facts that Salt Lake City headquarters the LDS church there was always potential for misunderstanding and conflict. Thomas was advised that if anyone did raise the question about him not being LDS he should allow the board to respond. As it was, only one letter appeared in the local press wondering why the district had hired an "outsider." During his tenure Thomas enjoyed a cordial relationship with the Mormon community and its leaders. The board had indeed chosen an expert in conflict management, someone who could defuse potential conflicts.

THE MAKING OF A MODERN SUPERINTENDENT

Prior to Thomas's appointment, the nine people chosen to superintend the Salt Lake City schools, Mormon and non-Mormon, had been more or less ethnically homogenous: eight were of British, and one was of Danish ancestry. Given his surname of Thomas, most people assumed he had his roots in Wales, but the new superintendent was born in Bugnara, Italy, in 1926, and his birth name was Mario Donato DiTomaso. His father, Luigi Pasquale DiTomaso, had emigrated to the United States early in the twentieth century, became a citizen in 1912, and around 1920 returned to Italy to marry Rosina Manna. Under the law in effect at that time Luigi's wife automatically became a U.S. citizen, so Mario and his brother Luigi were born in Italy as U.S. citizens. In 1931 when Mario was in the second grade, the family moved to Pittsburgh and then to Chicago Heights, Illinois. To avoid the prejudice often raised against Italians, Luigi changed the family name to Thomas, and his second son became known as M. Donald Thomas. The third son, born in the United States and named Andrew Thomas, eventually became a professor of Italian at Wayne State University and is now known as Andrea DiTomaso.

The young Italian-speaking immigrant experienced some prejudice in America. He was even introduced to his school teacher as the "new dago from Italy." When he asked what that meant, his father deflected the issue by saying, "Dumb teacher, she doesn't know how to pronounce Diago. You are part of the history of Italy and Diago was a famous Italian explorer and you're part of that." Thomas attributed much of his success in life to the positive attitude cultivated in him by his father.

Thomas graduated sixth in a class of some 500 from Bloom Township High School in 1945 and received a football scholarship to the University of Dubuque. He was not really a star player, he recalled, but "I was mean as hell." During his high school years Thomas abandoned the traditional Catholic faith of his family, becoming a member of a Protestant church. The minister encouraged him to develop his speaking skills, and the congregation helped him financially when he

---

3. Material relating to Thomas's life before coming to Utah is based on M. Donald Thomas, Oral History, 16 Aug. 1991, Special Collections, Marriott Library, University of Utah, and on a telephone conversation, 27 Apr. 1992.

went to college.

In the next few years Thomas was involved in a variety of educational experiences—as a high school English and speech teacher, as a principal, and eventually as a superintendent. He capped his professional preparation with a doctoral program at the University of Illinois. In 1969 he was appointed superintendent of an urban district, Greater Amsterdam, in New York, and in 1972 became superintendent in Newark, California.

Newark, according to Thomas, was in disarray, with a mediocre attitude toward education. Board and staff meetings featured irrelevant speeches and ethnic jokes, but Thomas in typical fashion accepted the situation as a challenge. He moved to decentralize the system and to exclude the board from interfering in decision-making about curriculum, personnel appointments, and personnel evaluations. In the process, he pressured at least one principal into retiring and had to face a board that did not like him. They eventually, however, supported his notion of shared governance. His success with shared governance in Newark most attracted the Salt Lake City board to Thomas. A California visit by some Salt Lake board members convinced them that Thomas would meet Salt Lake City's needs. His experience in handling conflict and his focus on decentralization secured him the position, which he assumed on 1 July 1973.

Something New Under the Sun:
Political Calm and Economic Stability

Thomas gave those who worked under him the general impression that he had superb verbal skills and had "great ability to talk and work with people." Even people who felt that they were being manipulated by his command of language and persuasive manner came away from meetings admiring his ability to get what he wanted and to make participants in the meeting feel involved. From the very beginning Thomas was direct about the district's problems and he expected others to be direct with him. He had a vast store of data and professional knowledge at his command. He kept up to date in his field through voracious reading habits and expected others to be similarly informed.[4]

The arrival of a more charismatic and more personable superintendent did not reverse bad situations immediately: scores were still declining, the budget deficit was growing, and the school population was still sinking (and continued to do so until around 1980). Within a short time, however, in Patricia McLeese's words, "political calm and economic stability" began to work their way through the school system. By adhering to guidelines set up by the board, savings were achieved through closing additional schools. Administrative costs were further reduced by natural attrition and by making available an early retirement plan for aging administrators. During Thomas's administration a total of 12 schools

---

4. Impressions of Thomas's working style were derived from oral history interviews conducted with teachers and former teachers and other school personnel. See Oral Histories of George Henry, Dean Collett, Patti O'Keefe, Don Bailow, and Amy Engar in Everett Cooley Oral History Project, Special Collections, University of Utah.

closed, six because of population decrease, two for not meeting safety codes, and four to make way for new schools built between 1976 and 1978—an important sign to the community that the district was still vital. One can only imagine the disastrous results if Arthur Wiscombe had asked for an increase in the property tax mill levy or the issuing of bonds for school renovation during his tenure. Yet within a few years of Thomas's appointment, Salt Lake City residents responded favorably to a request for a mill levy increase and approved a $30,000,000 bond issue to improve the physical plants. The success of these changes was attributed by John Crawford to the fact that patrons and other members of the community were involved in and informed about the decision making process from the very beginning.

A major contributor to the district's fiscal stability was the newly appointed Business Administrator, Gary Harmer, who not only balanced the budget, but also produced a reserve account for the district. The previous Business Administrator had not, in John Crawford's opinion, been on top of things financially. Harmer had a successful career with the Utah Education Association and was reluctant to leave that position, but the persistence of President Crawford paid off and Harmer accepted the task of rebuilding the district's financial structure.

One difficulty the district faced was that under the state funding formulae the district lost money every time a pupil was absent. Under a creative innovation—the "absence reclaiming program"—the district required and arranged for children who had been absent to attend school after regular hours and on Saturdays. In this way Average Daily Attendance rose to a high of some 97 percent, and the district reaped from the state millions of dollars which otherwise would have been lost. Unfortunately for the district coffers, the state department of education soon caught on and changed the rules to disallow Harmer's creative "reclaiming" of lost revenue. In any case, stabilized conditions helped promote a climate of acceptance for the plans and innovations of the new superintendent.[5]

SHARED GOVERNANCE AS AN IDEA

The board expected Thomas to pay significant attention to improving the central administration's relations with teachers, patrons, and the community as a whole. While the board did not understand all of shared governance's implications for their own legal responsibilities, some early discussions with Thomas had centered precisely on the notion, and it would become a major defining characteristic of Thomas's tenure.

In fairness to previous administrators it should be noted that for many years close cooperation between the school and its patrons had been encouraged. Certainly superintendents such as L. John Nuttall approved of involving patrons in the schools, but his personal sense of authority combined with his professional

5. Patricia McLeese, "The Process of Decentralizing Conflict and Maintaining Stability: Site Council Enactment, Implementation, Operations, and Impacts in the Salt Lake City School District, 1970-1985," Ph.D. dissertation, University of Utah, 1992, 496-97; Thomas, Oral History, 16 Aug. 1991; John Crawford, Oral History, 26 May 1992.

stature prevented him from sharing it with teachers. M. Lynn Bennion, on the other hand, expressed a great deal of faith in involving more than just educators in shaping school policies. But Bennion was not likely to forget that he had the responsibility to provide leadership—in the absence of which a system can become chaotic. He was, however, able to balance between abdicating his belief that leadership was crucial and the assertion that authority knows best.

According to Patricia McLeese, while Arthur Wiscombe served as assistant superintendent under Lynn Bennion, he and other district administrators envisioned the School Community Councils they established as a means of giving schools a greater say in governance. This move was related to Wiscombe's efforts to meet the demands of minority patrons and their students. It would also counteract what was perceived as the "minority dictatorship" of the whole school district by patrons of East Side schools. Increasing the degree of local decision making for Wiscombe was a means of making "district governance more democratic and district educational programs more effective with minority students." Consequently, when Don Thomas came into the district, there was some precedent for decentralizing decision making, especially in terms of curriculum decisions. While the conflicts of the day overwhelmed Wiscombe, he still apparently had some mechanisms for decentralization in place by 1973, and perhaps even as early as 1967.

The foregoing underscores the fact that innovation in education is usually a matter of evolution over time. Thomas himself acknowledged that what he did in Salt Lake City grew out of the American principle of "consent of the governed," which holds that society is best served when those governed have some say in determining the policies that will govern them. Without such support and input, a leader can do nothing. In Thomas's view, schools could not be closed nor boundaries changed in a unilateral way. While Wiscombe did make attempts to involve people (the shouting matches which erupted at public hearings on the closing of schools was to him evidence of public participation), his decision to close schools was not seen as one that emanated from the "will of the governed." Wiscombe asserted his leadership when difficult decisions had to be made, making himself a lighting rod that drew pent-up hostility and increased polarization in the community.

John Crawford believed that for too long the management of the Salt Lake schools had been based on an adversarial relationship. He liked Thomas's shared governance approach, an extension of the traditional notion of "local control" of public schools, an enshrined perspective in the United States, "based upon a basic belief that citizens (including parents) have a fundamental responsibility for education. Moreover, it is believed that [educational] interests are better served when lay persons determine educational policy than educational bureaucrats."[6] Crawford's commitment to this ideal catapulted him into taking a stand against what he saw as unwarranted arrogance on the part of the board and the superin-

---

6. L. L. Cunningham, "School Boards and School Councils," T. Husen and T. N. Postlethwaite, eds., *The International Encyclopedia of Education*, vol. 8 (Oxford: Pergamon Press, 1985).

tendent in assuming they knew what was best for the district. He believed Thomas could help fix what was broken in school government. Without any formal policy on shared governance, but with the board's informal approval, the new superintendent began to involve as many people as possible in decision making at all levels.

Thomas initiated his program of shared governance by inviting significant personnel to attend his staff meeting on a regular basis, not just as observers, but as full voting members empowered to make decisions. By including such individuals as the president and executive secretary of the Salt Lake Teachers' Association, their counterparts in the administrative association, and the president of the classified employees on the "Superintendent's Cabinet," Thomas greatly broadened the decision-making base and increased the information available from professional colleagues, as well as increasing the number of people who might be held responsible for whatever decisions were made.

Input from schools came through School Improvement Councils and School Community Councils. The SICs in elementary schools were assigned the responsibility of providing "orderly and professional means of improving the educational program and conditions within the school." They consisted of faculty representatives, the principal, secretary, and custodian. In secondary schools additional personnel were involved, such as representatives of the counselling staff, advisors to student government, and various academic and non-academic staff.[7]

To insure that the SIC would become actively engaged in the decision-making process, individual members could introduce any item of business for council discussion; minutes were to be kept of recommendations and actions, then disseminated throughout the school; the council would meet at least once a month, and the chair was to be elected by the council. While each SIC had responsibility for its own school in terms of procedures and programs, these had to be consistent with the board's policies and were "subject to ratification by the faculty of the school and approved by the superintendent." The SIC was not empowered to go beyond local concerns and issues judged to be outside their scope had to be referred to the central administration and teacher association, or the chair could take the issue to the superintendent.

Thomas further extended the idea of shared governance through School Community Councils, giving patrons representation in the decision making process. The SCC for each school included the members of the SIC plus the PTA president and first vice president. The latter two, in collaboration with the principal, nominated three community members, who in turn nominated another three community members, making a total of eight community members on each SCC. In selecting community members of the SCCs, consideration was given to equitable minority and geographic representation. The councils were also given the power to appoint additional ad hoc committees and to report the findings of

---

7. Stanley R. Morgan, "Shared Governance in the Utah Public Schools," Position Paper, Salt Lake City School District, May 1979, 2-3.

such committees to the council. Like the SICs, minutes of meetings were supposed to be kept and distributed to the members and, of course, councils were required to work within the "guidelines of the Board of Education policy, budget, ethics and law."

The superintendent wanted SCCs to be actively involved in the decision making process. When he delivered the charge to the school representatives on School Community Councils he expressed some of his ideals and hopes for their role in school governance:

> Schools operate best when there is close cooperation between home and school. Shared Governance is a method for establishing that cooperation. . . . The School Community Council extends local decision-making to each local school unit. It is there that decisions can best be made concerning those items that augment Board of Education policies. Recognizing Board policies, abiding by state and federal regulations, staying within the budget limits, and promoting ethical practices, the School Community Councils are a tremendous asset to the Salt Lake School District and make a significant contribution to the operation of our schools.[8]

SICs and SCCs were, as mentioned above, introduced to the district prior to Thomas's arrival, but Thomas did sharpen and focus their role. Certainly the number and variety of items they dealt with during his tenure and the degree of authority delegated to local schools increased markedly compared to the years 1970-1973.[9]

SHARED GOVERNANCE IN ACTION

Thomas tended to keep out of the decision-making process as much as was legally and professionally permissible. In one instance, the issue of whether high schools should continue to operate a flexible scheduling program (wherein students were required to be in school only when classes on a particular topic were necessary) led to acrimonious and extended debate that pitted teachers against principal, students against faculty, or non-academic faculty against parents and academic faculty. When one group appealed to the superintendent to resolve the issue for their stymied SCC, he refused to intervene and instructed them to solve it at the local level; no district policy was involved. Eventually each school reached a similar decision to abandon flexible scheduling, although by quite different routes.

In another case, one junior high school had gone through much turmoil over a lack of students' accountability for their behavior. Police calls were common, but did not reduce the tensions or improve low academic achievement. SCC initiatives led to a complete overhaul of all the school's policies. New poli-

---

8. Cited in Morgan, "Shared Governance," 5-6.

9. McLeese graphically illustrates the increase in authority delegated to school councils in a chart summarizing "the policy-making authority delegated to sites" and suggests that there was about a 100% increase in such delegation between the early 1970s and 1976-78 and another 100%+ increase by 1985. See McLeese, "The Process of Decentralizing Conflict," Table 8.1, 503.

cies implemented by the SCC brought an immediate reduction in police calls and academic promotion improved by some 20 percent. All this was accomplished without top-down directives.[10]

Even issues beyond the purview of individual schools were seen as being amenable to shared governance at an inter-school or district-wide level. As early as the mid-1970s there was talk among the district leadership of the need either to close one high school or three junior high schools. An ad hoc district-wide committee recommended that the district's grade system be changed from K-6, 7-9, and 10-12 to K-6, 7-8, and 9-12. Ninth grade students would be assigned to the first year of senior high school, reducing pressure on junior highs by permitting three of them to close and changing the remaining six to intermediate schools.

Because such decisions were made on the advice and consent of the governed, the closures "were accomplished with less difficulty than had ever been experienced by the district in the closing of any twenty-three previous schools." Stanley Morgan attributed this to the high involvement of significant sectors of the community in the decision making process as did Thomas, who also attributed it to allowing market forces to determine the outcome of deliberations. One Community Council (Roosevelt Junior High) was so attuned to the market realities that they actually petitioned the board to close the school, which Thomas interpreted as the "ultimate in the consent of the governed."[11]

While the district during the Thomas years reflected a more up-beat and cooperative tone than the previous administration had enjoyed, it would be wrong to attribute all of the change to shared governance. As happens often in education, improvements can sometimes be brought about simply because the issues are being talked about and attended to by those in power. According to McLeese, the whole concept of shared governance was very controversial throughout the years it was tried in the district. In only one of the schools she observed did it lead to a new and creative vision as to what schools should be about. In this particular instance the School Community Council determined that their school should be "sluff free, fight free, failure free and fear free" and policies were implemented at the site level which indeed made headway in producing such a school, for a time at least.[12]

Even such an enthusiastic proponent as Thomas admitted that he had difficulty working with principals who resisted shared governance in their schools. At times he had to persuade teachers not to resist the notion of evaluating teachers through School Community Councils.[13] Such instances remind us that mandated democracy is not quite what the liberal theory of democratic government is supposed to mean. However, in the eyes of the board and the superintendent,

---

10. These examples of how shared governance was perceived were mentioned in a conversation with Pat McLeese, 28 May 1992.
11. Thomas, Oral History, 16 Aug. 1991.
12. Conversation with Pat McLeese, 28 May 1992.
13. Thomas, Oral History, 16 Aug. 1991.

even "top-down democracy" is probably better than the social, political, and educational chaos they perceived as the legacy of the previous administration.

In practice, shared governance had the potential of giving self-serving leaders more power; they could claim that the "people" were behind the decisions that they had actually engineered. This "tyranny of the majority" made the shared governance ideology just as destructive of good decision making as overt, top-down, centralized governance. Others were uncomfortable with the idea because it seemed to contradict the traditional notion of professionalism, which held that the superintendent was in charge of principals, who were in charge of teachers, who were in charge of students. Abandoning the "natural" order of things and involving teachers too much in the governance of schools forced teachers to lose interest in their primary responsibility, the classroom.[14] Response to the concept depended in large measure on the personal dispositions of participants. In spite of some resistance to shared governance, the vast majority of principals, teachers and parents apparently responded positively to it. In time, Thomas was recognized as a promoter of the idea in school districts across the nation, although in Utah the idea was limited to the Salt Lake District.

When Thomas initially broached the issue of having the board adopt a formal policy statement about shared governance, some resistance occurred on the grounds that it went against the board's own legal authority to govern the schools. This was overcome when the board was assured that parents serving on SCC would be appointed, not elected, and the councils would not have the power to fire teachers. Like many other professional educators, Thomas was anxious to increase his professional stature and national visibility by demonstrating outstanding accomplishments as a school leader. This very natural disposition was probably part of the motivation in getting the board to approve a formal policy statement on shared governance. On 16 May 1978, the board approved a statement which met Thomas's request for official approval of what he had been doing for the last five years. It stated: "It is the policy of the board that each council participates actively in the decision-making process for the school rather than in an advisory capacity. The council, like all other governance or administration units of the district, operates within the guidelines of Board of Education Policy, Budget, Ethics, and Law."[15] Such a statement, enshrined as an official board policy, was necessary for the district to be considered for the prestigious list of model cities put out by the National Committee for Citizens in Education, a private group to promote citizen involvement in public schools. At the core of this group's rationale was the belief that the professionalization of education had deprived parents of a sense of ownership in their children's education. Thomas, one of this organization's board members, was perceived as one of the most open

---

14. George Henry, Oral History, 9 Apr. 1992; Dean Collett, Oral History, 28 Apr. 1992.

15. Excerpt from Board of Education, Minutes, cited in McIeese, "The Process of Decentralizing Conflict," 367.

superintendents in the nation for including parents as decision makers in schools. He was recognized by the National Committee as a "pioneer" in the area of site-based management.[16] His endeavors came to fruition in Salt Lake City in 1979 when the district was designated as a model for "site based governance" by the NCCE.

Widespread representative involvement was not an end in itself. Shared governance was rather the means of making public schools more effective in serving children. Although shared governance has become something of a trend nationally, there is little long-term empirical evidence showing a connection between shared governance and concrete benefits accruing to children. It is assumed, probably not without good reason, that parental involvement in schools *will* benefit students. However, specific evidence (apart from the anecdotal accounts discussed above) confirming or denying this will have to await future studies. By the end of his tenure in 1984, Thomas claimed that student achievement in the district had improved—for eighth graders "we were about two years ahead of norm achievement levels"—but even this cannot be tied to one particular innovation.[17] Perhaps the most that can be said is that traditional learning proceeds more effectively when the schools are operating in a calm, non-threatening environment.

ASSESSMENTS OF SHARED GOVERNANCE

In 1985, after shared governance had been implemented in Salt Lake schools, Betty Malen and Rodney Ogawa of the University of Utah's Department of Educational Administration attempted to determine the extent to which parity of power had been achieved in the city's schools. Taking as a starting point the policy's explicit intent to give administrators, teachers, and parents "equal power in the determination of school level matters," they wanted to know how well it actually worked. Based on extensive interviews and a close study of attempts at implementation, they concluded that their findings "clearly demonstrate that parity has not been realized" and that "Site councils have not redistributed decision making authority at the building level." In spite of many expectations and claims to the contrary, "[t]raditional authority relationships have not been altered by the Shared Governance Policy." Malen and Ogawa identified a number of weaknesses: the councils did not reflect the ethnic diversity of the community; the councils varied greatly in the way they followed the "explicit guidelines" designed to promote effective operation of the councils; too many councils did not meet regularly, did not disseminate minutes, and did not prepare agendas for meetings; the councils tended to enhance principals' authority rather than share it; principals tended to use the councils as a means of defusing potentially controversial issues; and, ultimately, principals retained control over management of schools, while teachers retained control over instruction. The net result was that

---

16. Telephone conversation with Chrissie Ewen Bamber, Assistant Executive Director, National Committee for Citizens in Education, Washington, D.C., 2 June 1992.

17. Thomas, Oral History, 16 Aug. 1991.

decision-making authority in any meaningful sense was *not* altered by shared governance practices. The discrepancy between the intent of the shared governance policy and its actual realization generated "complex and troublesome issues" which the researchers felt would have to be addressed by the district in order to make shared governance more than a good idea.[18]

In spite of such negative results, however, Malen and Ogawa did not dismiss shared governance as worthless and futile. The School Improvement Councils were viewed by principals as performing an important function as sounding boards, safety valves, as a source of teacher input and staff support, and a means of improving relations. Teachers saw the councils as important sources of information and as giving them a voice in the school. Much more ambivalence about the School Community Councils was expressed by educators, partly because they feared too much parental interference in the classrooms. Parents, on the other hand, seemed to appreciate having access to information about the schools and a voice (even if somewhat circumscribed) in what went on in them.

By simply giving parents a good feeling about what they were doing, the councils gained pragmatic value. As John Crawford expressed the idea, when a school leader promotes a free flow of reliable information to patrons and invites their input, it becomes less likely that new initiatives and recommendations will be rejected or that a hostile relationship will develop between the officers and the patrons of the schools.[19]

In addition to the pragmatic consequence of including patrons in school deliberations, shared governance tended to decentralize conflicts and "got the district off the hook" by reducing pressure on the central administration to resolve issues immediately. Two potentially explosive issues that were "disarmed" by involving local councils in their resolutions concerned which teacher should leave a particular school and what programs should be cut. Multiplied by the number of schools in the district such decisions had the potential of being a real district "donnybrook," but when split up among the schools, they were effectively neutralized as far as the district was concerned. Based on her study of the shared governance policy in Salt Lake City, Pat McLeese has suggested that at the district level, decentralization of conflict was perhaps the most important practical result of the policy and may have more long-term significance than the transfer of power. Others have referred to this as the "share the blame" function of shared governance and have suggested that the policy's major weakness is its use mainly to deal with unpopular decisions. Given the complexity of governing schools one can hardly blame Salt Lake City's chief educator for wanting to share some of the "negative glory" accruing to him by dint of his participation in the affairs of a seventy million dollar corporation employing some 1,200 teachers and administrators and trying to meet the needs of 25,000 students and their par-

---

18. Betty Malen and Rodney T. Ogawa, "The Implementation of the Salt Lake City School District's Shared Governance Policy: A Study of School Site Councils," Report Prepared for the Salt Lake City School District, Aug. 1985, 38-39.

19. John Crawford, Oral History, 26 May 1992.

ents.[20]

Actual results aside, Salt Lake City's implementation attempts took on a life of their own and were perceived by outside observers as more successful than similar attempts elsewhere. For example, one study of Salt Lake's shared governance in teacher evaluation, conducted for the Rand Corporation, asserted that while the concept had been tried in many areas between 1974 and 1984, with varying degrees of success, its relative success in Salt Lake City could be attributed "to the homogeneity of the culture, or at least to the unintentional suppression of divergent groups." This particular research saw a particularly close "fit between Mormon culture and shared governance." The superintendent's ability to convince patrons, teachers, and administrators of the efficacy of shared governance succeeded in large measure because it was "consonant with the organizational and relational styles his patrons were accustomed to."[21]

Like the schools in "Mormon country," local Mormon wards have a great deal of responsibility for their own affairs, even though they are tied to a hierarchical and centralized system of governance in matters theological. Among other factors the Rand study indicated helped make shared governance a success in Salt Lake City were: the widespread use of lay leadership in initiating and carrying out religious, social, cultural, educational, financial, and artistic responsibilities; the tendency in Mormon culture to avoid confrontation and to rely instead on consensus building; and the "notion that a higher [ecclesiastical] authority might ultimately reverse a local decision."

Even the mundane fact that shared governance requires much time fits into a meeting- and family-centered culture used to spending a great deal of time in councils and on its children. Shared governance, to work at all, depends on "cultural supports for volunteerism, participation, and collective responsibility for child development," factors readily available in Mormonism's emphasis on "education, conformity, and cooperative endeavor." The Rand research also suggested that Thomas personally fit into the religious/cultural expectations which permeated the schools: "Thomas, like the hierarchy of the Mormon church, retains ultimate control, and is unabashedly hortatory."[22]

The Rand study also said that "the fit between Thomas's contrivance and the culture of public education seems more difficult." By this they apparently meant that the bureaucratic structure of public schooling had difficulty dealing with a system that tended to short-circuit long entrenched procedures and make what were perceived to be end-runs around the entrenched bureaucracy. Thomas admitted that up to the time he left the district some principals did not share his vision of shared governance. Some had difficulty going directly to him with problems because of their previous socialization into a more hierarchical chain of command. Administrators at the district level, who had become accustomed to

---

20. Conversation with Pat McLeese, 1 June 1992; Henry, Oral History, 10 Apr. 1992.
21. Arthur E. Wise et al., *Case Studies for Teacher Evaluation: A Study of Effective Practices* (Santa Monica, California: Rand Corporation, 1984), 46.
22. Wise, *Case Studies for Teacher Evaluation*, 7, 46-7.

their place in centralized decision making, found it almost impossible to give up the power and titles which had accrued to them. Even the Salt Lake Teacher's Association, while very supportive of shared governance in adjudicating the removal of teachers judged incompetent by their peers, was caught in a double bind when it provided legal funds for teachers so removed to challenge the action. But as Thomas was wont to say, no system is perfect: shared governance did not guarantee that no tensions would ever arise in a system as complex as the public schools.[23]

In light of public support and administrative resistance, it is not unreasonable to see Thomas as an educational reformer attempting to counteract the "one best system" mentality, which David Tyack has demonstrated permeated much educational thought of the late nineteenth and early twentieth centuries. In counteracting this mentality in Salt Lake City, Thomas, an outsider, pushed the community back to some of its own cultural roots and values. He was also resisting the inherent bureaucratic tendency to promote "over conformity." Ironically, shared governance came into conflict with a highly centralized school bureaucracy that had also been promoted by the Mormons, in the early 1900s.[24]

What Are Schools for and What Is Worth Knowing?

Just as many doubt that there is any one best system of organizing schools, so too, it appears, there is not one type of teacher or strategy that is efficacious in every situation. For example, when Patti O'Keefe began teaching in Salt Lake in the early 1970s she resisted using the Sullivan whole language approach to reading, but eventually decided that to reject it out of hand would harm those students who needed that particular approach. The nub of the whole issue for her was the realization that a teacher needs and should have access to a multitude of approaches, rather than relying on one approach to answer all the needs of the mixed groups that inhabit a typical school.[25] Public schools, even in relatively homogenous cities such as Salt Lake, find a wide array of needs and talents among their students. One of Thomas's innovations that stimulated dialogue and discussion was his promotion of the theme that "Every Child Can Learn." This posed, in essence, a challenge to each teacher to plan the classroom experience with a wide variety of student needs and capacities in mind. This idea certainly encouraged a broader conception of school aims and also helps explain the kinds of comprehensive reform Thomas encouraged teachers to develop. O'Keefe reflected on this as "the era when we started really recognizing that we could engage in professional dialogue and discussion about teaching and learning and the context of the school and . . . [identify] some of the things that might contribute

23. Wise, Case Studies for Teacher Evaluation, 47; Thomas, Oral History, 16 Aug. 1991, 71.

24. For the history of the emergence of highly centralized bureaucracy in American schools see David Tyack, The One Best System: A History of American Urban Education (Cambridge: Harvard University Press, 1974). The idea of "bureaucratic over conformity" is discussed by Robert K. Merton, Social Theory and Social Structure (Glencoe: Free Press, 1949), 197-200.

25. Patti O'Keefe, Oral History, 29 Oct. 1990.

to make it a more effective [learning] environment."[26]

Teachers who came to Thomas "bright eyed and bushy tailed with sparkling enthusiasm" could run new ideas for programs by him and find ready acceptance and encouragement to proceed. Of course, he expected teachers to be professionally responsible for their plans, but he tended to endorse "any and all innovations" that teachers could convince him helped increase the learning of their students. Thomas really believed that schools could make a difference in the lives of young people. He repeatedly expressed concern that while educational reforms initiated by the *Nation at Risk* report of 1983 stressed academic excellence and apparently boosted the achievement scores of the bottom quartile of the student population, this was not happening among the students in large cities, where most minorities lived. The lack of progress was due, in his estimation, to city systems being too bureaucratic—a view that fits well into his notion of site-based governance.[27]

His basic concern for the classroom reinforced the notion that Thomas was very much a "hands-on" advocate. He organized workshops to help teachers hone their skills. At workshops he did not hesitate to join discussion groups and become involved in talking about different approaches to teaching. He knew teachers' names and was not above engaging in good natured kidding when he met them in various settings. His disposition to be genuinely interested in teachers was probably the basis for the comment made at the farewell banquet in his honor when he left the district in 1984. After a number of dignitaries had spoken and praised his work in the district, the President of the Salt Lake Teachers' Association simply said that Thomas's major contribution was to make teaching a profession in Salt Lake City. Frequently he and his wife Fran received bouquets of flowers as marks of appreciation from teachers who appreciated his support of their professional aspirations.[28]

But Thomas was not just a hands-on enthusiast, exuding fast-fix gimmicks for teachers. His practical side was firmly rooted in a sophisticated view of learning that was much influenced by his graduate work with David Ausubel of the University of Illinois. Ausubel, a pioneer in the cognitive approach to learning, viewed the learning process not as a matter of conditioning students to respond to discrete stimuli, but as a process of intellectual growth and development brought about through relating the learner to the context in which the details can be understood. The memorization and recall of discrete facts in isolation from their context was not, for Ausubel, the way children should be taught.[29]

This approach to teaching is clearly reflected in the kind of curriculum Thomas pursued in the Salt Lake District. In his view, to meet the needs of the broad spectrum of student ability, the best way "is *not* to concentrate so heavily on the

---

26. O'Keefe, Oral History, 29 Oct. 1990.
27. Thomas, Oral History, 16 Aug. 1991.
28. Oral history interviews with O'Keefe, Henry, Engar, and Thomas.
29. For an overview of Ausubel's approach see his *Educational Psychology: A Cognitive View* (New York: Holt, Rinehart, and Winston, 1968).

basic skills. . . . [I]f you want to teach basic skills it's better to teach them through algebra than general math. . . . If you want to teach grammar it's better to teach it through John Steinbeck's literature than to teach it through [focusing on] basic skills." In his opinion the schools had done quite well in teaching the basic skills didactically, but had not done so well in linking the basics to "high order thinking skills." Basic reading skills taught and learned alone and apart from thinking skills represented for Thomas only one limited aspect of the teaching/learning process.[30]

Even with all his persuasive skills, the superintendent could not convince everyone to embrace the point of view on the holistic, Ausubelian model. Given the diversity found in a large school district, Thomas's own reluctance to impose one way of doing anything, and his willingness to allow teachers to experiment, it would have been too much to expect him to reshape the teaching approaches of generations of teachers and principals. In a sense, he may have been prevented from establishing a more holistic approach district-wide because he had convinced teachers that they should be involved in governance. With that orientation, imposition of a prescribed program from the district office would have been well-nigh impossible.

"PLURALISM GONE MAD"

Thomas's early exposure to Ausubel and to the history of education under James Anderson at the University of Illinois served him well when he took issue with criticism of public schooling that surfaced during the late 1970s. Much of this was based on a revisionist interpretation of the American educational past, which attempted to counterpose the traditional, sometimes euphoric and romantic view of the public schools with what the revisionists saw as a more realistic assessment. The rhetorical view glorified the public schools as giving everyone equal opportunity in America and serving as a foundation for a democratic society. The realistic view stressed the failure of schools to meet the needs of America's dispossessed—the poor, minorities, and women.[31]

Thomas believed both extremes did injustice to the intent and record of the American public school. He rejected the notion that the only way to redeem the schools was to open them up to greater diversity of perspective and to forego making any moral or ethical claims on them. He argued that "pluralism gone mad" was weakening the schools through establishment of separate courses for minority students, the stress on immediate relevancy in class content, proliferation of courses, the promotion of moral relativism, and "confusion between education and job programs." Instead of improving educational opportunities for America's minorities, this warped program, according to Thomas, had "created confusion, ambivalence and fear." What the nation needed was not such a nega-

---

30. Thomas, Oral History, 16 Aug. 1991.
31. As examples of revisionist history, see Samuel Bowles and Herbert Gintis, *Schooling in Capitalist America: Educational Reform and the Contradictions of Economic Life* (New York: Basic Books, 1976); Joel Spring, *The Sorting Machine: National Education Policy since 1945* (New York: David McKay, 1976).

tive assessment of schools, but a "renewed emphasis on the historical traditions of our nation, based on the democratic principles embedded in our national documents." Admitting that such a task was not easy, he affirmed that with aggressive educators committed to "narrowing the gap between principles and practice" the nation's schools would not need to be "dismantled in order to improve them."[32]

Thomas argued that expecting schools single-handedly to resolve complex problems such as racism, poverty, and social injustice was completely unrealistic. Better to help alleviate such problems by teaching "students to think, to get jobs, to appreciate freedom and to understand the principles of democratic government. These are the functions that schools can perform well. Other educational goals should be assumed by other social agencies. When such a balance of responsibility is established, both public and private agencies will do their jobs better."[33]

At the very heart of Thomas's educational philosophy, and an essential component of the public school's role in American society, was what he (and others) have referred to as the "American ethos," a tradition-shrouded statement of liberal sentiments and assumptions he believed should undergird public schools: self worth, the value of democracy, faith in reason, respect for knowledge, and equal protection under the law. These principles, if adhered to and promoted in public schools, would provide the diversity of American society with the cohesive social glue required to keep it from falling apart. Such a perspective would allow public schools to balance their aims and purposes between promoting individual rights and the public good.[34]

Given the kind of culture in which Thomas served as superintendent, his resistance to radical pluralism can be easily understood. If shared governance (partially) succeeded because of the close fit between it, Thomas, and the local culture, his ideas for curriculum also fit very nicely into the general conservative outlook of the era and area. His affinity with the values of Mormon culture explains not only the curriculum he promoted, but also why he never felt any pressure exerted on him from the LDS church. He occasionally had breakfast with the LDS Commissioner of Education, Neal Maxwell, to discuss general school issues, but in none of these contacts did he ever experience pressure. Thomas had the impression from his visits with church leaders that they were anxious to avoid controversy. In addition, some points of contention during Wiscombe's tenure were now fading—in June 1978, for example, the church abandoned its long-held denial of priesthood to males of African descent. As Thomas reflected on his relationship with the LDS community he remarked: "What I did was appropriate for the times in which the Mormon Church was changing. . . . [W]hat I did and what they were doing was just kind of congruent . . . it was not a chal-

---

32. M. Donald Thomas, *Pluralism Gone Mad* (Bloomington, IN: Phi Delta Kappa Education Foundation, 1981), 18.

33. Ibid., 19-20.

34. Ibid., 28.

lenge; it was a complementary thing to what they were doing."[35]

His cordial relationship with LDS leaders and the community did not mean that Thomas overlooked instances when some teachers overreached the bounds of propriety and initiated prayers in classrooms or had discussions that verged on promoting particular religious doctrines in the classroom. In one instance, when a principal asked for assistance with a teacher who was telling children about Jesus' virgin birth, Thomas attempted to approach the issue from a First Amendment perspective. The teacher responded: "Well, Dr. Thomas, don't you believe in the Virgin Mary?" Thomas emphasized that his belief or disbelief was not the issue; the real issue was that in public schools "We can't under the First Amendment be teaching children about the Virgin Birth." Aside from a few other instances, Thomas had to counsel principals or teachers about separation of church and state only three or four times in eleven years. From Thomas's perspective, his situation was unique in Utah in that as superintendent he was cautioning *against* overlapping state and church functions. Thomas had a sense (probably accurate) that prayer and religious teachings were more common in Utah's rural school districts. It was unlikely, he believed, that rural Mormon superintendents would counsel against these practices as he did in Salt Lake.[36]

EQUITY AND STANDARDS

The same knowledge and assertiveness Thomas used to broach the issue of church and state also characterized his response to the education of minorities. From his point of view, to educate the minority child as a minority instead of as an individual was harmful to the child's sense of self. One teacher told Thomas she had not disciplined a black student for throwing rocks until the child's third throw because she believed "Blacks are used to throwing rocks . . . and have to get that out of their system." "That's nonsense," retorted Thomas. "[I]f a child throws a rock, you interfere and discipline him the first time, because if you let him throw rocks three times you are reinforcing that he can throw the first two, and he will get away with it." The teacher tried to excuse herself by saying that she didn't want the NAACP to harass her, to which Thomas responded: "The NAACP doesn't want their kids to throw rocks."[37]

The worst thing an educational system could do for minority students, in Thomas's mind, was to think that equity and fairness meant the absence of standards. No one would be helped in the long run by this permissive approach. Thomas believed that nothing should be done for minority students "that they reasonably can do for themselves." When teachers inflate the grades of minority students as a gift they in fact say: "You poor dumb kid, I'm going to have to give you a better grade." To do this under the guise of help would be counterproductive. In the opinion of one African-American teacher, these condescending ap-

---

35. Thomas, Oral History, 16 Aug. 1991; telephone conversation with M. Donald Thomas, 27 Apr. 1992.

36. Thomas, Oral History, 16 Aug. 1991.

37. Ibid.

proaches led to students unprepared in reading and basic study skills and who lacked a sense of self-discipline.[38]

With large infusions of federal funds Thomas recruited more African-American teachers to teach not only special classes, but the regular curriculum. And while applauding cultural diversity, he drew firm lines at what he saw as an unwarranted broadening of the canon. He dismissed claims that, simply because a person was African-American or hispanic or Italian, he or she should be included in the study of history. Thomas believed in a mainstream of values and ideas, and only those contributions that enhanced the culture of the mainstream were considered worth knowing. He wanted to avoid stereotypes and the trivialization of cultures, often saying that he didn't want Italians to be known only for eating spaghetti. Choices had to be made. Not everything from every group could or should be included in the curriculum.[39]

Thomas encouraged personal interaction between members of the minority community and school personnel and seldom missed an opportunity himself to show his support for cultural diversity as an important aspect of the curriculum. For example, he made sure that he was invited to the annual South High Awards Banquet and always made a point of promoting that school's diversity as one of its strengths. When principals called him in sheer panic because Alberta Henry, an assertive African-American community activist Arthur Wiscombe had appointed to the district staff, had arrived at their school ("She's in my school. What shall I do?"), he advised them to take her to lunch and get to know her better. Over a series of district-sponsored Saturday "soul food" dinners, he had community members share with principals their stories and their visions of community. The most important effect of this community interaction was to counteract the notion that minority students were incapable of meeting high academic and personal standards. That attitude for Thomas was wrong, morally and pedagogically. To accept it was to create a vicious cycle of lessened expectations on the part of teachers and substandard performance on the part of students.[40]

ENCROACHMENT ON PREROGATIVES

During his years in Salt Lake, Thomas reportedly received repeated job offers, many of them more prestigious and with better pay than the Salt Lake superintendency. But, in the words of one president of the board, Wayne Evans, "he remained singularly dedicated to his job here," and had implemented every commitment he had made to the board in 1973.[41] A decade later, however, a number of circumstances combined, leading to his surprise resignation from the superintendency to take up a major role in a massive educational reform package in South Carolina.

A person as forthright and committed as Thomas could not, of course, fail to

---

38. Ibid.; Henry, Oral History, 9 Apr. 1992.
39. Thomas, Oral History, 16 Aug. 1991; Henry, Oral History, 9 Apr. 1992.
40. Thomas, Oral History, 16 Aug. 1991; Henry, Oral History, 9 Apr. 1992.
41. "S. L. School Superintendent Resigns," *Salt Lake Tribune*, 28 July 1984.

ruffle some feathers during his long tenure. Shared governance, in its tendency to share the blame for problems as well as the credit for solutions, may have helped deflect criticism onto Thomas himself. Not until he had been in Salt Lake almost five or six years did he begin to feel uneasy about the directions he was receiving from the board. In 1978, John Crawford, shortly before stepping down as president of the board, had presided over a "brief meeting" during which the board reappointed Thomas for another term. Crawford praised the superintendent for his "unselfish devotion to students, parents, teachers, the board and other administrators" and the vote of re-appointment was unanimous. John Crawford ran a "tight ship" as president of the board, and Thomas acknowledged that much of his own success in Salt Lake City could be attributed to Crawford's work and his abilities.[42]

With Crawford's departure in 1979, Thomas began to sense a lack of support. Two of the new members added to the board at the election of November 1978, Tab Uno and Susan Keene, caused Thomas to feel that the days of John Crawford's kind of board was over, as they violated the 1973 board's agreement to give him maximum freedom to implement policies. Thomas deeply resented the encroachments Uno and Keene were making. Within eight months of their coming on the board, both Uno and Keene were identified as the major cause of renewed factionalism. Words such as "circus," "zoo," and "menagerie" were used to describe the proceedings as the two new members asked surprise questions the staff were not prepared to answer and engaged in "public attacks" on the administration and the board. In addition to disrupting board meetings, Uno and Keene reportedly sent out newsletters to their constituents, openly attacking the board and its policies. Although some observers saw Uno and Keene as "obstructionist agitators" determined to promote conflict in the district, others, Thomas included, blamed a weak board that sat quietly by and allowed its two most aggressive members to set the tone of the meetings.[43]

Others felt that the board's two mavericks served the needs of their constituents by raising hard-to-answer questions about school funds and other issues. Instead of debating the issues openly, the majority on the board came to meeting with their minds made up, their votes already cast and without any disposition to listen to new facts and arguments. One patron who supported Uno and Keene complained that the board seemed to be more willing to spend money on new facilities than on new educational programs. Both Uno and Keene believed that the board had become an instrument of Superintendent Thomas, and they accused him in meetings of manipulating the agenda to fit his needs. They felt he should have less power and that the board and local schools should have more. Keene voted against reappointing Thomas in January 1980.[44]

---

42. M. Donald Thomas, "A Preeminent School Chief Reflects on What Makes a Board Member Exemplary," *The American School Board Journal* (Apr. 1985): 31, 44.
43. "Factions Hinder Results at Board of Education," *Salt Lake Tribune*, 6 Aug. 1979; Thomas, Oral History, 16 Aug. 1991.
44. "Two Minority Members Seek More School Board Powers," *Salt Lake Tribune*, 7 Aug. 1979.

For his part, Thomas was in no mood to compromise with his critics. He had always fended off board members who tried to encroach on his responsibilities. In similar circumstances some superintendents would have organized "retreats and all that nonsense," but Thomas would have none of that. He wanted to be left alone to do his job. If it was not self-evident to the board that he should be in charge, he did not want to have a role in such a system. Things improved, however, helped perhaps by Uno's decision not to run for reelection in 1982 and the apparently successful efforts of the rest of the board to neutralize Keene's continued hostility toward Thomas.[45]

"Excess High School Capacity"

From 1959 to 1981, Salt Lake's school population declined steadily until it reached around 23,000, forcing Thomas to close eight schools in ten years (the two previous superintendents had closed some 20, combined). Of the schools Thomas closed, three were junior highs. At the same time he built three new elementary schools. After 1981, the school population showed a slight increase, but had stabilized at around 24,000 students. After so many years of decline, the board's decision to rebuild East High School after fire destroyed it in 1973 must be seen as a result of political pressure from East's powerful patrons rather than sound economic or educational reasons. The fact that the entire city population had declined during the 1960s from 189,454 to 175,885 should have been enough to caution the board against rebuilding East. However in the face of an emotional campaign that "East will rise again," led by such influential cheerleader alumni as Professor J. D. Williams, Mayor E. J. "Jake" Garn and board member Dan S. Bushnell, the irrefutable logic of demographic shifts was refuted by political clout. East High School was rebuilt, just as the need to start closing secondary schools loomed into view as an issue.[46]

Thomas claimed he would not have recommended rebuilding East had he been superintendent, but it was a *fait accompli* by the time he assumed office. However, he still had to deal with the realities of shifting demographics. For Thomas, the best way to do that was to close old schools that could not be upgraded and to build new schools that combined the populations served by two old schools. For example, he closed Douglas and Webster elementary schools in 1978 and replaced them with the new M. Lynn Bennion Elementary School. In line with his basic belief in freedom of choice, Thomas also continued to promote a district policy (in effect since the early 1960s) of open enrollment for secondary schools. Students, if they wished, could attend school anywhere in the city. The rising number of minority students coming into the city schools, the deterioration of central city residence areas, and the movement of middle-class families to suburban areas combined to make East and Highland High Schools more desirable for white, lower-middle-class residents. This "white flight" meant

---

45. Thomas, Oral History, 16 Aug. 1991.
46. Data on school closing compiled by Juanita B. Wainwright, Superintendent's Office; Clark Brimhall, Oral History, 22 Aug. 1990.

that West and South High Schools began to suffer from a dearth of college-bound students. A self-fulfilling prophecy was thus set in motion: as college-oriented students fled the west side schools, South and West were perceived as unchallenging academically. As a result, fewer people under the open transfer policy opted to attend West and South. The whole process was exacerbated by the inescapable fact that as the 1980s progressed, the district simply had, in the words of John Bennion, Thomas's successor, "excess high school capacity," just as it had excess elementary capacity under Wiscombe.[47]

There was understandable reluctance on the part of administrators and the board to close an institution that had come in many ways to be identified with the community, if not for the academic abilities of its "Sterling Scholars," then certainly for the rich emotional attachments generated by sports, music, and the esprit de corps youth peer groups engender. While closing an elementary school brings protests from a limited area, high schools take in a larger area and a different combination of patrons and politics. So sensitive was the board of education on this issue that sometime in the 1970s they actually passed a mandate that there would *always* be four equal high schools in Salt Lake City. When Thomas advised that such a policy was unwise, the board warned him that he did not understand Salt Lake City and that "[p]olitically you cannot close a [high] school." If he did he would "get people coming out of their retirement and out of their graves to fight for their school."[48]

Something, however, had to be done. Partly because of demographics and partly because of the open transfer policy, the "critical mass" of students needed to keep high school programs viable at West and South was declining precipitously. One strategy adopted around 1975 changed the junior high schools from serving seventh, eighth and ninth graders to serving only the seventh and eighth in a "Middle School." Ninth graders were then transferred to high school as the freshman class, making the high school a four year institution. (The four year high school was, incidentally, a common pattern in the days before junior high schools were touted as necessary for the social and mental health of students aged 13-15.) In this way, two ends would be served: first, the reduction of the junior high to two grades would save money by closing a number of such schools; second, when the 9th grade moved to the high schools, the high school enrollment would automatically be increased, and it would be possible to sustain comprehensive academic offerings.

While closing South High School may not have been part of the agenda of the meetings dealing with the future organization of the junior highs, closing Lincoln Junior High in 1975 was preceded by talk of the need to perhaps close South. From Don Barlow's perspective, the decision to close South in 1986 was "almost inevitably the result of what we did with the junior highs [in 1975]." But, without a transfusion of ninth grade students from junior high feeder schools, closing South would have become an issue earlier than it did. As a result

---

47. Bennion, Oral History, 11 Aug. 1991.
48. Thomas, Oral History, 16 Aug. 1991.

of the middle school reorganization, Thomas was able to close three junior high schools in 1975 and one in 1982. The reason recorded was "decrease in population," but covertly, it was also to save money and to give the high schools a "critical mass." Another less-publicized reason had to do with athletics. While ninth graders were in junior high they could not play football, but transferring them to high school enhanced the senior high football teams through providing the students with an extra year of training. A number of prominent individuals (including board members) apparently exerted pressure to enhance their sons' athletic participation in this way.[49]

Closing junior highs kept South High open for a few more years, but the problem of declining population would not go away. In spite of valiant efforts to stave off the inevitable—including the innovative Danforth Foundation moral education program and a U.S. Department of Education citation that singled out South as an exemplary urban school—it was clear at least by 1980 that the option of closing South would have to be considered in the immediate future. While Thomas was probably technically correct in asserting that closing South was not an item he discussed with the board, at least as far as formal public meetings are concerned, it is also quite evident that patrons of South High, individual board members, the principals of Highland High and South High, and other administrators had thought much about the issue.[50]

In December 1983 the board began preparing the public in a series of meetings at each high school to discuss the issue of "open enrollment." One option discussed during these hearings was the possibility of closing a high school and redistributing its students among the other schools. Another option lay in rescinding the open enrollment policy and changing boundaries to make each school equivalent in numbers of students. The South High community immediately recognized that their enrollment declines made them most vulnerable.

A massive campaign swept South, involving students, faculty, administrators, and alumni to demonstrate concern for the school's future. Even LDS wards were involved in the campaign to inform the community members of the importance attached to the hearing at South. A special school assembly featured a casket from which the "student body" emerged, signifying the determination that the school should not die. At the public hearing held on a cold and snowy 13 December, over 1,400 people sporting "I Love South High" buttons crowded into South High's auditorium to protest any attempt to close the school. According to Principal LaVar Sorensen, "more people attended the South High hearing than all the other three schools combined." And for good reason—no other schools were vulnerable.[51] The highly charged hearing "very politely, but forcibly, told the

---

49. Don Barlow, Oral History, 4 May 1992.

50. Conversation with Larry Johnson, 18 Aug. 1992; Thomas, Oral History, 16 Aug. 1991; Al Church, "Public Education Policy Analysis: Open Transfer in the Salt Lake City Schools," Research Paper, Department of Educational Administration, University of Utah, 15 Dec. 1983, 13-14.

51. LaVar L. Sorensen, "School Closure Dilemma" [December 1983]. This statement was prepared for the National School Public Relations Association; LaVar L. Sorensen, Oral History, 8 Sept. 1992.

Board of Education not to close the school." But as events unfolded in the late 1980s, not even strong community enthusiasm could prevent South's doors from closing.

Closing West High, on the other hand, was successfully avoided. West's problems included a relatively weak School Community Council and the continual movement of middle-class families away from the "natural" West high attendance area. Had these conditions continued unabated West would likely have closed, as Thomas expected, but several important events intervened: in his last few months as Superintendent, Don Thomas appointed the successful principal at Bryant Junior High, Harold Trussel, to head West High as of 1 July 1984. Trussel, an Ed.S. graduate of the University of Utah, had succeeded in changing the academic climate at Bryant. When he took over at West High he brought to the school a sense of discipline and high expectation the school for so many years had lacked. One of his first tasks was to get an effective School Community Council in place, and, with the help of strong community-minded individuals such as Paul Hanks as the SCC president, he began to transform West High School's image and reality. Within a few years test scores began to improve and conflict over minority issues declined. Trussel pressured the board to chose West as the home of the district's prestigious International Baccalaureate program. Classical art work began to adorn hallways and a new sense of pride was instilled in many of the students.[52]

In the early 1980s Thomas told the board, in response to movement in that direction, that social engineering was not the solution to Salt Lake City's problems. However, the perspectives of Susan Keene, Tab Uno, and Ronald Walker—representing, respectively, the Central City, lower Avenues, and upper Avenues—won out. The board set boundaries that would (theoretically at least) achieve equity in terms of ethnic composition, income distribution, and social class representation. In Thomas's view, Keene came to the board with an agenda—to achieve economic and social balance by putting five African-Americans here and ten there; four people making $100,000 here, ten making $30,000 there. Using a computer, Keene tried to distribute the exact number of minorities and the same income levels to each school. This was "[t]he dumbest thing you could do," in Thomas's estimation; it simply did not work. Thomas claimed that as a result of the closed boundary policy, the African-American dropout rate increased, GPAs dropped, and there was an increase in the suspension rate among black students.[53]

Nor was Keene's way something all African-Americans wanted. Thomas reported that the leadership of Salt Lake's NAACP told him that "there is equity pretty much behind every child . . . we want to decide where we want our children to go," whether to a predominantly white school or to a school in which African-American students were more concentrated. For Thomas, the way to achieve genuine equity was through open enrollment and parent choice, and by

52. Barlow, Oral History, 4 May 1992.
53. Thomas, Oral History, 16 Aug. 1991.

organizing magnet schools to provide opportunities directly linked to college or occupational preparation. But Salt Lake City was simply too small for the magnet school concept. The best solution would be to focus on the comprehensive model of the high school with open enrollment—a practice which, according to Thomas, achieved ethnic balance by bringing more African-American students into East High and more hispanics into Highland. However, the board sought socio-economic equity through mandating a policy of closed boundaries. The tension over this issue led ultimately to Thomas's resignation in July 1984.[54]

AN UNCERTAIN BOARD

In January 1984, in spite of increased tension between some board members and Thomas, the superintendent was told that his reappointment the following June was certain. However, when the board met to formalize this in June 1984, some uncertainty surfaced. Salt Lake City's popular mayor, Ted Wilson, praised Thomas to the board and urged them to work out their differences and retain him. Two board members (Kump and Walker) who had prior to the board meeting been identified as considering abstaining on the vote to reappoint Thomas, reported that they had received 53 telephone calls from citizens and a few administrators who urged them to abstain in the vote. Six professors at the University of Utah, though, had called them in support of Thomas. When the votes were cast, four voted to retain, one was opposed, and two abstained, giving the impression that only a bare majority favored Thomas staying on.[55]

Some popular discontent with shared governance may also have played a role in Thomas's resignation. Parent groups at East High charged that discipline was lax and the principal, Jack Hart, resigned complaining that shared governance had stripped him of his power to make decisions with alacrity.[56] In June 1984 parents charged Thomas with circumventing shared governance when he quickly appointed the new principal for East High. Why, they asked, were principals and the board unable or unwilling to make necessary decisions? Thomas acknowledged that the process was imperfect and cumbersome. To remedy this, he suggested the creation of a "central office clearing house from which information and explanations of the process can be delivered faster. You need a source of information broader than the superintendent."[57]

Just over a month after he had received another two-year appointment, on 27 July Thomas announced that he had submitted his resignation to the board in order to accept a position implementing an educational reform package in South Carolina. His decision to leave, he said, was "complex." Although his wife de-

---

54. Thomas, Oral History, 16 Aug. 1991; McLeese, "The Process of Decentralizing Conflict," 498-99.

55. Patricia McLeese, "The Attempt of the Salt Lake City Board of Education to Appoint Wayne Evans Interim Superintendent," Research Paper, University of Utah Department of Educational Administration, 1985, 5-6. In a 1992 conversation with the writer, Carolyn Kump expressed some regret that her abstention had such far reaching consequences in perhaps forcing Thomas to resign. It was, she said, the one vote she was least proud of.

56. "Close Vote Keeps Thomas as City Schools Chief," Salt Lake Tribune, 6 June 1984.

57. Ibid.

scribed him as having been bored of late with his responsibilities in Salt Lake City,[58] the differences between him and the board played a major role in his decision to leave. As he was quoted by a newspaper reporter: "There has been an inability (on the school board's part) to set priorities that were clear and congruent with my abilities. The board's uncertainty was certainly part of my decision to leave" and to accept a $15,000 reduction in salary. Thomas had passed up an offer from the Danforth Foundation in June that would have paid more money than he was getting. He turned down another position in California because his wife did not want to leave Salt Lake. Between the time the board reappointed him and his resignation (5 June and 27 July) he received a personal call from Governor Richard Riley of South Carolina inviting him to come to South Carolina for a meeting to discuss his potential involvement in implementing the South Carolina reform legislation. Riley offered him the position of "state deputy for public accountability." He tendered his resignation to the board, and they, by a vote of six to one, agreed to release him from his contract. The single vote cast against releasing him came from his long-time nemesis Susan Keene; she was consistent in her opposition to him to the very end.[59]

While the board embarked on a search for a new superintendent, in order to promote a sense of stability, on 2 August they voted to appoint the president of the board, advertising executive Wayne Evans, as interim superintendent. The state legislature had recently repealed state regulations allowing a non-credentialed individual to be state superintendent. Consequently, the attempt to get the state to approve a waiver of the credential requirements for Evans split the educational community into "pro-waiver" proponents (led by Evans's business colleagues) and "anti-waiver" proponents (led by district and state administrative personnel). Thomas supported Evans' candidacy, perhaps to show some measure of support for those who had supported him. The only board member to oppose Evans's appointment was Carolyn Kump, who, between 1979 and 1983, was the first woman to serve as vice-president and then as president of the board. Based on her past experience, she did not believe it prudent to mix administrative and policy-making functions. In addition, Kump argued that the appointment was a violation of Utah state law, which allowed an uncredentialed person to serve as superintendent for no more than eight weeks provided that "the supply of qualified, certificated personnel has been exhausted."[60]

In spite of the clear illegality of the move, the board voted to make Evans Interim Superintendent, but the action was nullified when the State Committee on Certification unanimously denied a waiver to Evans, a decision subsequently upheld by the State Board of Education. The board then appointed George Brooks, the amiable and much respected Personnel Director, as Interim Superintendent. Brooks made it clear that he was *not* a candidate for the position and that he was

---

58. "S.L. Superintendent Resigns," *Salt Lake Tribune*, 28 July 1984; "Superintendent Takes Post in S.C.," *Deseret News*, 27 July 1984.

59. Telephone conversation with Carolyn Kump, 12 May 1992; Thomas, Oral History, 16 Aug. 1991.

60. McLeese, "The Process of Decentralizing," 360-61.

only willing to serve until a permanent replacement was found.

To get rid of the "uncertainty and confusion" surrounding the series of administrative transitions, the board contracted with Harold Webb Associates of Evanston, Illinois, an executive search consulting firm, to screen applicants for the position. In a brochure announcing the vacancy and stressing shared governance, Salt Lake was described as a city of 162,000 people, seventy percent of whom were Caucasian and thirty percent representing a wide variety of ethnic groups: hispanics, Pacific Islanders, Southeast Asians, Native Americans, and blacks. While fifty percent of the city population were identified as members of the LDS church, "virtually every other major denomination is represented." The brochure pointed to a healthy economy, which since 1974 had posted an unemployment rate two percent below national rates, with service and high-tech institutions playing a dominant role in the local economy. In spite of its small-town friendliness, the city also housed a major symphony, the renowned Mormon Tabernacle Choir, and hosted numerous social and cultural events.

Educationally, the city was boosted as having the second highest literacy rate in the country for cities of 100,000 or more and "Utahns, on the average, complete more years of schooling than any citizens of any other state." Acknowledging the city's decline in school population, the brochure said that 27 schools had been closed during this period "with extensive community input"(?), and that in 1981 there had been a gain of some 200 students. With 36 schools: 4 high schools (grades 9-12); five intermediate schools (grades 7-8) and 27 elementary schools (K-6), the district served 24,400 students through 1,200 certified teachers and other educational personnel, supervised by some 80 administrators and supported by almost 2,000 non-academic personnel. The per pupil expenditure was listed as $2,528 and the entire operating budget was listed as 7.3 million dollars.[61]

This public relations advertisement reflects the influence of M. Donald Thomas, the Midwestern "outsider" who presided over a system rapidly becoming more attuned to the larger society. As the brochure indicated, Thomas's replacement should "continue the present non-adversarial relationships with teachers of the system . . . possess a demonstrated record of successful and economical management of a school system . . . generate genuine equity of educational programs for all segments of the school community . . . work with the 'Shared Governance' plan of management which is operative in the district," be "sensitive to the religious and ethical culture of the community," and "support the educational concerns of minorities, handicapped persons and women."

M. Donald Thomas was not just a name on an organizational chart nor a person following orders from the board. He brought to his superintendency an energetic and infectious enthusiasm for the role of public schools in Utah's capital city at a time when morale was lowest in the district. It was a time too when schools nationally were being tagged as not only ineffective in meeting the de-

---

61. A copy of this brochure, prepared by Harold Webb Associates, is in the files of the Superintendent's Office.

mands of the age, but were regarded by some as detrimental to students. In the long term, it must be left to the generation that matures in the early years of the twenty-first century, and their historians of education (with their particular ideologies and agendas), to judge whether the children of Salt Lake City in the period from 1973 to 1984 were well- or ill-served by the schools Thomas attempted to shape into participatory democracies. Whatever precise interpretation is arrived at then, there can be little doubt that the exuberant personality and professional expertise of M. Donald Thomas will be recognized as having left an indelible mark on the development of Salt Lake City's public schools.

10

"TAKING IT A YEAR AT A TIME"
The Administration of
John W. Bennion, 1985–94

The months immediately following Don Thomas's resignation saw the district in some disarray as its affairs were administered by a brief succession of temporary replacements. Everyone involved was pleased when in the spring of 1985, the board finally settled on a permanent replacement—the superintendent of the Provo, Utah, district, Dr. John W. Bennion.

John Warren Bennion was born in Salt Lake City in 1936 into a home that exuded commitment to education. His grandfather, Milton Bennion, for many years had served as Dean of the University of Utah School of Education. His parents, Katherine Snow and M. Lynn Bennion, were deeply involved in the educational and cultural life of the community, his father serving 24 years as superintendent after having administered the LDS church's seminary programs. The Bennions lived next to the University of Utah, and John spent his first six years as a student at the progressive William Stewart School, the "lab school" located on the university campus, after which he attended Bryant Junior High and East High School. Restless to begin his higher education, he left East after his junior year and enrolled as a philosophy major at the University of Utah. His university experience was interrupted by a two and one-half year "mission" for the LDS church in West Germany after which he completed his bachelor's degree in philosophy and English (with a teaching certificate) in 1961.

Bennion's first teaching assignment in the neighboring Granite School District was to organize and teach experimental courses in philosophy and social ethics, which his grandfather Milton had done at the University of Utah in the early 1900s. The data collected during this experience became the basis for his Master's thesis in history and philosophy of education. In 1962 he received his Master of Arts degree from the Department of Educational Administration.

The following year, Bennion married one of his former philosophy students at Granite High School, Sylvia Lustig, and shortly thereafter accepted an assistantship to study for a Ph.D. in philosophy of education at Ohio State University in Columbus. Concerned, like his grandfather, that theory be relevant to real life issues, he eventually shifted his focus from the philosophy of education and decided to work toward a degree in the Department of Educational Administration. His Ph.D. was awarded in 1966.

From 1966 to 1968, he served as an Assistant Superintendent for Curriculum in Elgin, Illinois. In 1968 he was appointed as Assistant Professor at the Uni-

John W. Bennion

1985–94

versity of Indiana in Bloomington but left after less than a year; academic life was not how he wanted to spend the rest of his career. He much preferred to be on the front line administering public schools rather than teaching others how to administer them.

In June 1969 he was chosen as superintendent of Brighton, New York, a small district with a heavily Jewish population and an unabashed commitment to supporting the public schools serving its 4,500 students. The small-scale enterprise meant that Bennion was able to develop a close working relationship with the principals, whose role he envisioned as being more akin to instructional leaders than system managers. Another benefit was that bureaucracy was minimal. Brighton gave Bennion the opportunity to try out some of his ideas on curriculum development, and he, his wife, and their two sons put down their roots as relatively permanent residents.

During his tenure at Brighton, Bennion was appointed to the superintendency three times by the board's unanimous vote, and not once did the community fail to support the annual budget requests (and tax increases) he asked for. He also continued to communicate his thoughts on contemporary school issues. Reflecting his continued interest in philosophy as a means of understanding and dealing with the real world of teacher negotiations, curriculum development, and educational reform, he contributed an article to *School and Society* that spelled out his ideal relationship between the reflective, detached perspective of the philosopher and the "nitty-gritty" demands made by the school system.[1]

Bennion also administered the affairs of the LDS ward in Rochester, New York. Being bishop broadened and deepened his commitment to his religious community; he found opportunities to assist LDS people struggling with their religious orientation in a secular world far from the supportive environment of Utah. As a member of the LDS church, he was forced to confront the church's practice of excluding males of African descent from the ranks of its lay priesthood. In an appearance before the New York State Civil Rights Commission to answer charges of bias relating to the employment of an African-American teacher, Bennion satisfactorily made the point that his actions as an administrator, not the belief system of the church to which he belonged, should be the criteria by which he was judged. The commission found no evidence of racism in his administration.[2]

For Bennion, ten to twelve years as superintendent in one location is probably a maximum. He believed that change of challenges and perspectives benefits both the institution and the individual. Accordingly, in 1979 he accepted a posi-

---

1. "The Superintendent as Philosopher," *School and Society* 98 (Jan. 1970): 25-7.
2. The LDS church changed its practice with respect to males of African descent in June 1978. In common with many other LDS members of this time, Bennion was acutely uncomfortable with the church's ban. Around 1977, he sought a meeting with President Spencer W. Kimball to express his concerns about the impact of the practice on the church in places with large African-American populations. He was not at all encouraged by what President Kimball communicated to him at that time and held out little hope of a change in church policy in the immediate future. Conversation with John Bennion, 25 Aug. 1991.

tion as superintendent in Bloomington, Minnesota. The family (now consisting of five boys) uprooted itself with some difficulty from New York, in the second year of a three-year contract. The minutes of the Brighton Board of Education recorded that "he will be greatly missed" and that he left with the Board's best wishes.[3] The process of leaving what had become a genuine home was more traumatic than the family expected, and they hesitated to put down their roots as deeply in Bloomington as they had in Brighton. After a year in Minnesota, Bennion was praised for centralizing the delivery of educational services and for increasing contact between principals and teachers. He was also cited for dealing with community problems, including enrollments that were falling fast, schools that had to be closed, and teachers laid off. In a "system fraught with difficulties for a school administrator," he had "established himself as a good listener, as well as one who acts decisively once he has all the facts."[4]

In spite of what appears to have been a successful first year in Bloomington, questions about the new assignment arose. Bennion realized that Bloomington, with some 16,000 students, had a more entrenched bureaucracy than he liked and less personal contact with principals and schools. Consequently, when the superintendency in Provo, Utah, opened up during the first year in Bloomington, Bennion decided to investigate the possibilities of returning to Utah. A visit to Provo and two interviews with the board convinced him that the district was interested in developing "high-quality educational programs," and when the board expressed interest in having him come to Provo, he accepted. The family had scarcely unpacked their boxes in Bloomington when they were on the road again, enacting a sort of reverse diaspora, returning to their homeland after receiving higher degrees and professional experience outside of Utah.[5]

THE PROVING GROUND OF PROVO

Given Bennion's basic interest in curriculum, instruction, and staff development, he quickly found in Provo an excellent opportunity to try out some of his skills. In his estimation, curriculum development in the district had been haphazard, with pockets of excellence here and there in which good principals and teachers had taken it upon themselves to be innovative. On the other hand, the less capable principals and teachers were doing only mediocre work, with no sense of accountability. Drawing on his experiences in Brighton and Bloomington, Bennion began implementing "effective teaching" programs in Provo. One surprise he discovered in Provo, which had *not* been mentioned in the board interviews, was that the district had a deficit of some $900,000. His plans to implement new programs were seriously threatened by the lack of resources. His immediate need was either to raise taxes or cut the existing programs.[6]

---

3. Brighton (New York) Board of Education, Minutes, 8 May 1979.
4. "Dr. John Bennion gets a good grade," *Sun Newspapers* (Minnesota), 11 June 1980.
5. Background information on Bennion's life was derived mainly from Oral History, 11 Aug. 1991, and my personal recollections. I have known him since 1961.
6. Bennion, Oral History, 11 Aug. 1991.

After deciding to pursue a tax increase in October 1981, Bennion received a second surprise: in spite of much rhetoric about Utah's commitment to children's needs, most Provo citizens firmly opposed any tax increase. This outright opposition came to Bennion as something of a "cultural shock." Among the largely Jewish population in Brighton the annual school budget had invariably been passed, usually by a two to one margin. For the first time in his career as a superintendent he now heard charges of "inefficiency, waste and fat" being hurled against the schools. More troubling was the outright "denial of real need in the district." In Brighton the people had held him and the schools to high expectations, but they were also willing to match their level of expectation with high financial support, something Provo residents were not willing to do. As a consequence the leeway levy was defeated, with 54 percent of the voters saying "No" to the tax increase.[7]

Bennion saw the lack of support as rooted in an almost endemic skepticism about government in general and public schools in particular. For Utahns, government seemed to be an alien institution out to get citizens' money. Conversely, in New York and Minnesota "the attitude was more that the government is us and the means of collectively doing things that we can't individually do for ourselves that are important for us."[8] Frequently at budget hearings in Brighton he would hear people ask "Are we doing enough?" instead of protests that "We're trying to do too much."

Bennion also saw the reluctance to support schools as tied to the economics of having large families, supporting Mormon missionaries, and paying tithing to the LDS church, in addition to a desire to have the material artifacts of the "good life"—campers, boats, and such. Given their financial priorities, Bennion believed many probably couldn't afford a tax increase and that they used "inefficiency and waste" to justify their unwillingness or inability to increase taxes. A certain provincialism also operated in Provo—those who had experienced well-funded school systems outside the state were more willing to support increased funding, while those who had lived in Utah all their lives often did not realize the importance of smaller classes, improved libraries, and the materials and support services necessary to ensure an adequate school system. The people in Brighton, New York, would have considered Provo's schools as "in many ways an educational disaster area; they wouldn't tolerate them."[9]

When a second attempt the following month to raise the tax base lost by a larger margin than the first (57 percent), Bennion realized something dramatic had to be done to break the logjam.[10] If public funds were to be made available, voters had to be convinced that the schools were taking seriously the questions raised during the leeway campaign. At this time, the notion of "career ladders" was being discussed in Utah as a way of increasing teacher earnings, and Ben-

7. "Provo Voters Veto School Tax," Provo *Daily Herald*, 7 Oct. 1981.
8. Bennion, Oral History, 11 Aug. 1991.
9. Ibid.
10. "Provoans Hand School District Second Rebuff," Provo *Daily Herald*, 26 Nov. 1981.

nion helped develop the legislation that was put into effect in every district in 1984. Before it became a statewide practice, however, Bennion recognized it as a way of resolving his funding problems.

One aspect of the career ladder proposal, known as the "Job Enlargement Component," held that pay could be significantly enhanced if teachers were able to work longer than the traditional nine months. Standing alone, this might never have been accepted, but Bennion grafted the notion on to another innovation—the year-round school. He proposed that the Provo School District could save money by establishing a number of year-round schools in place of constructing new buildings. The money not used for bricks and mortar could be channelled into pay for those teachers who opted to work beyond the traditional academic year.

The Provo Chamber of Commerce was enthusiastic, and voters were asked to approve this "efficiency" measure. Citizens approved the new arrangement by a two-thirds majority, and Provo became the first district in Utah to establish year-round schools and fully finance the career ladder.[11] The district and Bennion received statewide recognition. A joint project involving Brigham Young University's college of education also showed promise as a creative approach to preparing teachers and administrators. In 1984 the professional journal *Executive Educator* designated Bennion as one of the nation's top 100 public school executives. His work in Provo was apparently resonating with national interests.

When the Salt Lake superintendency opened up late in 1984, Bennion had already made a strong contribution to the Provo schools and was not looking for a new position. His reluctance to uproot his family once again added to his mixed feelings about applying. In spite of his reluctance, he did see some advantages to Salt Lake, including a much larger financial base. With this, he knew the district could supply some of the things necessary for an enriched programs, including computers, more textbooks, and other supplies. He also liked the district's programs for accelerated learners, full-time elementary librarians, lower class sizes, and the higher salaries for teachers. It was still a far cry from what he had been accustomed to in New York and Minnesota, but it was considerably better than Provo, convincing him to become, initially at least, an "informal" candidate for the position.

For his first interview, Bennion went to Denver, preventing undue publicity and speculation. Later, one to one contacts with acting superintendent George Brooks and business manager, Gary Harmer, encouraged him to pursue the possibilities further. The board itself visited Provo and discussed Bennion's performance there with the staff, board members, and parents.

One of Bennion's major concerns was the lack of a cohesive district-wide curriculum—a natural result of the decentralizing tendencies inherent in shared governance. Bennion told the board that he would want more "continuity and articulation" in the district curriculum. He talked about "developing opportunities for teachers to enlarge their repertoire of teaching skills" and his desire to

---

11. "Provoans OK School Reform," Provo *Daily Herald*, 28 Mar. 1984.

promote the career ladder concept in Salt Lake City. The board liked his perspectives, and eventually invited him to accept, as the unanimous choice of the board, the superintendency of Salt Lake City School District.

In March 1985, John Bennion assumed complete responsibility for the district schools—only sixteen years after his father had retired from the same position. In his acceptance speech to the board on 8 January 1985, Bennion joked that perhaps he, too, should retire immediately, after having received much praise in Provo. He also said he hoped to bring about "a genuine educational mecca in the Salt Lake District." Little did he know then that in the ensuing years, "retirement" would indeed become more attractive and that the pilgrimage to mecca would be almost indefinitely postponed.[12]

ON THE EDUCATIONAL FRONTIER

When Bennion interviewed for the Salt Lake City position, he did not get the impression that the board had any particular problems they wished him to deal with. He was, of course, familiar with shared governance, and it was Bennion's view that the system contributed to variance between schools' responses to the state core curriculum—particularly in light of reforms Utah and other states were busy implementing in the aftermath of the *Nation at Risk* report of 1983. In essence, the report claimed America suffered deteriorating academic quality in public schools and that this "rising tide of mediocrity" had destroyed the gains made in the aftermath of the Sputnik-inspired reforms of the mid 1950s. Linking America's trade deficit with Japan and declines in "the intellectual, moral and spiritual strengths of our people" to the lack of high academic standards in the schools, the report called for a return to the basics, which it saw as the best way to meet the needs of the nation and its students.[13]

Bennion became superintendent just as the reform movement of the early 1980s got underway, and much of what he did must be seen in the context of this "back to basics" movement. He was not, however, simply indulging in a knee-jerk reaction to these "new" demands. To say the least, the connection between the U. S. trade deficit and its public schools is tenuous, and many educators rejected other conclusions of the *Nation at Risk* report as well. While we were students at Ohio State University in the 1960s Bennion raised questions with me about the problems inherent in having schools assume responsibilities for all of society's ills. Sensitive as he was to the progressive notion of schools helping to bring about a good society, he was convinced that expecting too much of the schools resulted in essential basics being ignored. By "basics" Bennion certainly did not mean a return to rote learning. His notion of "basics" involved higher order thinking skills and dispositions. A major aim of schooling should be to promote in students the ability to think logically, clearly, and creatively so they

---

12. "Acceptance Speech Given by John W. Bennion at the meeting of the Salt Lake City Board of Education Meeting, January 8, 1985."

13. National Commission on Excellence in Education, *A Nation at Risk* (Washington, D.C.: U.S. Office of Education, 1983), 5-7.

can deal with increasingly complex ideas. Without some proficiency in this area long-term success would evade students after they left school. At first blush, this may be seen as a typically middle-class formulation of the aims of education, but Bennion did not limit its applicability to the college bound or those from the East side.

Like Mortimer Adler in his *Paidiea Proposal*, Bennion holds that everyone could benefit from raising her or his intellectual capabilities. Thus, to deny minority students equal access to "critical thinking" was to practice an insidious form of racism. For John Bennion, "the real frontier in American public education" was the challenge to improve the effectiveness of education in the lives of the urban "at risk population." He was intrigued to know whether a lack of "supportive home and neighborhood environment" could be compensated for by schools, thus "break[ing] the cycle of poverty, ignorance and despair" endemic in urban populations, including Salt Lake City's. The possibility of facing these challenges in his home town had attracted him to the superintendency there in the first place.[14]

Bennion is enough of a realist to recognize that many of the problems that beset students do not originate in the schools. He is also something of an idealist (with a pragmatic bent), in his belief that if schools limit themselves to focusing on a few basics (clear thinking and creativity, for example) they might be able at least to *start* the process of critical thinking in the lives of individuals. That was his reasoned faith, and it was with this perspective that he began his tenure in Salt Lake City.

GETTING THE LAY OF THE LAND

In the year following Bennion's appointment, the board of education approved a set of district-wide goals that laid out in some detail what the new superintendent hoped to accomplish. These focused on honing teachers' skills through the popular "Effective Teaching" program; improving the evaluation process for all professional personnel; and cultivating a "close, cooperative, mutually supportive working relationship" between all segments of the district, including the refinement of the shared governance concept. In addition, major curriculum emphasis was planned in the area of mathematics in K-8, social studies, and English, with special focus upon teaching writing in all areas of the curriculum. Also included were long-term plans for a comprehensive testing program, a study of "an automated comprehensive student information management system," and the formulation of a "comprehensive staff development program that integrates components presently operating in the district and responsive to the educational mission of the Salt Lake City schools."[15]

One of the things that troubled Bennion as he became familiar with the landscape he had inherited was the "curious thing" entitled "review of services,"

14. Bennion, Oral History, 6 Sept. 1991.
15. District-Wide Goals for the 1986-87 School Year, approved by the Board of Education, 19 Aug. 1986.

part of Superintendent Thomas's democratic efforts to make certain everyone in the district would be listened to. By simply filing a complaint with the central office, someone could count on a committee being formed to investigate the issue. According to Thomas, if a person submitted a complaint they had to sign it and be willing to stand by their allegations. Nine-tenths of all complaints were dismissed at this stage because most people were not willing to pursue something that might lead to a court suit against them. The process, as Thomas had introduced it to the district, was based on the assumption that no one is perfect and that even administrators can make mistakes for which they should be called to account.[16]

In early conversations with the central office staff, Bennion became familiar with the process. Although he agreed about the need to address such complaints, he was troubled that the process consumed so much time. His staff reported that they spent half their time on review committees. As a result of the "review of reviews" he initiated, the process was refined and specific requirements were built into the process: the aggrieved party was required to write out the complaint *in detail*; arrangements were then made to have parties meet face-to-face and attempt to resolve the issue; the person under review was given the opportunity of making a written response to the initial complaint; if no resolution was reached, an third party would arbitrate, instead of having a committee discuss it. If a third party were unable to resolve the issue, a committee could be appointed. The early stages of Bennion's plan dried up most of the complaints, reducing the energy the reviews had been consuming.[17]

Certainly John Bennion brought a different personality and style to the superintendent's office. While Thomas had been gregarious and personal in his demeanor, Bennion was noticeably less so. He came out of a more reflective philosophical position and would, unlike Thomas, hesitate to give quick approval to an innovation. Bennion's more restrained and reflective approach made it difficult for teachers and others to relate to him and his programs. He was perceived as being intellectually talented and as trying to stay above the fray of political battles. This perception was reinforced by his modifying the open-door policy of the previous administration and directing that questions should work their way through the system rather than coming immediately to him.[18] His wariness about shared governance caused many teachers to fear he would "make shared governance a thing of the past." Teachers, administrators and parents interpreted his public statements as intending to "recentralize and reprofessionalize policymaking" in the district. While principals may have seen this as a step toward freeing *them* from too many external restraints, teachers seemed suspicious of Bennion's long-term aims. They feared he would reverse the degree of profes-

---

16. M. Donald Thomas, Oral History, 16 Aug. 1991.

17. Bennion, Oral History, 11 Aug. 1991.

18. This discussion of Bennion's leadership style is based on oral history interviews conducted with John Bennion, 11 Aug. 1991; Patti O'Keefe, 9 Nov. 1991; Don Barlow, 6 Apr. 1992; George Henry, 10 Apr. 1992, and "Be Fair with Bennion," *Salt Lake Tribune*, 3 Mar. 1988.

sional esteem and power which had accrued to them during the tenure of the former superintendent.

Bennion's first public statement to make headlines, just a few days after he assumed the superintendency, did nothing to allay teacher fears. The news item dealt with his belief that teachers were too isolated in their classrooms. They could be helped by having meaningful evaluations by principals. Bennion's intent was not to constrict teachers, but to lay out what he saw as a crucial dimension in improving teaching. He held that "effective teaching" was predicated upon principals transforming from plant managers into educational leaders. The proposal to involve principals directly in the classroom struck a raw nerve. Combined with Bennion's announcement that he would be reviewing the concept of shared governance, it convinced many teachers that the Camelot of widespread innovation, shared governance, and independent professional teachers of the Thomas era were over.[19]

CAREER LADDERS

Bennion saw the career ladder reform he had implemented in Provo as a way to increase teacher performance by relating it to teacher earnings. The program's four components, which, it was hoped, would enhance teachers' salaries *and* classroom competence were performance bonus, job enlargement, extended day, and career ladder steps. Performance bonus generated the most controversy because it was tied to a system of evaluation or pay for merit. Teaching quality was supposed to be enhanced "by paying bonuses to teachers rated as the best in the school or district." Teachers would "qualify for a bonus generally through a positive principal evaluation supplemented by additional lines of evidence that verify excellent practice." While some districts using this type of system actually improved teacher skills, others attempted to "carry out the letter of the law," and teacher morale plummeted.

Historically, teachers have resisted any imposition of evaluation-based pay. One Utah teacher in the 1980s responded to the career ladder plan in words typical of teacher response to any kind of merit proposal: "I didn't apply. I know I'm a good teacher . . . but why should I risk the envy of my friends and colleagues for $200. For all I know, it will disappear anyway next year, but I'll still be working with these people."[20]

According to an external evaluation of Utah's Career Ladder System done in 1987, it was precisely because "career ladders" had the potential to effect change "in such a long entrenched system of work and pay" that it stirred up such strong feelings. This analysis claimed that in spite of the controversy, career ladders

19. Patricia McLeese, "The Process of Decentralizing Conflict and Maintaining Stability: Site Council Enactment, Implementation, Operations, and Impacts in the Salt Lake City School District, 1970-1985" Ph.D. diss., University of Utah, 1992, 361, 493-94; Don Barlow, Oral History, 6 Apr. 1992; "Bennion Unveils Plans for Bringing S.L. Teachers Out of Isolation," *Salt Lake Tribune*, 18 Mar. 1985.

20. Cited in McLeese, "Process of Decentralization," 17.

were indeed changing "the teaching profession and the ways in which schools are organized to teach students." Because of its impact on "every teacher, principal, school and district" Utah's Career Ladder System was identified as "a model that deserves national attention."[21]

It may have deserved "national attention," but when John Bennion became superintendent in Salt Lake in 1985, career ladder reform had not garnered much enthusiasm. Bennion's attempts to implement it received mixed response—some Salt Lake City schools adopted it while others resisted it. In Bennion's view, the resistance was in part due to the district's large size and the fact that shared governance had made implementing district-wide policies more difficult. When he brought in two new central staff administrators, Jack Keegan and Mary Jean Johnson, to implement career ladders they were perceived by teachers as "too much top-down leadership infringing on [the teachers'] professional prerogatives," a further attack upon shared governance. Resistance to Bennion's initiatives was also rooted in an egalitarian mind set in the teaching profession that resists qualitative differentiation among teachers.[22]

What started as an attempt to increase cooperation among teachers instead became a matter of "pandering for dollars." Also, bureaucracy seemed to have taken over the whole endeavor. But much worse was the effect on teacher relationships: "If my incentive for money is stronger than my need to be collegial, I'm not going to go and help you be a better teacher if in the process you are going to take the money that I want."[23]

In spite of these negative responses to the career ladder program and in contrast to the direct opposition to the merit plan of the 1930s, after six years in operation a survey of 602 Utah teachers indicated considerable support for the policy, with 75.5 percent of those surveyed favoring its continuation and only 14.3 percent opposed.[24] This widespread acceptance of the program is reflected in the amount of money which was made available to the district as a result of its being implemented. The largest percentage of Salt Lake City's share in the state appropriation (46 percent) was used to enhance "Career Ladder Steps," which were designed to offset the traditional tendency for teachers to gain salary increases by leaving the classroom and becoming administrators. Under this component, teachers were given differentiated professional status on a number of levels: Level 1 being "Provisional Teachers"; Level 2, "Career Educator"; Level 3, "Teacher Specialist"; and Level 4, "Teacher Leader." In five years it was theoretically possible for faculty to reach the top level and receive around $4,360 extra salary. The downside was that not everyone could possibly become a teacher leader—only about ten percent.

What had been heralded in the 1980s as something to resolve the issue of

---

21. Mary Amsler et al., *An Evaluation of the Utah Career Ladder System* (San Francisco: Far West Laboratory for Educational Research and Development, 1988), 2.

22. Bennion, Oral History, 11 Aug. 1991.

23. Barlow, Oral History, 4 Apr. 1992.

24. John D. Ross and David E. Nelson, *A Follow-up Statewide Survey of Teacher Opinions Concerning Utah's Career Ladder Program* (Salt Lake City: Utah State Department of Education, 1991), A-5.

teacher accountability changed within a decade from being a "wildfire" of educational reform in 29 states to a "movement" in only seven states, including Utah. In some states the program had been legislated but not funded and in others different aspects of the career ladder idea were being implemented. While there was noticeable lack of uniformity in implementing the idea nationwide, in 1991 more than a half billion dollars was paid to teachers through various aspects of the plan.[25] Whether the program was actually making teachers more accountable may be open to question, but teachers *were* getting more money through it.

A 1987 study of the program in Utah recommended that the program should be continued, but the merit pay component should be eliminated. The competition involved "elicits more negative than positive responses from those it seeks to motivate." Other aspects of the program were recommended for retention and further development with "Job Redesign" helping redistribute salaries as well as improving "performance and retention of teachers." "Job Expansion" was deemed to be of value because it seemed to have a positive effect on teaching performance, although it did not "alter salary or status reward." The "Extended Contract" was judged similarly. This study emphasized that the program's success depended on the availability of "effective administrative leadership": "School administrators must exert leadership to ensure" that such issues as the credibility of those rewarded as well as the "inherent energy drain" related to the process "are thoughtfully and successfully addressed."[26]

One crucial question persists: Did the Career Ladder Program have any impact on students? The study just cited did not deal with the issue and in the view of one of the researchers "career ladders only have an impact when the activities being paid for are directly tied to the core functions of teaching and learning in schools and provide teachers with leadership opportunities."[27]

Just as John Bennion was getting geared up to promote the career ladder concept in Salt Lake City, it was overshadowed by the need to consider closing a high school.[28] In the early 1970s, economic realities not only derailed Arthur Wiscombe's educational agenda, they led to his dismissal. Even as Wiscombe closed elementary schools, there was intermittent, guarded talk of closing South High; as early as 1969 one real estate agent was telling persons buying homes in the South High district that the school might be turned into a community college. Seventeen years later, when John Bennion was faced with a similar predicament, it almost ended his tenure as superintendent in Salt Lake City.[29]

---

25. Southern Regional Education Board, "Career Ladder Clearinghouse," (Atlanta, 1992), 1, 16, 44.
26. Betty Malen, Michael J. Murphy and Ann W. Hart, "Career Ladder Reform in Utah: Evidence of Impact—Recommendations for Action," Occasional Policy Paper, Graduate School of Education, University of Utah, Jan. 1987, 31-3.
27. Conversation with Ann W. Hart, 27 July 1992.
28. Bennion, Oral History, 11 Aug. 1991.
29. Early mention of the possible need to close South High are cited in Ingrid Oxaal, "Closing a High School: Student Activities in the Temporary Organization," Ph.D. diss., University of Utah, 1990, 38.

MANEUVERING IN "AN EMOTIONAL MINE FIELD"

During his interviews with the board Bennion had received the distinct impression that the public hearings on open enrollments during the last years of the Thomas "had put the issue [of closing a high school] to rest." Bennion was all too familiar with the difficulties Arthur Wiscombe had faced when he began closing schools between 1969 and 1973. If Bennion had been told he was expected to close a high school, he would have respectfully declined the proffered position. He enjoyed challenges but he was not inclined to martyrdom.

Nevertheless, he had barely gotten his feet on the ground by 1986—implementing career ladders and other reforms—when in the summer and fall of 1986 he and the board began to set the stage for one of the most divisive political struggles the district had ever experienced. Closing a high school, and the boundary changes it heralded, loomed on the educational horizon until it eclipsed everything else he was attempting to do. The ensuing struggle even made him question whether he should continue as superintendent.[30]

From a purely economic perspective, Salt Lake's high schools were grossly inefficient: they all offered expensive programs in languages, science, mathematics, and history. At South and West, some of the advanced placement courses only had five or six students enrolled. In addition, many of the district's overall high school programs lacked the critical mass necessary for an effective learning environment.

These problems, compounded with increasing statewide pressures to cut back on funding, convinced the board that unless programs could be made more efficient, the district's entire secondary program would suffer. The board reached consensus on the need to close a high school sometime in the fall of 1986, and the evidence—based on programs, test scores, student numbers, the homogenous nature of the student body, and the large number of "at risk" students— gave credence to the view that South High should be that school.[31] While the staff refined the bases for its recommendation, rumors about an impending closure began to spread. The board would have to go public with its intentions before they had sufficiently planned.[32]

"FRUSTRATION AND RESENTMENT"

On 1 February 1987 Bennion recorded that he was "struggling with a number of difficult problems at work." First was the need to find a new location for the open classroom program, since patrons and teachers at Rosslyn Heights had requested it be moved out of that building. The other issue was the need to close

---

30. Bennion, Oral History, 6 Sept. 1991.
31. Marjory Boyden chaired the district's Equivalency Sub-Committee which prepared the "Equivalency Interim Report," 18 Nov. 1986. The data in this report became the basis for deciding which high school should close.
32. The discussions about the need to close a high school were not officially "on record" because they were exploratory in nature, hence there is no written record of what transpired during these discussions. Bennion, Oral History, 11 Aug. 1991, and a conversation with him on 25 Aug. 1992.

one of the high schools. On this Bennion wrote: "We are moving rapidly towards announcing a plan to close a school and put students now attending 5 high school bldgs. into 4 bldgs. It will stir up controversy and opposition. Just how much, I don't know. On top of all that the state is in great financial difficulty and the legislature right now seems more inclined to make cuts than to raise taxes."[33] Linking the need to close a high school to the state's financial exigencies was, no doubt, a response to a recently proposed legislative plan to force school districts to be more efficient. Under this legislative mandate, districts that did not fill their schools to at least 70 percent capacity would be denied state appropriations for insurance and utilities. While designed with low-enrollment schools on the east side of Granite school district in mind, the plan had the potential to affect the Salt Lake district with its long-term decline.

This seems to have been on Bennion's mind on 3 February when he made his initial public presentation on the subject. He talked about the threat to the district's resources if insurance and utility appropriations were reduced. While enrollment had steadily dropped since the 1960s, there had been no reduction in the number of high school buildings maintained. Based on staff recommendations, Bennion announced that the board had decided to consider closing South High School. When this announcement became the stuff of headlines and TV sound bytes beginning that evening, he knew precisely how much "controversy and opposition" the proposal had stirred up.[34]

The rumor mill had disseminated the news before Bennion made public his plan. The principal of Highland High, Delbert Fowler, announced the closing to his faculty, and teachers at South had heard about the proposal from their colleagues at Highland before it became a media event. The issue had already dominated classes at the school and a "feeling of despair" prevailed among students. At the board meeting, students, patrons, and teachers listened to Bennion give the economic rationale for the proposed closure. What sounded logical to Bennion and the board caused an uproar at the meeting, and no amount of assurance that this was a proposal and not a decision could assuage the ire among patrons.

The issue divided the community, East side pitted against West side, affluent vs. less affluent, a deep-seated contention in the city even if not always expressed. Ellen Marsh, a Spanish teacher at South, said South always got the hard raps. To the suggestion that closing South would give Highland and East a better ethnic mix she responded: "That's bull. Most of the racial kids live on the West side." Adrian Saputo was sadly confident that South—not Highland or East—would close: "If you have money, you have rule of the whole world." Others commented after the meeting that the decision was tinged with class bias and racism. Said Rachel Howard, secretary of the sophomore class: "We're the one that doesn't have BMWs parked in the parking lot. We have all the minorities."

---

33. John W. Bennion, Journal, 21 Feb. 1987.
34. *Deseret News*, 26 Jan. 1987. See Jan Keller's "South High Closing" packet for details of meeting of 3 February through 16 June 1987. The packet is available for examination at the Superintendent's Office.

Lori McGarvey, a cheerleader for the South High Cubs, worried that while the minority students felt welcome at South, they would have difficulty fitting into the other schools. "What's going to happen to them?" she wondered.

One South junior, Will Potter, feared that what he wanted to say about the board could not be printed; he did manage to comment: "They're not even going to give us a chance. They're always slapping us down. . . . They just want South out." Advantages that would accrue to the remaining schools meant little to South students. They did not believe that this was only a proposal; in the opinion of student body public relations director Kris Draper, it sounded "like they've already made up their minds." Given all the studying and discussion that had preceded the announcement, it would be hard to disagree with her that there was any realistic chance that South would be spared. As Bennion and the board realized within a few days, logic had little to do with feelings of frustration and resentment that would build up in the community in the ensuing weeks.[35]

Part of the community resentment was rooted in the ideal of shared governance, which had made community members feel they should be involved in decision making. Although the board and Bennion did get input from ten members of the important Equivalency Sub-Committee (including representatives of all four high schools), whose report helped convince the board of South's weaknesses, they did not follow the usual shared governance procedures, causing the chairman of South's School Community Council, Larry Failner, to protest the decision to consider closing South. To the board president, Keith Stepan, he wrote: "[R]egardless of the ultimate decision with regard to the closing of one of the city high school facilities, the underhanded method employed by the board to announce its intent should be recorded as one of the most irresponsible acts ever perpetrated by an elected school board in the history of the state." Failner demanded a public apology from the board for the manner in which the board had handled the issue, asking them to give assurance for a full disclosure "any future actions prior to public announcement."

An alumnus of South, honors history teacher George Henry, was also dismayed over the manner in which the decision was made. Henry reportedly left his history class with "tears streaming down his cheeks" because he didn't know how to explain the board's actions to his students: "It's really hard to teach kids that the democratic process has kind of passed them by." For him, South had played a special role in helping many kids succeed who otherwise would not, and he grieved that with its closing this role would end. Although Henry was sufficiently aware of the problems the school faced, he could not understand the board's *modus operandi*. Why, Henry asked John Bennion at the stormy South High meeting, had they allowed the announcement to be heard over the TV?

---

35. "Proposal to close South High angers students, faculty," *Deseret News*, 4 Feb. 1987; "Plan to Close South High Riles Youths," *Salt Lake Tribune*, 4 Feb. 1987; conversation with Sue Southam, English teacher at South, Spring 1993.

This smacked of "insensitivity beyond imagination."[36]

President Keith Stepan rejected the charge that the board had intentionally avoided involving community people in the decision. The district was faced with a real dilemma of either reducing programs and getting rid of teachers, or making better use of buildings. It had to act—and act fast—to stem the flow of money into unproductive programs.[37] In spite of Stepan's denial of deliberate exclusion, it seems apparent that a strategy was adopted in the board's meetings with staff and with the Equivalency Committee of *not* being completely frank about what was going on. For instance, when the equivalency report was discussed at a meeting of the Highland High School Community Council on 10 December 1986, there was no hint that closing *any* school was in the works. The minutes simply said that the report "pointed out some strengths and weaknesses of each school. It was emphasized that the data would be used as a tool for improvement and for identification of problems."[38] It was this lack of frankness that the South High Community Council Chair objected to as being inconsistent with shared governance philosophy.

Even though it recognized closing a school was necessary, the *Salt Lake Tribune* chided Bennion and the board for insensitivity to community feelings. According to the *Tribune*, this was another instance of arbitrary decision making without consulting the people most involved—the residents. The editorial concluded: "When people most directly impacted believe they've been excluded from decision-making on painfully wrenching changes, achieving those changes becomes needlessly more confused, disorderly and potentially flawed. With prompt and punctual public involvement and support, however, prospects for a well-constructed transition can be considerably brighter."[39]

Bennion and the board were emphatic in stressing that the recommendation had only been arrived at after intensive study and debate. The possibility of good decision making would have been destroyed if discussions from the study sessions with the board during the fall of 1986 had come out in bits and pieces, lacking context. In keeping the discussions about the issue confidential until a concrete proposal was ready, the board hoped to avoid the kind of "turmoil caused by public hearings three years ago on whether to close a high school." According to Bennion, "There was absolutely no consensus [in 1983], and there couldn't be in that situation. There's too much emotion tied up in the neighborhood high school" for school community councils to arrive at a decision which in reality affects not just one school, but the whole district.[40]

Even a decade before the 1983 deliberations, the district's leaders were unwilling to take a stand "against public pressure" and make a controversial deci-

36. "South High's Students Daunted by Plans to Close School," *Salt Lake Tribune*, 5 Feb. 1987; Henry, Oral History, 9 Apr. 1992.
37. "South High's Students Daunted by Plans to Close School," *Salt Lake Tribune*, 5 Feb. 1987.
38. Highland High School Community Council, Minutes, 10 Dec. 1986.
39. "South High Lapse," *Salt Lake Tribune*, Feb. 1987.
40. "School board says it discussed closing South but didn't break any laws," *Deseret News*, 21 Feb. 1987.

sion against rebuilding East High after it burned, which seems to have exacerbated the situation for future superintendents. Again, the board avoided the issue of declining numbers in 1983 by closing enrollments, hoping against hope that this would resolve a deep-seated problem which resisted even the best democratic efforts of shared governance. The issue is succinctly summed up by an editorial comment of the Salt Lake *Tribune* which, in looking over the history of the issue, noted that "Short-sighted decisions by former school officials doomed South High."[41] In 1987, John Bennion wanted the board to make "long-sighted" decisions that would enhance the educational future of the Salt Lake City public schools rather than have them inherit an "emotional mine field."[42]

On 15 February, Bennion recorded that the days since the announcement on South High's future had been "extraordinary"—never had he "been involved in such an emotionally charged issue." When he made the announcement "the effect was explosive. . . . Parents, teachers and students at South reacted with great emotion. I have become the target of their frustration and resentment. A petition has been circulated for my resignation."[43] Previous charges of violating shared governance agreements were repeated at public meetings at South High. When the chair of the South High School Community Council, Larry Failner, proposed that a petition be circulated calling for Bennion's resignation it brought "a roar of approval from the audience." Failner added a new dimension when he urged the board to hire an outside, unbiased party to examine all four high schools and come up with a recommendation.

At a 17 February board meeting, 75 placard-waving protestors crowded outside the board offices. Police had to clear them away until the meeting got underway. Inside, a petition containing 1,200 names demanding Bennion's ouster was presented to the board. Charges were leveled that the superintendent had lost the public trust, and that the board had acted illegally in not making public its meetings on South. Furthermore, teachers filed a grievance because they had not been consulted on the issue, and seven patrons in turn spoke out against the proposal.

In the midst of the critical response was but one ray of support: Glenda Gaudig, who as chair of the Glendale School Community Council was originally scheduled to speak against the closure, changed her mind and instead made a statement supporting the measure. From her knowledge of the situation at South she had concluded that quality of education there left much to be desired, and while she recognized the importance of sentiment and school spirit, she could not let these "stand in the way of quality education."[44]

From state and community leaders outside of the schools there were also expressions of support. Governor Norman Bangerter called Bennion's office and left word that he appreciated having some of the political heat taken off him at this

---

41. "Plan 99 Rates Highest Grade as S.L. High School Answer," *Salt Lake Tribune*, 15 Mar. 1987.
42. "South High's Students Daunted by Plans to Close School," *Salt Lake Tribune*, 5 Feb. 1987.
43. Bennion, Journal, 15 Feb. 1987.
44. "South High Petitioners Seek Ouster," *Deseret News*, 18 Feb. 1987.

particular time: "They are mad at [me] for raising taxes and mad at you for trying to save some money," the governor's message of support read. A neighbor and prominent business leader, Mike Leavitt (later governor of Utah), and his wife, Jackie, wrote to encourage John to stand his ground: "The admiration of the masses will be earned by enduring the criticism of a mindless few."[45]

Board member Steve Boyden rejected the call for Bennion's resignation; he was simply following board policy. The board had decided to consider closing South because of the benefits that would accrue to the schools if some $800,000 were saved—benefits such as smaller English classes, summer programs for at-risk students, and improved alternative programs for students who didn't do well in regular classes. Based on staff research, the board had concluded that with South due to lose another 100 students over the next four years, it would have too few students to "operate a sound, cost-effective educational program." Perhaps he was technically correct when he said closure was at that point just an option, but given what is known about the "Reorganization Plan" of 3 February, it's doubtful that many people accepted the statement at its face value—South's community knew its days were numbered—and so, too, did the board and the superintendent.[46]

VALUE CLASHES ALONG DISPUTED BOUNDARIES

For Bennion, with his central focus on educational improvement through better instruction in the classrooms, closing South was necessary. It would have been "unconscionable to put money into bricks and mortar when it could go into programs." He urged the board to make a definite decision by 17 March; if closure was decided upon he would need time to make necessary adjustments to accommodate the students who would have to attend the other schools. As that deadline neared, however, it became quite obvious that the question was less "Should South be closed?" and more a matter of "What shall the new high school boundaries be?" On 1 March Bennion wrote:

Most people seem to be assuming that South will close and are now debating what the new boundaries should be. Some people argue for as little change as possible; others say that major boundary changes should be made to bring about a similar mix of students in 3 high schools. I think there is a middle ground between these two positions which I hope the board will eventually reach. Board members are presently being bombarded from many different, conflicting interest groups.[47]

Bennion's personal reflection mirrors what happened at a meeting called by the Community Council for 23 February at Bryant Junior High School. Some 500 people assembled to discuss the changes proposed in the district. There was

---

45. Telephone Message to Dr. Bennion from Governor Bangerter, 13 Feb. 1987; Mike and Jackie Leavitt to John and Sylvia Bennion, 4 Mar. 1987.

46. "South High Petitioners Seek Ouster," *Deseret News*, 18 Feb. 1987; "South Patrons Take Fight to School Board," *Salt Lake Tribune*, 18 Feb. 1987.

47. Bennion, Journal, 1 Mar. 1987.

unanimous agreement on only one thing—South High should close—but after that there was protracted "heated and emotional" debate on the issue of boundaries. Prior to this meeting, four plans had been put forward as "best." The guidelines prepared by the staff at the request of the board identified size, minority composition, median income level, and student achievement level as the criteria, but plans 1 and 2, which would be least disruptive of schools, would leave West as the school with the dominant minority population. On the other hand, plans 3 and 4, while giving more balance in terms of ethnicity (but certainly not equal balance), were viewed as being most disruptive.

At the Bryant meeting, another plan was unveiled—plan 5, or "The People's Plan," which took the position that the best way to get equity in each of the categories was to send *all* the students living on the Avenues and the exclusive Federal Heights area to West High. Under this proposal West would have around 2,000 students; East, 1,942; and Highland 1,920. In terms of minorities, West would have a minority population of 22 percent; East, 24 percent; and Highland, 20 percent. Using the number of students who eat free lunches as a measure of wealth, all the schools under Plan 5 would have 19 percent of their students receiving free lunch. In terms of academic achievement, West would have a percentile ranking on the California Achievement Test of 58.66; East, 62.15; and Highland, 67.59. Plan 5 certainly was an expression of an effort to make equity more than just a rhetorical phrase. In the words of Jaynie Brown, who helped put it together, "the people's plan," if adopted by the board at its next meeting, would mean that for once Salt Lake City had people in it who "are more concerned about being fair than about being No. 1." Chris Robinson, a graduate of East, also favored maximum equity, so West students would have the same chance as the "elitists" who attend East.

Bill Bowling, a resident of the Avenues who claimed that he had moved there in 1985 so that his children could attend East High, saw Plan 5 as "grandiose sociological meddling." To try to bring about socio-economic equity was, for Bowling, "categorical sociological nonsense," and should not interfere with deliberations about boundaries. And so the evening wore on with a revival of old fears about property values on the Avenues being lowered if students there had to attend West, countered, of course, by the claim that equal educational opportunities would actually stabilize property values. The official "booster" for the revitalized West High, Principal Harold Trussel, told his potential patrons from the Avenues and Federal Heights that he planned to make West one of the top ten schools in the nation within a few years and that its music and academic programs were excellent. If the *status quo* is kept, he claimed, students from Salt Lake City's more affluent districts would miss an important opportunity to "associate with people different from themselves."

Trussel's appeal was countermanded by the East High Principal, LaMar Sorensen, who had served as West's principal from 1980 to 1983. Taking the mantle as loyal protector of the "East turf," he told Avenue patrons that they were "the heart of East High." If "the people's plan" were adopted and Avenue students left East for West, "we would suffer severely." East's academic program would be destroyed if any but plan 1 were to be implemented. Ron Walker, the board member whose constituents were on the Avenues and Federal Heights, spoke in favor of a plan that had many of the elements of plan 5 and told the group that it was "less important now to preserve the *status quo* than to find a solution to the district's problems of inequality."[48]

By 7 March, the board had reached consensus on the need to close a school. Although most board members refrained from mentioning South by name, it was a foregone conclusion that South would close at the end of the 1987 academic year. Facing this reality, South's principal, LaVar Sorenson, said students at South were hurting and "wondering which garbage truck is going to pick them up."[49]

As the 17 March deadline loomed for a final vote on closing South, a majority on the board began to have qualms about disturbing the *status quo*. No one really thought that South should *not* be closed, but the board had felt the sting of public rebuke for their handling of the issue. Four of those who had been part of the unanimous decision to consider closing South High (Matheson, Kump, Boyden, and Minson), now began to wonder if they needed more time to reconsider the issue of South High and to get more input from the community in the deliberations. Stephen Boyden suggested that perhaps South's students should be allowed to attend any school they wished. In this way, the thorny issue of realigning high school boundaries could be deferred.

The boundary issue seems to have been the real source of ambivalence. Although few admitted that their views on this issue were rooted in their social class or that bias against minority groups was influencing their positions, those on the West side were acutely sensitive to class distinctions and even racism. As Bennion noted: "Value clashes have reverberated across the city with a fury. Prejudices, stereotypes and irrational fears have sprung up like mushrooms on a water soaked lawn." City Councillor from the west side, Earl Hardwick, expressed his reaction to the emerging bias at one of the many early hearings on the boundary issue. He felt embarrassed for the citizens of Salt Lake; the message adults seemed to be sending their children was that particular schools do indeed represent particular social and economic values—desirable ones on the East and undesirable on the West. Talk of declining property values on the Avenues if students from that area attend West and reference to "undesirable" students at South and West, sent a message of acceptable prejudice to children. It represented, to Hardwick, "an elitist attitude that shows total lack of sensitivity and responsible social conscience. The setting of social, economic or racial boundaries by the people of this valley stands as a message to the rest of the world that bigotry and social class structures are alive and well in Salt Lake City."[50]

In reporter Marianne Funk's view the proposed closing of South had forced the community to "confront the sharp social divisions" between East and West

---

48. "South closure agreed upon, but not boundaries," *Deseret News*, 24 Feb. 1987.
49. Peter Scarlett, "School Board on Verge of Closing South High," *Salt Lake Tribune*, 7 Mar. 1987.
50. Bennion, Journal, 28 Mar. 1987; "Many stigmas once forgotten are resurfacing . . . ," *Deseret News*, 15 Mar. 1987.

Salt Lake. The old adage that schools are a mirror of society was as true in Salt Lake City as anywhere else. By their very nature, schools send a message that middle-class values, high socio-economic status, and especially the notion that ultimate power resides in the white-dominated political system, are what ought to be, and that schools exist to promote these orientations. Some would argue that the hidden curriculum of public schools is, in fact, to communicate that dividing the world into haves and have nots is a legitimate and necessary function of schools—some schools prepare leaders, while others prepare workers. Bowles and Gintis, in their analysis of the function of reform in the development of the schools, express a dominant theme of radical critics of the American public schools when they conclude: "U.S. education is highly unequal, the chances of attaining much or little schooling being substantially dependent on one's race and parents' economic level. Moreover, where there is a discernible trend towards a more equal educational system—as in the narrowing of the black education deficit—the impact on the structure of economic opportunity is minimal at best."[51] In this view, the response of the East side community councils on the issue of boundaries was consistent with the dominant ideology of those who wielded much of the political and economic power of Salt Lake City. This is a reality hard to avoid, but one must also recognize that in spite of it, American schools have also been given the almost impossible task of making a flawed system better. This idealism seemed to underlie the original decision to close South.

When the board met to make its final decision on 17 March, the consensus so evident the week before had evaporated. Three members of the board (Stepan, Walker, and Keene) favored closing South immediately to minimize further trauma and get on with realigning the boundaries. Another group (Matheson, Boyden, and Kump) now wanted to delay the closure on the grounds that more community input was needed. The person representing the South High area, Colleen Minson, wavered between the two options, but finally sided with those who wanted to delay closure on the ground that it would enable the district to do some long-range planning for the future development of the three remaining high schools. She also recommended that an independent professional consultant be called in help make the decision about which high school should be closed or even consider the possibility of the establishment of two high schools. In response to Susan Keene's charge that the board was capitulating under pressure from East side interests, Minson denied that she had changed under pressure. Keene, for her part, was reported to have believed that there was collusion between patrons of South, who wanted to keep their school open, and patrons on the Avenues, who didn't want their children to go to West. According to Keene, both benefited if South were not forced to close. It was, she was reported to have said, in the interests of the "rich and powerful to keep South open." According to Sue Southam, then an English teacher at South, the Eastside citizens wanted to keep South students out of *their* community.

For Ron Walker, on the other hand, the only thing that could explain the

---

51. Samuel Bowles and Herbert Gintis, *Schooling in Capitalist America: Educational Reform and the Contradictions of Economic Life* (New York: Basic Books, 1976), 35.

evaporation of consensus was that board members had confused closing South with the boundary issue. There *was* indeed pressure being exerted on the board and the board *had* become embroiled in the implications of boundary changes for their home turf. Lorna Matheson, who had supported the original move to close South, was now quoted as saying that to move hastily would "be premature and a Band-aid solution." To the notion that the board had moved in undue haste, President Stepan retorted that the problem was not that they moved too fast, but that they moved "five years too late." As far as he could tell, there was just as much sentiment in the community for equity as for maintaining the *status quo*, and the board should act accordingly and follow through with its original decision.[52]

Up to a few minutes before the meeting on 17 March, Superintendent Bennion tried in vain to effect a compromise behind which the board could unite, but "the board became hopelessly divided [and] the best that we could do was to postpone the decisions until next summer on the closure and fall on the boundaries." Bennion found the process of debating and wrangling over the issues "terribly draining, time consuming and unproductive." He was anxious that he and his staff should attend to educational, rather than political issues, and publicly expressed keen disappointment when the board unanimously opted to postpone the closing until spring of 1988, unless the consultant recommended the closure of a different school or no school at all. Postponing the inevitable would simply exacerbate the issue.

In the meantime, a citizens' committee would work with a professional consultant to accept or reject the closure decision by the end of the summer. If accepted, a boundary committee would formulate proposals by October. However, there were still voices in the community calling on the board to follow through with their original intent to close South and reminding them that failure to act in years past had not resolved the issue. Exhausted by the ordeal, Carolyn Kump told those assembled at the board meeting that "I personally don't feel we went through the process right, and you have my apologies.[53]

The conflict board members experienced fulfilled the prediction made by an editorial in the *Deseret News* a few weeks after the original decision had been announced. The *News* cautioned: "If the Salt Lake City School District thinks closing a school is grabbing a tiger by the tail, wait until it tries drawing new boundary lines for the remaining three high schools."[54] And again when the board decided to postpone the closing to let tempers cool "and a clearer perspective to prevail" the *News* warned that postponement was not likely to change the attitudes of turf protection and polarization by which "the community at times

52. "South High decision is probably months away," *Deseret News*, 17 Mar. 1987; "School Board May Abandon Today's Deadline on South," *Salt Lake Tribune*, 17 Mar. 1987; conversation with Sue Southam, Spring 1993.

53. "Board Vote to Keep South High Open Until '88," *Salt Lake Tribune*, 18 Mar. 1987; "South High will close in 1988—if citizen's panel agrees," *Deseret News*, 18 Mar. 1987. See also Board of Education, Minutes, 17 Mar. 1987.

54. "New boundaries could improve S.L. Schools," *Deseret News*, 25 Feb. 1987.

threatens to come apart at the seams." In a remarkably frank statement the editorial averred that "[n]othing can be gained by resolutely clinging to the idea of preserving the status quo. What's needed now is to arrive at the best plan possible and then to execute it with firmness and resolve."[55] That is what Bennion and the board attempted to do over the next ten months, but before the issue could be called resolved in any way, the community tiger not only swung its tail vigorously; it bit back.

In addition to selecting a citizens' committee, the board also appointed as a consultant an expert in closing schools: Dr. George Garver, of Livonia, Michigan, who had supervised the closure of 22 schools—including a high school. From his perspective, it was possible to establish with almost scientific precision *which* school should be closed. However, school boundaries were a different matter because of the "subjective" emotions involved in telling people where they should go to school. For this reason, Garver steered the citizens' committee clear of boundary decisions: they were to deal with one question only: Does Salt Lake City need to close a high school, and if so, which one should it be? The boundary issue was thus put on the back burner, but the heat was never quite turned off. Garver's committee met at least once each week in the late spring of 1987. They first reviewed on paper the figures regarding declining enrollments and made comparisons of programs at each of the high schools.

With a clear picture of the "objective" data in front of them, the committee, under Garver's direction, then visited each high school to get a feel for the on-site situation. Theoretically, the committee was trying to determine *which* of the high schools would be closed, but it is difficult to believe that anyone ever seriously considered closing East or Highland. Nevertheless, the committee did attempt to be "fair" and to look at everything without prejudice. Don Barlow recalled the visit of the committee to Highland High when "we put on our best dog and pony show" as if there were any real chance that the committee would decide to close the newest, and what he and others regarded as the "most effective high school in the city in order to keep South High open." All this was done "with tongue in cheek" because no one really believed that closing other schools was a real option. Barlow suspected that "everybody in South High School knew that too." However, board member Susan Keene mentioned Highland as a distinct possibility on occasion, in part because its real estate value on Seventeenth East and Twenty-First South would be a windfall to the district. Don Barlow's response to this suggestion was "Come on, lady, have a clue." The committee deliberations were perceived as a means of softening the blow: It certainly could not be said now that the community had not been consulted.[56]

According to George Henry, who served on the citizens' committee and also taught history at South, the committee's real aim was to produce a community-based rationale regarding South's future. During all the deliberations in the

---

55. "Delay won't soften tough S.L. school decision," *Deseret News*, 18 Mar. 1987.

56. "Close Schools? It's Tough Advice to Give," *Salt Lake Tribune*, 25 May 1987; Barlow, Oral History, 4 May 1992.

spring of 1987 the economics of the situation tended to dominate everything that went on in the committee. South simply did not have the kind of established residential community the other schools had. This lack of community was further manifest in the fact that while 70 percent of East's students were within walking distance of the school, some 70 to 80 percent of South's students were bused.

South was the "natural" school to close—ultimately it was more expendable because of the nature of its constituency. South's boosters, including its last principal, LaVar Sorensen, could muster emotionally compelling arguments about its importance to the community, its rich cultural diversity and pluralism, and its role in giving students who might never have succeeded a chance to succeed. It even had a physical plant in better condition than East's. But Garver instructed the committee to avoid emotional issues and stick only to the facts in the case. In light of the "objective and detached" report given to the board, there was no other conclusion but that "South High will close as of May, 1988."[57] And, after a roller coaster spring in which student and faculty spirits rose and fell with every rumor, that is precisely what the committee reported. On 16 June, the board unanimously voted to follow the committee's recommendation and sweep away the school on State Street. When the final, long expected announcement was made "the adjustment and healing process began. South High Cubs made their last year their best."[58]

The healing may have begun for the students and faculty at South, but for the district as a whole, and for the superintendent and the board, what lay ahead would be even more divisive than was the initial decision. John Bennion's reflections on the first half of the year were a succinct portent of what would occur over the course of the next half year:

> The last 5 months have been the most trying and difficult of my entire [seventeen year] professional career as a school superintendent. I have been at the heart of some extremely difficult emotional issues. . . . My frustration level has been higher for a longer period of time than I ever remember it being. I would not want to stay on as supt. in Salt Lake City very long if conditions remain as problematical as they have been during the last five months.

In addition to the boundary and closure dispute, there were problems associated with the open classroom program and the overriding pressure from the governor, legislature, and state board for school systems to "squeeze more blood out of the turnip." "I wish," Bennion concluded on 1 July, "I could see some light ahead. With state conditions such as they are and the volatile boundary issues about to heat up again, I am taking my job a year at a time."[59]

---

57. Henry, Oral History, 9 Apr. 1992; Barlow, Oral History, 4 May 1992; Bennion, Oral History, 11 Aug. 1991; LaVar Sorensen, Oral History, 8 Sept. 1992; "'Big Bad South'" to Leave a Special Sports Legacy," *Salt Lake Tribune*, 1 July 1987. LaVar Sorensen was a cousin of LaMar Sorensen, principal of East.

58. Audrey E. Anderson et al., *South High School: A History, 1931-1988* (Salt Lake City: Associated Students of South High, 1988), 30.

59. Bennion, Journal, 21 June, 1 July 1987.

"Deep and Passionate Division" over Freedom and Equality

Keeping previous criticism in mind, the board made sure the resolution of the boundary issue would involve community representatives and public input. From the initial attempts to settle the boundary issues, however, the board had been badly split, not only on where boundaries should be drawn, but over what criteria should be used to determine them. The split community quickly returned to the fore as soon as the board set out the criteria to be used as a means of achieving that most elusive of all social aims—equality.

Ostensibly, the board closed South to create better opportunities for all the city's high school students. In their "Statement of Purpose," board members clearly enunciated this ideal when they agreed to create three high schools, equal in "academic standards, extracurricular programs, staff, learning climate, and student achievement."[60] While generalities are easy to achieve consensus on, however, problems emerge when agreement on the specific means of accomplishing these ends are sought. American commitment to the ideal of equity may be a basic social value, but that has not prevented it becoming a contentious and divisive issue. The difficulty lies in determining what the expression "equality" means. Does it refer to *input* equality, *output* equality, or equality of *process*?

By 1 September, a bare majority on the board (four to three) had agreed on the criteria to determine the new boundaries, and a series of five open hearings was scheduled to gain public input. That the board was badly split in itself suggested that resolution would not come easily. Still, they seemed to go along with the group of 50 patrons attending the first meeting at Northwest Intermediate School in late September, which encouraged the board to "do the right thing" in the face of political pressure to delay.

These public hearings allowed people to vent feelings on many sides of the issue. The factions divided between those who wanted to maximize equality and those who wished to minimize disruption. The latter held the position that boundaries should essentially be left as they were, even if this did not create equality. To them, perfect equality was an idealistic chimera. On the other hand, the former held that sending all of the Avenues students to West High was the only way of ensuring equality. This either/or perspective proved to be difficult groundwork on which to build a compromise.

Bennion felt the pressure from neighbors and as an alumni of East High to espouse East's cause. The hearing at Clayton Intermediate on 13 October was especially difficult for the superintendent. His closest neighbors in his LDS ward spoke out against any change and expected him to "come on like gangbusters in their interest," but Bennion resisted being an advocate for East.[61] He was convinced that West needed a climate and programs that would bring it up to par with Highland and East. Some disruption of family traditions might have to be

---

60. "Hearing Views 'Balancing' High Schools," *Salt Lake Tribune*, 1 Oct. 1987.
61. Bennion, Journal, 27 Sept., 11 Oct., 18 Oct. 1987; Bennion, Oral History, 11 Aug. 1991. See also accounts of public hearings in *Salt Lake Tribune*, 7 Oct., 14 Oct., 20 Oct. 1987; *Deseret News*, 7 Oct., 14 Oct. 1987.

tolerated in the interest of all the schools becoming relatively equal. However, he did not think it had to be all or nothing with regard to the Avenues. By disposition Bennion was not an "either/or" person, but as early as October it was becoming clear to him that there was very little basis for compromise. He seemed to be single-handedly left to represent the interests of the city's schools as a whole. He recognized, as did Alexis de Tocqueville a century and a half earlier, that the ideals of freedom and equality are a heady mix in the American experience. If anything were to be accomplished, some accommodation and balance between the two ideals must be achieved.

The board, however, was "being strongly pulled in many different directions" by their respective constituencies. In retrospect, Bennion felt that had the board been elected at large, instead of by only a segment of the community, they might have had a more inclusive vision of what the schools needed. In an attempt to defuse the situation, Bennion recommended that as an alternative to major boundary changes the board should create a model high school at West by expanding the International Baccalaureate Program established at the school in 1986. Essentially, a liberal college program for advanced students, the program as Bennion and his staff envisioned it would also have been supplemented with "intensive instruction in such areas as computer science and business." Although some board members liked aspects of the program and thought it "nifty" and "exciting," the cost and the target population raised major hurdles, and the idea, designed in large measure as a "peace pact" to end "the boundary war gripping the district" died aborning. The majority on the board (Ronald Walker, Susan Keene, Colleen Minson, and Keith Stepan representing areas of the city which served South and West) were, according to Bennion, more "inclined to do major surgery on the boundaries." The remaining three (Carolyn Kump, Lorna Matheson, and Stephen Boyden representing Highland and East) were adamant that the boundaries remain unchanged. The superintendent described the public hearings held at Hillside and Bryant as "many emotional voices . . . heard on different sides of the issue. Some called for complete equality; others pleaded for a least disruptive approach."[62]

THE CITIZENS' COMMITTEE ESTABLISHES BOUNDARIES

In the following months, the board and the superintendent tried to reach a compromise. Although board members maintained a civil attitude toward each other, it was clear that "feelings were strained." At the conclusion of the meeting preceding the boundary committee being given its charge, the board adjourned "frustrated and without clear direction."[63] However, the majority was determined to push its advantage, and on 27 October the board by a vote of four to three gave the citizens' committee the task to realign the high school boundaries. This

62. Bennion, Journal, 20 Sept., 11 Oct. 1987; Bennion, Oral History, 6 Sept. 1991; "Proposal to create academy at West is met with skepticism," Deseret News, 23 Sept. 1987; "Board Studies Plan for 'Model School' at West High after Closure of South," Salt Lake Tribune, 23 Sept. 1987.
63. Bennion, Journal, 25 Oct. 1987.

was to be done to meet a criteria of equality: all high schools would have no more than a variance of four percent in student achievement scores; no more than twelve percent variance in minority population; and no more than a variance of 200 in total student population.

In response, Carolyn Kump warned the board that to meet these criteria the district would have to shift half its students to new high schools. Lorna Matheson argued that the boundary committee had been given an impossible assignment; at least it could not be done "without massive, massive disruption." Susan Keene defended the majority's decision as necessary to achieve a "balanced mix of resident high, low and middle achievers." If this were not held to, claimed Keene, "some very lopsided schools" would be produced.[64]

Armed with specific criteria of what would constitute equality, the citizens' committee went to work. The newspapers gave them an encouraging send off, the *Deseret News* and Salt Lake *Tribune* both praising the board for taking a controversial stand in favor of equity in the city's schools. Somewhat critical of East High patrons who had put up "fierce resistance" against the idea of disturbing boundaries, the *News* noted that "Salt Lake residents have paid lip service to the idea of equality." Given the fact that South had made a great sacrifice in the district's efforts to promote equity, "it would seem unfair not to ask others to share in the sacrifices of realignment." Doubting the possibility of getting absolute equity in all the criteria, the *News* editorial nevertheless felt that the creation of three high schools with "about the same academic mix would benefit every neighborhood and all the students." Saying that "prejudices, fears, and threats to fight to the end" did nothing to help the schools, the editorial concluded. "What is needed is cooperation, a sense of community, and a willingness to make the school system one of the best—for everybody." In a similar vein, the *Tribune* referred to the board's "courage and wisdom" to see beyond the "inevitable storm of neighborhood protests and criticism." Warning that the board's close vote "could still collapse under pressure," the editorial lauded them for taking "the high road on a tough boundary decision" designed to prevent "recurring boundary problems," and provide more equitable opportunities for the city's students.[65]

During the next six weeks as the committee attempted to arrive at a consensus, divisions in the community and board became more and more apparent. Picketers appeared at board meetings bearing signs that read "Say No to Communism," and a regular schedule of protests was published and distributed to high school community councils by those who opposed any realignment. Patrons were asked to "cruise" their cars on South Temple at particular times to show how congested that street would be if Avenues students used it during football games at West, and a letter-writing campaign got underway to steer the

---

64. "Strict rules set for revising school boundaries," *Deseret News*, 28 Oct. 1987; "S.L. School Board Sets Guidelines for Boundaries," *Salt Lake Tribune*, 28 Oct. 1987.
65. "Equality should be goal of new S.L. school lines," *Deseret News* 25 Oct. 1987; "Salt Lake City School Board Process Bolsters Boundary Process," *Salt Lake Tribune*, 1 Nov. 1987.

board away from "social engineering." Some parents threatened to send their children to Granite District's Olympus High, and others complained of the dangers inherent in having their high school students drive across town to West High from the Avenues and Federal Heights. Some expressed dismay at their children attending school near industrial lots ringed with barbed wire fences. One even suggested that changing the name "West" might ease the pain of attending the school. Underlying these comments was implicit hostility to those of a different social class: "If they wanted better schools for their children, they'd move as we have done." It was asking too much, some averred, to have Eastside students attend West High in order to stimulate those who chose to stay on the west side.[66]

At one tension-charged meeting, the student-body president of South, Kimberley Hall, and Joey Borgenicht, president of East, spoke out against what they perceived to be increasingly a "parent problem," not one centered in the schools or in their students. Borgenicht pleaded, to no avail apparently, for parents to "step back" and tone down the rhetoric. Hall charged that parents were overreacting and that they needed to start working together: "It has become a war that reeks of bigotry and selfishness. Everything is my child, my school, my neighborhood."[67]

Minority groups also perceived the resistance as rooted in racism. In response, a new group which appeared on the scene in late November. The "Let's Make it Work Coalition" went public with its claim that many statements made at meetings carried racist overtones. The Reverend France Davis of Calvary Baptist Church claimed that parents who vocalized their fears about their children associating with "blacks, Polynesians and the less economically affluent" further divided the community. Katherine Simon wondered if "we have stooped so low as to become a dictatorship of the 'haves' over the 'have nots.'" Responding to the "racism" charge, Joy Orton, chair of the East Community Council, denied that racism existed at East High and claimed that East already had a high proportion (20 percent) of students who were minorities.[68]

After weeks of charge and counter-charge, the district was far from peaceful. Bennion, on the eve of his fifty-first birthday, had never had so many people upset with him, he reminisced, and he longed for a resolution. If the boundary dispute was not soon over, and if the Utah legislature failed to support the career

---

66. The furor created by the decision to realign the high school boundaries is documented in some thirty articles that appeared in Salt Lake City newspapers between 28 October and 15 December 1987. No attempt has been made to cite them all here, but a few representative pieces are "Parents March to Protest School Boundary Decision," *Deseret News*, 4 Nov. 1987; "Parents Vow to Remove Children from School to Protest Realignment," *Deseret News*, 12 Nov. 1987; "If School Lines Go, We Do Too, Cry Parents," *Salt Lake Tribune*, 18 Nov. 1987; "Use Heads Instead of Hysteria to Solve City School Problem," *Salt Lake Tribune*, 22 Nov. 1987. As a member of the Highland High School Community Council during 1987-88, I observed the community divisions at close hand.

67. "If School Lines Go, We Do Too, Cry Parents," *Salt Lake Tribune*, 18 Nov. 1987.

68. "Coalition Aims to End Battle Over School Boundaries," *Salt Lake Tribune*, 23 Nov. 1987; "Coalition Accuses School Boundary Foes of a Racial Motivation," *Deseret News*, 23 Nov. 1987.

ladder program adequately, he was tempted to consider moving back to the vicinity of Rochester, New York, where a number of excellent suburban districts, including Brighton, were looking for new superintendents: "The New York economy is strong and the political climate much more hospitable than Utah. I would much rather function as an educator than a manager of conflict and political broker. . . . I find it difficult to pursue the education agenda because of political cross currents and conflicts. . . . It would not be difficult for me to go back [to New York]."[69]

Nor would it have been difficult for some to reverse their support for closing South High. Steve Boyden did precisely that when he told the board at the end of November that he would now "rather have South High open" even if it meant the district had to lose the $600,000 in state appropriations. No doubt similar sentiments went through the minds of the members of the citizens' committee, which now had to share the criticism previously directed at the board and the superintendent. No matter what they did, or what decision they arrived at, the boundary committee was in a "damned if you do and damned if you don't" position. They succeeded in getting the board to make the criteria a bit more flexible in allowing the four percent achievement variance to range from six to eleven percent. Of course, the committee was not dealing with the entire board, only the majority of four. They alone seemed to be involved in any of the negotiations involving criteria. The remaining three simply voted against any change, an attitude roundly criticized by the *Deseret News*.[70]

By December the committee had reached a decision. However, they could not get the necessary 9-3 vote on one plan. Instead, by a vote of 8-4 on one plan and 6-2 (with two abstentions) on the other, they submitted to the board two unendorsed maps. The first (eventually tagged as "Plan G") called for an achievement level variance of 8.23 percent; a minority variance of only four percent, and an overall population variance of no more than 104 students. While this plan would necessitate the movement of some 19 percent of the district's students, the percentage of students requiring busing would rise only eight percent. In order to meet these criteria, Plan G required *all* students living north of South Temple to attend West High, including Arlington Hills and Federal Heights. The alternative, "Plan P" (approved in a 6-4 vote, with two abstentions) called for a student achievement variance of 11 percent; a minority variance of seven percent and a population variance of 159; to accomplish this, West's boundary would extend eastward to Virginia Street, thereby splitting Arlington Hills from Federal Heights and sending one part of these very affluent areas to West and the other to East.

The lack of the stipulated 9-3 majority on either plan indicated that community divisions had also become part of the committee's final deliberations. The committee actually split into two caucuses—representing the east side and the

---

69. Bennion, Journal, 22 Nov., 20 Dec. 1987.

70. "School Boundary Panel Drawing Up 3 Maps," *Deseret News*, 1 Dec. 1987; "S.L. High School Equality is Still Ideal Worth Pursuing," and "Any School Boundary Act Will Draw Fire," *Deseret News*, 2 Dec. 1987.

west side. Apparently those representing the Northeast Avenues section refused to give any plan the necessary 75 percent approval unless Arlington Hills and Federal Heights were left undisturbed and within East High's boundaries. It was argued by one resident of Federal Heights that to split these areas and send one to East and the other to West would split people of the same class and even lead members of LDS wards to attend different high schools. School patrons in the northeast section of the Avenues were certainly not going to give up without a fight to preserve what they perceived to be their sense of community. However, they ran into a new reality; east side interests no longer dominated the board. Redrawing the boundaries to exclude a large portion of a very affluent area exacerbated what the eastsiders perceived to be a further diminution of their political power and traditional prestige.[71]

As if the board did not have to contend with enough maps (some twenty-four had been submitted since the beginning of the dispute), Stephen Boyden made another proposal. As a way of resolving forever the dispute over boundaries, he seriously suggested that East High should be closed and that all students living north of 900 South Street attend West High and all students who lived south of 900 South should attend Highland High. A number of parents agreed with this new two high school plan; they would prefer to see East closed than have their children receive an inferior education after East's academic tradition had been, in their view, destroyed. The superintendent immediately went to work on the way in which such a proposal might be implemented, but the citizens' committee regarded the proposal as a "slap in the face" after the time and energy they had put into the plans submitted to the board. Ultimately the plan to close East (and another one to close *all* the high schools and build one new high school for the whole city) was tabled for lack of time.[72]

Finishing off the "year of the boundary debate," board president Keith Stepan and a member of the East High Community Council, Robert Wright, gave Salt Lake residents a Christmas treat by debating the major points of dispute in the *Tribune*.[73] As his year ended, Bennion recorded that the "high school boundary issue continues to dominate my life. The boundary committee became divided and could not reach a consensus. They submitted two maps, but did not bridge very well the east and west sides of the city."[74] The "exhausted community" left that task to a somewhat discouraged superintendent and a badly divided board.

On 13 January, at the last public hearing on the issue, the two plans were

71. Telephone conversation with Paul Hanks, 3 Sept. 1992. Hanks chaired the Citizens' Committee and also taught LDS seminary at East in the 1960s.
72. "Boundary Drama Gets New Twist: Close East," *Deseret News*, 16 Dec. 1987; "Parents Would Rather Close East than Lose Hundreds to West High," *Deseret News*, 18 Dec. 1987; "School Board Must be Joking with East High Jettison Idea," *Salt Lake Tribune*, 23 Dec. 1987; "Closing Two High Schools has Merit," *Deseret News*, 23 Dec. 1987.
73. "Cross Fire: 'Equity' Plan Under the Gun," *Salt Lake Tribune*, 21 Dec. 1987; conversation with Sue Southam, Spring 1993.
74. Bennion, Journal, 20 Dec. 1987.

once again discussed. Annette Tanner, chair of the Highland Community Council, spoke in favor of "P" because it was the least disruptive of the two plans and the only "alternative that would have the support necessary to bind this valley back together after a process that has literally torn it apart." Michael Ortega, a westside neighborhood organizer for the Salt Lake Citizen's Congress, spoke in favor of "G" because it was the only alternative that would "eliminate the east-west stigma."

A University of Utah professor spoke in favor of "G" also, saying the charge that it is "social engineering" should be discounted because when the board decided to close South, that act was "*de facto* social engineering." Robert Wright opposed the whole notion of trying to create equity by making schools the same saying that it couldn't be done given the diversity within the city. T. H. Bell, former U.S. Secretary of Education, whose own children would now attend West, expressed the view that although the community seemed fractured, once the board decided, the wounds would heal and the "difficulties will be behind you." Those speaking for the west side (and a minority from the Avenues) favored Plan G, but most of the speakers at this final hearing favored Plan P, including representatives of Federal Heights.

The formal minutes of the board meeting of 19 January seem anti-climactic as they record the business relating to agenda item "3b. Decision on High School Boundaries" in thirteen sparse lines. A motion to adopt Map G was made and seconded, followed by a substitute motion to adopt Map P. The latter was defeated by a vote of four to three, and the former, Map G, was adopted by the same vote. Prior to the vote, the members had one more opportunity to say why they were doing what they did; Minson spoke of the need to equalize educational opportunity and of the need for maturity in accepting the final outcome of the vote; Walker spoke of fairness and of his belief that East would continue to be an excellent school; Kump recognized the need to give West a critical mass of achieving students, but feared that East would be stripped down in the process. Boyden lamented the failure of the board to have had the foresight five years before which could have produced two excellent schools. That, he felt, was the only way to promote long-term equity. Matheson said that Map G did not represent true equity and too much was being asked of East.

The superintendent, for his part, said that although the past months had been difficult, he felt that the district now had a much deeper awareness of the kind of high schools it wanted, and commented on how easy it was to agree on general aims, but how difficult to agree on means. In response to a question from Carolyn Kump, Bennion said that he believed that both "G" and "P" could be used in meeting the ends of equity. He cited Martin Luther King on the need for a spirit of unity and hoped that the district's energy could now be used to implement whatever option was chosen. Personally Bennion did not think the boundaries needed to be drawn as tightly as they were, but it appeared to him that the more the East's representatives persisted in affirming their opposition to "G," the more the others on the boundary committee became resolute in making it the only choice.[75]

Reminiscent somewhat of a classical tragedy, John Bennion recorded the formal conclusion of the boundary dispute with a terse "The deed is done . . .," followed by his observation that he feared "the issue may still fester."[76]

THE CONTINUANCE OF "SNARLING RESISTANCE"

In the ensuing weeks, as Bennion feared, the issue continued to fester on several levels—among community opponents of the action, among the Salt Lake Teachers Association, and among the minority of three on the board. There was, however, also considerable support for Bennion's stance and for his attempts to arrive at a middle ground resolution. Emma Lou Thayne, Utah poet and writer, called on the words of John Bennion's uncle, Lowell L. Bennion, in an eloquent appeal for community support of the resolution. Citing the venerable teacher and community activist as saying "never let the things that matter most be at the mercy of the things that matter least," Thayne went on to appeal for diversity within the city schools: "No one group or time—certainly not one area of the city—has a corner on brains, character, personality, potential, frailty or disaster. And moving with credible change often takes a lot more courage and quality than any snarling resistance ever did." A city that put principles ahead of property values and education ahead of territorialism would indeed be focused on the things that matter most and would take on "the challenge of the new boundaries with bigness, not smallness and send our children off with the same."[77]

Those who had opposed any change in the boundaries met the day following the board decision and discussed ways by which they could undo the "damage" done to East High School. Invitations to a meeting to discuss "The John Bennion Style of Administration" were passed out at the conclusion of the board meeting, and a group of some thirty people assembled in a room at the University of Utah Olpin Union on 20 January. Dee Vincent, a local school patron who had played a role in governance activities, stated that some sort of organization was necessary to determine whether patrons had any recourse to reduce the voted leeway and initiate recall proceedings against the board. She also noted that flight from the district was now underway. Complaints of "fat in the administration" were raised, and assertions were made that basics, not equity, should be the focus of the district. When it was mentioned that Bennion might leave if the leeway were reduced, a voice piped up with "That would be a small price to pay." Wide ranging discussion of the procedure to be used in transferring to another district, a proposal to boycott the schools, whether Carolyn Kump had been cautioned against undermining the board's narrow decision, the need for a poll of some sort—took up much of the meeting time, but ultimately leaders

---

75. Board of Education, Minutes, 19 Jan. 1988; F. S. Buchanan, notes, Board of Education meeting on redrawing boundaries, 19 Jan. 1988; Bennion, Oral History, 11 Aug., 6 Sept. 1991.

76. Bennion, Journal, 20 Jan. 1988.

77. Emma Lou Thayne, "Diversity Counts," *Salt Lake Tribune*, 1 Feb. 1988. A letter of support signed by some thirty citizens was also delivered to Bennion on 7 Feb. 1988.

were appointed to head a group called "Citizens for Better Schools." They were given the task of determining what, if any, legal actions should be pursued.[78]

By March the group had collected enough money and legal advice to take action, and subsequently they filed suit in the U.S. district court seeking an injunction against the board on the grounds that they acted illegally in distributing students among the three schools on the basic of achievement scores; that balancing minority enrollments violated the Utah State Constitution, the U.S. Equal Education and Opportunities Act of 1974, and the Civil Rights Act of 1964; and that busing east side students through "hazardous industrial and commercial districts" exposed them to unnecessary risk. The group's claim that they represented thousands of patrons was rejected by the president of East's Booster Club, Wynn Johnson, who said it was more realistically only tens of people. As far as he could tell most people had by this time accepted the decision made by the board in January.[79]

U.S. District Judge David K. Winder apparently accepted the decision's legality too. On 22 July he rejected the request for an injunction, agreeing, in effect, with the board's attorneys that the board had acted within its statutory authority; that it did not violate any federal laws in assigning students or prescribing school boundaries; and that "the board's decision was not arbitrary and capricious and not an abuse of the board's discretion." Winder dismissed all claims against the board "with prejudice" and remanded the issues dealing with the Utah Code and Utah Constitution to the State Court.[80]

THE SUPERINTENDENT AS LIGHTNING ROD

Legality notwithstanding, the months following the final decision gave no respite from the aftermath of the boundary dispute. "Gloom . . . pervades the East High Community. Many feel that East High was done in. I see the disappointment in our neighbors' eyes," Bennion wrote. Efforts to get the legislature to pass an open enrollment law (supported by former superintendent, M. Donald Thomas), failed to get out of committee, but only by a single vote, and some parents petitioned the board for special exemptions on which schools their children should be allowed to attend. The superintendent even began to consider some other kind of employment because of his weariness over the boundary dispute. A sort of malaise swept over him as he tried to be "enthusiastic" about his work in a state that seemed so penurious:

> It is getting to seem like a losing battle to me. I am running out of creative ideas for improving the quality of education with less and less money. I am tired of the negative attitudes towards public service, public education and taxes. The legis-

---

78. F. S. Buchanan, "Salt Lake City School Boundary Dispute, notes made at a meeting called to discuss the John Bennion Style of Leadership," 20 Jan. 1988.

79. "Salt Lake Board Sued Over Changes in Boundaries," *Salt Lake Tribune,* 5 Mar. 1988; "Lawsuit Seeks to Prevent Redistribution of Students," *Deseret News,* 5 Mar. 1988.

80. For documents dealing with the suit see Stephen Boyden Papers, Special Collections, University of Utah.

lature is in session and I have no interest in spending time there. I am not well matched for the highly political role I am presently in. I would much rather spend my time in educational program improvement.[81]

With the boundary dispute settled Bennion apparently thought he could now focus on education instead of politics. It was not to be; within a week he was in the headlines again when the Salt Lake Teacher's Association released a letter to the board in which they criticized his leadership and reported that they had recently passed a motion of "no confidence" in him. The letter specified a number of problematic issues, including "teacher morale, trust of central administration, more direct and open communication, continued attempts to circumvent the shared governance process," the imposition of regulations and programs which were stifling creativity, lack of teacher involvement in reform, increased teacher workloads and a diminution of "pride in being part of the district team of professionals." Although the SLTA president, Karline Grief, claimed that she had informed Bennion about the letter before it was sent, he would have preferred to sit down with the teachers to discuss their grievances before they were made public. The board's vice-president, Stephen Boyden, reported that the board took the matter seriously and wanted to be fair to the superintendent and the teachers. He suggested that perhaps the boundary dispute had caused neglect of teacher concerns and that this was one way of promoting a greater focus on "the things that really count."[82]

For Bennion, teacher dissatisfaction stemmed from more than the boundary dispute, although that must surely have heightened the tensions. There had been some rising hostility between teachers and the central administration following Don Thomas's resignation and prior to John Bennion's appointment. Some of this had its roots in teacher objections to School Community Councils having a say in how teachers should be assigned to a school. The appointment of George Brooks as interim superintendent apparently calmed some teachers' fears of having their decision making power diminished, but Bennion's appointment may have exacerbated their concerns, and his appointment was "less well accepted by district employees" who had become so used to the style, manner and personality of Thomas.[83]

As Bennion pondered the complaints, he saw teacher dissatisfaction as stemming from his introduction of innovations they apparently perceived as threats to their professional status: a "more systematic approach to curriculum development, teacher supervision and evaluation, a multi-year study of effective teaching, and a more comprehensive student assessment program." When these perceived threats combined with "other irritants" such as the change in the transfer policy, changes in the health insurance policy requiring stricter adherence to the contract, a lack of salary increases over two years, the closing of South, the

81. Bennion, Journal, 31 Jan., 14 Feb. 1988; "Ex-Superintendent Urges Open Enrollment," *Deseret News*, 15 Feb. 1988.
82. "S.L. Teachers Enter Vote of No Confidence Against Bennion," *Deseret News*, 28 Feb. 1988.
83. McLeese, "Process of Decentralizing Conflict," 361.

protracted debate over boundaries, and changes in the elementary mathematics program, it is clear why the representatives of the district's teachers lashed out at Bennion. According to the president of the SLTA, Karline Grief, some teachers were upset over the motion, but she thought the majority would have agreed with it.[84]

The week following the "no confidence" letter, Bennion met with the SLTA leadership. Although he felt better personally after having had an opportunity to tell the teachers' representatives that he thought the letter "was inappropriate and inconsistent with agreed upon procedures," and although he had received numerous supportive gestures from a wide range of people, still the impact of the "no confidence" vote, coming as it did on the heels of the divisive debate over boundaries, caused his respect for the SLTA leadership and his enthusiasm for his job to reach a "low ebb." He seriously considered the option of resigning. As if things were not difficult enough in the midst of all the teacher related criticisms, the "Group for Better Schools" filed the lawsuit discussed earlier. Although in July that particular issue was resolved in the district's favor, its initial filing in the spring of 1988 simply exacerbated the litany of explosive issues which had made the past year "the most wrenching of [John Bennion's] career."[85]

The board as a whole did not publicly demonstrate its support of the superintendent during this particular teacher issue, although a number of individual members privately empathized with him. Bennion did, however, take some solace from editorials in the *News* and the *Tribune* which both labelled the teachers' attack as unfair. The *Tribune* criticized the teachers' association for undermining the whole notion of "review of services" by going over the superintendent's head to the board. Acknowledging that the teachers' complaints should not be minimized, the editorial attributed part of the difficulty to the fact that the teachers had become accustomed to former Superintendent Thomas's "flamboyant" personality and had difficulty relating to Bennion's "more reserved and, possibly, less democratic" style.

In a similar vein the *Deseret News* criticized what they perceived to be teacher "arrogance" in giving the impression that "Bennion is somehow supposed to be at the mercy of the teachers and their opinions." Noting that the teachers had held out hope, given that both teachers and Bennion were "professionals," that a successful resolution of the issues would be found, the *News* opined that in taking the position they had, the "teachers' association didn't look very professional on this one." Also a supportive column by Twila VanLeer charged that Bennion had been made a "scapegoat," and that confrontational tactics such as "no-confidence" votes would not help resolve the issues. Mirroring some of Bennion's own thinking at this time that he might "throw in the towel," VanLeer concluded that if this should happen, "Salt Lake's loss could become some other district's

---

84. Bennion, Journal, 28 Feb. 1988; Bennion, Oral History, 6 Sept. 1991; "Bennion, Teachers Take 'First Step' to Reconciliation," *Salt Lake Tribune*, 7 Mar. 1988.

85. "Bennion, Teachers Take 'First Step' to Reconciliation," *Salt Lake Tribune*, 7 Mar. 1988; Bennion, Journal, 7 Mar., 13 Mar. 1988.

gain."[86]

One observer of the Salt Lake City schools, Peter Scarlett of the *Salt Lake Tribune*, has noted that a major component in the dispute with the SLTA was Bennion's style of management and his personal disposition to be reflective and careful in what he would say off the cuff. He was not a "glad hander" and would have "done a lousy job in sales." The teacher complaints about him were based more on perceptions than reality; indeed, in Scarlett's view, Thomas's approach to administration might have been ultimately more autocratic than Bennion's. Although Bennion's personality gave the impression of aloofness, he was essentially very democratic in his attempt to have everyone involved weigh all the evidence before coming to an decision. He strove to keep his own emotional responses in check and wanted others to do the same.[87]

Many meetings of the board continued to be mini-replays of the boundary dispute and Bennion expressed distaste for the persistent polarization between the "equity" faction and the "free choice" faction. As mentioned previously, the board as a whole was not very supportive of him publicly during the teacher fracas, and the minority three members cast votes against the renewal of his contract in the late spring of 1988. For Bennion it was another low point in his career, but he also was able to understand it, in retrospect at least, as a typical response of board members whose constituents were frustrated by the board's decision: "the superintendency is a symbol of the district and a visible object of expressing that frustration; the superintendent either caused the defeat to occur, or didn't prevent it from happening. [Consequently] there's a natural tendency for people who feel frustrated and disappointed, to think that new leadership is needed since the old leadership didn't produce what they had desired."[88]

Before the vote was taken on his re-appointment, those who planned to vote against him (Stephen Boyden, Carolyn Kump, and Lorna Matheson) encouraged him to seek other work opportunities, in light of the controversies he and the board had been involved in. They had lost; their constituents were upset, and now, in reaction, they either blamed him for what had happened or feared for the future. However, the other members of the board who had regularly voted for maximum equity (Keith Stephan, Susan Keene, Colleen Minson, and Ronald Walker) apparently did not agree that Bennion should be dismissed. By a slim margin of four to three, he was reappointed to another two year term beginning 1 July 1988.[89]

---

86. "Be Fair With Bennion," *Salt Lake Tribune*, 3 Mar. 1988; "Attack on Bennion Was Unfair," *Deseret News*, 4 Mar. 1988; "No Confidence Vote Was Unfortunate," *Deseret News*, 9 Mar. 1988. See also A. L. Gallegos letter, *Salt Lake Tribune*, 14 Mar. 1988, in which he chides the SLTA for lack of specificity in its criticism of Bennion.

87. Conversation with Peter Scarlett, 28 July 1992.

88. Bennion, Oral History, 6 Sept. 1991; Bennion, Journal, 10 Apr. 1988.

89. The momentous decision to retain Bennion was recorded in a terse three-line item. See Board of Education, Minutes, 21 June 1988; also "School Board Gives Bennion 2 More Years," *Salt Lake Tribune*, 22 June 1988.

A TAPERING OFF OF "CEASELESS CONTENTION"

Shortly after his reappointment, Bennion was invited to speak at a Sunday meeting in the LDS ward his family had attended in Provo. He took the occasion to bring some closure to the turmoil of the past two years by putting the whole issue in meaningful perspective, not only for the congregation but for him and his family. Taking as his texts Mormon scriptures that focused on the need to "esteem our neighbors as ourselves and to seek the interest of our neighbors as well as our own" he said that he had gained a new appreciation of the importance of this in community life. During the boundary dispute, there were few who transcended their own narrow borders and "identified with the general community interest." As he reflected on this, he realized that a key measure of the extent to which individuals have "religious and moral maturity" is in their ability to go beyond their narrow circle of concerns and be able to identify with and be responsive to the needs of others outside of their immediate circle.

Another insight he arrived at was how careful one must be in thinking one is always right in "dealing with difficult and complex issues." Closed-minded individuals are not good listeners or learners, he said, and they increase in intolerance by their unwillingness to consider other points of view.

At a third level, he said that the dispute had reminded him that the ideals which some Mormons (and others) hold, frequently collide with the ideals of other Mormons. Such ideals cannot be held in an absolute sense; perfect equality would, he claimed, end in a concentration camp and perfect freedom would result in chaos and gross inequality. Difficult as it is, people must try to navigate some middle road when these irreconcilable ideals collide.

Finally, he said that the controversy had reinforced in him the notion of religious and moral obligation for the rich and powerful to plead the cause of the poor and powerless. The former know how to work the system to their advantage, while the latter do not. Without concern for those who are powerless, there is grave danger of diminishing opportunity for those children who are "at risk."[90]

In large measure, this sermon was the blueprint from which he worked during the days he may have been tempted to give in to his most powerful and strident opponents. He was forced to act politically, but behind it was a very strong sense of social justice, firmly rooted in and supported by religious and moral principles. He used the occasion to teach and to affirm his own commitment to important social ideals. His social philosopher grandfather, Milton Bennion, would have surely said, "Amen."

In the months that followed the split vote on his re-appointment, Bennion continued to feel "exhaustion and depletion" from the "ceaseless contention." He was, he said, more aware than he ever had been about what "burnout" really meant. In terms of his professional duties, one ray of light seemed to lighten the gloom—the idea of refining the shared governance procedure through imple-

---

90. John W. Bennion, "Insights Gained from the High School Closure and Boundary Issue," Sermon given at the Edgemont 10th LDS Ward, Provo, Utah, 21 June 1988.

menting site-based decision making. This appears to have been the most interesting aspect of his work as 1988 drew to a close. He was anxious to get some agreement on this as a means of giving school personnel a more effective voice, even though it was evident that some administrators and teachers were able to see how they could implement site-based decision making while others seemed more cautious.

As he met with teachers in the spring of 1989, he was puzzled by a shift in their thinking. Previously they had complained over too much "top-down" decision making; now the leadership seemed to be complaining that the "bottom-up" type of involvement was not adequate. Bennion proposed a partnership between the board, staff, parents, business, and community leaders that involved individual schools setting academic goals for students. This, when achieved, would result in substantial bonuses to teachers "in exchange for some specific achievement goals in reading and math." Once again this appealed to the superintendent's competitive instincts and his belief that there should be some sort of link between how well students performed and the kinds of rewards their teachers received.

Teacher representatives discussing this notion were not impressed by what appeared to them to be the dreaded "M P" words—"merit pay." They countered with a proposal which eliminated "any measurable achievement goals" and insisted on a performance bonus regardless of any increase in student achievement. In addition, they wanted salary increases to put Salt Lake City teachers above the average for the Western states—a request Bennion felt was simply "beyond the district's means." Bennion was highly disappointed that as a group teachers "are not risk takers. They would like some of the blessings of the free enterprise system, but they tend not to be competitive by nature." In addition to the resistance of the Teachers' Association to any kind of significant measurable goals, Bennion was also disappointed that they were still not willing to rescind the vote of no confidence.[91]

Despite some continued doubts about his future as a professional educator, he found satisfaction in teaching a class in philosophy of education for prospective teachers in the Department of Educational Studies at the University of Utah. He found the challenge of dealing with ideas about what education *should be* to be "a different kind of challenge than what I experience as an urban school super-intendent."[92] On occasion during the previous two years he must have sometimes longed for the detachment and tranquility of the "ivory tower," but John Bennion was much too committed to shaping his part of the world to seek an escape from the real world of the urban school district. He had come to Salt Lake in the hope of making a difference, and to that task he returned in an attempt to complete what he had begun.

As outlined in his early comments to teachers and the board, Bennion be-

---

91. Bennion's reflections on the meetings with the SLTA are found in his Journal, 28 June, 24 Nov. 1988; 9 Apr., 20 Aug., 27 Aug., 26 Nov., 3 Dec. 1989.
92. Bennion, Journal, 26 Nov. 1989, 15 Jan. 1990.

lieved that the central purpose of school is to give individuals the means and tools whereby they can achieve a meaningful and purposeful existence. He believed, in fact, that there is (or should be) an inescapable connection between what a student learns and what a teacher does. Career ladders and effective teaching strategies with clear and explicit objectives were one side of the equation—the input side. Now he focused upon ways to determine what happened to students in terms of the learning outcomes. The traditional means of doing this were, of course, standardized tests. While necessary in any assessment, they were by no means sufficient. If, as survey after survey seemed to show, too many students were graduating "only semi-literate and ill equipped to cope with the demands of higher education, the world of work and citizenship responsibilities," it seemed to John Bennion that some means had to be found to articulate what students were supposed to know in order to function in these areas. The central question which everyone needed to ask was "how well are students learning what is fundamentally important for them to learn and what can we do to stimulate higher levels of learning, particularly among students who are not progressing well."[93]

To answer this question demanded more than scores. It required on the part of the teacher "a history" of student output which could be evaluated within the context of the school's own environment. One means of doing this, and one which was being tried in a number of Salt Lake City schools as the district celebrated its centennial in 1990, was the "Portfolio" approach. Using student portfolios, teachers collected on a regular basis samples of student work in, for example, writing. They then analyzed them to determine the extent to which the learning outcomes contained in the student's portfolio meshed with what the student was supposed to be learning. Teachers could see before them a history of what students were actually doing (or not). This approach also enhanced the communication of student academic status to parents. The portfolio approach to evaluation is time consuming, subject to the vagaries of all evaluative procedures, and not easily tied in to a score. But it promises some way out of the reductionist fallacy so often associated with traditional grading or testing practices. In a very real sense, it also holds promise of making the individual student the focus of assessment by not "tagging" the student a success or a failure, but instead offering opportunities for success at the student's own rate. Whether large numbers of teachers will pursue the portfolio concept long enough to enable the process to be fairly evaluated is debatable.

As one peruses some of the papers Bennion has written, there can be little doubt that he is an educator who believes that teachers *do* count and that schools *can* make a difference. He rejects the pessimistic notion so common among philosophers and historians of education in the 1970s that schools are "ineffectual and all but impotent." He holds that the school's primary role is one of intel-

---

93. Bennion, "Student Assessment—The Propelling Force in the Educational Restructuring Movement," Paper delivered at the Utah Association for Supervision and Curriculum Development, 7 Oct. 1991.

lectual stimulation and that expecting it to fill social and other services blunts that primary focus. But Bennion also believes that as poverty and inequality of opportunity became more and more evident in the lives of many children, the school can help bridge the opportunity gap caused by "dysfunctional families, poverty, language barriers, unstimulating home and neighborhood environments, child neglect and abuse and the over-indulgence in T.V., videos, video games and other mindless pass times outside of schools." In Bennion's words: "the 1990s will test anew the proposition that schools can learn to effectively compensate for instability and limited learning opportunities outside of the school. . . . If we fail, our failure may mean the demise of the American dream itself."[94]

In June 1990 and again in June 1992, just as the district celebrated its first century of service to the people of Salt Lake City, the board of education unanimously appointed John W. Bennion to his third and fourth terms as superintendent. The first board election after the bruising closure and boundary dispute did not become, as some had predicted, a referendum on the board or on the district's eleventh superintendent. In the fall of 1991 at the annual meeting of the Utah Education Association at the Salt Palace, Dr. Don K. Richards, on behalf of the Utah School Superintendent's Association, named John Bennion as the "Utah Superintendent of the Year," and nominated him for consideration as "National Superintendent of the Year." In his letter of nomination, Richards praised Bennion for his "dedication, bold vision and willingness to try innovative approaches." John Bennion, he said, "is the kind of dedicated and dependable leader you search for."

In words so different from what his entries about educational matters had reflected since February 1987, Bennion recorded in his personal journal that the meeting before the UEA at the Salt Palace "was all very nice. . . . This recognition is gratifying after my being such a controversial figure in Salt Lake City for several years."[95] It was a typical low-key Bennion comment, but the award compensated somewhat for the turmoil of 1987 and 1988. His executive secretary, Jan Keller, commented that he was always willing to let people try new things, "and if they fail, he says, 'well, that didn't work,' and puts it into perspective." Only in the long perspective of history can John Bennion's efforts to make a difference in Salt Lake City public schools ultimately be judged, but perhaps, more than any superintendency in the history of the district or even of the state, Bennion's tenure may be seen as a case study of the ways in which public schools, for good and ill, are a reflection of the ideals *and* the biases that pervade the community.

As the Salt Lake School District's first century came to a close, John Bennion attempted to focus public attention on the need not only for excellence in the curriculum, but also on equity of access for all children. The learning lag in in-

---

94. These observations are based on remarks made by Bennion at an orientation for new teachers in the district on 14 Sept. 1992.

95. Twila VanLeer, "Bennion wins a new label: Utah Superintendent of the Year," *Deseret News*, 9 Oct. 1991; Bennion, Journal, 13 Oct. 1991.

ner-city schools compared to student achievement in affluent neighborhoods had become one of his main concerns. He felt that low achievement in inner-city schools greatly reduced opportunities for urban children and increased polarization between the affluent and the undereducated.

After eight years as superintendent Bennion was granted a sabbatical leave which he spent teaching a class in ethics at each of the city's three high schools from September 1993 to January 1994. During this period Assistant Superintendent Mary Jean Johnson served as Acting Superintendent—the only woman to have done so since M. Adelaide Holton's brief stint as Acting Superintendent in 1899. On 1 September 1994 Bennion left the superintendency to accept a professorship in Urban Education at the University of Utah's Graduate School of Education. There he hoped to create opportunities for urban educators to learn to stimulate higher levels of student achievement.[96] For Bennion, the frontier of public education in metropolitan areas is the revitalization of urban schools in general and the improvement of low-income schools in particular. The extent to which these ideals are realized in the district's second century will indicate whether anything was learned from the turmoil and friction the district went through in the late 1980s. Perhaps knowledge of the tensions and strains of these years will prevent these struggles from becoming a template for Century II of the Salt Lake City public schools.

---

96. "Bennion Continues Tradition, Confronts Inner-City Ills," *Continuum: The Magazine of the University of Utah* 5 (Summer 1995): 34.

EPILOGUE
A Centennial Perspective

Public schools mirror the societies that maintain them, however much we would wish otherwise. Although reformers have over the years tried to make schools shape the "good society," their efforts have been frustrated by the inescapable fact that schools tend to follow, rather than precede, social and cultural change. Consequently, when Salt Lake City harbored a relatively hegemonic Mormon society, the schools tended to reflect that community. Even if the textbooks were essentially the same as those used throughout the nation (e.g., the McGuffey *Readers*), the fact that almost all students and teachers were Mormons shaped the climate of the district schools and gave them the appearance, if not always the content, of Mormon parochial schools. As closely tied as these schools were to their environment, the changes that occurred in Mormonism during the last two decades of the nineteenth century (making it more mainstream in its perspectives on marriage, politics, and economics) were also reflected in the kind of schools that served the Mormon communities. As John S. McCormick has observed: "Salt Lake became less and less isolated, and its population became more and more diverse, subjecting the kingdom to increasing stresses and strains. The inevitable conflicts intensified, until towards the end of the century, the Mormons were forced to accommodate themselves at last to the realities of mainstream America."[1]

One of those "realities"—a veritable touchstone of "true Americanism"—was the notion of free, tax-supported public schools. The Mormon church opposed the establishment of these schools initially because they saw them as a threat to Church dominance. And in a very real sense, the non-Mormons supported them for the same reason: with public schools functioning throughout Utah, or so the rhetoric held, Mormonism's grip on its people would be weakened. Public schools would, it was believed, accomplish what years of Protestant missionary work had failed to do. This was a typical American perspective on the power of schools to correct what ails society; in this case America would be "cured" of Mormonism by having Mormon children attend public schools.

For almost three decades following the establishment of public schools in Salt Lake City (1890-1920) there was a clash between those who demanded a free secular school system, with no formal church influence, and those who believed that if Salt Lake City were to have public schools they should serve and be shaped by the Mormon community. In this clash the Free Masons played a prominent role and perceived themselves as duty-bound to keep the public schools from becoming an extension of the Mormon church. Within this volatile context,

---

1. John S. McCormick, *Salt Lake City: The Gathering Place* (Woodland Hills, CA: Windsor Publications, 1980), 31

the superintendents kept the schools on an even keel. Each was a capable executive officer; three of them were "outsiders" and not members of the dominant faith: Jesse F. Millspaugh, Frank B. Cooper and Ernest A. Smith. The lone Mormon during this period was D. H. Christensen. He and Millspaugh, a Congregationalist, were perhaps most responsible, by virtue of their long tenure, political savvy, and high degree of professionalism, for keeping the schools from being completely submerged in the heavy swell of politics that surrounded every school board election. Smith was apparently inundated by it.

As McCormick notes, the Latter-day Saints were "forced to accommodate" themselves to the new realities. But in doing so they effectively blunted the school as an instrument of change and sought to turn it to their own purposes as an instrument of reproducing the community that supported it. An obvious way to do this was to hire only locally trained teachers—the very opposite of the policy followed in the 1890s when "outsiders" outnumbered "insiders." This strategy succeeded so well that by 1914 a national survey team criticized the elementary school teacher corps as being too inbred. Nowhere was the intent of having Mormon teachers dominate the schools more clearly stated than by David O. McKay, LDS Commissioner of Education, when he proposed to the Church Board of Education the active recruitment of Mormon teachers for Utah's public school as a counter to the influence of non-Mormon teachers: "Now is the time to step right in and get teachers into these public high schools and eliminate the spirit which dominates the schools now."[2]

Sometime in the 1920s a "gentlemen's agreement" emerged between the Masons and Mormons. The Masons were assured control of district finances while the Mormons were assured the superintendency. Indeed, from the 1890s until the 1950s the Masons had a firm grip on the district's finances through the office of the Clerk-Treasurer and from 1920 until 1973 all five superintendents (George N. Child, L. John Nuttall, Jr., Howard S. McDonald, M. Lynn Bennion, and Arthur C. Wiscombe) were members of the LDS church. During this period there was very little public wrangling over church-school entanglements. These appointments fulfilled, as far as the superintendency was concerned, what David O. McKay wanted for the public schools serving the Mormon community.

However, a larger set of educational interests transcended the local Mormon or Masonic communities. Salt Lake City's schools became more mainstream than might have been expected. While certainly not bastions of radical progressivism (few American school districts were), the schools of Salt Lake City under the leadership of a variety of Mormon superintendents, with their roots deep in Utah's religious culture, remained aware of the ebb and flow of national educational reforms. For example, in 1918 the National Education Association's "Cardinal Principles of Education" helped shift the public school curriculum away from the traditional academic emphasis toward a more social-centered emphasis.

---

2. General Board of Education of the Church of Jesus Christ of Latter-day Saints, Minutes, 3 Mar. 1920. Cited in James R. Clark, "Church and State Relationships in Education in Utah," EdD diss., Utah State University, 1958, 269.

Within two years that shift began to be reflected in the Salt Lake District—at least in the published reports. When educational efficiency became the watchword in the late 1920s, George Child promoted it even to the point of reducing the years spent in school from twelve to eleven. Somewhat paradoxically, this "successful" reform was abandoned in the 1940s partly to recoup the loss of larger and heavier twelfth graders, which had put the city's football teams at a disadvantage when they competed with non-city teams. Again, community values shaped the schools.

When the depression of the 1930s took the nation to the edge of despair, L. John Nuttall, Jr., modified school programs to provide young people with hope and opportunity. Eventually, a Vocational Center and Evening High School were established at West High providing a direct link between students and local businesses. The public schools' responses to new social, economic, and political situations reinforces the idea that schools have almost no choice but to mirror their communities.

Demographic changes also place new demands on schools—some positive and some negative. For example, for M. Lynn Bennion the increase in a highly homogeneous population and the economic expansion after World War II made for an exciting and exhilarating professional experience. The system expanded and the perceived needs of the "cold war" funnelled additional funds and ideas into the schools. On the other hand, in the late 1960s and early 1970s Bennion's successor, Arthur Wiscombe, felt nothing but uncertainty and pain when he faced a declining school population, a steady loss in school revenues, and consequent closure of schools as the city took on some of the characteristics of large urban centers. Wiscombe's appeal to the historic Mormon sense of community led nowhere as he struggled to resolve the district's social and economic problems.

Salt Lake City's schools in the twentieth century were not avant garde, but neither were they in the backwater of public schooling. Given the conservative nature of the community, the schools were relatively progressive. In the 1970s M. Donald Thomas's interpretation of "shared governance" (the idea of maximizing community involvement in the schools) put the district in the national spotlight as a model of shared governance. Ironically, although Thomas was the fourth non-Mormon to be superintendent, his success with shared governance was attributed by some observers to the way in which his leadership style dovetailed with the expectations of Mormon school patrons: although much local initiative was promoted, he was ultimately in charge. Nevertheless, there was widespread satisfaction with the increased community involvement in school governance during Thomas's tenure.

As the Salt Lake City schools approached their centennial during the administration of John W. Bennion, they underwent as divisive and convulsive an event as they had ever experienced—the combined closing of South High School and the related realignment of the boundaries of the other high schools: West, East and Highland. Nothing in the schools' history came close to being as potentially divisive: not the election of a usually non-Mormon majority to the board from

1890 to 1940; not the small pox vaccination fracas of 1900; not the released-time seminary issue of 1943 or the ouster of Superintendent Arthur Wiscombe in 1973. Like six of his predecessors, Superintendent John Bennion was an active member of the Mormon community, but Salt Lake City had changed and his religious affiliation was irrelevant to the situation. New realities crowded in on the schools—the realities of a significant number of minority students; social class division; plummeting test scores among "at risk" students; the perception of weak programs; the pressure of state mandates in the efficient use of school buildings. The board was badly split on the issues, but no one ever mentioned religion as a factor: there were, in fact, committed Mormons on both sides. The ability and willingness of an earlier generation to accommodate to new legal and economic realities was replaced by a need to accommodate to the urbanization of "Mormon Country," with all that implied for equality of opportunity and access to the American dream for an increasingly at risk school population of urban children.

Ironically, it was a similar aim which some of the early non-Mormon advocates of public schools had in mind in the 1880s as they struggled to establish public schooling in Utah. They then perceived Mormon children as being depraved by their exposure to the "evils" of Mormonism and therefore severely deprived of the opportunity to participate as citizens in the American Republic. In a century the aim had come full circle, with people of all persuasions now challenged to come to grips with the issues of poverty, urbanization, and ethnic diversity.

The motto adopted by Salt Lake City in its successful 1995 campaign to gain the Winter Olympics for the year 2002 was "The World is Welcome Here." That notion is light years away from the fortress mentality of an earlier generation of Utahns, which saw its quasi-public schools as a bulwark against the "world." Once again schools as the mirror image of society comes to mind. The society that lies ahead, for all the promise of technological sophistication, will not be less complex than the past, nor will its schools. In their second century, Salt Lake's schools will be called upon to meet the challenges that the "world" will bring to the valley, a world in which the city now has a recognized place.

Hopefully Salt Lake City's schools will meet these challenges with the same spirit of creative accommodation that led an earlier generation to accept the idea of free public schooling for all children, even though it meant giving up the use of schools to promote strictly Mormon aims. The public school cannot, of course, be a panacea for all society's ills; but it still is called upon to help society at least address the problems of gangs, drugs, teen pregnancy, illiteracy, racism, and bigotry, as well as promote higher order thinking in all students across the curriculum. Given the nature of a pluralistic society, consensus on issues is difficult to achieve. In this sense "accommodation" is a necessary feature of a public school system that serves diverse interests, but whose parents, teachers, and administrators have the courage, energy, and vision to work together for the greater good and for the sake of the schools' most important clients: children. John S. Welch, a Salt Lake teacher and administrator in the first decade of the twentieth century, eloquently expressed the ideal of public service for children when he said:

> At the altar of childhood where the eternities meet to sum up the past and preface the future I kneel in humble though blind adoration. I dedicate whatever of energy and strength; of insight and intellect; of integrity and fidelity of purpose, I may possess. To it I sacrifice personal ambition, social prestige, bodily welfare. In so doing I know that every thought through every deed is sown into some soul for seed.[3]

However faintly this ideal may be achieved in the real world of the schools, it is still at the heart of the public school idea and is still the credo which committed educators try to teach and live by. The need for such ideals is unlikely to diminish during the Salt Lake District's second century.

---

3. Welch's statement, entitled "My Creed," was included in a memorial tribute paid to him by D. H. Christensen in 1910. See *Twentieth Annual Report*, 1910-11, 126.

INDEX

released-time credit, 186
Community Life in Salt Lake City and Utah (Worlton), 159
Communist scare, 180-81
Congregationalists, 12, 133, 152, 153
Corbett, Anna L., 102
Corporal punishment, 121, 206
Counts, George S., on politics of boards of education, 157
Cowles, LeRoy, 136
Crawford, John, 195, 209, 212, 213, 214, 217, 218, 221, 222, 228, 236
Crawford, Marilyn Reiser, 195
Cremin, Lawrence, 177
Critchlow, E. B., 42, 52, 61
Crowther, George L., 152
Cuban, Larry, 118
Cubberley, Ellwood P., 39, 76, 98, 101, 130; conducts survey of Salt Lake district, 70, 84, 123; uses factory as school metaphor, 124
Cummings, Byron, 66, 68
Cummings, Horace H., 18, 38
Cummins, John, 188, 212-13, 214
Current Events, 146
Curriculum Foundations for the Public Schools of Salt Lake City: focus on child needs, 177; reflects Cardinal Principles, 178
Curriculum: spelling, 14; child centered emphasis in, 33, 42, 50-51, 82, 98, 100, 118, 119, 148-49; 177; 290; practical focus of, 33, 98; sex education, 83; sewing, 102; foreign language 95, 102; physical education, 96-97; for atypical (special education) students, 102-103; vocational education, 101-102; 111, 127-28, 140-41, 149, 205; Utah history, 106, 205; subject/teacher-centered, 120, 144; athletics, 146-47; social emphasis in, 178; teacher involvement in planning, 205; cold war and, 288
Curriculum reform, 48, 72, 75, 76, 82, 100-103, 111, 115-17, 144-46, 178, 287. *See also* Reform
Curtis, Genevieve R., 162, first woman elected to board, 152
Curtis, L. H., 212
Curtis, Lindsay R., 152
Curtis, Ray T., 162
Cushman, C. L., 145
Cutler, John C., 42

Daily Worker, 180-181
Davis, Moses, 90
Davis, Rev. France, 272
Decentralization, 215, 222

Decline of the West (Spengler), 165
Democratic ideal: 116; in progressive curriculum, 145, 162; in shared governance, 222, 225
Democratic Party, 59, 61, 65
Democratic Women's Club: sponsors first woman candidate for board, 42
Depression (1930s), 111, 129, 130-32, 288
Dern, George (Governor), 132
Deseret Alphabet, 14
Deseret News, 29, 32, 35, 37-38, 43, 47, 51-52, 55, 59, 60, 67, 89, 94, 113, 120, 125, 156, 174, 185, 212, 215, 266, 271, 273, 279
Dewey, John, 59, 90, 95, 97, 99, 119, 130, 165, 177, 189
Discrimination: racial, 198-200, 232, 258, 264; religious, 60, 65-66, 69-70; social class, 162, 173, 193, 196, 232, 258, 264-65, 272, 289; gender, 19, 71, 80-81, 102, 123, 232
Diversity, 276
Dixon, Aldous, 167
Dooley, James, 199, 201
Driggs, Howard: at NEA 1920 conference, 108; on writing performance of S.L. students, 121
Dropouts, 139, 207-208, 240-41
Durham, G. Homer: on Mormon political power, 170
Dwyer, Rev. Dr. Robert J.: on released time seminary, 157

East High Booster's Club, 277
East High Community Council, 272, 274
East High School. *See* Schools
Eaton, George, 123, 129, 146-47
Eberhardt, A. E., 137
Edmunds, George F. (Senator), 22
Edmunds-Tucker Act, 25
Edwards, Miss Rachel: first woman candidate for board, 42
Elections. *See* Board of education
Efficiency, 34, 84, 94, 99, 111, 125, 250, 262, 287
Eighteenth Ward Seminary, 7-10
Eliot, Charles W., 32, 48, 97, 99, 126, 127
Ely, Richard T.: on Mormon social organization, 86
Emerson, Ralph Waldo, 3
Enrollments. *See* Schools
Episcopalians, 12, 156
Equality, 2, 101, 269, 284
Equality of Educational Opportunity, 138, 140, 141, 196, 213, 232, 234, 240, 269, 270, 271, 275, 284, 285. *See also* Reform and Curriculum reform

ABOUT THE AUTHOR

Frederick S. Buchanan was born in Stevenston, Ayrshire, Scotland. In 1949 he and his parents migrated to Utah. Six years later he entered the University of Utah and graduated in history and English. He taught U.S. history and literature at Bountiful High School (Utah) for three years and received a Ph.D. from Ohio State University in 1967. After three years at the University of Toledo, Ohio, he joined the University of Utah's Graduate School of Education in 1970 where he is a professor and teaches history of education in the Department of Educational Studies. In 1963 he married Rama Richards of Ogden; they are the parents of five sons.

His major areas of academic interest are history of schooling in Utah and the Scottish-Mormon connection. He has published articles dealing with response of the Old Order Amish, the Order of Aaron, and the Mormons to public education. In 1989 he received the Mormon History Association's Steven F. Christensen Award for Best Documentary Book: *A Good Time Coming: Mormon Letters to Scotland* (University of Utah Press). He also received MHA's T. Edgar Lyon Award for Best Article in nineteenth-century Mormon history: "The Ebb and Flow of Mormonism in Scotland, 1840-1900," published in *Brigham Young University Studies*.

Year	Average Daily Enrollment
1890-91	3870
1895-96	8951
1900-01	10483
1905-06	12918
1910-11	15817
1915-16	19555
1920-21	24189
1925-26	29032
1930-31	31942
1935-36	32326
1940-41	30931
1945-46	31059
1950-51	34635
1955-56	40391
1960-61	40315
1965-66	38186
1970-71	33521
1975-76	26524
1980-81	23425
1985-86	24769
1990-91	24897
1994-95	25083

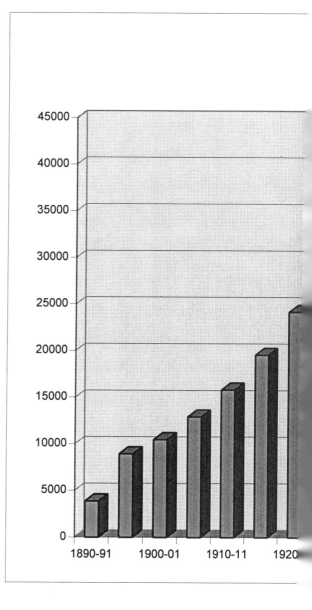

Student Enrollment Profile of Salt